Carol —

Keep the !

[signature]

GRANDMA'S JEWELS

Grandma's Jewels

AND THE LEGACY
BEHIND THEM

by Joyce Oglesby

XULON PRESS | XULONPRESS.COM

AND THE LEGACY BEHIND THEM

Visit Xulon online at www.XulonPress.com.
Visit *Joyce Oglesby* at www.JustAskJoyce.com.
Visit Legacy Pendant at www.aestheticsinjewelry.com.

Grandma's Jewels
and the Legacy Behind Them
by *Joyce Oglesby*

Printed in The United States of America
ISBN 9781498401814

Author photo copyright © 2013 by Cornerstone Photography.
Savannah photo copyright © 2013 by Ashley Baumann Photo & Design.
Designed by Terry N. Wilson Jr. at: tnwilson@kgldcable.com.
Edited by Dr. Dennis E. Hensley.

Published in association with Beyond This Point Ministries, Inc.,
PO Box 786, Corydon, IN 47112

www.xulonpress.com

Dedicated to those who sacrifice and persevere for the preservation of a strong family legacy.

Chapter 1

The jewels would be secured, but not without one more soft stroke of a hand over the brilliance of their beauty. Hand-designed and created in Italy, the necklace was adorned with 136 stones–92 round brilliant cut white diamonds and 44 egg-shaped, pigeon-blood-red ruby sapphires. It was common knowledge the stones were natural, not simulated. Because all the stones were naturally obtained, it added to the immense quality and value of the necklace. The carat weight of each diamond was 7.86 and each ruby 65.60. Set in their gold encasements, the rubies' purple hue exploded into their vivid red quintessence. The 16.50-inch necklace was the perfect length for a woman's décolleté. Measuring 6.25 at its widest point, it would poise itself upon a neck in intimate fashion. The triple-strand matching bracelet was a gratifying offspring of the necklace. The quarter-size earrings brought balance and elegance, and the ring was an exquisite work of finger art. The glorious rubies and the VVS1 clarity of the diamonds were telling of the monetary significance

9

of the jewels, but the intrinsic worth—its original owner.

The overstated red plush velvet case rested nicely inside the custom-made waterproof box designed for protection. The combination lock was secured and tumbled. A sturdy 22-inch strand of hand-soiled hemp was knotted through the latch. Once placed in its shallow grave, the loose end of the hemp was fastened to a three-inch portion of a root of the custodial oak where the soil had eroded from underneath it, pulling the hemp snug against the earth that held it securely as it grew, and carefully concealing it from the casual observer's eye. The broken earth was returned to its rightful position and packed firmly atop the box. Leaves then were carefully arranged to disguise the ground's fresh disturbance.

There now. You're safe. No one would even think to look here. But I'll be back to check on you. Now rest, my beautiful, long-coveted riches, secure in the knowledge that you are mine. She wanted me to have you. Grace told me herself, "You will be the heir to the jewels I possess someday." But with this family, it might not be so. Besides, this is the best way, just in case she changed her mind.

The mighty oak guarding its secret treasure melded into the midst of the grove surrounding it on Bay Street, its branches sprawling over Savannah's quaint streets, interlocking fingers like sisters strolling on both sides of a babbling creek. What was it about this place that held a soul captive? Much of its charm was certainly found in these majestic oaks. Great beards of shaggy Spanish moss hung from those branches, accenting the ancient Southern architecture of the famous historical downtown squares with their cobbled streets and rustic carriage lamps.

A dog barked in the distance muffled only by the sounds of footsteps against the sidewalk. The surreptitious dwelling securing the jewels faded into the distance as it witnessed the shadow glancing back into the damp early morn. An umbrella opened and joined the silhouette of the lone figure outlined underneath the street lights. The mist turned into rain and rolled off the trench coat and umbrella. As it beat upon the impressive oak, its mighty branches could not shield the jewels' resting place. However, the leaves pressed down with each drop, providing the necessary shelter.

*   *   *

OUTSIDE TURNER'S FUNERAL HOME,
SAVANNAH, GEORGIA, OCTOBER 15, 6:30 A.M.

"Hold on there, Ma'am, you can't go in there," the officer announced, throwing his arms out to block any attempt at passage. Yellow crime-scene tape encircled the entire block where Turner's Funeral Home set, as well as the parking lot extension the next block over. Turner's was the largest and most prestigious funeral home in the Savannah, Georgia area.

Nora could hardly believe her eyes. She knew Grace Willingham was a beloved woman in the community. She expected a crowd, but not at this hour and certainly not in this manner. She was looking for a quiet moment while no one was around. That Grace was admired was quite evident by the numbers of candles, flowers, and posters lodged against the temporary barriers. Angry mourners and curiosity seekers were babbling amongst themselves in outrage. To an unsuspecting visitor, something was amiss at the funeral home, and whatever it was appeared shocking.

"What's going on? What's happened? Is everything all right?" Nora Willingham was confused. She had traveled from Spain, setting aside important agendas for this funeral. She had every intention of getting inside, viewing her grandmother and visiting with her family. But from the looks of things, it appeared someone had been shot or at least severely injured. "I'm part of the family, Officer. I have to go in," she insisted.

"I'm sorry, Ma'am. No one's going in, and no one's coming out until the investigation is concluded."

"Investigation? What investigation? What's happened? I need to know. Please, let me go in there, Officer! That's my family!" Nora's voice drowned out the buzzing conjecture of friends, acquaintances, and the inquisitive townspeople who had gathered in memory of Grace Willingham. "Officer, that's my grandmother. I need to be in there." Nora continued to insist on passage into the premises.

Nora Willingham was the journalist daughter of James Willingham and granddaughter of his mother, Grace, the deceased. Her long auburn hair cascaded in soft curls over her shoulders. It complemented her beautiful big brown-black eyes peering out of luscious lashes. Those qualities paired with her perfectly-formed body might have convinced a lesser man, but Jarrod Phillips was a veteran of the Chatham County Sheriff's Department with a rookie reputation. He was a willing and likable officer who took his job seriously, but had never moved up in rank. Though lacking in qualities to excel, he wouldn't be swayed by a sexy smile, pleading whimper, or long tanned legs protruding from a short skirt. He kept his eyes fixed straight ahead so as not to be distracted by her gripping beauty. "I wish I could help you, Ma'am, I really do, but I have my orders. No one in, no one out."

"But why?" Nora insisted. "Just tell me what's going on. I have a right to know. Is someone dead? I mean, of course, besides my grandmom. But, I mean, did someone get shot? Is anybody seriously hurt? Was there a heart attack? Just say it, please. My relatives are in there. I beg you, Officer, tell me now. I don't think my heart can take this." Nora dramatically patted her chest drawing attention to her fullness.

Phillips had attempted to answer Nora's first, second and third questions, but there would be no interrupting her once she was on a roll. "Excuse me, but you must be from out of town, Lady. Did no one call you? I can't believe you haven't heard, seeing's how you're family and all. The whole state of Georgia is in an uproar over this thang. Your grandma's jewels have been stolen."

"What!" Nora was stunned. "Who? Why? Have they caught them? You mean they stole the jewels off her person?"

"Yes, Ma'am, that is correct, right off her dead body. The second viewing was when it happened. Once it was discovered, they shut down pert-near two whole city blocks. They're blocked off until the officers do their interviews and investigation. No one in—"

"Yeah, yeah, no one out. I heard you. But, the funeral was scheduled for this afternoon. So, they're just going to stop a funeral? That's insane! They just can't do that." Nora felt rage welling up inside her. Her grandmother deserved better than this. What depraved mind would have taken Grandma's jewels? Never mind that she believed Grace's intentions were to leave them to her. That wasn't important, at the moment at least. Her mind was racing and her stilettos pacing. She simply had to come up with a means to get inside that funeral home and find out exactly what was going on.

Chapter 2

The boisterous thunder from the early morning's unexpected storm had broken the silence that had finally settled
inside the viewing room at Turner's. The clap was deafening,
as though uttering displeasure and mourning over the fate of
Grandma Grace's passing. It woke almost everyone with a jolt,
but Madelyn's baby with upsetting commotion. The child had
cried himself to sleep and been fitful most of the night. Now, his
incessant whining would serve to agitate the already-frustrated
captives and rob them of a couple hours' sleep after tossing and
turning on couches, chairs and in corners in vain attempts to
find slumber.

"I need to go get my baby some formula," Madelyn demanded
of Lieutenant Harrington.

"Just let me know what you need, and I'll send a runner to
get it, Hon," he appeased.

"I'm not your Hon. He needs a bath and a change of clothes!"
she snapped. "He's spit up everywhere and tussled all over me.

15

We both need to get cleaned up."

"Sorry, Ma'am. Can't do it. The investigation is still ongoing." He handed her a piece of paper and a pen. "Write down what you have to have. I'll make sure you get it."

"This is ridiculous!" she murmured. Nevertheless, Madelyn hurriedly wrote down Enfamil 2 and Stage 4 Pampers, 22 to 37 pounds.

"If you could get me the money, Ma'am, I'd appreciate it."

"That's another thing. I didn't bring my purse in. There's money in it outside. Just let me go to my car and I'll get it and come right back. I'll leave the baby here with you if don't trust me to come right back. It'll only take me a minute, Officer."

"Ain't happening, Ma'am. See if someone will let you borrow the money. If not, I'll see what I can do."

Madelyn turned on her heels and stomped over to Kareem, shaking him from his slumber. "Hey, wake up. I can't believe you're sleeping through all the commotion anyway. I need money to get Bryson some formula and diapers."

Kareem mumbled under his breath, giving Madelyn a drop-dead look. He groggily reached into his pocket and pulled out a wad of cash. She reached for the roll. Even in his dazed senses, he yanked it back, took a twenty and handed it to her. "Bring me the change," he admonished. "When we goin' home? I'm ready to bust outta this place. It's creepy being in here with a corpse."

"No time soon. Best I can tell, anyway. And I need a fix, bad. You have anything?"

"Are you kidding? With these cops around? You're out of your head, Woman!" Kareem whispered. "Go take care of what you need to do." He settled back down and adjusted positions, not wanting to be bothered by such trivialities.

Madelyn was used to doing everything for the baby. Kareem rarely touched his child, yet was more-than-deservingly glorified over having a boy to carry on his name. Madelyn made her way back to Lieutenant Harrington, handed him the bill, and once again inquired when they would be allowed to leave.

"Go have a seat, Ma'am. You'll know as soon as I do. Believe me, I want it to end as much as you do. We'll get these things back to you as soon we can." The officer took the money over to one of the rookies on duty and the mission of quieting Bryson began.

*   *   *

INSIDE TURNER'S FUNERAL HOME, OCTOBER 15, 6:15 A.M.

Coffee, sausage, egg and biscuits, and donuts were placed in the kitchen area for the stirring, weary relatives and friends of Grace Willingham. It wasn't their idea for this all-night vigil. Most of them were only involved because the crime had taken place under their very noses. In fact, the likelihood of Grace Willingham's jewels being taken by more than one person was a stretch, at best. Although, there could have been an accomplice who might have acted as a decoy, scouting out those coming near and shielding the thief as he or she removed the jewels from Grace's corpse. Those were variables the officers were trying to uncover in the interviews being conducted.

Nick Willingham leaned against the door frame of the double-door entrance to the parlor. A funeral viewing was a most familiar setting to him, as he had been funeral director and owner of Turner's for the past three years. This time, however, there was an attachment he had never experienced. He would be officiating a family member's services. Nick had apprenticed under Richard Turner for two years, then bought the old man out. He had made a couple of enemies in the deal. The two gentlemen who had worked at Turner's for more than 15 years had planned to take over when Richard retired. When Nick dangled the million-dollar check in front of the long-time bachelor's face, Turner and his rumored male companion caught the next plane for Belize, and no one had seen either since.

The funeral home was holding its own under Richard Turner's management. Richard had invested a respectable amount of money into its presentation, but he was lacking in style and elegance. Nick had spent almost as much toward improvements as he had paid for the funeral home. He stayed true to the Southern plantation appearance outside, but combined its architecture with simple, symmetrical forms of neoclassical ancient Greek and Roman structures. Inside he incorporated a more contemporary flair with a touch of expensive European décor. He was able to ship several pieces of statement artwork and decorative vases from France and Italy to add to the upgraded style at Turner's. An extended portico with an elaborate tower and several pronounced columns were added to the facility. Cobblestoned walkways mimicked the ones at River Street in order to add to the Savannah ambiance. Nestled near the Ardsley Park area on Waters Avenue, he influenced the socially elite of this Southern city to make provisions for pre-planning. His relaxed and unpretentious personality invited the more modest citizens to utilize their services as well. Under Nick's professionalism, Turner's quickly became the number one provider service for departing loved ones in Chatham County.

Nick was one of two grandsons of Grace Willingham. He had often given thought to what this time might resemble—laying Grandma Grace to rest. He knew it would be chaotic, given the family history, but he didn't know exactly how it would play out. He found himself quite amused but calm.

When Nick and Grace would discuss her funeral arrangements, she would always recite one wish: "I want it to be a celebration, Nick. No tears, no sadness or sorrow for me. No video cameras and no pictures. And don't you let them make a spectacle of me, Nicholas Albert Willingham! I'm counting on you. Oh, and don't you dare let them sing dirges at my funeral. I want it snappy and glorious. I'm going to a better place, and I want everyone to celebrate that with me."

That was Grace Willingham—always positive, forever joyous, and constantly anticipating her new life after death. Grandma told every stranger about her *upcoming trip*. She painted a picture of "abundant living," a place "where a soul couldn't help but be happy all the time," and a location "where it makes you wonder what took you so long to get there." Her description invited the unsuspecting to walk slap dab into an opportunity for Grandma Grace to share the Plan of Salvation. Rumor had it she was responsible for more of the twelve-thousand-member congregation at her church than Brother Ralph, who had been preaching the Gospel at Bethel Christian for forty-some-odd years. It was little wonder Grace Willingham was such a revered woman in the community, even had the unique jewels not been a part of her elaborate history.

Chapter 3

"Interview Headquarters" at
Turner's Funeral Home, October 15, 8:01 a.m.

Lead Detective Bruce Masters rolled up his sleeves and took a sip of coffee to wash down the sticky sausage biscuit he had inhaled. He was going on very little sleep, so he grabbed a second cup of brew for backup. Grandson/funeral director Nick had helped him assimilate the somewhat convoluted family tree and give the few details he knew about the friends who happened to be entangled in the temporary confinement at Turner's. The theft had taken place at 17 past 1300 hours Friday and folks were tired. Best he could figure, he had a full day ahead of him yet, possibly spilling over into the following day, Sunday. He would do his best to wrap up this aspect of the investigation today. Folks didn't like you messing with their Saturdays. But handling a case claiming the spotlight of the entire state and likely to gain at least national attention if not beyond, the detective had to make sure no stone was left unturned. Best he could hope for was that people would be cooperative. It would make his job a lot easier, and get them all back in their beds no later than tonight. But the detective's orders were, "No one in, no one out until the last person goes through a thorough-and-sifting interview."

"Officer Ricks, bring in Mr. James Albert Willingham," Detective Masters announced as he settled into his interview headquarters.

"Sure thing, Sir," and Ricks scurried out to retrieve the son of the deceased Grace Willingham, and Mayor of Savannah, Georgia.

*   *   *

"INTERVIEW HEADQUARTERS" AT
TURNER'S FUNERAL HOME, OCTOBER 15, 8:05 A.M.,

"How ya doin', Jim?" Masters stuck out his hand and offered a gripping shake.

"Been better, Bruce. Been better." Jim seated himself and looked across the oversized maple desk. Jim was unaware of the sentimental attachment Nick had to the desk. The wood used to make the desk was cut from Grace Willingham's property. The light-color wood provided a touch of traditional mixed with the more contemporary style of the white leather executive chair. A Chinese Elm Bonsai complemented the abstract art piece offset to the right of Jim's view of the desk. A contemporary curved-glass dual frame displayed photos of Nick, his mother and Grace Willingham in one frame, and Nick with a lovely French maiden in the other. A small vertical organizer for file folders was within reach of an executive's hand. The first folder bore the label of Grace Willingham. The workplace was clean and organized with a distinctive flair of success. Jim liked that, as he was a stickler for organization himself.

Jim's eyes wandered as he assessed the pleasing and expensive office décor. The showcase wall consisted of impressive architecturally-designed buildings. Below the artwork was a striking vintage mechanical drafting table with cast-iron supporting base and complete with tools for the trade. *An odd hobby for an undertaker*, he thought. Other decorative pieces reflected an appreciation for abstract art from the staggered-height trio of columns donning effigies of Donatello's sophisticated Gothic version of David on the left, Andrea del Verrocchio's version of young David with the head of Goliath at his feet positioned on the right column, and in the middle set the masterpiece of David by Florence's favored artist, Michael Deangelo. *Obviously, Europe captured this boy's heart. Must have been his senior trip with Grace.* Jim's eyes looked at the exquisite hardwood flooring in young Willingham's office. The reflection in Nick's office punctuated his personality even more prominently than the atmosphere of the updated eye-catching funeral home décor.

"I don't know that I've ever been in Nick's office. He has it fixed up better than Ol' Man Turner. And pretty expensive taste, I might add."

"Yeah, well, it's about the only place we could have privacy, Jim, 'less'n we held it in the embalming room. Figured the ladies wouldn't like that too much." Masters chuckled at the thought. Jim smirked thinking he wouldn't take too kindly to the idea himself.

Detective Masters continued. "I need to read you your Miranda Rights, Jim."

"That's not necessary, Bruce. I know what they are."

"Gotta, Jim. You know the rules."

"Whatever." Jim was irritated. "Let's just get this over. I need to leave."

"You have the right to remain silent. Anything you say can be used against you in a court of law. You have the right to have an attorney present now and during any future questioning. If you cannot afford an attorney, one will be appointed—"

"Bruce, it's me. I have—" Jim thought how ridiculous this was since Bruce knew who their family lawyer was.

"—to you free of charge." The detective waited for a response. Jim sat silently annoyed, arms folded, scowling at the process.

"Do you wish to have your attorney present, Jim? Yes or no? I need an answer, please, for the record."

"I don't have anything to hide, Bruce. Nothing. Let's just get going. Please."

"Is that a no?" he pressed.

"That's a no, Bruce. Okay? That's a no." Jim repositioned himself and crossed his legs.

"Thank you, Sir." Masters continued. "Jim, I gotta ask you some questions. And I don't want you to take offense at anything I ask today, now, 'cause you know I have to do my job. A lot of these are routine questions. I'll be asking everyone else some of the same ones, but I have to do this. You know that, don't you?"

"Well, I guess. It kind of depends on what you'll be asking me, Bruce. I mean, I can tell you right up front, I didn't take the jewels. That should be all you need to know. So, ask away and we'll get outta here a lot sooner." Jim squirmed in his chair, uncertain of what was coming next.

The detective cleared his throat and began. "Jim what time did you get here— Oh, yeah, meant to tell you, Jim, this is being video-recorded. Have to have it as evidence in case there's a trial. You understand that, don't—"

"A trial! Are you kidding me, Bruce? When you find the jewels, whoever did this will just be hauled off to prison. Or should be. I mean, it'll be obvious that—"

"Now, Jim, you know everyone is innocent until proven guilty, and everyone is entitled to a fair trial if they don't plead out."

"Now, doggone it, Bruce. That just seems like a colossal waste of the taxpayers' money. And besides—"

Masters pulled his glasses off and leaned in closer. "Jim, you're the mayor of this town. You know how it works. Just because it's Grace Willingham doesn't exempt this family from goin' through the motions of the justice system. Now, let's get started or we'll be here a week from tomorrow."

"I'm not staying another night, Bruce. This is ridiculous. Let's get going and get this mess over with. I have business to get back to, and we have to bury my mother for Pete's sake!"

"Calm down, Jim. We'll get Grace in the ground. We may have to put her in cold storage until we do, but we'll get this done and go on about givin' your mama proper esteem. Have you seen the crowd out there? They all want to pay respects to Grace Willingham. If I don't get through with this process soon, we're liable to have a riot on our hands. That was one loved woman, your mama."

"Yeah, yeah, I know, *everybody* loved Grace." There was an undisguised snarl in Jim's voice and a slight roll of his eyes before he remembered he was being videoed. He thought better of himself and quickly softened his tone, "She was a great woman, and she's going to be missed by an awful lot of folks."

"Now, Jim," Masters began again, "what time did you get here yesterday?"

"One o'clock."

"Now, you're sure about that, Jim? You weren't here for the initial viewin' by the family, were you?"

"Oh, yeah, that's right," Jim corrected himself. "I got here a little late for that. I think the family gathered at twelve, but I got tied up downtown and didn't get here until about a quarter till, ten till one. Valerie was here on my behalf. The family didn't like . . . Never mind."

"No, go ahead. Did you have something else to say, Jim?" Masters was seemingly curious but had a general understanding of why the family would object to Valerie's presence.

"No, no. Ask your next question, please." Jim was irritated with himself for his loose tongue.

"What was so important that you would miss your mother's viewin', Jim?"

"I just got held up, Bruce. Okay? I mean, I am the mayor of this illustrious city. Just things. You know, busyness." Jim readjusted himself in the chair, turning away from Masters and the direct angle of the camera.

Masters stopped writing and peered over the rim of his glasses "Well, let's just cut through the chase, Jim. You and Grace didn't have a real good relationship, did you?"

"You know we didn't, Bruce. Why are you—"

"Told you I gotta do my job, Jim," Masters interrupted. "Did you and Grace have a good relationship? Yes or no? Simple question."

"No." Jim was short. He didn't know what Bruce was driving at, but if he thought he was going to get into his personal life, he had another think coming. It wasn't like the whole town didn't know most of his business anyway, but there were a few sacred secrets he intended for no one to know.

"When's the last time you and Grace saw each other?"

"I don't know. I can't remember that, Bruce. I'm a busy man." Jim was quick to offer his response.

"One week? One month? One year? Two?" Masters pressed for an answer.

"I told you, I don't know when I. . ."

"Well, do the best you can, Jim. Take your time. Didn't mean to interrupt you there, but we've got as much time as we need here." The detective laid down his pen and leaned back in his chair with his hands behind his head.

"It's been at least a year," Jim confessed.

"Maybe a little longer, Jim? More than two years, would you say?"

"Well, you seem to know already. Just write down what you want, Detective."

"Need an answer, Jim. Two years? Closer to three or longer?"

"Probably so, Bruce. I mean, come on. I've just been a busy man since I got elected. And especially with all the refurbishing of the downtown area."

"Shame, a real shame," Masters uttered under his breath.

"I'm sorry? What did you say?"

"Never mind. Tell me, Jim, when you saw your mama the last time, did the two of you get into any kind of an argument?"

Jim paused, not wishing to go there, but his mind took him anyway.

*   *   *

GRACE WILLINGHAM'S FRONT PORCH, FEBRUARY 17, THREE YEARS PRIOR

Grace Willingham sat on her veranda sipping a glass of home-made cucumber lemonade. She knew it was her son's favorite refreshment. She had a pitcher made for him, iced down, and a glass waiting to be filled. She recalled summers when he was at home. As soon as the cucumbers came into season, she kept a supply made up for the boy. He would come home sweaty from playing and head straight for the refrigerator. She anticipated his arrival every day and welcomed him with an open door. She came to love the clammy kisses on the cheek from him and his tag-along buddies as they rushed past her headed for the refreshing concoction. The boys would down a gallon of her special brew in a heartbeat, which kept Grace's heart in rhythm.

"Morning, Mama." Jim's voice brought Grace back from her daydreams.

"James, honey, I'm so glad you came by. Here, have some cucumber lemonade. It's good and fresh. Made it 'specially for you this morning." Her voice was loving and kind.

"No, thanks. Gotta get going. Lots to do today. You wanted to see me?" Jim was looking toward her but never caught Grace's eyes. Had he done so, he would have seen the wound he had inflicted upon her spirit turning down a taste of her special recipe. Her arthritic hands had ached and even trembled with the labor-intensive ordeal of peeling and slicing the cucumbers and extracting the necessary juice with the lemon press. She had offered prayer as she prepared it, hoping the potion would take him back to a "remember when" moment when he was a forbearing young boy who respected her as a woman of great faith. Instead, he gazed above her head as though he was looking through glass.

"James, sit, please. Let's talk. You and I have not had a soul-searching talk in an awful long time. I miss my time with you, Son. We've had our differences, but you know my heart. There is unconditional love here for you. Always has been. It doesn't matter what you've done in the—"

"Stop, Mama. Don't go there. There's been too much. I didn't come here for one of your lectures. You sent word that you needed to see me. I thought it was something of importance, not another sermonette. So, spare me. You and I will probably never have a relationship like we did before. I mean, you took me out of your Will. What does that say about what you think of your son, Mama?"

"What I think of you and what I have in my Will don't have anything to do with one another, James. What are material possessions? I wish you wouldn't dwell on—"

"You just don't get it. Look, I'm not the man Dad was. I never will be that man, Grace." Jim knew it irritated his mother to show her disrespect by addressing her in that manner, almost as much as it irritated him to be addressed as James. "I didn't even know him, really. I was too young to remember when Dad left us. All I have are stories from you, and you try to make him out to be some kind of hero that I really can't verify because I never knew the man. Okay? All I know is I am not that man. Give it up, Mama. And I don't want God on your terms either. I believe. I just don't live and breathe Him every minute like you, Mama."

"James, I wish you wouldn't say that because you haven't tried living the life. And, you don't have to be your dad. I've never said you did. You've accomplished much, but you've also made some very poor choices along the—"

"Mom, I know that. You've told me over and over what a rotten individual I am. And it doesn't—"

"James Albert Willingham, I have never said any such thing to you. People hear what their heart wants to hear at times."

Jim knew his mother was right, but he was intent on making his point to her. "It doesn't matter what I accomplish, Mama. It will never be enough in your eyes because I don't believe the way you do." Jim was becoming agitated that the subject of religion was being broached again by Grace. She had managed to bring hundreds if not thousands of people into church, but it was clear it ate at the very core of her soul that she couldn't get her son baptized. He dared not say it aloud, but he thought—*I refuse to give up the life I have for something I can't even see.* And then, as always, it spooked Jim when Grace ostensibly read his thoughts.

"Son, remember this: The character of a great leader is defined when he abandons an idea of truth for the reality thereof."

"Bye, Mama. I have to go. I have a meeting at three o'clock." And with that, Jim turned on his heels and walked off the porch of his childhood home and the dwelling place of Grace Willingham, his beloved mother, forever.

"Come again, will you, Son? I'd love to visit with you for

a while." Jim was opening the door to his car as she raised her voice and her bottom out of her front-porch rocker and continued her appeal, "I love you, and God loves you, too, James Albert Willingham II. Don't ever forget Whose you are." Grace sat back down and began to pray. A lone salty tear made its way to the glass of the tasty brew nested in her lap.

*   *   *

"Do you need me to repeat the question, Jim?" Detective Masters asked.

"I–I'm sorry, Bruce, what was your question again?"

"I said when you saw your mama the last time, did you two get into an argument?"

"The answer is no. There was no arguing." Jim was solemn but firm.

Detective Masters pulled a document out of a folder and started to speak when Jim interrupted.

"Look, if I need to take a polygraph, Bruce, I will. I don't have anything to hide. I didn't take those jewels. Can I just get out of here? I need to make a phone call." Jim stood and pushed back his chair and headed for the door.

"Sure, sure, Jim. Didn't mean to upset you. We may need to talk again, but for now, you can go. Of course, you can't *leave*-leave you understand. No one in, no one—"

"Yeah, yeah, got it. Thanks, Bruce. Hope this ends soon."

"Hey, Jim," Bruce said, stopping him, "I am really sorry for your loss. Your mama was a great woman."

"I know. Everyone knows." Jim was unsure why his heart met

with a stabbing pain of regret at his response.

"Just leave the door open, Jim, if you would," and Detective Masters yelled out for Officer Ricks to bring in the next person to be interviewed—the daughter and oldest child of Grace Willingham.

Chapter 4

"Mornin', Gladys." The detective stood as his next witness entered the room.

"You obviously got more sleep than I did if you think it's such a good morning, Bruce Masters," Gladys scowled.

"Have a seat, Gladys. We need to talk," Masters said, pointing to the larger of the two chairs.

"This is ridiculous, Bruce Masters. You've got the wrong person in this chair, Mister," and Gladys Faye Willingham-Murphy wriggled her rear-end into the smaller chair.

"I don't get it, Gladys. I would think you and Jim would be delighted that we're conductin' this investigation. Don't you want to get to the bottom of this mystery?" he asked.

"I can't speak for James, but I believe y'all ought to be questioning all those other folks in that room, but you started off with Mother's children? That's unforgiveable!" she hastily protested.

"Gladys, I need to advise you—"

"Honestly, Bruce, I'm very offended at the insulting nature

of this procedure. We are griev— I am grieving over the loss of my mother, and you have me in here questioning me like I'm a common thief! How dare you, Bruce Masters. I'll have—"

"Gladys, I need to read you—"

"—your badge for this. I would never think of stealing jewels off my mother's dead body when she would obviously will them to me. I'm the most likely candidate for those. I'm her only daughter— Well, only blo— I'm her only daughter. It's reasonable that they would be left to me. I should have those jewels. I mean, I wouldn't steal them anyway, mind you."

"By the way, this is being videoed, Ma'am. You need to realize that up front," Masters firmly informed.

Gladys began smoothing back her hair and straightening her blouse. She assumed perfect posture and crossed her legs at the ankles. She realized how she might have unintentionally incriminated herself and immediately reined in her rage. She fumbled for a handkerchief from her purse and dabbled at her nose and eyes as if emotions were getting the best of her. She needed to compose her thoughts and be careful not to let her uncertainty of Grace's wishes get in the way of this interview procedure. "Oh, and I look a frightening mess, Bruce. Do we have to have that thing on? I don't want everyone seeing me cry."

"Yes, Ma'am, I'm afraid it's the rules. You look fine, Gladys. You've been under duress. Everyone's gonna understand that," he reassured her in his professional tone yet trying to put her at ease in order to effect a credible interview. *It'd be a shame to waste the time and not get one shred of evidence that might lead me to my villain,* he thought.

"I'm sorry, Detective. I'm just so upset about Mother's funeral.

This should be a respectable time for her, you see. She deserved that much. She was a good person," Gladys shared through her sniffles.

"I agree one hundred percent, Ma'am, but Miss Grace herself would want a thief brought to justice. And that's what we intend to do. We owe that much to your mama."

"Then she'd just try to win his soul to Jesus."

The detective chuckled, because it was the truth, although Gladys sounded a bit snide in her comment.

"But, Bruce, why in the world would you suspect that I—"

"It is standard procedure. I have to do my job, Ma'am, that's all. I need to read you your rights before we proceed any further. You have the right to remain silent..."

Detective Masters was trying to be tender. After all, he was on camera as well. He was well familiar with Gladys's pretentious spirit. He reflected antics she had pulled on her friends back in high school, dragging them into her latest drama only to betray their loyalty. That gal was a viper. Back then she was a looker, not a knockout, but a young girl who would please the tease, and you don't have to look like much to turn a young boy's head for that. She had worked her charm on many a gullible young male. The guy who made it that far was hoping to get into Grace's Will and lay claim to her jewels. Bruce was grateful he had not been victim to a bleeding heart by "the" Gladys Willingham. *She turned many a head in her good ol' days, but she ain't seen one of them days in a lot of years,* he thought to himself.

What gene Gladys's character developed from was a real anomaly to Masters today. She had been a lovely girl outwardly in high school, but something had happened that spent those good looks in short speed. He had only caught rumor of some female who outsmarted her wits, but his memory failed him now as to whom she was. He recalled the girl was related in some way, but he couldn't quite pull up the connection. He was obviously tired and processing was slow. His mental computer worked faster on a normal day. He would give that point more thought later, or see if he could get it out of Gladys now. *Might not be the appropriate time to find out who crossed this woman. Timing is everythin' when you're trying to nab a criminal.*

Whoever had outsmarted Gladys really worked a number on her, and that was the beginning of the end. She had lost something that day, which only served to make her a lot meaner. She married an unlikely candidate who became an alcoholic. An unhappy marriage, a barren womb, and a sour spirit might serve to rob any woman of her charm. It seemed to have imbalanced more than hormones in Gladys Faye Willingham-Murphy. If you compared her to the high school yearbook, you couldn't pick her out of a lineup today if your life depended on it. The cute gal from bygone days was someone Gladys would long to return to until her dying days.

She surely hadn't held her beauty like her mama, and Grace certainly was familiar with hard times. Gladys never shared the charm or spirit of Grace Carissa Willingham. Jim was the spitting image of his dad from what I hear. But poor Gladys, if there'd ever been a family misfit, she fit the bill. That girl would chew you up and spit you out in a New York minute and never feel an ounce of remorse for her actions. Just a hard, bitter woman, that Gladys. No wonder Ralph took to drinking. I suppose it'd drive any man to drink. Masters shuffled papers. Gladys was feeling uneasy at the silence.

"Should I get my attorney? Perhaps that would be wise." Gladys had entertained the thought before coming in.

Bruce realized he had gotten lost in thought. "I apologize, Gladys. I was thinking about another case there," and he cleared his throat. "You certainly have the right to call a lawyer, and we can suspend if you—"

"Wait a minute. I haven't done anything. Why would I need an attorney, for Pete's sake! Just get this over with, would ya, Bruce? I want to get back out there with Mother, God rest her soul," and she began to sniffle ever so slightly.

"Gladys, are you sure you wanna proceed? I mean, we can stop and let you call Shawn Allen and get him in here to represent you. I want you to understand that." Masters didn't want anything to be compromised in any way. Sometimes the most unsuspecting person turns out to be the perpetrator.

"No, no, I'm fine. Just proceed." Gladys readjusted and focused on Masters.

"Gladys, you're the one who discovered the jewels missing off your mama, correct?"

"Yes. It was the strangest thing. I had been in the receiving line and had just looked at Mother. They were on her then, Bruce. They looked so beautiful. The line was really slow because people just wanted to gawk at Mother's jewels. Even so, it would be rude to rush everyone. So, we just let people take their time."

"Gladys, did anyone stand there long enough that it would've given you concern? I mean, maybe a family member that you mighta noticed?"

"Oh, Bruce, Madelyn was hanging all over that casket. She

and that African-American druggie of hers. I'm so certain she did this. She was forever going over to Mother's. I'm sure she was worming her way into Mother's good graces just trying to get her to will those beauties over to her. I never have trusted that little girl, never have." It was true. Gladys had never cared for Madelyn. She was a disgrace to the Willingham family as far as Gladys was concerned. Her tattooed body simply disgusted her. She wondered if perhaps she shouldn't have pointed the finger so quickly, but dismissed the thought with another. *It's the truth, and I've been dying to say that for a long time, so there.*

"Did you notice any friends who mighta lingered around the casket?" Masters inquired.

"Oh, my goodness. There were so many who paid respects that first hour. I don't even know if I can remember who all came through. Come to think of it, I did notice that Melissa Fitzgerald was at the casket for an extended period. Even James mentioned it. I didn't think she'd ever stop talking to us. We never knew she had such an admiration for Grace. It did seem a little odd, I must admit."

"Think, Gladys. Did you see the jewels on your mama after Melissa moved away?"

"Oh, let me think. Did I see them after that?" Gladys considered her answer carefully. *Be careful, Gladys, pointing fingers erroneously can cause a lot of hard feelings. Remember?* She had been down that road before a time or two. "Gee, Bruce, I'd hate to say. I know others came after her. I want to say they would have said something if the jewels had not been there. But you never know how people react to things like that. They might have just thought we wouldn't be stupid enough to put them on her. I didn't want to. It was not my best judgment. But that was Mother's wishes, and Nick follows the letter of the law on his agreements when making funeral arrangements. None of what we wanted mattered. I could have wrung his neck off even with his big toe, making this funeral a celebration instead of wake. Now look at it. It's a complete disaster!"

"Any other family members you might be suspicious of, Gladys? Jim's been pretty angry with Grace. Took him out of the Will I understand."

"As well she should have, Bruce." Gladys leaned over and lowered her voice. "Jim has disappointed all of us time and time again. People may believe he's a great mayor, but everyone knows he's lousy at choosing his women." She leaned back in her chair. "Now, what did you— Oh, yeah, no, I don't think Jim would have done that kind of thing. He has his faults, but no, I don't want to think that. I won't let myself." Gladys straightened up in her chair and brushed both sleeves with her hands.

"Well, Grace did take him out of the Will? You know that, don't you?"

Gladys sat up in her chair. "What? What did you say? No, I don't believe that. Mother never told me that for sure, but then, she didn't talk too much about her private affairs. Well, how about that? I had heard that myself, but never knew for sure. So, she did do it after all. Well, well, well."

"You didn't know, but it sounds like you thought she might. Tell me about that, Gladys." Masters settled back, figuring this could be a story he needed to take in.

"I think it was Valerie—and she might be someone else we should consider here—but Mother had seen women come and go in James's life. Grace loved Annie. We all did. She was good to James. Better than he deserved. But then, everyone knows that. He has children scattered around every county in these parts, and there are several who lay claim to his heritage but haven't been able to prove paternity. I'm sure Grace's fortune has a lot to do with their accusation. I mean, it's clear that everyone wants a piece of that pie." Gladys was rolling through her story, barely stopping to breathe.

"There was something that happened between Mother and James. I never knew what it was. He's never mentioned it to me either. You know Grace. If she didn't want to share something, her lips were buttoned. If anyone ever wanted to share a confidence just to get it off their chest, Grace was who they went to. I declare, that woman was a saint. Mother always said, 'A secret is a silent friend until it finds its voice.'"

Gladys caught her breath and continued her recitation. "But it was about five years ago, maybe a little more, that Mother and James just drifted apart. I'm not quite sure why. Like I said, she was lock-jawed about it. Would never tell me a thing. If I ever brought up James, she got real quiet, like her heart was troubled. For the life of me I couldn't get a thing out of her, though. It's kind of driven me crazy not knowing, you know. Mother's always talked to me about things and I just..." Gladys paused, considering her contradiction. "Well, I guess I wouldn't know what she didn't tell me, now, would I? How silly to say that," and she gave a nervous giggle.

She caught her uneasiness and quickly resumed. "Anyway, I had mentioned to mother that if something was going on with her and James, she might consider taking him out of the Will. Not that I wanted everything, mind you. I simply made the suggestion because she seemed so distant from him. It was something I felt like might settle her down a bit. You know how you wouldn't want someone to walk off with an inheritance who wouldn't even go to see you for months or years on end. I mean, James was her only son. How could he do that to her? It's heartless, I tell you, simply heartless."

Masters leaned forward, realizing that Gladys didn't reveal anything helpful. It was clear, however, that she would hope to be the benefactor of all of Grace's wealth. She didn't fool him any. *You've been waiting for Grace to bite the dust for a long time. Betcha never dreamed your mama would live as long as she did. She was a healthy button, that gal. Took care of herself. Always did. And what a way to go—in her sleep. Peaceful, beautiful smile on her face, the coroner said. Just lying there like an angel, content, and at peace with her Maker. What a way to live and die.*

"Gladys, how long were you standing at the casket when you discovered the jewels were gone?"

"Oh, I–I–I don't know, Bruce. You know how when you've seen something, it's like—Well, it's like you see but— It's like you know they're there, or should be there, so you don't notice them after a while."

"Well, but it seems those would be somethin' that would catch your eye anytime you'd walk up, don't you think? I mean, Miss Grace didn't wear those things every day. They were a special occasion-type occurrence for her, from what I understand."

"Oh, Mother only wore them on the anniversary of hers and Daddy's wedding. Every year, it was a beautiful thing. She'd gussy up and have candlelight dinner, just her, and in a strange sort of way, him. She'd set a dual place setting and sit and have conversation with him, just like he was sitting in that chair across from her. Never wanted to be disturbed, but you could see her from the other room. It was the only time she excluded the kids from any meal. She fed us ours, now, don't get me wrong. But she'd clean up that kitchen and be done with us for the night. It was her time with Daddy."

"She really loved that man, didn't she?" Masters affirmatively questioned.

"You know, I guess she did. Wish I could have known him more. I remember a few things about Daddy, but I was pretty young when he went away. All the events of that season in our lives are kind of a blur to me. But since it all happened, she has never said anything but good things about Daddy—and really everyone involved in the unfortunate events." Masters was a bit surprised at the softness in Gladys's voice. He had never seen that side of her. There was tenderness there. What a shame. It must have been lost when her dad exited the picture. You have to wonder what could have been different for this family without the chain of events surrounding the Willingham legacy.

Masters hated snapping her out of her serene moment, but he had to get back on task. There were many more witnesses to be interviewed and, at this rate, he would be interviewing another two days.

"Gladys, so how long were you standing there before you discovered the missing jewels? And, go ahead and tell me what that looked like, you know, how you responded to your discovery."

"Oh, it couldn't have been long, maybe thirty seconds, a minute, possibly two."

"Well, that's a wide range there, Gladys. Was it thirty seconds or two minutes? Could it have been longer?" he pressed her.

"Good grief, Bruce, I don't know. It could have been less, could have been more. I mean, come on, I'm grieving over the loss of my mother!"

"I understand, but think. It's important. Could it have been long enough to, say—"

"Don't you dare go there, Bruce Masters! Don't you dare! I did not and would not think of doing such a thing. They were going to be mine anyway." Gladys made her way out of the chair with effort and was obviously rattled. "I would have never put them on her to start with. People didn't need to gawk at them like they were on display in a museum. They were a family heirloom. But now, they're not here. And you men need to find them. Do you hear me? You need to find them and soon. We have to bury my mother!"

"Just this one last question, Gladys. How did you announce it?"

"Well, I screamed. I just announced they were gone, 'The jewels are gone!' I yelled. And then I fainted. I mean, gosh, I don't know what relevance that has to do with anything. I just said, 'They're gone!' and I screamed and fainted." She was puzzled at why such a trivial incident might matter in the whole scheme of things.

"Okay, Gladys. Thank you for your patience. I don't want you leaving until I talk to everyone here. Okay?"

"Oh, Bruce, how long will that be? I'm awfully tired. I need to get home, and I mean, we have to bury Mother. It's supposed to be this afternoon. Now what? We have decisions to make.

I just need my rest and to get my senses about me. Let me go home and—"

"I'm sorry, wish I could accommodate you, but no one in," and Gladys chimed in with Masters, "no one out."

"Ricks, bring me Ashley Willingham," Masters yelled out, and then muttered under his breath, "I need a change of pace."

Chapter 5

Nora turned right off of Victory Drive and into the mile-long drive leading to Grace Willingham's place. The pavement was still damp from the early-morning rain. The hardwoods and spindly pines peeked out from the acreage on either side. But it was the moss-laden bravura oaks that summoned visitors to the majestic tranquility of the antebellum homeplace barely seen in the distance. The house was stately but accommodated no stuffy, elaborate décor. The furnishings were simple comfort with impeccable taste. In the good ol' days with GG–Nora's special name for Grace, the spacious white two-story home complete with wrap-around porch resounded with voices of energetic, creative imaginations of every grandchild, whether legitimate or not, encouraged by a woman who loved each of them more than life. Rockers lined the porch, each bearing the hand-painted name of a grandchild. Labeled as tacky by some, the simple gesture of an assigned spot on GG's porch swelled the heart of each of her special youngsters, especially those, like herself, shunned by public scrutiny.

Nora gazed upon the eighty-acre tract of property surrounding Grace's home. These woods became a storehouse of memories as trails were blazed taking its explorers to coastal creeks, neighboring monuments, and magnificent pre–Civil War homes. Nora recalled the thrill of camping adventures in these woods with Grace Willingham. GG was amazingly energetic and always wearied the kids long before she ever succumbed to exhaustion. Nights under the stars with Grandma Grace never ended without a fabulous story from her. Some were stories of bygone days with an impressionable history lesson attached. Others were fashioned from her own fictitious tales that kept all ages spellbound and eager for the upcoming chapter at the next campout.

Nora was breathless gazing upon the place she held so dear. She slowly made her way up the steps, allowing her hand to glide along the rail savoring the thought of the hands of her GG that had brushed it millions of times. To the right was the Spanish mosaic tile table for two. That was GG's Barcelona purchase. Spain was Nora's choice of travel. Each grandchild enjoyed that very special time with Grandma Grace—their choice of a trip abroad. Nora treasured her Parc Güell souvenir salamander, the symbol of Antoni Gaudi's work.

Nora hoped GG would have left the table to her. Many glasses of cucumber lemonade had been shared between the two of them, along with much conversation during those difficult teen years. GG always had the right words to soothe a wounded spirit at the hands of a mal-intentioned suitor or an injudicious best-friends-forever betrayer. She could almost hear GG say, "God's best is always waiting in the wings of our worst."

It was a stab in the dark that Nora might actually enter the house, but lucky for her, GG had not changed the secret hiding place for the key to the homeplace—under the last rock by the first step. She was a woman of her word. She had assured Nora if she ever needed a place to come and crash when she wasn't home, there would be a key waiting to welcome her. For that, Nora was grateful. Otherwise, she wouldn't have this private time to wrap herself in the memories the two of them had shared. Being denied entrance into Turner's to pay respects might have been a blessing in disguise. Here was GG's spirit. It was here where Nora learned to love GG. Here was where her childhood values and morals were shaped and her career established. It was Grandma Grace who opened the eyes in her mind to possibilities for success.

Nora was an unlikely candidate for that according to the likes of folks in this historic place. But not in GG's eyes. She saw something in Nora, as she did in every grandchild, which was beyond success. It was GG who introduced Nora to *"the plans I have for you," declares the LORD, "plans to prosper you and not to harm you, plans to give you hope and a future."* Nora smiled as she could still hear the ringing of GG's voice in her ears.

Nora slid the key in the door and turned the handle. She made her way to the sitting room, picked up a Grandma-scented throw pillow, and buried her face. It was the first time since she'd left Spain that she had allowed herself to cry. She was trying to be strong because GG wanted everyone to celebrate her demise, but Nora couldn't help herself. She would celebrate GG's Heavenly reunion, but she would miss the times with her grandmother.

Nora found herself regretting not having traveled home for more than five years. GG never pressured her to return, but Nora knew in her heart Grace Carissa Willingham should have been honored with a visit from her granddaughter. Grandma told her, "Career and life should never be too busy for family." Nora was feeling the sting of truth to GG's wisdom, especially to honor one who invested her life in preparing those she loved for the plans the Lord had for them.

*   *   *

"INTERVIEW HEADQUARTERS" AT TURNER'S FUNERAL HOME, OCTOBER 15, 8:55 A.M.

"My turn, Detective?" The petite blue-eyed blonde unassumingly eased into the room. Her captivating smile resembled the essence of the lady lying in state. This beautiful gal embodied Grace's personality—gentle as a lamb but tough as nails when necessary. The two qualities collided to develop the diplomatically-kind-while-disassembling-your-thoughts trait unique to Grace and now replicated in Ashley Renee Willingham.

Bruce Masters got out of his chair and raced over to greet her. "Ashley, how ya doin', Sweetheart?" He gave her a respectable hug and led her to the chair closest to him. He positioned himself catty-cornered across the end of the impressive maple desk, swinging one leg as he prepared to interview the beloved granddaughter of Grace Carissa Willingham.

"I'm distressed over all this, quite honestly," Ashley began. "Grandma deserved a better send-off than this. I'm beside myself over the whole ordeal. I've gone over scenario after scenario, retracing people that came through yesterday morning, analyzing the time and course of events, and attempting to envision who was standing near the casket when Aunt Gladys had her screaming and fainting episode. I'm baffled, Detective Masters, really baffled over this one."

"Please, Ashley, call me Bruce. Really, it's okay."

"Who would have pulled such a farcical stunt, Detective? They have to know they'll be caught, and when they are—"

"You'll take them down, won't ya, Tiger?"

Ashley turned up a Grace Willingham half smile at the right corner of her mouth, graciously accepting the compliment. Ashley had enjoyed a short but promising career. She had already gained a victory in one of the largest awards by a Chatham County jury—a nice hefty 26-million-dollar verdict. No other lawyer in Savannah, Georgia would take on the case. The poor plaintiff came to Ashley, who had just hung her shingle two months prior. But, hungry lawyers take on the most unlikely cases. Initially, the green attorney was the laughing stock of the Chatham County Bar Association, especially by the 23-lawyer-strong, smug, and prestigious veteran firm of O'Neal & Hunter. But they weren't laughing so heartily once the defendant they had represented for three decades became Ashley's most loyal client some two months after the verdict came down. She was glad Grandma lived to witness that hallmark in her career, especially since Grace was ultimately responsible in helping Ashley find her passion for law.

"Grace loved you, Girl. You were the apple of that woman's eye, I'm tellin' ya. She was so proud of you, always boasting about her Ashley Dahlin'. Nuttin' haughty, mind ya. You know Grace. She didn't do things that-a-way. Not gonna rub nothin' in the face of nobody, even those most deserving. But she got in her praise in a mighty dignified manner."

Ashley would have cringed at Masters's butchering of our beautiful English grammar, but rather, her eyes filled with tears. Grandma Grace boasted of all her grandchildren. *That* was her style. It was part of her beauty. Whether she approved or disapproved of someone's lifestyle, well, that was between Grace and God. You could never go there with Grandma. If she had nothing good to say, disapproval was introduced to silent prayer. It wasn't uncommon during overnight stays for Ashley to witness it firsthand. Grandma's kneeling posture was Ashley's first exposure to strength and poise in times of duress. The disclosure would manifest itself to equip Ashley's passion to fight for justice while staying calm in the midst of strong-arm attacks on human decency from a corrupt world.

"Are you okay? Do you think you can press on? Don't mean to rush your private thoughts. Take more time if—"

"No, no, Detective. I'm sorry. I'm fine. I know you have a full day."

"Let's do this thing right, Ashley. You have the right to remain silent," and Masters continued the recitation of her Miranda rights.

"Ashley, I understand that you prepared Grace's Will?"

"I did, though under objection," Ashley replied. "I didn't think it was a good idea for me to know everything Grandma was planning, but she's so fair. Always has been. Who could defy her intent regarding the inheritance she would dispense to its recipients? But you and I know, in a family who has known its share of turmoil, it can and will be done. With three siblings to divide it between, if there can be—"

"That's right, Ashley, there *are* three children. Have you

heard from Carmen yet? I meant to ask Nick about his mom and when she might arrive, and it completely slipped my mind until you just mentioned it. Of course, your dad nor Gladys mentioned her at all. It's a crying shame how all that came down, Ashley. Your grandmother took Carmen in and loved her like her own, adopted her, and then she runs off with some hoodlum. Pert-near broke Grace's heart, she did. Seemed like she took it as a personal failure, although she never should have. It weren't her fault. You can't shake them roots that come along with adopted children sometimes, regardless of how wholesome the environment they grow up in." On its surface, Masters's observation had merit.

"That's true, Detective Masters, but you can't forget the roots of her own flesh-and-blood children. How do you explain that?"

Ashley's point was well taken. Jim had to be a huge disappointment to Grace. And, well, Gladys couldn't have brought her much joy either with her constant stirring up of hornets' nests around the community. You'd never know they were children of the fine lady Grace Willingham was.

"I believe Nick has been in touch with Carmen and she's en route. She was coming for the funeral, but there's not one… for now, at least. I've spoken to Nick about arrangements for a delay. I think he's anticipating your investigation being completed today, midmorning perhaps, tomorrow at the very latest, and perhaps we'll do the funeral on late Sunday afternoon." Ashley had cause for pause, and then broke out in a slight chuckle.

"Amused?"

"Grace always said she didn't deserve it but would love to be buried on The Lord's Day. I find it humorous that even when she's gone, her legacy is being blessed. I can just see her doing her "happy dance" and furiously clapping those sweet little hands in applause at my sudden revelation. She was always sharpening my fact-finding skills."

Masters chuckled, too, but had to get down to business. Time was wasting. "Ashley, other than your dad, who else was at odds with Grace Willingham?"

"You mean family? Friends? Acquaintances? She didn't have too many enemies, you know that. She wasn't angry at Dad, just terribly disappointed in his poor choices in life. But she never stopped loving him."

"Oh, no, I know, I know. I didn't mean to imply that any indifference was Grace's doin'. I've never known a more fair and equitable woman than your grandma." Masters wanted to dispel any ambiguity about Grace's reputation. *Don't need this little cookie as my enemy.*

"No, I understand. I'm just saying it wasn't an ongoing argument at all between Grandma and Dad. There was only distance because Dad chose that course. As far as other family members, Nora hasn't been home for years to see GG, as she always referred to her. I find that odd, too. They were so close. I know Grandma talked about Nora calling her from time to time and how well she was doing in Spain. But then, again, you'd never hear it from Grandma if she was disappointed in any of us. But, I know Nora idolized that woman."

"But I haven't heard anyone mention Nora's presence. She hasn't been here. If she loved her so much, where is she now?"

"No, I haven't seen her, but I heard one of your officers mention a few minutes ago about the 'hot frame' who tried to come in insisting she was family. So, Nora may be in town. She would definitely fit the description, whatever that means."

"Well, that eliminates her, I suppose," Masters concluded.

"Unless she had someone here as a plant to carry it out. I mean, we can't dismiss any angles, Detective." Ashley didn't want to sound accusatory by any stretch, but Nora was always secure in the fact that Grandma Grace was willing the jewels to her. It never settled well on Ashley's spirit about her assumption, but she had kept that matter to herself all these years.

"Is there any reason to suspect her, Ashley? I mean, you would know."

"You know I'm not at liberty to divulge anything about that Will, so don't ask me." Ashley set her jaw, sitting up straight in her chair and readjusting her position. Personal or not, she would never forget the oath she took as an attorney. "That will all be disclosed when the Will is probated and disclosed."

"I'm sorry, I didn't mean to imply that—" *She's a smooth one, that girl.* Masters knew he'd never weasel anything out of her that might give him a clue who was to be the recipient of those jewels. Although, if pressured, he would have to admit curiosity was killing the cat.

Ashley seemed to have concealed the reality of the situation from the detective. Truth was, she didn't have a clue who was the recipient of those jewels. Could be her, could be Nora, could be someone else. She was curious during the whole process of drafting the Will. Grace was her own woman, and she was a calculated one. When Ashley asked if Grace had overlooked anything before the Will was finalized, her response was quick: "If you're talking about my jewels, Ashley, I have that already taken care of. You won't have to worry about that. It will be revealed at the appropriate time."

If Ashley hadn't seen the jewels herself at the wake, she would have believed Grandma had given them to the church. She hadn't seen her with them on since hers and Grandpa's last anniversary. Best of Ashley's calculations, other than the day they had been gifted to her, the yearly ritual to pay homage to her love for Grandpa Albert were the only times they had seen daylight. All in all, the jewels were worn at least sixty-two—no, no, make that sixty-three occasions.

"No offense taken, Detective," Ashley reassured him. "Now, as far as friends, I never heard Grandma speak ill of anyone, so if there was a friend sideways with her, it was news to me. Acquaintances, now that's another story. You know Benny who worked here at Turner's for years was really sweet on Grandma. He was a nice enough man, and a good business person, I suppose. I understand he and Thomas had planned to buy out Richard Turner when they got the funds together. But, of course, that was before Nick came to town. I know Benny pursued Grace pretty hot and heavy there for a while until he ran fate with her gun. She had it propped up by her tea table on the front porch one day. It's no unfounded rumor. I was there and witnessed the whole thing. When he drove up, she asked me to step inside, which I did, but I peered through the window to see what set Grandma's jaw sideways.

"I have never laughed so hard in my life once I got to my room. Heaven knows I would have never laughed around Grace about that. But you should have seen Benny Fulkerson's eyes when Grace pulled that double-barrel shotgun on him. She said, 'Benny, I've told you my last time I have no interest in any man.

I'm flattered that you think I'm worthy for you to be my suitor, but I want no part of it. I fell in love once, and it was for keeps. Now, I hate to resort to this measure, but apparently there's some part of no you don't understand. So let me say this one last time: Don't come calling on me again. I'm happy to be your friend, but I won't ever be your mistress. Do we have an understanding?' Benny jumped in that car so fast, and all you saw down that mile-long trek out of Grandma's place was a blue streak. I know Grace would have never brought harm to the man, but she got her point across."

"Benny never reported that incident. That all sounds pretty innocent, though, don't you think, Ashley?" Masters was digging for her angle, if there was one.

"Maybe, maybe not. After the pomp and circumstance surrounding the jewels, it didn't take long for the men to come around once the dust settled. Dad said when he was younger, and they were on speaking terms, Grace was constantly turning away proposals. She believed they were only after the jewels, not her. Funny, she never saw in herself the beauty that was obvious to everyone else. Her thought was, 'You're only as beautiful as what comes out of you.' I can almost hear her saying it now. There is an awful lot of truth to that."

"Indeed, indeed. So you think Benny could be someone we should talk to, eh?"

"Oh, I don't know. I'm just saying, if jewels were the only things he was after, could be. He was in the viewing room at the time of the theft. They say he always loved her and was taking it hard, but I didn't witness too much emotion. I know he always wanted to see those jewels, though. I've been told he had made mention of that to several folks in town before he met up with Grandma's gun." Ashley and Masters snickered in unison.

Masters thought that an interesting point and made note of the observation. "Anything else, Ashley? I mean, I didn't ask you if you were all right with Grace. I just assume you were, seeing's that you're her attorney and all, not to mention her favorite grandchild. I mean, you've taken care of her business since then, from what the rumblings have been around town."

"Grandma Grace always taught me what people don't know they make up, Detective. You should know that by now yourself. Grandma used to say, 'People conjecture about a lot, and somewhere in the assumptions lies the truth . . . or the lie.' One thing we know, the truth always surfaces. If not now, there will be a day of reckoning."

Masters nodded as if to agree with the profoundness of such a young professional. There was more depth there than any amount of schooling could have instilled in her. She learned well under the tutelage of Grace Carissa Willingham. He showed Ashley to the door and thanked her for her time.

"Ricks, get me Madelyn Joy Willingham."

"Will do, Boss. Be right back." Ricks scurried to retrieve the next witness.

*   *   *

"Interview Headquarters" at
Turner's Funeral Home, October 15, 9:13am,

"Come on in, Sweetheart," Masters motioned with hearty

invitation.

"I ain't your sweetheart. Sir." Madelyn had a sharp tongue, and had she chomped on it like she was masticating her gum, it might have tamed it a bit. Her motto was "to take nothing off nobody." She'd had a couple of scraps with the law already, and Masters was well aware of her discontent for the system. She also was no stranger to the courtroom. Between drugs, domestic violence—both giver and recipient— and bounced checks, she kept the seats warm in the criminal justice division. A newcomer would be hard pressed to understand why Madelyn was shown such mercy and received a slap on the wrist rather than serving serious time for her behavior. The townspeople had a good sense for it, however, but always failed to vote their conscience when elections rolled around and someone had the audacity to oppose the incumbent's seat of judge or mayor.

"How's Connie these days, Madelyn?"

"Haven't seen her in a month of Sundays. This has nothing to do with my mom. If you want to talk about or to her, you can catch her on the street corner. You probably have before. She's pricy, though, you know."

"I need to read you your Miranda Warning, Madelyn. You're most familiar with that, but it's standard procedure."

"Just get on with it, Bruce, Madelyn snipped.

"'Detective' to you, young lady."

"Whatever."

He recited the Rights. "Let's skip all the bull and talk about where you were in the funeral parlor when the jewels were stolen, Madelyn. Do you remember where you might've been? Oh, and by the way, you know this is videoed. For your protection." *And mine*, he thought.

"I was sitting in some chairs with Kareem."

"Where was your baby?" Masters inquired. He knew without a baby in hand, it would be easier to swipe those jewels.

"I think Ashley had relieved me for a minute. The baby had been crying and I was worn out. Kareem never does anything to help me out. He's such a jerk." Madelyn chewed her gum harder as she crossed her legs, hiking her skirt so it left nothing to the imagination of an onlooker.

Masters was careful not to let his eyes wander. He had to remember this was videotaped. But Madelyn was truly a beautiful girl. A delectably tempting body and anyone would love to— *Her body's a roadmap of tattoos, and she's got rainbow-colored hair for Pete's sake, Masters! Still, what a piece of handiwork. C'mon! What are you thinking? Dismiss the thought, Masters. You can't go there anymore. Those days are gone. You're a happily married man now, and a new Christian.*

"How long did Ashley have the baby— What's his name, again?" The detective wanted to try to tenderize the session a bit, and if the girl had half the heart of a true mother, he knew she would cave when he talked about her baby.

"Bryson. Like you care. I know what you're trying to do. Won't work. Get on with it."

His jaw stiffened, and Masters set about his work. "So, answer my question, then, Madelyn. How long did Ashley have the baby?"

"I don't know how long. Not long enough in my estimation. I was worn out when I got here, and I'm completely frazzled now. I need to go home. My baby needs a change of clothes.

He's peed through his diaper and smells like a cesspool. I need to get outta this place." Madelyn's agitation was mounting. She needed a fix, and if she had to spend one more hour here, she might blow a gasket. She wished she had refilled her script bottles before heading out; those would've helped until she got the big hits. But, who would have thought someone would be in lockdown at a funeral home? This was insane! She had already found a means of escape, and if this didn't end soon, she'd be making her way out. Doing such would only draw more attention to her. She had to play this cool or she'd be in more trouble than her prostitute mama could work off in trade. Half of the justice system in Chatham County was in Connie's bed, but only a fourth could be attributed to trade for the legal predicaments in which Madelyn found herself.

"You won't be going anywhere, Lil' Lady, until we question everyone here at least once. And if we find out anything we need to call you back for because you weren't up front the first time around, it'll just delay it even more. So let's get through this process here, and you just need to chill and put on your best funeral parlor behavior. Don't care how bad you need a fix this time, Madelyn, there are some big stakes resting on this one. Mama can't help you this time. So when we're done here, relax, take care of your baby, and just remember no one in, no one out."

"If I hear that one more time, I may spit in someone's face. Ask me whatever you need to and let me get back to my baby. He's crying outside and people are irritated."

"When did you and Kareem go up to the casket to pay your respects to Grace? Did you go together? Did he go with you and stand there with his back to you and give you a moment with her? Did he even bother to go up at all?"

"Which question do you want me to answer first?" Madelyn had done this a time or two and knew the rules about compound questions. "Never mind. I can probably answer them all before you could recall what you asked."

Masters could get crossways with this witness given another ten minutes. He had to keep his cool with her or she would storm out of the room. He needed any tips he might glean from Madelyn, but she was a tough one. Her antics were well known. *She's one who needed a couple of woodshed visits way back when. Of course, I guess when you have the parade of men comin' and goin' out of Mom's bedroom for as long as this little gal witnessed it, she's entitled to some anger issues.* Her father, Jim Willingham, never showed concern for Madelyn. The paternity battle for this one was nasty. The DNA unequivocally asserted Jim as the father. As much as Jim would have liked for his involvement with the prostitute to go away, no one dared disrupt the course of legal events. Everyone agreed, including Jim, it had to go down any way Connie called it. She had a long blackmail list of justice officials that had participated in her services. If anyone inter-fered with her pursuit, there would have been a run on broken and wrecked marriages in Chatham and ten counties beyond. *Men get really foolish when it comes to sexual pleasures. But to be talked into videos and believe she wouldn't keep a copy for herself? Seriously? Goes to prove the power of sex over stupidity and book knowledge—it trumps every time!*

"We paid respects several times. Once when it was just family. Once when Gladys and Jim were receiving guests. And then, once when some lady was talking to Gladys incessantly.

Everyone was too polite to go around. I didn't need an invitation or permission. As much as the family doesn't like it, she is *my* grandmother, too, so I took liberties. Granny Grace often said, 'It's easier to get forgiveness than permission.'"

Madelyn knew the context Grace intended with that statement. She was always trying to sell Madelyn on Jesus. She so wanted to know the man that gave Grace Willingham her tenacity, because it looked better on her than it did Madelyn. Grace was loved, revered, and respected. And truth be told, it didn't matter that she had wealth. She was loved for her character. Strangest phenomenon. Madelyn had never known anyone who loved so unconditionally like Granny Grace. If Jesus could do that for her, there might be a chance for Madelyn. For sure no one else forgave Madelyn for what she did. No one would give her a chance. But she could always count on Granny Grace. Regardless of how tight Madelyn's clothes were, or the color of her hair, or how many tattoos or piercings she got, Granny Grace seemed to look at Madelyn's heart. Madelyn had filled Granny's apron with tears many times, just resting her head in her lap while Granny sang "What a Friend We Have in Jesus." Now that she's gone, Madelyn had little hope for ever feeling loved like that again.

Secretly, she hoped she was in the Will, that somehow Granny let the world know that Madelyn had been shafted by Jim Willingham and that Grace would make up for what should have been rightfully Madelyn's. Even if the ol' gal comes through, all the money in the world can't make up for being deprived the benefits of a father. Madelyn would always long to feel the tenderness of a dad's embrace, the protection a father provides his little girl, the daddy-prince dances with his Cinderella baby girl, and to know the feeling of a father who looks at his daughter with pride rather than disdain.

"You okay, Madelyn? You need a moment?" Masters handed her a box of tissues.

Madelyn refused and quickly brushed the tears away with her hands. She really needed a fix. Her emotions were getting the best of her. Where did this come from? Was it Granny Grace or Jim Willingham?

"Where was I? Oh, and Kareem went with me twice. I went once alone. Did he stand with his back to me? I don't know. I was focused on Granny Grace's jew–I mean, the flower–I mean, the ribbon from the grandchildren in the casket area. I noticed it said 'Grandma Grace' and thought about me and Nora who don't call her that. That's where my thoughts were. I couldn't say if Kareem had his back to me or not. I didn't take notice."

"Did you have the Baby–let's see, what's his name?–Bryson with you at any time when you went up?"

"Yeah, once. I know he won't remember it, he's just barely seven months, but I wanted Granny Grace to see him and Bryson to see her. I mean, I know she can't *see*-see him, but…"

"I gotcha. I gotcha." Masters's voice was gentle. He found himself feeling pity on Madelyn, but still not trusting her. She was a pro at manipulating men. He wouldn't fall prey to that, but he was a man of compassion.

"I just needed a moment with my Granny, Detective. That's all." Madelyn was filled with regret. She had promised Granny Grace she'd bring the baby to visit. Grace wanted to hold her great-grandchild. After being clean for a few months before Bryson's delivery, she hit the drugs heavy afterward. Madelyn was too strung out and Grace Willingham would have known immediately. She would have given Madelyn a fit and had prayer meeting over her. She might have gone so far as to get Bryson taken away, and that would have been the end of their relationship. Madelyn wanted to preserve what was special between her and Granny Grace, so she stayed away. Now, there was no chance of fulfilling the promise she had made to her Granny.

As wretched as Madelyn was, Granny Grace always opened her home and her heart to accept Madelyn. She fondly remembered Granny's comforting words: "A heavy hand never met a receptive heart." Grace Willingham's hands were tender and it opened up Madelyn's heart to receive love. If she could break free of these drugs, become self-sufficient and not have to depend on a man, her heart might learn to know this Jesus Granny loved. Those jewels were her ticket out of this flea-bitten town. Surely Granny Grace knew how much she needed them.

"Thanks, Madelyn. I think I got all I need here. We'll get back with you a little later if we need to. Hopin' to wrap this part of the investigation up soon so you can get that boy of yours settled down."

Madelyn turned to leave when Masters spoke again. "Hey, lay low with your use, Madelyn. He's a fine-lookin' kid. Don't lose him to the system. There are lots of wanna-be moms and dads out there, but the foster homes usually get these kids first. It's a rough way to go for these young'uns. Get some help, but get clean."

Madelyn was silent, but appreciated the concern in Bruce Masters's voice. No enforcement officer had ever encouraged her to clean up; they only wanted to paw at her. If she could just find the strength, the support, the means to get clean, she would jump at the chance. No one wanted it more than her… except, of course, Granny Grace.

Chapter 6

827 VICTORY DRIVE, OCTOBER 15, 10:15 A.M.

It would have been futile to attempt to enter at Turner's, according to Nick. Since Carmen was already in town, she took a detour to the Willingham homeplace instead. No blood roots, yet grounded in a heritage that should have turned out differently for her. It had been many years since she had been forced from this home by James Willingham. Time and Grace had helped her lay aside her anger, bitterness, and hatred for that man. How befitting that Grace Willingham would introduce her to the grace of her precious Lord and Savior. Where might she be without the mercy and redemption she found at the foot of the Cross? She shuddered at the thought.

The pathway of splendor looked as she had remembered it at sixteen, save for the stately oaks that labored with added history bearing upon their elaborate branches. Their shade was respite from the September heat and still-sticky humidity of this grand historic area. Oh, how she missed Savannah! How she had loved this home and the comfort it provided until...

She welcomed the numbing emotion of the memory of

65

her running down this lonely path that God-forsaken day. She understood at this moment better than ever before what Grace meant when she said, "Sometimes numb is good. It's a safer place than mayhem." The violation of that wretched time period would destroy Carmen's fairytale rescue from congenital chaos. As painful as it was to come to an abrupt end, she was grateful for the season she had with her adopted mother–Grace Carissa Willingham.

Her eyes smarted. The source: pain or gain? Carmen was uncertain which, but it was bittersweet. She would go through every minute of the pain once more for the gain of strength, confidence, love, and forgiveness she had found in her temporary dwelling at the Willingham homestead.

She stepped out of her car slowly, taking in the panorama of memories brushed upon the landscape. She was certain if the birds would silence, she could hear the voices of Grace's three children echoing in the camping areas and trails they blazed on this eighty-acre homeplace. She ambled up the stairs leading to the porch where she had so often sat as a little girl. She and Mom Grace would sit for long hours watching the stars and fireflies. It's where Mom would bring her when she had nightmares of her childhood. The sexual abuse by her family was overshadowed by victory now, thanks to the tenderness of Grace Willingham and her familiarity with Jesus and what He could do in the life of any individual who allowed that intervention. Grace herself had overcome obstacles and was confident that Carmen could do all things through Christ who would give her the strength she needed. Grace was right. But then, Grace was seldom misguided.

Carmen entered slowly not wishing to startle whoever was

inside. She was uncertain who she might find, but didn't care. She had enough stones to face her giants now. "Hello? Anybody here?"

Nora got up from the couch a bit groggy. "Oh, hello. I'm sorry, I must have fallen asleep. I'm Nora Willingham, grand-daughter of Grace. And you are?"

"I'm Carmen, daughter of Grace. Good to meet you finally, Nora. Long trip from Spain, eh?" Grace had kept Carmen up to date during her mother's visits to California. "So you are the Nora your grandmother loved dearly. I have heard much about you. And you are as beautiful in person as Mom described you, and even more so than your gorgeous pictures. When did you get here?"

"Earlier this morning. Did you come from the funeral home?" Nora suddenly felt a surge of hope that she might be able to get in to pay respects to GG. She was longing to be there.

"No, no. Nick told me they're doing an investigation and no one in, no one out."

"Yeah, I got the same line when I went by," Nora snarled. "I tried my best strategies for getting in, but they have that place surrounded. There must be every law enforcement officer three counties over guarding that place. You would think it's Buck-ingham Palace!"

"Well, there is some validity to that, you know." Carmen grinned and began looking around. "It hasn't changed much since I left, except for some new pictures and artifacts from Mom's travel with the grandkids. So Spain captured your heart, did it, Nora?"

"Oh, yes. Grandma was a wise one. What an impeccable

read she had on people. Her instinct for God-given gifts guided most of her grandchildren into a career path, at least those of us who would listen. But, I loved it when GG would start pulling out the history and geography books and would take hostage our thoughts as we'd travel across the globe. She made places come to life. But Spain, ah . . . there was something about Spain." Nora embraced herself and twirled around the room like a giddy school girl. "I love it there! I do! I probably won't ever come back, except for occasions like these."

"Nick was the same way, Nora. France captured his fancy as Grace recognized his penchant for art. He studied abroad for a while, but promised Mom he would come back and fulfill his agreement with her. The two planned the Turner's Funeral Home purchase. Mom never wanted Richard Turner's hands touching her corpse, and definitely not Benny Fulkerson who had planned to take over after Ol' Man Turner retired. Benny was unrelenting in his quest for Mom's hand. She couldn't bear the thought of him possibly–well, you know. Obviously, neither can I."

The image flashing in Nora's head was quite repulsive, and she quickly diverted the thought. "I'm sorry I never got to know you, Carmen. I would have enjoyed the company of a less contentious aunt. There was much speculation about why you left so abruptly. Why did you keep it a secret all those years? Getting pregnant at a tender age was no crime. Why didn't you just–" Nora had many questions surrounding the scandal, and Grandma Grace never breathed a word about the details.

"It's a really long story," Carmen interrupted. "Threats for my safety. A baby that I needed to consider. Mom's heart and health. I didn't want to cause any trouble, and I knew the news would break her heart. But *she* sought *me* out, in case you didn't know. Tracked me down like a hunting dog. I've never seen such determination in a person, regardless of what it was she set her mind to. But, Mama Grace knew me. It was as though she was a blood mother rather than my adoptive mother. And, she knew what my heart was made of because she helped fashion it. Her intuition saved my soul. And Nick's."

"Threats for safety? Well, I would love to hear all the details. We can fix a cup of tea and sit at GG's tea table until we get clearance to head to Turner's. I think somehow GG would like to know the tradition is being carried on. I'll bet she hasn't changed where she stashed her English teas."

The two made their way to the kitchen. Grace's favorite Italian apron was laid across a chair. In unison they picked it up and buried their faces, first breathing in her essence, then, weeping together over precious memories they each shared with the woman who was a legend in her own time.

*　　　*　　　*

"INTERROGATION HEADQUARTERS" AT
TURNER'S FUNERAL HOME, OCTOBER 15, 9:33 A.M.

Kareem dwarfed Masters, but his handshake was weak. The detective put his best grip forward to send the message all deadbeats needed to know about the strong arm of the law. It wasn't often that you would see officers shake the hands of shady characters like Kareem. But Masters was different. He was a recent convert. God had been working on his heart. He still struggled with issues. Masters could always tell when Satan got on his tail. But, he was discovering that showing respect, even to criminals, put folks on a different level. The handshake was a beginning. He had to stay at his tough-guy image for the most part, but he was coming to appreciate his new approach. And it was getting results.

Kareem's record was colorful, but his charges most always were dismissed prior to ever stepping before The Court. These sorts of things make officers on the force crazy. The Narc Squad starts to wonder "What's the point? Somebody is carting these thugs out the back door as fast as they bring them in the front." There had been much speculation as to whose pockets got dusted with the walk, but no one dared point fingers without being ready to lose his or her job. When you have a family to feed and you actually want to work for a living, you swallow a lot. It would take a fellow officer going down before heads would bang. The question in everyone's mind: Which officer would it be?

"Have a seat, Kareem." Masters never looked up from his paperwork and began reading Kareem his rights. "You want a lawyer, Kareem?"

"Don't need one. Ain't done nothing."

"You know this is being videoed."

"Don't matter. You need another shot of this pretty face. Go for it. You ain't even supposed to be holding us this long. You don't have a search warrant."

"We asked permission to search. No one objected."

"Well, you can't keep us here much longer. I know my rights." Kareem was careful not to say much more. He had a vested interest in finding the jewels. None of the family members were taking issue with the unlawful detention. The jewels were part of their inheritance, and it would behoove all of them to cooperate to the fullest extent of the law, and beyond the boundaries thereof.

"I'm sure you're well aware of all your rights by now. How long have you been with Madelyn, Kareem?"

"I don't know. Long enough to get her knocked up and have my boy." Madelyn was another passing fancy for Kareem. He had no patience for women. He just used them and disposed of them permanently. None of the permanent disposals had been pinned on him…yet. Besides, getting rid of dames he didn't need was a cinch. Make it look like an OD and it was a piece of cake. No one questioned if they did it themselves. Besides, having "friends" on the force helped. Kareem had eight other kids that he knew of, but Bryson was his first boy. His plan was to keep Madelyn around long enough to get the child self-sufficient. Then, he'd lose her when Bryson was older and after he got what he wanted from the Willinghams. Now that Grace had died, the child could complicate things. Madelyn irritated Kareem anyway. The girl was too feisty for his liking. He liked spunk, but wanted more submission. *Just do what I tell you, and you won't get hurt* was Kareem Reynold's philosophy with women.

"He's a fine-looking boy. I know you're proud of him." Masters wanted to keep a rapport going for now, but knew the tenor would change when he got more direct. "What is it you like most about Madelyn, Kareem? She doesn't really seem your type. She's a little more spirited than you typically keep around. What's up with that?"

"I don't …"

"Speak up for the camera. Gotta hear you or the interview's no good."

"I don't know. Just needed somebody to take care of my needs. She was available."

"The fact that she's Jim Willingham's daughter have anything to do with your sudden attraction?"

"I don't know what you're talking about, Man. You fishin' now." Kareem squirmed in his chair. He knew Masters didn't really care for him. He knew he'd been after his hide for a while. He was also well aware how close he was on the trail to Jim Willingham being his link to his walks out of the courtroom. His free ride in this town would be over if that cover was blown. He'd already gotten word to the big boss to back off the heat. If he kept pulling more law enforcement in his circle, someone was bound to blow the whistle and/or suspect foul play. If an undercover came in and involved the Feds, they could all be in big trouble. Hooking up with Grace Willingham's granddaughter was a smoke screen, and a risky one, but that was the nearest link he had to keeping Jim involved. And his nearest link to the jewels.

"Did you know Grace Willingham at all before you met Madelyn?"

Kareem ran his hands down to his knees as he shuffled his size 15 feet. Through a toothy-white grin he responded to Masters's question. "I didn't run in Grandma Grace's circles. I mean, come on. You fishin', you fishin'. But, I mean, I knew the lady. Madelyn intro'd us. She was something else. Cool. For an old lady, I mean. Cooked a mean meal, too. Mmh, mmh, mmh."

"How many times did you go up to the casket to pay your

respects to Grace?"

"I don't know, Dude. Once, maybe twice. I ain't much for dead bodies."

"Did you stand with your back shielding Madelyn so she could swipe the jewels, Kareem? You just need to come clean this time. Your friends can't dig you out of this one. Too much publicity surrounding the case. Bound to make national news by evening. Could be international tomorrow. You don't want to go there, not on this one. It's too big, even for your boss."

"Man, whatchu talking 'bout? I ain't stole no jewels."

"I didn't say you took them. I asked did you stand with your back to Madelyn while she made off with them?"

"You talking crazy, Man. I don't even know that I stood like that. I can't remember that."

"There are video cameras in this funeral home, Kareem."

"You talking jive now. If there was a video, you'd already have your thief." Kareem felt fairly safe in assuming that. At least, he hadn't noticed any, and it was always the first thing he looked for anyplace he entered.

Masters hoped the surveillance cameras would reveal some lead for his team. He had taken a longer break than he wanted from interviewing to see what he might turn up with his inspecting eyes. When he and Nick spoke initially, he met with heavy resistance. Nick wanted no part of videos. He had promised Grace there would be none. After Masters explained it wouldn't be used to film the event but to place surveillance cameras throughout the room, and definitely over the coffin, Nick acquiesced. They both saw the wisdom behind the plan now.

Masters was hoping whatever came back from inspecting the

videos would be helpful. He had his sergeant and Nick working on a frame-by-frame scrutiny at the very moment. From what he could tell, there were lots of folks bending over to get a really close look at those jewels. He knew it was going to be a lot to sort through in this case. Unfortunately, at some point, someone had adjusted the camera and took it off of Grace and the jewels. That meant someone was in the attic of the funeral home during the wake. Masters was beginning to realize that this saga was becoming an entangled web.

Masters continued. "Who's your link, Kareem?"

"I don't know what you mean. Link? Link to what?"

"How do you walk every time we bring you in? Scott free, I'm talking about. Not even a slap on the wrist. You just get off. No fine, no time. Nothing. Who's your link?"

"Like I'm gonna share my secrets with the likes of you. Are you done? There ain't much you can ask. I mean, we came to a funeral, somebody stole jewels, you're keeping us hostage. I mean, there are folks stacked everywhere out there. Leaning up against the walls in every room. We'll be here for days if you interview all those folks."

Masters already knew the ones who were near the casket at the time Gladys discovered the jewels were missing. The deputies had honed those few down. From what they were able to tell, there was only a very small block of time from when the camera was altered to the discovery. His men had searched everyone in the building outside the viewing room, and those folks were released and long gone. He would have never been able to fly in the face of protocol to that extent. But Kareem, obviously, had not been out of the room in some time or he would have realized no one else was around but his small group.

Going against protocol was not something to be taken lightly. He had considered the litigious nature of detaining people beyond the reasonable and allotted time. He worked around sequestration of the witnesses by assigning one man per two guests. They were given specific instructions not to discuss anything regarding the jewels. If they did, they could and would likely be a suspect. Such actions would cause them to be called back for interrogation rather than a simple interview.

Masters would never give Kareem the pleasure in knowing the interview process wouldn't be much longer. He'd rather irritate him, since it might be the only punishment he would receive for being the low-life scumbag he was. Masters didn't want to think those thoughts about people anymore, but at times, it was the only thought that surfaced.

"Yeah, it could take a while, Kareem. Hope you didn't have anywhere to go real soon." Kareem's face dropped. If he had to sleep on the floor with a dead body in the same room one more night, he would be none too sure about his civility. "But, hey, if you wanted to come clean, everybody could just go home."

"You smoking something, Man. You got nothing on me, Masters. Give it up."

"Get outta here, Kareem. But remember, I'm watching you."

Kareem sauntered out of the room. His pants hung five inches below his red plaid Calvin Klein's. Masters thought, *I'll be so glad when that trend is gone.*

"Ricks, bring me Valerie Smyth next. I mean, Valerie Willingham. Can't keep her names straight."

"10-4, Bruce."

Chapter 7

The shadows cast from the trees rendered depth to the day's calling upon those who would answer its plea to come and bask in the splendor. The massive weeping willow's branches waved in gestures of invitation to come and share its tales of days gone by. Aunt and niece felt privileged to share Grace Willingham's serene setting. It was the perfect place to converse as if they were forever friends instead of first-time acquaintances.

Carmen was a beautiful woman. Nora was mesmerized by her stark blue eyes, cold black hair, and luscious golden tan. She envied her eye color. Her brown-black eyes, while pretty, were just that—pretty. They weren't sensational. Carmen's were amazingly sensational! To her good favor, Carmen had held onto her youth in remarkable style. She looked to be in her late twenties, not early fifties. It was obvious she was not from Willingham stock, but Carmen sported more of Grandma Grace's qualities than either of the two children straight from her womb.

Nora fixed on Carmen's laughter. It was soulful and pure.

Not one of hilarity but rather of peace and confidence. They had only met for the first time a couple of hours ago, and in such a short time knew each other intimately. Related, yet not, Carmen laid claim to a bond with Grace Carissa Willingham that was kindred. For Nora, the bond with Carmen was immediate. Special. Attached. Comfortable. It felt as though they were nearest and dearest of sisters rather than relatives by adoption.

Here she sat in GG's chair where Nora had shared tea and conversation with Grace so many times before. Now, she was sharing her life's story with an aunt she had never met until today but felt she had known a lifetime. Strange sensations rushed through Nora's soul, as if Grace Willingham was present herself. It was the perfect setting, and she believed GG was smiling down with approval.

"So will you share your story? I mean, I don't want to make you uncomfortable at all. I know it's kind of common knowledge, at least among family, that Nick's father wanted nothing to do with him. Is that why you stayed away?"

"That had a lot to do with it, Nora, but it's ... complicated. I was a single mom in a strange town, very young, and it was tough to make ends meet. Had it not been for a local church loving me through it, I really don't know what I would have done. The women gave me a baby shower and found me odds-and-ends furnishings and a baby bed. The first couple of years were rough. I didn't know a thing about babies, but I made it through. Mom Grace found me when Nick turned six, and I'm grateful she did. I had my church family, but I felt so alone without my real family. It was a long, lonely season of my life. I thought I'd never see Mom again. She never gave up on me, and neither did God."

"Did you ever consider abortion? I mean, you were young, Carmen. I know GG would have never approved, but you left. She didn't have to know."

"But I would know. And God would know. I could have never done that. To silence a voice that had no choice would be unthinkable. I believe life begins at conception, whether you have a decision in the act or not."

"Are you saying you were raped, Carmen? Is that what you're saying? I'm sorry. I–I just never knew that part. I'm so sorry."

It's okay. It's forgiven. It really is. And besides, my life has been full with Nick. He's an amazing young man. It's been more of a blessing than a curse."

"Why didn't Grace bring you back home? I don't under-stand. "

"Like I said, it's complicated." Carmen would not renege on the agreement she had somewhat forced on Grace Willingham. If Mom Grace had taught her anything, it was that integrity speaks highly of a person's character. Once Grace understood Carmen's heart, they had agreed on a plan, and when things fell into place, the story would be revealed, but not until.

"Is this your first time back? I mean, all these years and you've never been back to Savannah? It's a big enough town that you could have avoided Nick's father, if he's even still around. Is he? Are you still afraid of him? Seems like a threat on two lives could have been appropriately handled by the law. Did you consider that? Have you ever established paternity? I mean, with DNA testing, it's a cinch. Is he a hoodlum? Does Nick know who his father is?" Nora's curiosity would not shrink. If anything, her interest was piqued beyond nosiness. The missing link to this mystery was of remarkable interest to Nora, but what could it be?

"Whoa, that's a lot of questions." Carmen wasn't surprised at the curiosity. She had considered questions would be plentiful when Nick arrived on the scene bearing the Willingham name, and most certainly once the townspeople laid eyes on her again.

"I'm sorry, Carmen. How rude of me. Please forgive me. Don't answer any of those questions. I'm embarrassed." Nora poured herself another spot of tea and tried to dismiss her intrusive behavior.

Carmen touched Nora's hand, reassuring her she was not offended. "It's fine, Nora. It really is. I'm sure people have speculated themselves into a tizzy over what happened to me and all the details behind my story. What they didn't know, I'm quite sure they made up. It doesn't matter, though. It's the past. I've put those demons behind me. It really is more Nick's cross to bear now, but he'll work through it. He's a good man. His faith is strong. It was tough on him growing up without a father, but God compensates in incredible ways. He's had some wonderful mentors in his life. That's why a church family is a good thing. You have found one, I trust, in Spain?"

Nora ignored the question. "I am sorry. It's not unlike me at all to inquire, you know. GG always told me I could ask more questions in one minute than most kids could think of in a week. She encouraged me to be inquisitive. I can still hear her say, 'Futuristic imaginations are borne only because history has laid an incredible foundation.' She did teach me manners, though. I apologize."

"Don't think a thing about it, Nora. It's fine. I will tell you, though, that Mom Grace knew everything. I didn't want to share it, but she finally pieced the puzzle together. It took her quite a few years to make her way to me, but she did. Everyone always thought Grace had to have things her way, but it wasn't that at all. Mom usually succeeded at whatever she set out to accomplish because she had spent much time in prayer. She had great discernment for doing what's right. She prayed to find me, and she did. Then, Grace and I left it up to God to show us the way. He worked all things together for the good of this situation. I have had a full and blessed life. It would have been much different had I come back with Mom. California was exactly where Nick and I needed to be. It's all good."

Nora was spellbound. "What strength you have, Carmen. And you've never married. You're a self-made woman—"

"Oh, no, no, no. No one is ever self-made. We can never think our accomplishments are anything short of God's blessings in our lives." Carmen's passionate faith mimicked Grace Willingham's. Not flesh and blood but of the same stock. It was the kind of tenacity that held up under the fiercest battles.

*   *   *

VIEWING ROOM AT TURNER'S FUNERAL HOME, OCTOBER 15, 11:20 A.M.

James watched Valerie enter the interrogation room. He could only hope she wouldn't overload her mouth. She had been known to cause a ripple or two in the paper by speaking out of turn about things she knew little to nothing about. The media seemed to always look for the weak link to target. And lately, it appeared as their aim was the mayor's office. He poured himself a cup of coffee. His gaze was drawn to the coffin. Why in the world wouldn't Nick take Grace and put her in cold storage until this thing blew over? The funeral was slated for a couple of hours from now, but clearly there would not be one today. Who knows, she may not be in the ground until this time next year at the rate this was dragging on.

Yet another humiliation! That's the thought that kept rushing through his mind. The Willingham family had had enough drama throughout the years. James had certainly contributed his fair share to the stage show, but now this—stolen jewels! Whoever heard of such a thing at a funeral? There had to be a better place to pull off such a heist. But for someone who had intentions of seizing the gems, the opportunities were few and far between. Who knew where she stashed them when she wasn't wearing them? He had plundered through the house on multiple occasions to try and figure that out. He even took the lockbox key once and had a heck of a time convincing Daniel at the bank that Grace had sent him there to check on something for her. When Daniel called to verify, Jim was glad Grace was out of town on one of her routine excursions. And eternally grateful she had never cared for a cell phone. At least that he was aware of. She said God was the only protection she needed. The woman was exasperatingly stubborn to a fault.

Grace was quite a woman in her day, before the two of them got sideways. What a sour turn of events for this family. Everyone else saw it as a legacy of greatness. Jim viewed it as a cursed inheritance. *Those who saw the richness of this family legend should try growing up without a father,* he opined. James astonished himself at the bitterness he still held onto after so many years. His cold heart, harkened by anger, began to thaw, and then sadden. *The Willingham name is strong. But imagine what it could have been. We could have been a normal family. Why would Albert Willingham throw away everything that mattered to him for a woman, and a woman he didn't even know?*

His thoughts halted. Isn't that precisely what he had done? He had thrown away everything that mattered to him for a woman—no, women he didn't even know. He chuckled under his breath. *Like father, like son.*

*   *   *

"James, I hope Valerie doesn't pull any more of her stunts. Her tongue is never reined in. Honestly, you can really pick them. I keep thinking maybe one day you'll land on another one like Annie, but I've about given up all hope for that."

James and Gladys conversed through pretentious grins, aware all eyes were fixed upon them. What the family members thought was of little concern to either of them. Both of them, however, always disquieted themselves over the curiosity of the public's eye of scrutiny about the Willingham family. The last thing either of them needed was to look suspicious, especially with a camera running.

"Shut up, Gladys. I'm in a mood already, and you don't want to go there with me. Number one, there will never be another woman like Annie. And number two, my business is never any of your concern, not my professional life and certainly not my personal. So crank your nose back in about six inches, or you and I will have major problems today."

Gladys huffed at her little brother's tone, giving no thought to hers. He had been disrespectful to her for years. There was a time their relationship had been better. James had every promise of being a well-respected man in the community. Once Annie got sick, all that went south. Something changed in him. He lost hope before she was even pronounced terminal. It's like he knew that she would be taken from him. His anger and resentment manifested itself in drunkenness and promiscuity. His business dealings became covert and questionable. Did his character blemish his personality, or was it that his personality flawed his character? She wasn't sure which came first, but she found it intolerable, shameful, and inexcusable. For him to take the Willingham name and mar the reputation Grace had established was reckless and unforgiveable.

"Let's set aside your indifferent regard for a respectable lifestyle, James, and talk about the matter at hand. Who do you think stole the jewels?" Gladys was now eyeballing James. If his eyes diverted from hers, she would inform the detective that he might have cause to investigate him further. She did take note of how brief the interview was with James. His title seemed to bring with it special privileges, not the least of which included to have the spotlight shifted to others and off of him. She didn't trust the law any more than she trusted James.

"Why don't you tell me, Gladys?"

"What? What did you just say to me?" Gladys's voice turned the heads of everyone in the viewing room. She didn't mean to bring attention to the conversation, but she knew what James was insinuating.

"Touch a nerve, did I, Gladys? We both knew you felt entitled to those jewels, but Grace was just as disappointed in your character as she was mine."

Gladys's eyes lowered away from James. James had pushed the right button. Her heart knew exactly what James meant, but she set her jaw and felt her claws release. "My character doesn't hold a candle to yours, James Willingham. I haven't disgraced the family name like you have. Your string of harlots sickened Grace and they sicken me. You managed to disrupt a family tree that yours and Annie's two kids should have preserved for Grace's inheritance. Now, God only knows who all of this inheritance will go to. Who can speculate as to how many people will march into this parade of heritage with DNA in hand claiming to be yet another kid of the rich and famous James Albert Willingham II."

"Yeah, well, I guess it's a good thing you could never have one in the mix. The world didn't need another Gladys—male or female for that matter. Who knows what we'd be dealing with between you and Ralph?"

James knew that chord would get her off key. He reflected on how heartbroken and angry Gladys had been for years about not being able to bear children. She had blamed the one that Grace always touted as the "God of Impossibles." After repeated attempts failed for adoption because of her no-account drunkard she called a husband, it cost her an extended season in the East Coast Counseling Center in Jacksonville, Florida. She couldn't cope with the idea she was never suited for motherhood and that all the apples had fallen from James's side of the family tree. James thought, *God surely knew what He was doing there. Although, Grace always said that's not how He operates.*

She had told Jim the same thing when Annie fell ill. Didn't seem that way to Jim. If God could fix things, why didn't He? It wasn't enough that he had to live without a father, but then God took away the one thing he loved more than life—his sweet Annie. In Jim's way of thinking, that was insufferable.

Gladys was struggling for a comeback when Nick interrupted the conversation. It was time to move Grandma Grace to a more suitable location since it was obvious the funeral would not take place as planned that afternoon.

"I'm sorry, guys, but we're going to have to move Grandma Grace. We're not sure how much longer the investigation process is going to take or even where this might lead us after they're through here. I'm sure the detective will sit down with you two and talk about what you want to do after this. But, I need to make sure on my end of things that we preserve the integrity of the body. I just wanted to make you were aware of what we're going to do. If you want a moment with Grace, I understand."

"Can you just give me a couple minutes?" Gladys was quick to ask. James acted disinterested and walked away.

"I'll be back in five to ten minutes. Take your time."

Gladys walked up to the coffin. She placed her hand on Grace's. "We're going to find who did this, Mother. You don't worry a second over this. I will get to the bottom of this. The nerve of some people!" Gladys let out a wail, dabbling her handkerchief to her eyes. She cast a glance to either side to see if anyone was taking note of her performance. No one seemed to really care. Was it because the jewels were gone, or because they were afraid to come near the casket now that there was such controversy surrounding their disappearance? She bowed her head in prayerful posture. It was a familiar stance. She used to do it every week in church, although it had been awhile. But this time, it was as though the spirit of Grace pricked hers.

She suddenly felt ashamed at pretending to be mournful. She *was* sad her mother was gone. She had become so adept at hiding her true emotions. She got up every day and put on her mask to face a meaningless world. That seemed nobler than staying locked inside a counseling center. It was her coping mechanism. If she could go back and change some of the things she had done in the past, she would. As her mother always told her, "No one gets to re-call history, but they can repeat it if they choose." Her heart felt so cold. It had been for as long as she could remember. Gladys knew she was going through the motions of life, but couldn't seem to find a new way of living. She was again reminded what Mother had told her many times: "When you want to make a change, you don't keep doing the same thing."

*   *   *

"INTERVIEW HEADQUARTERS" AT TURNER'S FUNERAL HOME, OCTOBER 15, 11:18 A.M.

Masters walked back into the interview room. Combing through individual frames of the surveillance video was really tying up his day, but it was necessary. He was hoping to get a sense of direction, and soon. Otherwise, he'd have to let everyone go before he found a real lead to the thief. For the time being, he had only suspicions of who it might be, but he hadn't narrowed it down to just one. That was not a good way to end the first round of questioning. He was known for sniffing out suspects with eyeball inspection. This clan was so colorful that he had to admit he was a bit bewildered for the moment.

He had covered the family members present, but he couldn't disregard the ones yet to come into town. He wondered if the news of Grace's death would smoke out Jim's only son. The prodigal boy had abandoned the family about five or six years prior. What a shame, too. James Albert Willingham III was as promising as Ashley. *For all the good Grace did for that boy, Jim undid it in a heated moment. Poor kid didn't have a chance to make something of himself living in the shadow of his dad. Be curious to know if he's gonna be in town for Grace's funeral.* That remained to be seen, along with the others unaccounted for thus far. Although, he had verified Nora was in town. That was one person he would surely have to visit.

Masters considered his interviewing of friends and acquaintances who had gotten caught in the fray of the viewing-room saga. *Poor folks. They were simply victims of being in the right place at the wrong time. Or, was it the wrong place at the right time? But, doggone it, I can't dismiss the possibility that one of 'em could be the culprit, even though my instincts point to a family. Especially this Melissa friend of Grace's. I can't come on too strong with her initially, but I gotta interview her. Then, there's Fulkerson. The ol' codger. I think he wanted to get his hands on more than Grace herself. I'll scope out those two possibilities.*

Masters knew the Chief would be breathing down his neck with the high profile of this case. The parade of media gathering was a good indicator of the significance surrounding the legacy of Grace Willingham's coveted jewels.

* * *

"Come in, Valerie. Looking good, Girl. You are looking good! Mmh, mmh, mmh." He knew the language that would loosen Valerie's tongue. It wasn't how he wanted to present himself, but a detective had to do what he must in order to crack a case.

Valerie threw her shoulders back and her hips out of joint making her way to the detective for a hug. He leaned in reluctantly, but she pulled up against him in order to get him closer to the fascination of her womanhood. Most men wanted the chance to figure out if they were real or augmented. Everything else might be counterfeit about her, but not those. And she wore them proudly.

Her southern accent was thick. "Why, Bruce, it's good to see you, too. It's been awhile," as she brushed her index finger to his chin. "Too long, don't you think?" She gave a wink.

"Oh, now, Valerie, that's been awhile. I'm a different man these days.

"Every man has a price, Bruce, and every man has a weakness."

"Not this one, Valerie. Let's talk about Grace Willingham. But before I do, you need to know this is videotaped."

Valerie pulled out her flip-up mirror she kept close at hand, then grabbed her lip gloss and reapplied. She was an image-conscious gal. Her platinum blonde hair bounced against her form-fitted apple-red dress. The flair had raised a few brows for a funeral. Her blue eyes against her air-brushed tan had lured more men into crossing the lines of temptation than she could recount. James was her seventh husband. All the others were already staring death in the eye. It took her awhile to get to the real gold, but her digging would finally pay off. She was young to have gone through as many men as she had. Only a couple months older than Jim's youngest daughter, Madelyn, in fact. Jim Willingham had never fared as well. Sporting the likes of her on his arm was far more than he deserved. She would wait this marriage out. It wouldn't be long now before she would land a chunk of his inheritance. She had convinced him not to write a prenuptial. He was easy. *But then again, what man isn't when it comes to me? Funny thing is, I'm the one holding the promissory notes. So much for no prenup!* Valerie smiled and returned her mirror to its safe haven.

I need to read you your rights, Val."

"Rights? Am I under arrest? I mean, what are you talking about? I haven't done anything wrong. Where's James? I want James in here. I don't like this a bit!"

"No, no. Calm down, Valerie. You're just being interviewed, not arrested. I really don't have to 'cause you're not being arrested, but I wanna cover all my bases with this high–profile case. That's all. I figured James had told you what to expect. I'm sorry. Didn't mean to upset you there, Lil' Missy."

Valerie sat down again and took some deep breaths. Her heart was still racing, but she quickly regained her composure. She didn't want to appear Nervous on camera, but it was a little too late for that.

Detective Masters recited the Miranda Rights. "Do you understand your rights, Valerie? You want to get a lawyer here? It's well within your legal right to have him enter the premises on your behalf if you feel it necessary."

"Did James get one?"

"No, he didn't."

"Then, I'm okay. I didn't do this. I had nothing to do with this at all."

"All right, then, let's get started. Where were you when Gladys discovered the jewels were missing, Valerie?"

"I don't remember that, Bruce, but I'm sure I was locked arms with Jim."

"Well, think, Valerie. Did you have to look across the room at Gladys, or were you at arm's length? How close were you?"

"Gee, Bruce, I don't know. It feels like we'd been there a year already. This has been such a long ordeal. There were so many people coming through, and still more wanting to come in and pay respects. I just don't know. I was worn out. I've never smiled so much in my life. Even in my beauty pageants. It was exhausting. I was everywhere in that room at different times. I knew an awful lot of men in there, and I'd stand in a corner and have a conversation with one of them and then look for Jim. I'd run into someone else nestled in between flowers and bushes and Ficus trees. Then, I'd go look for Jim and run into someone else I knew. Men were constantly pulling me aside to chat."

"I thought you just told me you were holding onto Jim?"

"Oh, well, I mean, you know, I didn't hold onto him every second. That's a silly notion."

"How many times did you walk away from Jim to talk to men, Valerie?"

"Gosh, I can't tell you that, Bruce. You know me, I just talk. I'm friendly. Of course, they could never talk to me while their wives were with them, so when they would break away for a moment, I'd walk over and speak and then walk back to Jim. I couldn't tell you."

"Oh, so you sought *them* out rather than them pulling you aside? Did I hear that right? Or, which was it? Maybe I misunderstood."

"Both. It happened both ways. I'm just a social butterfly. Everybody knows that about me."

"Yeah, we know you are, Val. We all know. So, do you know if you were standing beside Jim or talking to someone else when Gladys discovered that the jewels were gone?"

"Oh, yeah, I see what you mean. You know, I believe I was speaking with Charles Bennett when Gladys screamed. Yeah, I believe that's right, now that I think about it. Charles Bennett. He and I were chatting, because when she screamed, I immediately looked for Jim. It took me a minute to find him, as I recall, but I did finally make my way over to him."

"Where was Jim when you found him?"

"Near the double doorway. I guess. No, I don't know. Or, was he? Hmm. Let me think a minute. Was that the time when I was talking to Charles, or was I talking to Shawn Culvert then? Oh, gee, Bruce. Now you've got me confused."

"I got *you* confused?" Masters marveled at her perception.

"Maybe it was Shawn Culvert I had been speaking with when Gladys yelled. And maybe Jim was over near the harpist. Seems like that might be— Yeah, yeah, let me retract that. I was speaking to Shawn Culvert. Jim was by the harpist. I went over to him. Wait, wait. Or, maybe I was speaking with Freddie Jennings. Oh, my, I really don't remember."

Masters buried his face in his hands. Nothing much had changed about Valerie. She'd spin a web in a New York second and leave you dangling in her snare of confusion.

"Are you sure *you* were around when the theft was discovered, Valerie?"

"What are you insinuating, Bruce? You think I stole those jewels? You're dead wrong. Don't even suggest such a thing. How dare you!"

"Well, your story's full of holes, Valerie." He was hoping to have her throw Jim under the bus if he was the responsible party.

"Full of holes? How can you say that? I was just trying to tell you who I was talking to, Bruce. Full of holes? You can't pull anything out of that. You're on a witch hunt and you know it. Well, you won't get me tangled up in this one. I just married into a questionable family, but don't make me part of that suspicion. Jim certainly had his share of problems with Grace Willingham, but so did Gladys. Maybe you should look more at her than us."

"Us? What gives you the impression I would be looking at the two of you corporately?"

"Well, I mean, we are married. What do you mean, Bruce? You're confusing me. I think I'd better get a lawyer. Where's Jim? Get him in here. I don't want to say anything else. You're twisting things I say."

"I haven't twisted anything, Valerie. I'm just asking you questions."

"Well, I'm not answering any more. I'm not sure what you wanted to hear me say or what you were hoping to accomplish, Bruce Masters, but you're barking up the wrong tree. You need to figure out another angle. I don't know where Jim was when

Gladys screamed. But it's obvious to me, if she was standing over Grace, maybe she yelled after she swiped the necklace. Doesn't that make more sense than what you're trying to make it out to be? It does to me. This is an easy open-and-shut case as far as I'm concerned. I could have already figured it out. Gladys knew Grace wouldn't trust those jewels to her. Jim told me that."

"Oh, he did, did he?"

"Well, yes. Everybody knows Gladys isn't mentally capable of being the caretaker of those jewels. I mean, she was in lockdown in a mental institution for years."

"Months. And it wasn't really that kind of facility. It was a—"

"Whatever, Bruce. She was admitted because she was unstable. So, why don't you look at somebody like her? Jim didn't even speak to his mother. Hadn't for a few months."

"Years."

"Whatever. He's as entitled to those jewels as anybody. Whoever has the gems needs to return them to him. That's what I think. He's the rightful owner of those. They need to be left to his estate. He's the one with all the heirs. Gladys has no one but that drunkard husband of hers, who would probably do away with her just to get his hands on that fortune."

"You'd like that, wouldn't you, Valerie?"

"Like what? Gladys to be done away with? You're putting words in my mouth."

"I didn't say that. You did. I meant Jim to inherit the fortune?"

"Okay, I'm done. If you want more from me, you'll have to get with our attorney." Valerie turned and stormed from the room. She glanced back at Bruce for one last word, "And to think I actually liked you once. What happened to you?"

Masters sat back in his chair. He rested his chin between his thumb and index finger, stroking his cheek with his thumb. He nodded, thinking he might be getting somewhere. Finally.

Chapter 8

VICTORY DRIVE, OCTOBER 15, 12:00 P.M.

Jimmy Willingham's cold black hair was being tussled in the wind. His five–o'clock stubble was in need of a fresh blade with two days' growth and another fast approaching. He'd been traveling non-stop since he heard the news of Grace's passing. He was grateful he took the time to remove the doors and top to his rented Jeep Wrangler. Victory Drive demanded it. He threw back his head, took a deep breath, and savored the freshness of the surroundings. He missed Savannah!

His tears initiated the rite of passage to escape. He had kept the urge to weep at bay for hours. *Not now! Don't cry yet, Jimmy Willingham, you wimp!* He wanted no obstruction to this view. It was rich. It was pure. It held captive his fondest memories. This was the stretch of road that led to adventure and release. It was the path that brought him to comfort and peace. This thoroughfare invited him to more love and attention than he'd ever known. This was the highway to a haven of rest. It transferred him from brokenness to bravery and from Hell to Heaven. He wanted to once again capture every inch of its terrain. Nothing compared to the sensation of a trip to Grandma Grace's.

He hadn't really had time to cry, but he really didn't want that to happen now. He wanted this moment and the next ones ahead to be met with clarity and focus. He knew it was important to Grandma Grace. She wanted everyone to celebrate her new life. Jimmy wanted to honor that for her. *These are tears of joy, Grandma. Tears of joy. I can't stop them. They're spilling out of me, just like your love for me did. Thank you for what you invested in me, and all of us. Tears of joy. I love you, Grandma Grace.* "I love you, Grandma Grace!" Jimmy shouted as he turned down that long stretch to home. He wept with the imposing oaks that now blocked his view of the sky. *How they must miss you, too, Grandma. We will all miss you, Grace Carissa Willingham.*

James Albert Willingham III was a handsome, tough, authentic prodigy born to rule the trails. Grace Willingham perceived it when he was seven. She unearthed his bravery. Frightened of his shadow throughout his most tender years, she challenged the tenacious spirit she recognized within him to help him overcome many of his fears. Competitive to the bone, Jimmy would meet the obstacle courses she set at the campsites with great determination. Grandma Grace encouraged victory, but often allowed him to stumble into defeat. She singlehandedly helped him overcome his fear of losing, his lack of trust, and his dread of his dad. It was Grandma Grace who taught him how to be a man. It was Grace Willingham who allowed him to be secure in his somewhat fallacious wit. His Grandma made him secure in his Clark-Kent-in-a-Superman-body persona. He could still hear Grandma say, "You are a child of the King. Embrace every quality you possess as a gift from Him. Never apologize for the character God has placed in you. It is how you use your virtues that will set your course in life, Jimmy. Just because you are funny doesn't mean you're not intelligent. There will be those who laugh with you more than those who laugh at you. Be pleased you made everyone laugh. It brings healing and is really good for the soul." Jimmy would always be grateful for those reassuring words. Grace was his surrogate mother, but she never forgot she was a grandmother first.

"Today is the beginning of the best of your life," Grandma used to say to Jimmy. He came to believe it. He learned to believe in himself. She always told him he would seek to do God's work on a mission field. Why did he doubt her? Grace had always been right. At least, in things that really mattered. She was wrong that he would like cucumber lemonade.

* * *

827 VICTORY DRIVE, GRACE'S TEA TABLE,
OCTOBER 15, 12:15 P.M.

"Do you recognize the vehicle?" Carmen was straining to get a glimpse of the figure inside the open Jeep.

Nora was stretching and squinting to get a better view. "Not at all. Can't say as I've ever seen that one before. But remember, I've been gone five years myself. A lot has changed since I was here."

"I can't believe five years have gone by since you moved to Spain. It seems like yesterday when Mom was sharing her excitement for your decision."

"Nor can I. It has been the fastest five years of my life. I meet myself coming and going most of the time. I had planned to come back at Christmas. There wasn't any indication she was sick. She was healthy as could be. Died in her sleep is what I was told. Another of her prayers answered. GG always said, 'You have not because you ask not.' She would challenge us to pray for something, journal it, and watch it happen."

"She did the same for us, Nora. I only got to experience it for a few years, but it meant the world to me when I was out there on my own."

"That's Jimmy, Carmen! That's Jimmy Willingham! Oh, my. They got word to him. I was afraid he might have been out of reach. I've prayed so hard that somehow they would get the message to him. Thank you, Jesus! Thank you!" Nora stood and was clapping her hands with delight. O, how she, too, loved answered prayers. She knew if anyone wanted to be here for GG's funeral, it was Jimmy.

They rushed down the steps to meet him. Each took note that he approached the homeplace at a snail's pace, as though memories were slapping him in the face and waking up the sense that reminiscences were all any of them had left of the legacy of Grace Carissa Willingham.

*   *   *

TURNER'S FUNERAL HOME, OCTOBER 15, 12:10 P.M.

The smell of food was enough to get Bruce Masters out of the interrogation hole. He walked past the viewing room and saw that Grace had been moved. That was for the best. The family and few outsiders were stuffing their faces with a Nina's Diner delight.

He knew by midafternoon they would be antsy to get home to their own beds for the night. He couldn't say as he blamed them. Unless something turned up soon from the interviews he had left with the acquaintances, he would have nothing to hold these folks for. He was still hoping for some clue from the surveillance tape. Coming up dry there would make this case a tough one for him. This is one that he would love to solve before it spanned beyond the national media.

"Here you go. There's more where this came from." Ricks handed Masters a plate of food and glass of iced tea.

"Appreciate it, Ricks. You're doing a good job out there. You're a fine man and mighty fine deputy."

"Thanks, Sir." Ricks strutted back to his assigned post.

"Have you found anything yet?" Bruce inquired.

"Taking a break right now. Our eyes are bugging out of our heads." Nick and the sergeant were enjoying lunch. Nick swallowed and took a big swig of Nina's tea. It was the best in these parts. "There is one frame we want you to look at, though, Bruce. Can't say you'll find too much, but it's very close to the scene with Gladys. With the camera having been altered, it's hard to tell when exactly the theft took place."

Masters nodded in agreement. "What did we come up with as far as lapse of time?"

The sergeant was quick to show off his skills. "Best we can tell, forty-three minutes."

"What? Oh, man! Tell me you're kidding me. How many people would come and go at that casket in forty-three minutes? For all we know, the thief could have come in, paid respects and been out the door. The crook might not even be in this building."

Masters took a deep breath and pushed his plate aside. Whatever he had eaten before would have to sustain him through the rest of the day. This was not good news. A lot could happen in forty-three minutes. Who would have? Who could have? It could be any one of the 280,000 people who live in this county.

"Get some fingerprints off that camera."

"We did already," the sergeant assured. "They must've used gloves. The only prints on there were the guy who installed the camera."

"I want to interview him this afternoon."

"I'm on it."

"Nick, the camera was almost a good idea. Who has access to your attic?"

"Anybody could go up there. It's not locked up or anything. There's no storage up there. There's a door in the back room that leads up to the attic. And yes, they've dusted for prints there, too. Nothing. In fact, it was a wipe-down. They could tell someone had wiped the handle. Sorry, Bruce. For all of us."

Bruce kicked a chair. "I'm sorry, Nick. I'm trying to do better these days with letting my frustrations get the best of me. But, man, it could be anybody."

"How about the guest book? If we could narrow down the people who signed the book as they came through the door and match it up to the frames, it might turn up something."

"If they signed in, Nick. If they signed in. If you came in with the idea of lifting jewels off a dead body— I'm sorry, Nick, I didn't mean any disrespect." Bruce flushed.

"No, I understand." Nick took no offense.

"Seriously, if you came in with the intentions of stealing jewels off of a woman lying in state, would you sign your name in?" Bruce stressed his point again.

"I might, if I didn't want to be a suspect."

"Ah-ha. Good point. Great point, actually. Yeah, you guys comb through that book and see what you can turn up. In fact, we'll leave them out until the funeral is over, but we might need the books for a little bit afterwards."

"Sure, Bruce. Or I can make copies of the pages for you," Nick suggested.

"You know, you don't have to do any of this, Nick. We have plenty of deputies that could step in and relieve you."

"No, no, I don't mind. No other funerals are going on here right now anyway. I've got one on ice waiting, though. Do you have a sense when we might let the family know anything?"

"I'll do my best to wrap it up today, Nick. Just go ahead and plan your funeral. Now, with Grace's funeral, you'll have to talk with Jim and Gladys on that and see what their wishes are."

"Yeah, yeah, I will. As long as we're cleared to go forward with it. Are we?"

"Well, let me check with the Chief and see what he thinks. That's not my call. You know, of course, if this thing goes international, there might be some problems. I don't know that there would be. I'm just saying."

"Yeah, who knows what might turn up there?"

"Let me get back at it. I can't wrap it up sitting in here stewing over forty-three minutes."

Chapter 9

Jimmy masked his disappointment when Nora hugged him. He was looking forward to wandering around the old homeplace quietly. He chastised himself and wondered why he thought everyone would be at the funeral home in lockdown. When he picked up the paper at JFK International and saw the headlines, he thought maybe there might be a chance to steal away and get lost in nostalgia. He longed to commune with his memories of Grandma Grace in the silence of the place he had long cherished in his heart.

"Nora, you're back! So good to see you. You look great." Jimmy managed to muster enough excitement to disguise his disappointment.

"James Albert Willingham III, you are—"

"It's Jimmy. Surely you haven't forgotten how that grates on my ever-loving last nerve?"

"I'm sorry. I know. My apologies," and Nora gave a light-hearted curtsy.

"And you must be Carmen?"

"Jimmy, it is so nice to meet you." For a half second, they both stuck out their hands. Remembering their kindred likeness, they embraced in true Willingham style.

"Okay, so where have you been? GG knew but wouldn't tell. If anyone ever swore her to secrecy, you couldn't pry it out of her with a tire tool. She told everyone not to worry, that you were safe, but that's all she would share. Now, we're dying to know. Where did you hide? Have you been in the States all this time? I forget. Which country did you visit with GG? Did you like it enough to stay like me? Are you wandering aimlessly around the world? Are you in hiding? Did you get in trouble with the law and are having to avoid Savannah?"

"Nora, what a thing to say!" Carmen rebuked. "And, let's give Jimmy some time to catch his breath."

Jimmy was grateful for the save. Obliged! He had forgotten how many questions Nora was capable of yielding in one breath.

"You must be exhausted, Jimmy, if you're just breezing in today. Come and sit in your rocker. We had some tea earlier around the tea table, but we've been in a rocking fancy for the last couple of hours. What would you like to drink? Water? Hot tea? Believe it or not, there's a pitcher of Mom's cucumber lemonade in the fridge. I could get—"

"Never cared for it. I'll take water. Thanks, Carmen."

"Really? I never knew anyone didn't care for the lemonade. Grace was holding out on us about that."

"Yeah, she probably figured I'd change my mind one day. Likely not gonna happen now."

Jimmy's signature rocker was waiting for him. He sat down

gingerly, inviting the sensation once again. He had enjoyed many nights naming the constellations with Grandma Grace here on this very porch. They shared their time listening to the off-key synchronization of the crickets and bullfrogs, and watching the fireflies dance, twinkling like stars, as if they had been invited as part of a private audience. It was here that Grandma fascinated Jimmy with far reaches of the world that needed to hear a yet undeclared message. It was Grandma who unbridled a desire within his soul that would set him free from the emotional prison that held him hostage.

Jimmy Willingham aspired to please his dad in something— anything. For many years the strongest desire of his heart was to gain a fraction of the attention his father gave to other things. When his attempts failed, he tried what won his father's favor— alcohol, drugs, and sex. Yet, nothing satisfied Jimmy like the hope Grace created within him for greatness without remuneration. She would propel him to discover the one thing that would set him free to be his own man, yet be a slave to some greater cause.

"I'm sorry. Did you say something, Nora? I was deep in thought. I apologize."

Nora realized Jimmy's thoughts were exclusive. If it's the same Jimmy she had known in childhood, he would never share them.

"I asked if you were going to share where you had been all this time. You left town a couple of weeks before I departed for Spain. Just disappeared without a trace. When GG wasn't worried, I knew she held the answer. I knew it. Your dad was furious, Jimmy. I mean furious. I've never heard him yell at Grace like he did that day. She never let us stick around to help her out. As if she needed it. But, his rage was uncontainable that day. The neighbors likely heard it a mile away. Consequently, I didn't have to strain to overhear from upstairs."

"What, were you standing on the balcony like you always did to eavesdrop?" Jimmy chuckled remembering the antics of Nora.

"Well, maybe just a little on the balcony."

"We had some good times, didn't we, Nora?" Jimmy deliberately changed the topic. There was no need to talk about something that no longer mattered. Grandma Grace always handled herself wittingly, regardless of the situation. And James Willingham was a pathetic soul that he prayed for daily. It was all water over the proverbial dam now.

"Yes, we did, Jimmy. GG always made it an adventure to come here, whether working or playing. Do you think she ever got tired?" Nora reflected on how exhausted and bone weary she was at the moment. For two cents she would go upstairs to GG's room, climb under the covers and smell the line-dried sheets, and snooze for days. *Oh, somebody, please twist my arm to take another nap!*

"I'm sure she did, but it kept her young. I never thought of her as old. Did you?" Jimmy prompted.

"Not once. She was like my mom, not my grandmom. And, I know she was yours," Nora replied.

"Well, yeah. I was pretty young when Mom died. I can vaguely remember her, you know. Vaguely. I really only have one recollection of me with Mom." Jimmy's countenance sank at the loss he never really got to know but still strongly felt in the deep recesses of his heart.

"Care to share?" Nora was uncertain if he'd open up or not, but she couldn't help but ask.

"It was when she was her sickest. I don't even remember when she wasn't really. I mean, it's pretty amazing when you stop to consider that she gave her life for me. Had she aborted me like the doctor suggested, he might have saved her. She could have gotten some kind of treatment for her cancer early on. You know, Nora, if it had happened today, with all the advancement in cancer research, she might have made it."

"We don't know that, Jimmy. Only God knows that for sure," Nora comforted.

"Yeah, Grandma was really patient with me sorting through all that. It kind of messed up my head for a little while. But all along, Grandma kept saying that I had been set apart to do something great. I can hear her now, 'Annie didn't die in vain, James Albert Willingham III. Your mother's most important purpose at that time was to bring you into this world. That was her utmost desire. A woman without purpose is like a bird without a song—visibly there, but silently vanishing. She fulfilled hers. Now, the question is: Will you fulfill yours?'"

Nora and Carmen grabbed a Kleenex. "Here's your water." Carmen blew her nose and settled back in her rocker. "Mom loved Annie with all her heart, Jimmy. If there was ever a woman as good as Grace Willingham, Annie was her match. I never met her, but I felt like I did from hearing Mom speak of her all these years. Her heart was full of peace and joy. She loved life more than anything, but she never feared death. Her only remorse about dying was that she would leave you and Ashley behind. And Mom was right—Annie was happy to sacrifice for you. She wanted you, and so did your dad. Things would have been so different but for—"

"It's okay, Aunt Carmen. I understand more today than I ever have before why Dad chose the path he did. I've done an awful lot of thinking while I've been away. Life has grown me up."

Carmen was touched at the endearing title. It was the first official acknowledgement of kinship from one of Grace's grandchildren. Her heart melted into an admiration for this young man sculpted by the hands of Grace Willingham. She had done the same for her Nick separated by distance. Having become a dad-by-default early in her children's lives, Grace had honed her skills at assuming the roles of both. The two grandsons, devoid of a father figure as well, learned a lot about being men at the hands of a woman inspired and motivated by her love for the Lord.

"So are you going to tell us or not? Where have you been?" Nora was unrelenting in her quest to fill in the missing pieces of the puzzle in Jimmy's life.

"Africa. Zimbabwe. It's amazing there. I'm on a mission field."

"Get outta here! No way. Tell me it's not so!" Nora was more shocked than she imagined she would be at the news of where Jimmy had been displaced the past five years. "A missionary? You? Why on earth would you want to do something like that? How did you come to that decision in your life? I mean, you went to school to be a vet. What are you going to do with that degree now? You're just going to throw it all away to be a missionary? I mean, can't you do something equally as noble right here on home soil where it's not so dangerous? Why would you choose somewhere like Zimbabwe?"

"Okay, let me answer all your questions with one word. Jesus. Jesus is why. You should know that feeling, Nora. You've been saved."

Nora looked at Jimmy like he had three heads. She had pro-
pounded a lot of questions only to evoke one word? That was
it? He would say nothing more? It was clear he hadn't changed
a lot even if life had grown him up. They had been exposed to
the same tutelage—the discerning guidance of Grace Willingham.
Like Jimmy, Nora had been away from the family, on her own,
not just miles away, but worlds apart. He might not have come
to realize that Nora was a straddle-the-fence Christian. She had
learned the art of speaking the name of Jesus when she felt it
appropriate, but He wasn't a part of her everyday vernacular.
She wasn't sure she had swallowed the "fisher-of-men" concept
hook, line and sinker."

"That's wonderful, Jimmy." Carmen wanted to encourage
his efforts. "Nothing pleased Grace more than for her children
to come to know the one thing she invested her time in teaching them. Funny, isn't it, how she got the lessons in without us
knowing she was preaching to us?"

Jimmy paused his rocking. A calm swept over him. "She lived
it, Aunt Carmen. It was the subtly of her deafening example in
which she shared her faith. Her love and respect and kindness
never waned. It was always polished for the next beneficiary of
the message of grace by Grace."

*   *   *

"INTERVIEW HEADQUARTERS" AT
TURNER'S FUNERAL HOME, OCTOBER 15, 12:50 P.M.

"Melissa Fitzgerald, I presume?" Masters got up from his

desk to meet the friend of Grace Willingham. "May I call you Melissa?"

"Of course you may."

"And you call me Bruce. You're much younger than I had you pegged, Melissa." He had envisioned someone more Grace's age—late seventies, mid-eighties.

"Oh, well, thank you, Detective. I'm sixty, soon to be sixty-one. I'm no spring chicken."

"Have a seat, Ma'am, and we'll get started. I won't keep you long. Just a few questions and then, I'll get you back outside with the others."

"Are we going to be here long? My cats really are in need of attention. They don't like it when I'm gone this long. I didn't leave them a thing out to eat. Thought I'd be right back after the funeral. They'll have my place ransacked. It'll be stinking something fierce from the cat litter."

"I know, Ms. Fitzgerald. This has been tough on everybody. We're getting close to the end here, though. Hoping we can let you all go home by the end of the day."

"Well, this is awfully sad. Grace would be mighty disturbed if she had any idea this was all going on. She never wanted those jewels to be—"

"Hold on there, Ms. Fitzgerald. Let me read you your Miranda Rights before you start talking, if you would, please, Ma'am. Nothing to be concerned about. Just a matter of protocol. And just so you know, this interview will be videoed."

Melissa Fitzgerald was a plain sort of woman. No memorable face. A simple dresser. A quite common lady. Masters could see why Grace would take to her as a friend. Grace, as elegant as she was, was simple herself. She respected women who kept themselves up but didn't re-craft God's handiwork. As wealthy as she was, you'd never know it to look at Grace Willingham. She never flaunted her natural beauty and always made time to make people feel special. He could see where Melissa would have benefited from that.

"How long have you known Grace, Melissa?"

"Oh, I've known Grace longer than most folks give me credit for knowing her. I knew Grace before the second fire. I was just a spring chicken myself."

"Is that right? Didn't know that. How did you gals meet?"

"We met at the farmer's market down on Habersham. Struck up a conversation, and the next thing I knew I was sipping a cup of English tea with Grace. It was special. Albert had sent her some all the way from England, and she shared it with me. She later told me she didn't know what made her do that. She was kind of stingy with that stock once Albert was gone. But Grace and I spent many days sipping her special tea. It seemed that vessel never went dry." Melissa smiled contently at the thought of her tea times with Grace.

"Were you her best friend, Melissa?"

"Oh, I don't know that I was. I'd like to think that. But Grace was a friend to all. She devoted a lot of time to those grandkids of hers. Of course, after she reared her own kids. You know I was some twenty years younger than her, but I think she liked hanging around younger people. I suppose she'd count me as one of her dear friends, though. She certainly was dear to me."

"Did she tell you her secrets, Melissa?"

"Well, what do you mean? I don't know what kind of secrets

you're talking about. If you mean did she share her problems with me, then— Is that what you mean?"

"Well, yes, ma'am, for starters."

"Grace mostly listened to my problems. If she ever had any, you didn't hear it from her lips. She did most of her talking to the Lord. She taught me to rely on Him for the strength I need to accomplish anything. She was a remarkable woman."

"That she was, Ma'am. That she was. I was wondering—"

"You know, Officer, Grace Willingham had a window into the soul of those she loved. I wouldn't give anything for the time we spent together as friends. I watched her kids for her when she would go out of town. She'd occasionally let me clean her house. It was always clean. I think she just knew I needed the money, so she let me come in and tidy up the place a bit. She was a good—"

"I hate to interrupt you, Melissa. I really do. But if you're going to get home to those cats, I'm going to need to ask you some specific questions. I don't mean to cut you off. We all know Grace Willingham was about as special as they come."

"I understand. We could talk about Grace until Jesus came back and not exhaust all the good things about her." Melissa wanted the detective to know that she was somebody, too, simply by association with someone as well-loved as Grace Willingham.

"For sure, for sure. Did Grace ever speak to you about her diamond and ruby jewels?"

"I mean, we talked about how they came to be hers. As far as sharing their worth, it was none of my business, you see."

"Did you ever see Grace wear them?"

"Never laid my eyes on them before two days ago."

"Were you curious to do that, Melissa? I mean, ever since those jewels came into the possession of Grace, they have been the talk of this town. Everybody has wanted an up-close-and-personal look at those gems. What about you?"

"What about me? What *about* me?"

"Well, I mean, didn't you want to just see them, just touch them, and maybe try them on yourself?"

"No. You insult me."

"I don't mean to insult you, Ma'am."

"I never wanted what Grace had. I mean, I'd be lying if I said I wasn't curious. Sure, I was curious. But I wasn't going to compromise our friendship over some silly ol' jewels."

"Well, these weren't just any silly ol' jewels, now, were they, Melissa? These were pretty special. I mean, think about the legacy behind them. Weren't you curious just a little?"

"I've already answered that." Melissa's tone got curt.

"You spent a lot of time out at Grace's, I mean, when she wasn't there, didn't you?"

"Well, Grace let me keep her place up when she would go on her trips with her grandkids. I think it's common knowledge that she took them to the country of their choosing when they graduated. I watched her place for her during those times."

"She also took little jaunts out of town to Heaven knows where she'd go, from what I understand. Did she ever tell you where it was she would take off to?"

"Well, sure she did. She needed to let someone know in case something happened to her. She never carried a cell phone. Said there was no point in getting away if anybody could talk to her at any given moment. She resisted electronics. Can't blame her."

"Where would she tell you she would go on her out-of-town trips? Not out of the country, just out of town."

"Oh, if she took a fancy to go to the New England states in the fall, she'd go. If she wanted to go to the West Coast, she'd take off. She didn't care for Florida too much. Said she could get the same kind of heat here."

"So you looked after the place while she was gone?"

"Oh, I just went out and checked on things. Watered her plants, fed the birds, brought in the mail, things like that."

"Inside plants, too?"

"Oh, sure. Grace told me where the key was. I let myself in and let myself right back out."

"Did she ever tell you where she kept her jewelry?"

"You mean the stolen jewelry? I mean, Grace had other jewelry, you know. Nothing really elaborate. She still wore her wedding ring after all those years. I think she did that more to keep the men away than anything else. But it was just a simple band. Really nothing special. Of course, I never laid my eyes on those jewels until the day before yesterday. They're the most spectacular things I've ever seen in my life! I stood there forever just gawking over them. I don't know that Grace ever wore them but twice—the day she got them and at her death."

"A few more times than that, I understand."

"Well, I'll just say I never saw her wear them. And she never talked about them. She really didn't. She never was into material things. And a self-made woman like that, not once, but twice. Go figure. She just was Grace. Simple. Kind. Generous to a fault. She was full of love and compassion, and wouldn't say an unkind thing about a soul. You kind of could figure if she didn't like someone—she wouldn't say a thing about them. That was my clue of an unsavory character, and I kept my distance. I figured if Grace couldn't say anything good about them, they weren't worth my time to get to know."

"Did Grace talk to you about her Will, Ms. Fitzgerald?"

"Gracious no! That was personal to her. She never got into family matters with me. We just had a friendship." Melissa was not about to let this detective know anything of those private talks she had with Grace Willingham. Those were personal. Grace wouldn't share it, and she certainly wasn't about to. The questions this officer was asking were none of his concern. Whether she had laid her eyes on those jewels before or not, he didn't need to know.

"Well, I thank you, Melissa. I'm trying to wrap up this part of the investigation. Hopefully, you'll be home with those cats by dusk. I'll do my best. I promise."

Seemed innocent enough, but there was something Masters didn't trust in her kind face. He took note of the nervous twitch she developed while discussing her paying respects to Grace in the viewing room. He might have to revisit the housekeeping duties at Grace Willingham's homestead with Melissa Fitzgerald later on. For now, he had another mission—the Chief.

Chapter 10

Chief Griffin was on the phone but waved for Masters to come into his office. Masters knew the Chief was going to want answers he wasn't prepared to give. Not yet. Masters had never seen a case he couldn't crack. His career record was pristine. He didn't intend for this to become his first failure. The detective was looking at retirement in three months. He intended to go out in a blaze of glory. The likes of sticky fingers at a saint-of-a-woman's funeral was not going to mar his good name in this profession. Having been in law enforcement for practically his entire career, Masters was familiar with the nature of people. Folks would never remember all the big cases he had solved if this one got away from him. If it did, *that* would be his legacy. Bruce Masters would have no part of it.

"We should be able to have you an answer tomorrow. Just give us some time here, okay, Barrett. I've got my best men on this. Do I have your word–twenty-four hours more? Thanks, Sir. Appreciate the consideration." The Chief hung up the phone, took a sip of his cold Starbucks, and brushed the perspiration from his forehead into his hair.

"What have you got for me, Bruce? I'm counting on you with this. It is blowing wide open."

"Well, Chief, I—"

"Bruce, that was Terrence Barrett with the Attorney General's Office, as in U-S. Do you get it? The FBI wants to take over this case."

"What?! The FBI? That's not necessary, Chief. I can handle this. Why would they—"

"You know why, Bruce. Those jewels are making headlines all over this nation and across the seas already. You and I both knew it was a matter of time, a little bit of it."

The detective sank back in his chair. If the FBI got involved, Grace Willingham might never have a proper funeral.

"You've got twenty-four hours to crack the case, Bruce. That's all the U.S. Attorney General is going to give me. Then, the Feds take it over. Don't think for one second one of them, if not a couple or three, aren't already on the scene. We just don't know it. Yet."

"The surveillance cameras would have done the trick, but someone tampered with them, Chief."

"What? How? Who? When?"

"Those are all questions we're tryin' our best to get answered. Whoever did it knew they had to wipe down their trail. Left not a trace."

"How much down time?"

"About forty-three minutes best we could tell."

"Forty-three? Dadgummit! A lot of people went through that

visiting line in that length of time, Bruce."

"I know. How well I know. Could be anybody in a three-county area, Chief. Here's what we're doin'. We're takin' every camera frame-by-frame. Of course, right now, the only one that's been looked at so far is the one directly over the casket."

"You have enough people on it?"

"Well, it's only Sergeant Shaw and Nick Willingham."

"Nick? What's he doing that for? He's related." The Chief raised his eyebrows regarding that tidbit of information.

"He's been real helpful, actually. He's familiar with the whole clan of Willinghams and most of the friends. He's only been in this area about five years and knows most of the folks in all of Chatham County. Likable young man, too, I'll say that 'bout him."

"Have you considered this might be an inside job, Bruce?" Chief Griffin's voice became stern and indignant.

"Well, yes, now, I have." Bruce was hoping the Chief wasn't reading his thoughts. They did not coincide with his answer. He trusted Nick. There was something about the lad that he would stake his life on. Was he missing the obvious?

"You hadn't either, Bruce. I see it all over your face. You don't hide your feelings well these days, Masters. Get him off of that duty. If you need more men, call them up. We'll call in the GSP if we have to. The Georgia Boys won't mind giving us a hand to guard if you want your guys to help with the investigation." Griffin leaned over his desk to get closer to Masters. "Don't let me down on this Bruce. I'm telling you. Do not make me the laughingstock of the nation."

"We're lookin' into the security company that placed the

cameras. We're checkin' the registry of guests. I've interviewed most of the family members and guests. There's only one left now that I want to question."

"Turned up any clues at all?"

"A couple of questionables. Nothin' concrete, though. I landed a couple of really strong leads today. You know Kareem's in this mix."

"Oh, that's right. How's that looking? Any exchanges you've noticed with him and Jim?"

"Of course, I've been locked up in a room for two days, but Ricks has said they've dared not come near each other. They're onto us, I'm afraid."

Chief Griffin pushed his chair back and slapped his hands. This is all too coincidental–the timing of Kareem hooking up with Jim's prostitute's child. Do you have any probable cause at all so we could book him? He might not walk with this heavy-duty case."

"No. Judge Rowland would throw bricks at us with what I have, which right now is nothing more than the desire to put them both behind bars. Without prints or film, we got nothing. A big fat nada."

"I take it you've printed Grace? Nothing came from that, I suppose?" Chief Griffin was confident Bruce had taken care of that, but he wanted to cover all his bases.

"All over that one, Chief."

"Well, you've got twenty-four hours, Bruce. After that, it's out of our hands. I can't tell you how much I don't want that to happen. You understand where I'm coming from?"

"I'll keep you posted. We're doin' all we can, Chief. I'll wrap up these interviews. I want to question the ones comin' from out of town, and after that, I can't hold these folks any longer. I'm pushin' my luck now. Best I can do is assign surveillance to the ones I suspicion. Would love to go undercover with it. If we have enough manpower, I'd love to put one on everybody in that room."

"You can't take the whole force, Bruce. How many are you talking about?"

"You know I started my interview with the outsiders and worked my way to the family."

"Yeah, you kinda went at it backward, Bruce. But you always get your man. I've learned to never doubt your methods."

"Well, Chief, I intentionally allowed only twenty-five guests in the viewin' room at a time, not countin' the kids. With the family, that didn't allow for very many. It was a slow-go with the parade of folks wantin' to pay respects to Grace."

"Or to get up close and personal to those jewels. More nosey than respectable, I'd say."

"I don't plan to interview the overflow rooms unless you object. I couldn't rightly see how we could hold 'em, so I sent 'em all home but got their names and contact information." Masters exhausted himself thinking of taking on that task.

"Not necessary I wouldn't think. But, make sure you keep up with that record. Someone had access to those cameras. Find that one and you find your thief."

Bruce's gait was sluggish. He had lied through his teeth. He had not once considered lifting the prints from Grace! How could he have overlooked such an obvious piece of investigation? He wasn't about to confess to that oversight, not at this stage of his career. He felt a gnawing in his gut. He had tried hard not to stretch the truth since his conversion. What was that about? It came from nowhere. He was totally caught off guard. *Lord, forgive me, would ya? You know I'm just a sinner saved by grace. Help me stay focused. Please, Lord. This may be bigger than me. I could use a little help. Amen.*

Masters hit the quick dial on his phone. "Ricks, get Forensics to lift prints on the wrist, ears, and neck of Grace Willingham ASAP. What? That's right, they did move her already. Dog-gone it. Rotten timing. Doesn't matter. Get them in there now. Tell them to rush the report to me, too. Thanks. I'm on my way back." Masters ended the call. He needed some answers quickly. *Who would have had access to those cameras? To Grace? Who would be the least likely to be a suspect?* If he wanted to keep this case for himself, some pieces of this convoluted puzzle had to fall into place.

Nick? Masters had not considered Nick. He just didn't look the part, but things were beginning to stack up against him. First, there's his objection to the cameras. Although, Ashley also commented that Grace didn't want them. But, Nick has access to the attic. Of course, it would make sense his prints would be on any most everything around the funeral home, so why weren't they lifted? Who would suspect Nick? He was such a fine young man. Masters would reserve passing judgment on his character until the results from the latent fingerprints from the deceased came back. *Of course, he is a mortician. What are you thinking, Masters? Another slip-up! You never even asked Nick if he prepped Grace. I just figured he wouldn't do that, her being his grandmom and all. I'll have to wait and see. If the dusting and lifting comes up void, one of two things: our thief had gloves, or Nick or someone had wiped down the areas when they took Grace out of the room. That's gonna bust me if you're the thief, Nick. I'm bound to lose my faith in the human race altogether.*

Masters hit the redial button on his phone. "Ricks, me again. I want you to search through the women's purses in the viewing room one more time for any sign of gloves. What's that? Sure, check the men's pockets, too." Masters was thinking more women's, but why not. "Absolutely. Seize them, bag them, and we'll place them in the P&E room at the station. Oh, and, Ricks, it goes without saying but let me impress upon you: make a paper note of the owners of any gloves." In all his years of being a detective, one thing Bruce Masters had learned, it was 1 percent order and 99 percent check when it came to preserving the integrity of property and evidence. "Oh, and assign someone else to help with the surveillance films. Nick Willingham needs to take care of his funeral home business. Give him a break. Insist if he bucks you on it."

THE VIEWING ROOM, TURNER'S FUNERAL HOME, OCTOBER 15, 1:47 P.M.

"You already went through my purse yesterday. When are you guys going to be done with this interviewing and pawing through our personal belongings? I'm about done with all this. Where's Bruce Masters? Get him in here." Gladys's tone set the stage for other grumblings that emerged from the weary crowd.

"I'll need to take these, Ms. Gladys." Ricks was somewhat faint-hearted in his intent to confiscate Gladys's white gloves.

"Whatever for, Randall? Those are gloves Mother gave to me. I don't want you taking those. Please."

"I'm sorry. I'm just following orders." Ricks took the gloves and placed them in the plastic bag, sealed it, and with a permanent marker wrote the name of the rightful owner. "We'll try and make sure these get back to you, Ms. Gladys. That is, of course, if … "

"If what?" Gladys didn't like the sounds of what Ricks was implying, and especially since he didn't finish his statement. "If what, Randall?"

"Well, I mean, if we don't need it for any further proceedings or any part of our investigation or anything. I'll–I'll just let you talk to Bruce when he gets back. He should be coming any minute now." Ricks's timidity to stand up against the likes of Gladys Willingham was glaring. He had heard stories of her rage before and clearly wanted no part of any confrontation with her.

"You let me know when Bruce gets here. I'll have a word with him about this." Gladys closed her purse and grabbed a Turner's Funeral Home fan. The air conditioner was laboring to offset the afternoon heat that was bearing down on everyone. The room was filling with body odors and the stifling breath of twenty-plus people who had not brushed their teeth for now the second day. This sort of thing was unprecedented. What judge would allow folks to remain hostage for the span of two days to be questioned and searched and now re-searched? It was unthinkable to Gladys. She was sure if she polled the crowd, the consensus would be the same.

"Mr. Jim, you'll have to give me those. I'll need to bag them and label them, as well. Do I put your name on here?"

"Well, of course not, Randall. These are Valerie's. I just had them in my pocket for her." Jim laid the lace gloves in Ricks's hands reluctantly. Ricks was careful to label the owner as Valerie Willingham, but confiscated from the person of James Albert Willingham II.

"It seems like I'm missing somebody. Who's not here? The one with the baby." Ricks swallowed hard. *Whoever was in charge of watching her is toast. Masters will have his head!* "Is she in the restroom, Kareem?"

"I don't know. I ain't seen her in a while now."

The crowd was so relieved not to hear whining that the silence distracted the absence of Madelyn and Baby Bryson. Ricks grabbed his walkie-talkie. "Attention all posts. We have a missing person from Turner's Funeral Home. Repeat, missing person from Turner's Funeral Home. All posts be on lookout for a young female, approximately five-ten, a hundred and forty pounds, rainbow-tinted hair, multiple tattoos and piercings, dressed in short black dress and very high black heels. Time of departure unknown, but believed to be sometime between the hours of 0935 hours and present hour. Search every room of the premises. Name is Madelyn Joy Willingham." *Masters is going to have my head if this gal is gone.* Ricks's heart was racing at what he'd soon be facing.

*   *   *

TURNER'S FUNERAL HOME, OCTOBER 15, 2:10 P.M.

"We've looked everywhere and she hasn't turned up. I have Harrington and Willis going out to check her residence. Haven't heard from them, but I'll keep you posted."

Masters had barely crossed the threshold of the funeral home when the news was relayed. "Ricks, how did you let her slip by you? This is outrageous. Did anybody remember her goin' to the restroom? Have you pared down when she was last seen?"

"The girl was interviewed by you at approximately 0915 hours, out by 0935. Harrington said she came up to him several times after that complaining about needing to get her baby home. She'd pretty much stayed on his case since the lockdown. Last Harrington remembers was after lunch when she came out to go to the restroom. He got distracted when he followed Nick and his crew to take Ms. Grace to the back area. He didn't think anything about her being in there and apparently never gave second thought to knowing whether she came out. So, it seems to be sometime between the hours of 0935 and 1230 hours that she disappeared, best I can figure."

"That's a big block of time, Ricks. I ain't happy! Tell Harrington he's got to pin down the very last time he saw her. I don't want a guessin' game here. Forget the 0935. Figure out the time he last laid eyes on her. Hone it down, Ricks." Bruce's face was already flushed. He knew his blood pressure was on the rise again.

"Well, sir, I'll do my best. Harrington sometimes checks his brain at the door." Ricks gave a doleful look.

"Yeah, well, it's a good way to mess up a big case," Bruce snarled. "Go up in the attic and look. Make sure the girl's not up there. See if any windows were opened. At least I'd like to know how she escaped with no less than twenty officers surroundin' the place.

Masters dropped in his chair, exhausted, frustrated, and more perplexed than ever. Three pairs of gloves seized. Nick a possible suspect. And now, Madelyn on the run. Could this thing get more complicated? Yes, it could. Masters had every notion that within twenty-three hours and change, things might really become quite problematical surrounding the jewels of the late, great Grace Carissa Willingham.

Chapter 11

Jimmy opened the door to the building where Grace's children and grandchildren shaped their work ethics. Carmen and Nora followed behind. Things were a bit dusty, but nothing a good thirty-minute dusting wouldn't take care of. A few spider webs glistened in the evening sun. Multiple shelves with quart- and pint-size Mason jars were lined up ready to be filled. The apple peelers were bolted to the edges of the countertops. A dozen razor-sharp knives hibernated in their leather casing. Curly-soft maple and mahogany cutting boards lined the counter etched with deliberate wounds from coring and slicing thousands of apples from Grace's orchard. Overhead pot racks were mounted to the ceiling. Commercial pots and pans hung as witness to the hundreds of gallons of pie filling, jelly, and apple cider that materialized at the hands of the Willingham clan.

Next to the sink area set two bushels and a peck of plump red apples Grace had harvested in recent days. Nora made a selection, rubbed it intensely against her shirttail, and took a bite.

"Mmh, just like I remember them," she muttered through the mouth-watering crunches. Her mouth savored the bite knowing that GG's hands had plucked the apple from a tree.

"August through October was a busy time during my short stint at The Sugar Shack." Carmen slid her hand across the countertops. Splashes of red still frolicked about. It was Grace's favorite color. She maintained it had nothing to do with the rubies. Grace loved red as a young girl. The story was her mother suppressed any thought of wearing a red dress, as proper girls would never consider the possibility. Grace had more than made up for her deprivation. Her barn red bedroom applauded her passion for the color.

"I loved this place. Even when we wanted to be camping instead of peeling apples, it was the grandest place on Earth to be." Jimmy hopped on the counter, swinging his legs while he turned the apple peeler. "Peeling was my job until I could prove myself worthy to handle the knives. No fingers were going to be chopped off on Grace's watch."

"This was the place she made a small fortune. It took me a long time to understand why GG would continue to harvest her apples when she could have just gotten everything she made from Harvest Field. She sold them her secret recipe. It finally registered with me that it was the memories she was after by keeping the factory going at Sugar Shack."

"That was just icing on the cake, Nora. Grandma's main thrust was to instill a strong work ethic in each of us. Oh, Grace and I went round and round at times about my refusal to work. If I had made plans with my friends or had a last-minute date with a cute gal, we locked horns. And I will tell you, I never won.

I could boss my dad around anytime I wanted. It never worked with Grandma. Never could figure that one out in my head. And when I tried, it meant longer duty in this place. Then when fall was behind us, it was wood-chopping time. Every season brought toil for us in some way or another. What was that Proverb she always told us? 'All hard work brings a profit …'"

"'…but mere talk leads only to poverty.' Yeah, we heard the same verse," Carmen informed. "Aren't you glad she taught us how to work? It has served all of us well."

Nora and Jimmy nodded in complete agreement.

"How much did Harvest Field pay GG for her apple cider recipe?"

"Half a million dollars." Carmen remembered it well.

"For real? For serious? For positive?" Jimmy was flabbergasted. All these years and no one had shared that piece of information with him.

"Hey, that's my line," Nora chimed in.

"No, that's really Madelyn's line. I think we all liked it, though, so we stole it from her. Besides, the kids love it in Zimbabwe." Jimmy tussled Nora's hair. .

"For real, serious, and positive. It was 1972, and that was a lot of money then." Carmen remembered the lean years with Grace and on her own as a single mom.

"It's a lot of money now, Carmen! I'd give anything to have a tenth of that money. I could do a lot with that kind of dough in Spain." Nora's imagination ran rampant in a second realizing the publication obligations she had with her magazine.

"Imagine what I could do with that in Africa. They're starving there, Nora. I don't think Spain needs it nearly as much as the

Africans." Jimmy's humanitarian heart was passionate.

"What did she make off her apple pie recipe? They bought that one first." Nora's curiosity began to heighten.

"That was in 1957. The company stole that recipe for twenty-five thousand dollars, but that was a lot of money for a single mom rearing three children. We scraped by, and it all happened in our little kitchen, not in the nice amenities of Sugar Shack."

Carmen remembered how small their first house was. Grace had been a miser. In the backyard garden, she grew many of the fruits and vegetables they ate throughout the year. Her green thumb astounded everyone. It didn't stop with food, however. Her flowers were beautiful. From her azaleas to gardenias, hydrangeas to her collection of roses, springs and summers at the Willingham homestead were spectacular with fragrance and color. Her makeshift greenhouse was a showcase for rare and bountiful orchids. Carmen glanced at the wall of blue ribbons which evidenced Grace's natural gift of managing horticulture. Nearby was a framed *Southern Living* edition where Mom's horticultural abilities were featured. Six pages of exquisite beauty. The author headlined Grace Carissa Willingham as "A Woman of Resolve." Had Carmen not kept up her subscription of the magazine while in California, she possibly would have never known about the honor. Grace never made a big to-do over the article. But, it was a big deal to those who loved her. Carmen had framed the article and placed it under the Christmas tree that year when Grace came to visit her and Nick.

"The little house burned to the ground one night," she continued. "Mom pushed us kids to safety through a tiny bedroom window. She grabbed a box of keepsakes from her nightstand

and then crawled out herself. It was nothing short of a miracle that we escaped the blazing inferno. It was burned to the ground before the fire trucks arrived."

"I never knew GG had two fires. I knew of the one on this property."

"Mom bought this property after our first house burned. The house had been a rental, and the landlord never kept it up. He never cleaned the chimney, and the fireplace was our only source of heat. Another middle-of-the-night loss. The Sugar Shack was just that—a shack. It had quite a bit of renovations done to it in the little time Grace owned it. But, this is where we lived until the new house was finished. Mom was a shrewd woman. She lived frugally. If she found a penny on the street, she always picked it up. And she expected us to do the same.

"One of the many gentlemen who was sweet on her brought her all the fruit she wanted. We canned fruit and made jelly until we were blind! She set up a booth at the end of the driveway, and in less than two hours, we sold everything our hands could make in a day's time. Then, we'd start the process all over again." The money she made helped her acquire land one acre at a time. She planted an apple orchard immediately. She was a work in progress."

"Poor Grandma had to go through another fire. It's pretty amazing to think about all she's overcome in her lifetime." Jimmy tried to imagine the heartache that must have surrounded the starting-over process with three small children.

"Yeah, the second fire was a tough one. It was close quarters for a while living in this little space. I really didn't get to live in the new house for very long at all, but I fell in love with it in the short time I was there. But, Mom was a—"

Nora cocked her head and gave a questionable look at Carmen. "So why did you—"

Carmen didn't allow the interruption and continued her story. "Mom was a come-back woman, and she could drive a hard bargain. While the embers were still warm, she took the next train to Wisconsin, marched into the president's office at Harvest Field, dangled her apple cider recipe in front of his nose, and she took it from there. That was the recipe they were after from the beginning. No one could figure out her secret to the cider, even though many a poor soul tried. The apple pie had turned a tremendous profit for the company, and that man knew the half-million-dollar price tag would be an equally wise investment. He wrote Mom a check on the spot. She came back a well-set woman and began building the house we all love today."

Nora dismissed her thought. She would press Carmen for more details later. "Why didn't GG just marry someone and make it easy on herself? She was a beautiful woman. Petite. Shapely. Men were crazy about her." Nora felt herself puffing up a bit. She knew she had many of Grace's qualities, although *Lil' Sweet Ashley* was her replica. Nora tried hard not to resent Ashley. It certainly wasn't her fault she looked like GG. But Nora couldn't help herself. She had come to resent a lot about Ashley throughout the years.

"Mom always loved Albert. She gave that part of her heart to him. He took it with him and she never got it back."

"You never met Albert, did you, Aunt Carmen?"

"Oh, no, no, Jimmy, I didn't. He was gone before I came on the scene. I believe I was his replacement in a strange sort of way. I was lucky, though. No, I was blessed. Out of all the foster children she kept, she decided to adopt me. Me. She chose me." Tears filled Carmen's eyes. "After she made the decision, she decided not to be a foster parent anymore. I always felt sad for other kids who missed her tender loving care."

"GG kept foster kids? Really? What in the world for?" Nora couldn't imagine adding more chaos to a single-parent home.

"To make ends meet. But she always had a heart for children, too. I mean, come on, guys. You two have witnessed that affection firsthand." Carmen knew all the grandkids could relate to that kind of love from Grace Willingham.

"But who would want to take care of kids that aren't yours? I mean, they live with you day in and day out. It's not like a daycare-type situation where you can send them home at the end of the day." Nora did not share Grace's love for children. In fact, she was convinced she would never want any. But then, Nora had never loved a man deeply enough to know the thrill of creating life together as husband and wife.

"A foster parent?" Jimmy couldn't recall ever knowing that part of Grace's history. "Wow! I think that's awesome. Kids are exceptional in every way. Precious gifts from God. There are so many in Africa that I would love to swoop up and take home with me. But I can't. It's not that easy. So I love them every way I can. Touch. They love for you to touch them. A pat on the back. Touch their sweet cheeks. Wipe their slobbery mouths."

"Okay, now that's too much." Nora recoiled with disgust.

"There's nothing like it, Nora. Their little coal black eyes light up and their smiles break into warmth that invades your heart like nothing you've ever known."

"Ooh, what's happened to you? You're weird." Nora shook her head in total disbelief.

Jimmy wondered what had happened to Nora. She was not exactly dripping with sugar the way she always did when she was around Grandma Grace. More of the world had gotten into her since she'd been in Spain. It was clear he needed to spend some one-on-one time with her and find out where she was in her faith. Shallow, he suspected. But then, if Grace were here, she would remind him how judgmental it was for him to think such a thing.

*   *   *

INTERROGATION HEADQUARTERS, TURNER'S FUNERAL HOME, OCTOBER 15, 2:16 P.M.

Masters asked Benny Fulkerson to accompany him on his way back to Nick's office, his interrogation headquarters. He had to wrap up this interviewing and get on about putting the pieces of this complicated puzzle together. He had to get the Chief some answers and dispel the desire of the Feds coming to Savannah, Georgia, to stick their noses into his case. The thought turned his stomach.

"Grab yourself a cup of coffee if you'd like, Benny. I know I need some." He added three heaping spoons of sugar hoping to get a surge of energy. This was his midafternoon slump. *No time for that today,* he thought.

"Have a seat. How ya been, Benny? Haven't seen you around for a while."

"I just came into town for Grace's funeral. Didn't know I was going to be held captive here for two days."

"Well, you'll be happy to know you're the last interview today. We ought to be able to assess the information we have and, hopefully, you'll be on your way soon. No promises. Still working on a few things. Of course, with Madelyn's sudden disappearance, it might complicate things a little more. Who knows, you guys might be bedfellers another night."

"Perish the thought! Besides, I'd say you have your criminal right there, Bruce. Why else would she run? Should be as plain as the nose on your face. She's obviously the one who took the jewels. "Benny was emphatically irritated at the inconvenience that had been placed upon a lot of good people, including himself.

"There may be other reasons she'd take off unannounced, Benny. You're awfully quick to judge there, Mister. But hold on. Wait. Let me read you your rights. I don't want to get ahead of myself here." Masters read Fulkerson his Miranda Warning and informed him he was being videoed, neither of which made Benny feel comfortable.

"So I have a right to remain silent? I don't have to say anything?"

"If you wish. It is your right. You can get a lawyer in here if you'd care to. Do you have a lawyer in Savannah still? I could make a call and get someone down here for you real quickly if you don't."

"I know what people in this town thought of me and my obsession for Grace Willingham. I meant no harm to her. I know that little snitch of a granddaughter of hers made me the laughing stock when Grace ran me off her property with that gun."

"I hadn't heard a thing about that until today, Benny." Masters choked back a chuckle at the thought.

"I loved Grace. Since the day I first laid eyes on her, I have loved her. I wasn't Albert, but I could have made her happy. She, like everyone else, never gave me the chance because no one knew my roots. Then when they found out my past, they judged me. Seems I could never live down that reputation. Didn't matter where I landed."

Benny got caught up in the moment of heartfelt emotion for the love that never came to fruition in his life. He'd never been a man who could trust people. He was abandoned by his parents at age three and grew up in a boys' orphanage in Indiana. He had suffered at the hands of so-called counselors and aides assigned to protect and care for discarded kids. He had been molested repeatedly until he ran away at fifteen. Breaking free was the most glorious day of his life. He would go from town to town, trying to fit in society. He didn't mind working. He had worked and paid his way through mortuary school. When he got his license, Savannah was the place his body settled. His eyes had fallen upon Grace.

Benny had plans of buying out Richard Turner. He would have been sole owner had he been able to come up with all the money. He couldn't, so he was willing to share ownership with his cohort. Richard paid beans, and Benny ate a lot of them in order to save every dollar he could amass. Why he ever trusted the likes of Richard Turner to keep his word about selling the business would forever be a mystery to him. The man lived a deceitful life himself. Richard had invited Fulkerson to join in his secret lifestyle. Benny was a bachelor by choice. Not because he couldn't love. He did. He had loved Grace for as long as he could remember. He was nearly twenty years younger than Grace, but that never mattered to Benny. Grace didn't look her age anyway. They would have been a perfect fit. Given the age difference, he could somewhat understand why Grace might question his motives.

The only fault Benny had was he came into town as a wanderer, a stranger, and a huge suspicion to everyone. He had always tried to prove himself, but his greatest motivation was to win the hand of Grace Carissa Willingham. Grace broke his heart time and again by not allowing him to court her. *She could grow to love me,* was Benny's constant thought. He was confident in that. She never gave him the chance. He was the exception to the rule of persistence. It didn't pay off. It never seemed to for Benny Fulkerson. But he couldn't fault Grace for being a woman of steadfastness. It was one of the traits he admired most in her. She never let anyone take advantage of her or coerce her into something she had set her mind to. Ever.

Benny would have to admit that Grace did a better job at being self-made than him. He would have enjoyed sharing in her wealth. He often dreamed of it, as a matter of fact. But it was only part of the fantasies he shared in his dreams of Grace. If Masters asked the right questions, he could incriminate himself unintentionally. He wouldn't be able to deny his proclivity for wanting to see those coveted jewels. To his knowledge, no one in Savannah, other than Grace, had ever laid eyes on them save for two occasions. To win the woman's heart who wore them would have been quite the quest for a "nobody."

If Masters dabbled into his contempt for Nick Willingham, things might get even stickier for Benny. He had no use for the young punk. He practically stole the business out from under his nose. Had Benny been the rightful owner of Turner's Funeral Home, he would have been the one to touch Grace, to prepare her for her new dwelling place, and to place a kiss on the lips of the woman he had cherished all these years. He knew it was wrong to have such strong dislike for anyone, but Nick was another Willingham he had no use for.

"Benny? You want me to make the call? Or can we go forward?"

"I'm not going to answer any of your questions, Bruce. I think I'd feel more comfortable doing this with an attorney present. Don't get me wrong. I don't have anything to hide. I didn't take those jewels. I may be a nobody in the eyes of this town, but I am not a thief."

"Hold on, hold on, Benny. No one's accusing you of anything. Kinda touchy, aren't you?"

"I'm not talking anymore until I get an attorney. When you let us out of this make-shift jail, I'll talk with my counsel and come and give a statement then."

"Won't happen that way, Benny. You need to get in touch with your lawyer now and have him come here. You won't be going anywhere until we get your statement. Sorry, Bud. I hate doing that, but gotta do my job. You can step out and make some calls. Let me know when you're ready to get this done." Masters knew if his attorney said no way you're taking a statement from my client, it wouldn't happen. He would have to wait and see the caliber attorney Benny chose.

"My cell phone's dead. Hasn't been charged in two days."

"Ricks will take you to a phone. Or you're welcome to sit

right here and make some calls. But I need to step out for a few minutes. I'll get back with you shortly."

"I think I can find a phone here. I do know my way around this place. Remember? I worked here for twenty-two long, arduous years."

"I'm sure you know where most everything is in this funeral home, Benny. I'm quite certain you do." Masters made mental note that Benny also would know how to gain access to the attic. *This* was something he could give to the Chief.

Chapter 12

Madelyn glanced behind her looking for any signs of pursuit. She picked up the pace. Bryson was perched on her left hip, legs and arms dangling loosely. His gaze was fixed on his mother. He squealed with delight when she popped a kiss on his wet lips. His top two teeth were peeking through the gum. The black curly head full of hair complemented his enormous black eyes. He was a beautiful child and the joy of Madelyn's heart. She never dreamed she could love anyone with her whole heart, until Bryson. And to think she almost aborted him. But for Granny Grace, this child would be among the statistics of another "voice that had no choice." Those were Granny's words that pierced Madelyn's ears and penetrated her heart. Those and the fitful night before her scheduled abortion. The memory was vivid still. She brushed back a tear as the recollection moved her to a remember-when moment.

*   *   *

827 VICTORY DRIVE
MAY A YEAR AGO, 5:53 A.M.

The full moon's illumination and dawn's early light merged to light the peaceful path to Grandma's. Madelyn turned off her headlights. She didn't want to disturb Granny's slumber. It was far too early in the morning to be waking anyone who wasn't expecting a visit. Madelyn didn't fully understand why this woman loved her, but she was grateful Granny did. Had it not been for Grace Willingham, she would never have come to feel the significance of belonging to a family. Madelyn had learned to be self–sufficient at a tender age. It was fight or flight. Constance Beth Murray never had time for her. She was too busy entertaining the trails of unfaithful men who sought pleasures of the flesh. Madelyn never wanted for anything but never got anything she wanted. She wanted her dad to want her. She needed her mom to love her. She longed for time and attention from either. Connie never read her a book, never tucked her in bed at night, never fixed her a lunch, and never came to an event at school when she was young. The latter wouldn't happen until later.

High school was not the place Madelyn would have chosen for her mom to show her face at an event. But had Mom limited it to her face, Madelyn would have been happier. It was her cleavage, short skirt, and boots that drew the attention of the male students. Madelyn had never been more humiliated in her life. Her mother's indiscretion made Madelyn the target for jeering and callous remarks. Shortly after her mother's *appearance,* Madelyn was raped by the senior quarterback while his two friends held her to the ground, all the while taunting her with, "Like mother, like daughter." None of the school officials believed Madelyn's story. Connie laughed it off. Her only comment was, "If you gonna turn a trick, honey, you gotta get your money up front." Jim Willingham would have never cared to know. His only support of Madelyn was a Court-ordered check to Connie each month. Madelyn often wished she had shared the incident with Grandma Grace. There would have been justice served. Instead, the event turned Madelyn's heart toward the world. Granny had impressed upon her as long as she could remember about purity and abstinence. Now, she was tainted. It was shameful. Although she knew she had not invited the offense, an aura of guilt accompanied her shame. What if Granny didn't believe her either? It was not worth the risk. Their relationship was too important to Madelyn.

Within the month, Madelyn dropped out of school. Drugs, alcohol, and sex became her only escape. Her body became a canvas of expression. Each masterpiece conveyed a message of deliverance from a painful trauma she had endured. Grace never condemned her for having tattoos. She did, however, spill forth with beauty in the duty of her love for the Lord. She reminded Madelyn how her body was a temple of God, and how beautiful she was without all the covering. She spoke to her of inner beauty and all the attributes that accompanied it. Madelyn would rock in her special chair as Granny spoke of kindness, consideration, courage, and gratefulness. She encouraged Madelyn to have a gentle and forgiving spirit, and always to be mindful of unselfish love. Madelyn wanted to believe Granny when she told her, "It doesn't matter how the world sees you, Maddie. What really matters is how you see yourself. Always know that God sees you as He created you. You are a child of the King. Don't ever let anyone tell you any differently."

Madelyn got out of her car and quietly closed the door. The inside lights were still on. The last thing she needed was a dead battery, so she pushed up against the door with her thigh to close it tight. She just wanted to sit in her rocking chair and wait until Granny Grace started her day. She would have breakfast with her and spend a quiet day just lying around. As she walked up the steps, she noticed a candle glowing in the sitting room. Granny had a history of fires. She didn't need another. Madelyn scratched through the soil securing the vibrant Queen Elizabeth fern. Stuck down in the soil was her rite of passage to Granny's house anytime she needed a safe haven. Madelyn appreciated the trust behind the gesture of entrusting her to her very own key.

A shadow caught her eye and she pressed against the window for a closer look. She saw a lone figure kneeling in prayer. She stood motionless watching, not wishing to disturb the moment. Granny Grace never faltered. Her red kneeling pillow buffered her knees. The pillow had known Grace's presence many times, and it bore two hollowed-out indentations as a testimony.

Madelyn dropped the key. She fumbled between the back of the wicker chair and its cushion to find it. Granny opened the door. "Maddie, is that you?"

"I'm sorry, Granny. I hope I didn't scare you to death."

"No, no, child. Not at all. I've been expecting you."

"You have?" Her anticipation was surprising but comforting.

"Been praying for you, honey. All night. Right there," and she pointed to her cushion. Granny made her way to her rocker and Madelyn positioned her next to it. Ashley's chair had been the last beside Granny's. It was a ritual the grandchildren shared. One always checked out who had been Grace's audience before his or her consultation. Ashley visited her frequently. Of course, she and Jimmy had lived most of their lives with Granny Grace. Madelyn often wondered what it might be like to be in Ashley's shoes. She was the acknowledged daughter of James Albert Willingham II. The accomplished one. The beautiful one. The intelligent and most likely to succeed granddaughter of Grace Carissa Willingham. Everyone was proud of her. Madelyn would be, too, she supposed, if she wasn't so disgusted with her own life. She often wondered if Ashley had met with the obstacles Madelyn had faced how she would have fared. That was the God Madelyn had trouble understanding. Why would life be so easy for some and so difficult for others if He loved everyone the same?

"Life isn't always fair, Maddie." Granny reached over and patted Maddie's hand.

Madelyn looked up at the sky. *Are you kidding me?*

"What did you say, Granny?" Madelyn quivered inside. It was as though Granny could read her thoughts. How did she do that? It totally freaked her out. *Did* she have a pipeline to God?

"I said life isn't always fair. I know you must feel like you're the most abandoned child in the world. But you're not, honey. You are loved. I know you are troubled, Maddie. I pray for you every day. I don't know what happened that turned your heart away, but you abandoned God. He didn't abandon you. Everything you have experienced in life is the consequences of people's poor choices. You were fearfully—"

"And wonderfully made, yeah, yeah. All the days ordained for me were written in His book. That one hangs me up every time, Granny. You've explained it, but I can't wrap my head around that." Madelyn thrust her hands in the air in silent rebellion, then slapped her thighs and slumped back in her rocker. Madelyn's thoughts raced back to the day of her rape. She shook her head trying to erase the memory. *Where was God then? He ordained that for me? Thanks a lot, Lord!*

"Maddie, you have to keep reminding yourself that there are two forces at work in this world–Good and Evil. God gives people free will. People make poor judgment calls every day. Unfortunately, those bad decisions sometimes affect their circle of acquaintances, and always the very people they love most. But God works all things together for the good—"

"Of those who love Him and who have been called according to His purpose. I know those things, Granny Grace. I've listened to you all these years. I've read the Bible you gave me. But life—"

"Isn't fair, Maddie. Regardless, we are still called to be faithful. When we are, we have joy amidst the pain."

Madelyn was quiet for a moment. She drew her legs up under her chin, cradled her arms around them, and rocked. A muggy breeze caught her face, but it was welcome refreshment nonetheless. It was going to be another scorching August day in this God-forsaken town she lived in.

"I'm not going to do it, Granny Grace."

"I know you're not."

There she goes again! How? How did she know that? Yesterday Madelyn was going to abort. Only in the middle of the night did she come to her senses. How *could* Grace know that? She must have a direct line. How else could it be?

"I know my Maddie's heart. It's a good heart. There is so much good inside you, Maddie. You are part of me. There is a legacy of love in this family. We stand for right. I was confident God would hear my prayers. He never changes someone's will, but He will wrestle down your heart and mind until they are in sync with the Holy Spirit that lives inside you."

"I've been bad to God, Granny. Real bad." Madelyn was ashamed of her past. In just a few short years, she had managed to disregard all sense and sensibility regarding her self-worth. Since the rape, she had slept with at least thirty men and boys. She was going through the motions of life. It was meaningless. Kareem was another passing fancy. Who knew the contraception she had used all this time would fail. Now, here she was—pregnant! Madelyn had not even shared the news with Kareem. She was going to quietly get an abortion and that would be that. What changed her heart? Was it this praying woman beside her? Whatever it was, she was at peace.

"You know this decision means you can't drink or do any more drugs, Maddie. You have a baby living inside you. That baby depends on you now and will for the rest of his or her life. You have to keep yourself healthy. If you don't, you'll have a child growing up feeling abandoned, too. You have a true mother's heart. You don't want your child to experience the void you have all these years. You can break this chain, Maddie. But it's your choice."

"I don't think God wants the likes of me in Heaven, Granny Grace. I'm so ashamed of myself." Madelyn's head melted into her chest.

Granny reached over, lifted her chin, and brushed away the

tears trickling down her face. "No one goes to hell unless they want to, Maddie." Grace stroked Madelyn's hair as her sweet not-so-melodic voice broke into the words of Laura Story's song, "Blessings," 'What if your blessings come through raindrops'…"

*   *   *

Maddie. How I loved my special name. You really did love me. If no one else loved me, Granny Grace, you did. And I loved you, too. I'm sorry I didn't …

Madelyn took the final draw from her last cigarette and flipped the butt on the ground. She brushed the tears from her cheeks and fixed her eyes on the pavement ahead. She adjusted the doily and tied it more snugly under her chin. She had grabbed it off the bathroom side table to cover her tinted hair. She didn't care how far she had to walk in these ugly funeral home white satin slippers. She knew there was relief at home and she meant to get to it. She glanced over her shoulder at the sound of a siren. An ambulance was making its way to St. Joseph's. Just a quarter mile and she'd be home free. It looked like it might rain again today. She hoped to make it home before it did.

*   *   *

INSIDE TURNER'S FUNERAL HOME,
OCTOBER 15, 2:35 P.M.

"We found her exit." Ricks was in the basement of Turner's. "I'll be right down." Masters had been viewing the frames again, hoping to start linking some guest names with faces. "You guys keep it up. If your shift is up, don't leave till you get a replacement. We have to work around the clock, Boys. Just get 'er done."

The basement? There's a basement in this place and no one had told him that. Nick never said anything. Why would he not mention that? Masters didn't like what was stirring within him. He was a good judge of character. He didn't want to believe for a second what was stacking up to be suspicious regarding Nick Willingham.

Ricks pointed to the pile of clothes on the floor. Her boots looked as though she was walking out of them on her way out the door. Madelyn had slipped out of her scanty attire and helped herself to an outfit from the funeral home wardrobe selection.

"She went out this door. Not-so-easy access from the outside, but easy to unlock from the inside to get out." Ricks opened the door and led Masters outside. "It feeds back into a little courtyard area. But from here, looks like she hopped the fence on this side, away from the view of our posted guard. She probably watched him until he wasn't looking. Put this milk crate to step on so she could get over."

"How'd she do that with that baby?" Masters was confounded.

"Hoisted him over with this. He picked up a casket liner. There were some soiled ones in the basement. She probably laid him in it, let him down easy on the ground, and hopped over before he could get away from her. Pretty slick move."

"Did you comb the basement for the jewels?"

"Not yet. Just discovered this and called you immediately." Ricks was proud to have uncovered the mystery of Madelyn's escape route.

"If she took the jewels, she has them with her. She wouldn't have left them in that basement. But search it anyway. Could be anybody put them down there. Especially if they knew there was a basement there. I certainly didn't know there was."

"I'm on it." Ricks grabbed his radio to summons help.

"Have Harrington and Willis been to her place yet?"

"I don't know their status. I'll check and get back with you."

Masters walked upstairs. It was time to have a little talk with Nick. Madelyn was likely being orchestrated by Kareem, and the two of them would be high on the list of suspects. But Nicholas Albert Willingham would have some explaining to do as well.

Chapter 13

"You girls go ahead. I'm going to hang here for a few minutes, if you don't mind," Jimmy encouraged.

"No, not at all." Nora lied. She was thinking the same thing and was hoping for some time alone again. She did have her couple hours before Carmen's arrival, but weary from travel she had fallen asleep and not spent her time wisely.

"I may crash for a bit. I'll have my phone on, though, in case Nick calls. I'll let you both know if I hear anything." Carmen headed up the path toward the house.

"Are you all right, Jimmy?" Nora was hoping he would invite her in for a talk. Many seasons in their lives had passed since they were last together. They had definitely drifted apart. But then, Nora had drifted from everyone in the Willingham clan.

"Yeah, yeah, I'm fine. I'm bone weary and saddle sore, but I just wanted some private time before I crash. Doesn't sound like there's going to be a funeral today. I'll give it an hour or so here, and then head up to an available bed. Thanks, Nora. I do

155

want to talk to you, but later. If that's okay?"

"Sure, sure. Take your time, Jimmy. I totally understand." Nora reluctantly closed the door behind her.

Jimmy had waited for an alone moment since he'd arrived at Grandma Grace's. He'd prefer his rocker, but the Sugar Shack was as good a place as any, he supposed. He had shared a lot of poignant moments with Grace in this place many times when he was working off frustrations centered on his dad.

Jimmy made his way to the lounging area. It was a simple setting. A couch, chair, and a coffee table. No television. That was taboo in the Sugar Shack. You could play all the music you wanted, but it best be clean. If Grace heard anything questionable, and she did have a keen ear, it would be in the shredder, no questions asked. He thumbed through the collection of CDs when a stringed neck caught his eye. *Ah! She's still here!* He picked up his Giannini guitar and dusted it off. Grandma had bought his learner musical instrument for him when he was ten. It was great therapy. He quickly advanced to his Gibson, and then amassed other brands and models. When he left for Africa, he sold his impressive collection.

Jimmy began to strum his old friend. He was surprised how well he took to it again. He was reminded how much he missed the release his music provided. He was a bit rusty, but with practice, he'd be able to play again in no time. He had talent. Grandma said it was a natural God-given one. Grace loved to harmonize with him on both the old-time-religion and the contemporary songs. The two blended voices epitomized the theory that family harmony is unsurpassed.

He wondered if Grandma left his guitar to him in her Will?

Surely she would. And if she didn't, perhaps no one would object to his taking it. *The ol' gal's got a fortune here alone. How will she divide it all? Who did you leave those jewels to, Grandma? Well, it may not matter anyway. They're gone for now. I hope it doesn't matter to anyone, actually. It shouldn't. We never got to lay eyes on them but once anyway, so it's not like we're going to miss having them around. But, I understood why you did that, Grandma. The question is: Did everyone else? Did the others understand your idea of wealth and treasure?*

Jimmy hummed a few bars of the latest rendition of "Amazing Grace." He was slated to sing the song at Grace's funeral. He was hoping to have the composure to do it justice. If he could rein in his emotions and sing with celebration, that would be his desire. And Grandma's. She always wanted her passing to be festive. *I'll do my best, Grandma. I promise.*

Jimmy propped his guitar by the couch and walked over to the counter. He turned the handle of the apple peeler and closed his eyes. He visualized Grandma Grace standing there beside him, cutting the apples as he turned the crank.

*   *   *

THE SUGAR SHACK,
TWELVE YEARS EARLIER, 10:36 A.M.

"He makes me so mad, Grandma. I hate him. I hate him, I do."

"Number one, you know the rule about that word, young man. You're a child of God and you aren't allowed to hate. It's forbidden. Number two, don't ever say that about your dad. You don't hate him, Jimmy. There's not a fiber within you that's called to that emotion. Dismiss it from your mind. You can be angry at him, but you are never allowed to hate your father." Grace's direction was tender but stern.

"Yes, ma'am. I know I'm not supposed to hate anyone. I got that part, Grandma."

"It's *I have*," she corrected.

"But how could he be so cold-hearted? To me? I'm his only son, Grandma. I have wanted nothing but to have my dad say he loves me. I want to hear him say, 'Good job, Jimmy.' Do you know how much I want that? Do you know how much I *need* that?" Jimmy's tears kept tempo with every turn of the peeler.

Grandma was silent. She always knew to wait until composure was in place. "There's little need to speak when tears flood the ears," was her philosophy. Jimmy peeled a dozen apples before he could resume. "He hurt me this time. He really hurt me. I play my butt off in games, Grandma. I'm the best defensive back on the team. He's always there. He's on the Town Council. He comes to every home game. He's politicking. He wants to win next year's Mayoral election, of course. At last night's game, I made an interception and ran it in for a touchdown, Grandma."

"You did? Oh, I wish I had been there. I had to help out at the church for the Thanksgiving dinner at church tomorrow. You know I don't miss them if I can help it. I'm so proud of and for you, Jimmy!"

"Well, you would think Dad would be, too. But what does he do? He goes up to Zach Corbett and pats him on the back, tells him what a great game he played."

"Zach is the quarterback?"

"Yes, ma'am."

"He's the son of Cheryl?"

"Yes, ma'am, she's this week's flavor. That's embarrassing enough, Grandma. He split up their marriage. Do you know how humiliating that is? They call him 'home-wrecker,'" Grandma! He's the laughingstock of my friends. Or maybe I am. How does he get elected to anything in this town? I don't get it. He's all smiles and so kind and talkative to everyone else. But me. He doesn't give me the time of day." Jimmy paused, trying to swallow the lump in his throat and attempting to hold back the flood gates he felt opening. "I was right there, Grandma! I was right there! He looked over at me. I waited. Our eyes connected. He just nodded and walked away. That was it. That's all he had for me—a stupid nod? He just doesn't love me, Grandma. He doesn't love me. That really–it really hurts." Jimmy stopped peeling and buried his head on Grace's shoulder.

Grace stood holding Jimmy, accepting his emotions as her burdens. A tenth grader should never feel forsaken by his father. She could wring James Willingham's neck herself were he within arm's reach. Nothing challenged her heart more than pain inflicted upon a child's heart. And to know it was the likes of her son hurting this precious child. But then, he'd been hurting all of his kids for much of their lives.

Jimmy lifted his head and wiped his nose on his sleeve. "Why does he hate me, Grandma? Does he blame me for Mom's death? Is that why he has nothing to do with me, because he thinks I was responsible?"

Jimmy's eyes wanted answers Grace wasn't sure she was

capable of giving. She knew that question would come someday. A child begins to fashion his or her own reasoning behind neglect, abuse, or any form of abandonment. She immediately summoned help from within. *Help me out here, God. This child is as precious to You as he is to me. Please, give me the words. What would You say? Let it be heard through me. Amen.*

Grace coaxed Jimmy over to the table. She went to the refrigerator and got him a tall glass of her special fruit punch. It was his favorite drink, and Grandma Grace always kept a supply on hand. She sat the drink in front of him, along with a couple of homemade oatmeal-walnut-raisin cookies. Jimmy sat and stared as though he was frozen. His slumped posture painted the picture of the beaten-down spirit of a desperate young teen.

Grace situated herself across from Jimmy so she could look square on as she addressed his heartfelt issue. "Jimmy, your father is a very confused man. He knows what's right. He's running. And he's running scared. He's not angry at you. He only thinks he's angry at God, but that isn't it either. Your dad is angry at himself. And he's very ashamed. He's too full of pride to admit he's wrong. It's a bad place to be in life. Your father is a man who wrestles with many regrets. That can keep a soul hostage to a pattern of wrong rather than making a change for what is right.

"He's a lot like you, Jimmy, but in a different way. His dad wasn't around either. That's where his anger began. He played football and never had a dad there to see him. He would come home from games after watching his friends' dads pat them on their backs and tell them what a great job they had done. There were many days he dissolved into tears, too. He vowed he would never have a child that he would leave. And now, he's done exactly what he said he wouldn't do."

Jimmy raised his head in objection, but Grandma cut him off.

"I told your father sometimes people didn't have a choice in things that happen to them, but most of the time they do. It's how we as individuals handle our choices and others' choices for our lives, regardless of what those encompass. The heart may desire to do things the will refuses to allow, but it is still a personal choice. He was on a path similar to you—finding his way through a fatherless life. Then he fell in love with Annie and his perspective on life changed and he became more settled. He was a fine young man, just like you.

"Ashley came along. Life was good. Your mom and dad were thrilled to be expecting again with you. She always wanted the gender to be a surprise, but your mama was confident you were a boy. How right she was. Everything was different for her. She had pregnancy sickness with Ashley immediately. Not so with you. But something else plagued her body. She never had a single clue she had cancer until she went for a checkup to confirm her pregnancy. She had a decision—take the baby so she could have chemotherapy or have the baby and risk her life. She chose life—yours. When your dad found out it was a boy, he was so proud. But he was torn. He didn't want to give up either one of you. But he didn't have a choice. She did. She made the decision."

"Maybe she shouldn't have, Grandma. Maybe it was better I wasn't born." Jimmy was serious but distraught at the thought.

"That's nonsense, Jimmy. Who's to say she would have lived anyway? Could you? Could James? Could I? Of course not. The doctors couldn't even guarantee it. No one knows that but God. Your mother did what was right. You have a purpose for being here, Jimmy Willingham. Don't ever underestimate what God has ordained for you. You will be a mighty warrior for Him. I'm confident in that."

Jimmy took a drink of his juice and ate a bite of homemade comfort. Grandma always spoke words of hope. His heart still ached for his dad's approval, but he was certain he could never earn it. Now, it was his choice how he dealt with the situation with his dad. He would digest how that would look to him.

"Your dad will not be misguided forever, Jimmy. Keep your heart soft and receptive to him. You may be well into your manhood, possibly have a family of your own, but he will come back to his roots. I taught him well. I will not take responsibility for his behavior. He understands God's will for his life, but he has gotten caught up in the flesh. It's a very strong power, Jimmy. You resist it with everything in you."

Grandma never broke stride. She seized any opportunity she had for life lessons. "And this is as good a time as any for us to talk about some of what you are going to begin experiencing."

"Grandma, let's don't—" Jimmy could not see himself having this discussion with Grandma Grace. But what would he do with these kinds of choices in life? He had no dad who was willing to talk to him. Nor was James Willingham the shining example of wholesomeness either. But he knew Grandma. Once she set her mind to do something, God would be the only one who could redirect her thinking.

*   *   *

Jimmy blushed at the memory of Grandma's enlightenment

about the anatomy that day. But, he had to admit that it served him well. She left no stone unturned. But to say it kept him from dabbling in the fire, he was ashamed to say it did not. The ensuing years were his very rebellious years. Those years he had denied the advice about "choices" and resorted to alcohol, drugs, and girls to drown his miserable existence. With some of the shenanigans he had pulled, it was a thousand wonders he was a whole man today. In hindsight, he wished he had listened to the advice of Grandma. It could have spared him a lot of heartache and much regret.

Jimmy owed his life to Grandma Grace. His mom had fought a good fight, but lost the battle after four years. When Annie succumbed to the lymphoma which plagued her body, it was Grace that took Jimmy and Ashley to nurture. Looking back, Jimmy thought how difficult it must have been to divide loyalties—mom and grandmom. Grandmothers want to be just that. They have reared their children. How unfair it is to have to take on the responsibilities of another round of offspring, especially when an able-bodied parent is alive to do so.

His dad was in no condition to be the guardian of his flesh and blood. James resorted to alcohol immediately after Annie's death, but kept it confined to nighttime use. Within a couple of years, it had escalated into a chronic problem. Grace Willingham took matters into her own hands once she got whiff of his unthinkable conduct. Nine-year-old Ashley had called frightened because Daddy wasn't home and it was dark and they were hungry. That was the end of that. Grace packed up the kids' clothes and brought them home with her. James never objected and never asked for them to be returned.

How does a man who understands the pangs of establishing identity as a man neglect his own children? Ashley had worked out her differences with him. If Jimmy allowed himself, however, he could be angry all over again. He was grateful, beyond words, for his recall of Grandma Grace's words. They had sustained him. Those words had reminded him Whose he was. His earthly father might not care to lay claim to his worth as a person, but his Heavenly Father thinks he hung the moon! That was sufficient. In the meantime, he continued to pray for the day that Grandma assured him would come—a day of reconciliation between the II and the III heirs of the late, great James Albert Willingham I, the one who held the undying devotion of Grace.

Chapter 14

Madelyn was sitting on the floor with Baby Bryson, rocking back and forth, lost in thought, and humming *Amazing Grace*. He had been asleep in her arms, resting peacefully. She stroked his eyebrow lightly and ran her finger down the bridge of his nose. He was precious to her. How could she think of being anything less than a responsible mom? Madelyn had broken out of the funeral home, making her way back to get a hit. Sitting here with him, gazing upon his perfection, his innocence, his dependency upon her, it suddenly seemed unimportant to her. She had been almost two days without her sustenance. Madelyn was unsure of what came over her in her brisk walk home, but a feeling of breaking free was enveloping her for the first time ever.

She brought her legs under her and crossed them so that she could rest Bryson in the cradle they made. She stuck a bottle in his mouth, and he was content to nourish himself while watching his mommy with heavy eyes. She had been plundering through her memorabilia of Grace and gathered them around her on the floor. She looked through the few pictures she had of her and Granny Grace. She lingered with the picture of her in her special rocker on Granny's porch. She had spent many early mornings and late nights in that very spot. Rocking and thinking. Thinking and rocking. Mostly tied up in anger and bitterness.

What was it about Granny that could bring a soul to quiet rest? Grace had loved Maddie in those moments more than she'd felt loved by anyone. Now, those times were gone. Forever. How could she have been so reckless with her life that she would miss the opportunity to allow her precious grandmother to see this baby she cradled in her lap? Granny was excited over the birth of this sweet child. Madelyn let the opportunity slip away. For what? Drugs! Stupid, senseless drugs! Was she really *that* dependent on a substance that she would trade it for genuine love? She felt ashamed and convicted. Her mind flashed back to the porch, the rocker, and the words Granny spoke to her.

*   *   *

GRANDMA GRACE'S PORCH, DECEMBER 12, TWO YEARS AGO, 8:17 P.M.

"Maddie, you don't need drugs. You don't need men. Not those kinds of men. You can find someone who will love you the way you should be loved. Someone who will love you for the beautiful person you are inside. You have a baby growing inside you now." No one ever spoke straightforward to her like Grace Willingham. They only berated her, looked at her like she was a freak or with pity, but always with a judgmental eye.

"Granny, look at me. I have tattoos everywhere. I have more piercings than dogs have fleas. I have pink hair! I'm a rough and used-up girl for twenty-one. No one like you describe wants me, much less will love me like this."

"The Lord doesn't look at your tattoos or your piercings or even your pink hair today/blue hair tomorrow, Maddie. God looks at your heart. If your heart is as unsightly as your outward appearance, then you're in trouble. I'll be honest." Madelyn always respected the truth Grace spoke. "It is true that people judge by human standards, but God passes judgment on no one based on people's values. He'll take you just as you are, but you have to be willing to clean up your act. You can't purposely live in a state of sin and have a heart fit for the Kingdom. He doesn't work that way."

"I don't think I could ever clean up enough for God, Granny Grace. Once you're hooked on this stuff, it's hard to break free."

"Oh, pshaw. You're talking nonsense, Child! You can overcome anything you put your mind to, Madelyn Joy. Don't forget for one second that you're a Willingham, young lady. That's good blood. Forget the example your father has set. He's not in his right senses, but he'll come around someday. You know very well that you come from a long line of survivors. Do you remember what I have always told you about strength? Tell me what it is. I want to hear you say it."

"I know it, Granny Grace. I do know it."

"I want to hear it. When it's in your mind, it eventually flows to your heart. When it's in your heart, you'll believe it for everything it's worth. Say it to me."

"I can do all things through Christ who gives me strength."

Madelyn hurried through the phrase she had heard Granny say for as long as she could remember. She must admit it was these words from which she had gained her boldness. It was because of her belief in this truth that she mustered up the power to break away from her mother's control. Her problem was she ran straight into the arms of Satan. Once she found a way to escape her nightmare life at home, it became easier to escape through drugs and sex rather than ask for strength from the Someone she couldn't see.

"You are God's creation. Are you hearing me? No one can ever take that away from you, unless you allow it. You have better choices for your life, Maddie. Today is the beginning of the best of your life. Make it be so. I know you can do it, and I believe in you. I always have."

Grace was on her feet now and leaning over Madelyn's rocker. When Grace wanted to make a point, it was a square-on look. She patted Madelyn's face and then kissed her on the forehead. "You're my sweetheart, Madelyn. You're special to me. I love you more than life. You know that, don't you?"

"Yes, Ma'am, I do, Granny. I really do." Madelyn's eyes filled with tears. It always moved her heart when Granny told her that. She was the only one who had ever said those three words to Madelyn. The words had never fallen on her ears from any other person on earth.

"But I'm not the only one who does, Madelyn Joy. Your God in Heaven loves you more than I do, if you can believe that's possible. He loves you, Maddie. When I'm not here any longer to tell you that, you remember what I said. God loves you most."

*   *   *

ABERCORN TERRACE APARTMENTS, #14,
SAVANNAH, GEORGIA, OCTOBER 15, 2:47 P.M.

"Ma'am, it's the Police. Open up, please." Two officers knocked repeatedly at the door to get the attention of Madelyn Willingham. She ignored their persistence.

Madelyn laid the picture down. She picked up the journals and pens Granny had given her for each birthday. They had been her solace in times of deepest despair. There was more shocking life in these pages than one girl deserved. Madelyn clutched the snow globe Granny had given her the last time they were together, two days before Bryson was born. She gave it a shake and watched as the faux snow fell soft upon the Opera House in Sydney. She shook it again and watched until every flake was still. And again, and watched. And once again, and watched. She had dreamed of going to Australia since she studied it in school so many years ago. Granny agreed that if Madelyn would finish school and get her college degree to teach, by then Bryson would be old enough to go along. The three of them would enjoy Maddie's trip together. It was Madelyn's fault they never got to enjoy that time. She accepted the full responsibility. If it was the last thing she did, she would take Bryson to Sydney in honor of Grace Carissa Willingham.

Madelyn picked up her Bible Granny had given her. She opened it and began to read from her favorite book—James. "Consider it pure joy, my brothers and sisters, whenever you face trials of many kinds, because you know that the testing of your faith produces perseverance." She held the Bible high in the air. "I vow to you, God, today will be the first day of the best of my life!"

*   *   *

"Don't move, Ma'am. We'll let you know when you can stand up."

Madelyn was busy comforting Bryson who had been awakened. He was startled with the clamor of the door being kicked open by the police.

"Willis, search the rooms. I'll stay here and watch Ms. Willingham." Lieutenant Harrington stood over Madelyn pointing a gun at her head. Madelyn affixed her body to shield Bryson from any potential danger.

"You can put away the gun, Officer. I'm not going anywhere. Don't have any weapons. Just sitting here in a state of mourning."

"You're high, Madelyn." The Lieutenant was well aware of Madelyn's frequent visits to court. Her docile manner was a bit perplexing to him, even on drugs. He had been at this apartment many times before for domestic calls, only to haul her and/or her live-in to jail because of drugs.

Madelyn was calm amidst the confusion. "You won't find anything this time, Harrington. Give it up. I've been clean for two days. There's nothing here. I haven't disturbed the peace. You've broken in on me. I was just here with my baby. If you took me down for screening, whatever you find is residual. Won't hold up."

Madelyn had had a soulful moment from the time she walked into her apartment. She immediately flushed all drugs. Kareem would have a fit once he discovered how many thousands of dollars had been flushed down the toilet. She had taken the needles, tubes, bags, and bongs to the dumpster two complexes over. If they thought about looking there, they'd find them and could trace it if they so dared. But she was breaking free!

"Nothing here, Sir. Can't find a trace."

"Well, Madelyn, you must've been expecting us."

Madelyn ignored Harrington. It was not her usual conduct. In the past, Bryson would have been in his pack-and-play and she would have been in the face of this officer. She was as surprised at her actions as was Harrington. She gathered up her memoirs and souvenirs and placed them in their keepsake box.

"I need to look in this, please." Harrington took the box from Madelyn.

"Don't you break a thing in there, Harrington. I'll bust your head if you do."

"Don't give me a reason to take you in, Madelyn."

"If you think I took the jewels, you're wrong. They're not here."

"Oh, I wouldn't think you'd be stupid enough to bring them here, Madelyn. You knew someone would come looking for you here. Maybe you think we're that stupid. But you know where they are. I'm sure the detective is going to want to talk to you again."

"I'm quite sure he will. I had to get here and bathe my baby and get him changed. Kept telling you guys that. You wouldn't listen."

"He's a convenient excuse for you, isn't he? Kids come in handy when they're not in the way." Harrington was condescending in his demeanor.

"If you need me to go back, I will."

"Oh, now, that's different. Willis, get this, Madelyn's cooperating with us. How special. What, did you see the ghost of your grandma on your way here?" Harrington and Willis broke out in laughter. Madelyn would have spit in their face, but something was holding her back. Perhaps that's exactly what had happened to her. Something had grabbed hold of her heart and mind and spirit, and for the first time in her life, they seemed to be in sync with one another.

That's what Granny Grace had always told her. "Until heart, mind, and soul are in harmony, a gal's life will never find her way to peace." *So that's what this is? Peace. Finally! This is what serenity feels like.*

"Let me get my baby a couple of changing of clothes, diapers, and a couple of bottles, then I'll go back with you."

"Yeah, if you get the inspiration to stop along the way and show us where you stashed those jewels, you just do that." Madelyn walked into her bedroom. "Go with her Willis. I'll watch the baby and the front door. You never know if she's called some of her cronies." Harrington walked over to the trash can in the kitchen. He knew she had to do something. No bottles. No needles. Nothing. What did she do with those? She couldn't have cleaned up that fast.

"I'm ready. Let's go." Madelyn placed the items back in her keepsake and slipped it in the diaper bag hanging on her shoulder. She picked up Bryson and started walking for the door.

"Need your cell phone, Madelyn. We should probably check out who all you've called."

"It's been charging. It was dead. Remember? We've been locked up at a funeral home for two days."

"Get the phone, Willis. And check her records, too. She could've deleted every call or text off that thing. Need to find out who she called to let them know she was here. The drugs went somewhere. And so did the jewels. We'll find them. It's a matter of time."

"Whatever." Madelyn walked to the police car. She tickled Bryson under his chin and arms and down to his belly. He giggled with delight for the attention from his mother. Madelyn was more tender in her touch than before. She was amazed at the effect it had on her baby. Whatever had swept over her, she would not trade it for anything. And to think it took grandmother's death to bring her to her senses.

She stared out the window as the commission made its way back to Turner's. A lump gathered in her throat. There was still the matter of Kareem. She had felt his heavy hand before. She was uncertain what the future held and how he would take the course of things to come. She couldn't imagine Masters's plan, but surely this hostage situation couldn't go on much longer. Madelyn had no idea where she would go when they walked out of the funeral home. She knew it couldn't be Granny's place. Even knowing where the key is would not help her now. Kareem knew where it was, too. He had forced her to go there when Granny was out of town to look for the jewels. She knew they weren't in the safe deposit box. She had been there already herself. She had hit the bank just right and talked a newbie into letting her in. Knowing this, Kareem would have nothing else but to force Madelyn into the house. He threatened to burn the place to the ground if she didn't let him in. She felt awful. She knew it was an ultimate betrayal to Grace. Worse yet, she couldn't even change the hiding place for the key. Had she done so, Granny would ask questions. She was caught. And now, what Kareem would do, Heaven only knew.

Madelyn took a deep breath and attempted to swallow away her lump. *Come back peace. Don't leave me now. I like how you feel. I can do all things through Christ who gives me strength. I can do all things through Christ who gives me strength. I can do all things..."*

Chapter 15

"Will do, Chief. I knew we were milking this lockdown thing and it was a matter of time before someone blew the whistle on us. I'll dismiss them all right now and let them go home." Bruce Masters had been expecting this call. Benny Fulkerson had taken Masters up on the offer to call his attorney. *I'll betcha Benny wishes he'd done that sooner. We never would've been allowed to keep those folks at Turner's without some sort of court order or restraint, and the law wouldn't allow that.* Masters and the Chief had made a quick decision to try and smoke out the thief since it seemed logical the jewels would have been lifted by one of the folks in the viewing room at the time it was discovered they were missing. That time had to be close in proximity to Gladys screaming and fainting. Gladys was confident the jewels would be bequeathed to her. Consequently, she had kept a keen eye on the jewels the entire time.

"I know, Chief. I'm trying to get there. We do have some stronger leads. Madelyn, one of Jim's daughters, broke out and— Oh, you heard. Well, they're bringing her back here now. I'll let everyone go and see if Madelyn will stick around and give us another interview. If not, I think we have enough probable cause that the judge might issue a warrant for her arrest. It's a long shot. We've got to get somebody in jail for this to hold off the FBI and to keep the publicity down on this thing. I'll be in shortly."

Masters had been looking for Nick. He wanted to see for himself how Nick took being pulled from duty. He stuck his head in the viewing room and gave a quick glance. There was no sign of Nick anywhere. *Now, where would that guy go if his office wasn't available? This place is big, but it's not that big.*

Jim Willingham spotted Masters and made his way to confront him. He had had enough. It was time to let him and everyone else go home. "Bruce, hold up. I need to talk to you a minute."

"Whatcha need, Jim?"

"We're done. We're ready to go. This is ridiculous. I don't believe you can hold us here. You don't have anything on me or Valerie. We're not staying here another minute. And if you insist, I'll call my attorney. You guys are really pushing your luck with this illegal detention. Let us go, Bruce. It's over."

"Okay, Jim. You can go."

"And Valerie is coming, too."

"Sure, take Valerie with you. Get outta here."

Jim looked a little amused at the ease of accomplishing his mission. "Great. It's about time." He motioned to Valerie who was out of earshot but watching the exchange. She was quite amazed herself at the immediate response her husband elicited. She grabbed her wrap and Jim's suit coat from the coat tree in the back of the room. Jim waited, a bit puffed up at his commanding performance on behalf of himself and Valerie.

Masters turned from Jim and faced the crowd. "Folks, I just want to thank you all for your cooperation. You've been wonderful and very patient throughout this process."

"Did you find the jewels?" Gladys yelled out above the crowd.

"No, ma'am, we didn't. But we're closer." Masters had already surveyed the crowd and knew the location of each of the guests. He gave a quick scan for any sign of restlessness by his announcement, but would earmark his notes for any indication of vibes from his three suspects.

"We can go? I mean, we're free? I can leave?" Melissa Fitzgerald eagerly made her way to the door.

"Yes, ma'am. Everyone can leave. Thank you for your patience."

"Can I get my gloves back?" Melissa inquired?

"No, ma'am, I'm sorry. They're evidence," Bruce informed.

"Evidence? For what? I didn't—"

"Don't be worrying, Ms. Fitzgerald. I'll let you know if we need anything from you." Bruce turned to face the crowd again.

The twenty-plus participants in the would-be funeral for Grace Willingham scrambled to gather their belongings. They huddled at the door waiting their turn to exit their temporary prison. Jim wasted no time making an immediate departure. Gladys and Ashley lingered behind wanting a consultation with the detective.

"Did you need to talk to Bruce, Ashley?" Gladys didn't want her around to hear what she was going to say.

"No, no, Aunt Gladys. You go ahead. I'm sure you're exhausted."

"Oh, I've waited all this time. Another few minutes won't

hurt me. You go first."

Ashley was hoping to discuss business with Detective Masters privately, but she was well aware that when Aunt Gladys spoke, it was her way or no way. "Tell you what. I'm going to run home and spruce up a bit. I may give you a call later, Detective. If you don't mind, that is."

"Yeah, sure. But I'm not sure where I'll be, Ashley. I think you have my cell number. If I'm free, I'll certainly talk with you. If not, I'll call you back when I catch a minute or two."

"I have your number in my contacts. No problem. Get some rest, Detective. You deserve it." Ashley excused herself and walked away.

"Can't do that for a while, but I will. Take care yourself, Lil' Lady." Masters turned his attention to Gladys.

"What did you find out, Bruce? You wouldn't be letting us go unless you had some lead." Gladys was obviously unaware that she and the rest of the crew had been held on a wing and a prayer.

"Can't reveal that to you, Gladys. Still working on things."

"Did you find Madelyn? She never returned. Kareem just walked out of here without her. She did it, didn't she? I knew it. I knew she had sticky fingers. The more things change, the more they stay the same. She couldn't keep her fingers off of Ashley's things as a kid. Once a thief, always a thief. Did you find her? Did she have the jewels on her? What are you going to do—"

"Hold on, hold on, Gladys. You're jumpin' to a lot of conclusions there, Lady. However, I will tell you that we have found Madelyn. She is in our custody as we speak. That's all I know."

"She did it. I know she did it. I want those jewels in my hands when you recover them. They belong to me and I want them.

And they will not go back on Mother's body."

"Well, it won't work that way, Gladys. Don't get your hopes up. There'll be other procedures that will have to take place first."

"So you do have them! I'm so relieved."

"No, I didn't say that, Gladys. You're puttin' words in my mouth. I haven't said a word about the jewels being recovered, so don't go thinkin' or spreadin' somethin' I didn't say."

"Well, why are you letting everyone leave, then, Bruce? That's ridiculous. They have to be here somewhere. Someone has those jewels. I want them. They're mine! I want those jewels." Gladys's anxious thoughts invaded her calm. Her face reddened with rage. Her heart was racing. She had broken out in a fierce sweat.

Masters struggled to keep his patience. He had other things he needed to take care of. They didn't include the likes of Gladys Willingham. At least, he didn't think so.

"With all due respect, Ma'am, I'd say you might want to concentrate on rescheduling your mother's funeral arrangements rather than concentrating on those jewels. We're doin' our best to retrieve 'em. We'll keep you and Jim apprised of what's happening. But for now, I see the most pressing issue is givin' your mama a proper burial."

Gladys reined in her feelings. She realized how inappropriate and perhaps incriminating her exhibition must have appeared to Bruce. She didn't mean to come across greedy and materialistic, but she couldn't help herself in the matter of Grace's inheritance. She had no intentions of staying with Ralph for as long as she had, but couldn't very well leave until she had secured the financial means to do so. Those jewels would be safe with her and only her. They were her ticket to freedom and getting away from the misery she had managed to create in her life. A fresh start across the seas was something she had anticipated for years. She had always dreamed of Tuscany. She would have left long ago, but then, she would not have been able to monitor the comings and goings of Jim and his flock of kids around Grace. With every new Willingham grandchild, Gladys's share of the inheritance dwindled. It wasn't fair.

Then there was Nick. Gladys and Jim had not considered Carmen for years. But since Nick had joined the ranks of the family, Gladys had Carmen to worry about again. Like Grace, Gladys believed that money attracts the masses. Gladys had secretly feared that if Carmen had children, it was a matter of time before they made their way to Grace's fortune. Now it had come to pass. She could only surmise there could be more who would want to lay claim to a Willingham birthright. The best Jim and Gladys could determine, Carmen had never married. But whether she had any more illegitimate children was as much a mystery as Jim's surprise offspring. Discussing family with Nick was like prying blood out of an anvil. He gave up no information about his mother other than she was single. And he never discussed his life. Ever.

"Gladys? You okay?" Masters was curious what could be churning in that lady's head, but he really was hoping she would just leave.

"I'm sorry, Bruce." She grabbed for her tissue. "I'm just so upset about Mother's funeral. I need to see Nick and talk about arrangements. Did James leave? Where is James?"

"I believe he and Valerie have already left."

"That's typical. Well, I'll finalize Mother's arrangements

myself." Gladys headed to the administrative offices.

Masters yelled out, "Hey, if you find Nick, tell him I'm looking for him."

*   *   *

TURNER'S FUNERAL HOME, CREMATORY, OCTOBER 15, 3:17 P.M.

"Hey, Mom. I'm glad you made it in. Sorry I haven't been able to touch base with you, but things have been a little bit crazy around here this morning." Nick had stolen away to the crematory in order to have a moment from other ears.

"Nick, do they know anything yet?" Carmen was a bit groggy, having been asleep for longer than her usual power-ten. She could have used a good full eight hours, but that would have to come later.

"I don't think so. Last I heard they were looking for Madelyn. She managed to slide past watchful eyes and escaped through the basement. I heard on the scanner they apprehended her at her apartment and are bringing her back here. People are leaving now, so I suspect they'll be opening the funeral home soon. Not for guests, though. Grace is not out. I'm not sure how all that is going to play out to be honest."

"Can I come there? Will you let me see her?"

"Sure, Mom. Come on over and I'll get you some time with Grandma."

"Does she look beautiful, Nick?"

"Like an angel. Like I told you, Mom, she died in her sleep

with a smile on her face holding her Bible and a picture of Albert. Sweetest thing I've ever seen."

"I know you did a great job with her, Nick. She would be proud." Carmen's heart lit like a beacon. That was her boy carrying out her mother's heartfelt wishes.

"Are they onto anything yet? They haven't located the jewels, have they?"

"Not yet, Mom. I stayed involved for a long time. Then, something happened to cause the detective to remove me from the investigation. They gave me a lame excuse about my tending to funeral home business, but I know they have me on their radar."

"Oh, Nick. I'm sorry. Are you all right?"

"I'm fine, Mom. You know I can handle myself." Nick never let his mom know when he sweated the little or the big stuff. He protected his mom. He respected her above all women—Mom and Grandma Grace, that is. She had been given a real raw deal by her Willingham siblings. In his estimation, that was two raw deals too many for his precious mother. He never wanted to add to her burden, but he would help her any way he could anytime she asked. It was a privilege he considered an honor.

"Nick, Nora and Jimmy are here. Should I bring them with me or just come alone?"

"I mean, sure. I guess. They haven't seen Grace. I'm sure they'd like to be here. Besides, it might seem a bit suspicious if you just left them, not to mention pretty rude."

"They're really pretty neat, actually, Nick. I think you'll enjoy visiting your extended family again."

"If there's time. Not sure how preoccupied I'll be once we crank up the services again."

"When is that going to happen? Have they said?"

"I haven't talked with Jim and Gladys yet to finalize the arrangements for recommencing the services. I'm sure that's going to happen here very—"

"I want to be there, Nick. Don't let that happen without me. Stall them. Avoid them. Whatever it takes. She's my mother, too. I have as much right as anyone to be in on the decision. I didn't even attempt it when Mom died, and I have regretted not catching a plane immediately and standing up for my rights. God gave me a second chance to stake my claim. I'm not missing the opportunity."

"Uh, okay, Mom. If you're sure. Gladys is a force to be reckoned with. People avoid her like the plague."

"Gladys doesn't worry me any. Been there, done that one, Nick. She's not the one I dread seeing."

"I understand, Mom. But you know I'm here. I won't leave you."

"I know, Son. You've always been there for me. We're a team. But I'll lose you someday to a very lucky young lady. And quite frankly, Nick, I'm looking forward to that day."

"Yes, Mom, I know. You want grandchildren. So do I, but I had to find someone like you and Grandma. Haven't asked her yet. But I will. Soon. And when we are married, she's going to feel like a queen being married to Nicholas Albert Willingham."

Chapter 16

"Oh, Nicholas, there you are. I've been looking for you every-where." Gladys caught Nick as he was coming through the back door from the crematory. She was not the person he wanted to see, but he really couldn't avoid the conversation that would ensue.

"I want to talk to you about Mother's arrangements."

"Arrangements? You mean services?" Nick purposely attempted to agitate Gladys every chance he got. He took a little pleasure in dishing out what she always fed people.

"You know what I mean. I want to have Mother's services on Monday. We need time to rest and—"

"Where's Jim? We probably should all three discuss—"

"Don't need Jim. He left. He had his chance and he couldn't wait to get out the door. So, this one will have to be made by me alone."

"I'd love to Gladys, but legally I'm bound to include all family members in any decision about services." Nick was totally blow-ing smoke. He knew that was the farthest from the gospel he'd ever preached, but he was buying time for his mom. After all, he'd do anything for her.

"Well, that's all well and good, but if a family member has no interest in being here when decisions have to be made, then, you have to move forward. I don't know if I buy what you're selling me there, Nicholas." Gladys was a downright indignant at his resistance.

"Well, yes, Ma'am, I understand what you're saying. But Jim *has* been in on the decisions thus far, and we should probably keep that intact." Nick was grasping at every excuse he could conjure up in the moment. "I have to look at liability, Gladys. I can't afford to have someone come back on me legally with allegations of negligence. It wouldn't be good for business."

"Well, if I have to take matters in my own hands and call the paper and have it printed in there, I'll be—"

Nick was scrambling for a response to such an insidious contemplation on Gladys's part. But he knew she was capable and would follow through if he didn't come up with some convincing rebuttal. "I'm sure you could do that, but if it's decided it should be another day, you're going to alert an awful lot of folks and add further disgrace to an already reprehensible send-off for your mother and our grandmother."

Nick exasperated Gladys. She would love to slap his little smug face. She was ready to get everything behind her and press forward with her carefully laid-out plans, but she needed rest. She had been waiting for this day long enough. It was finally here and she didn't want the likes of this well-timed heir to Grace Willingham fouling up her strategy. She needed a day to get some things in order. Monday would be soon enough. But Gladys knew if she made too big of a stink, it wouldn't look good for her. She'd made enough enemies in this one-horse town. Gladys had created enough scandals to entertain folks for a lifetime. If she added yet another chapter of drama to Grace Willingham's book of life, she might well be flogged before she could make her exit. She didn't need extra attention drawn to herself.

"Very well, Nicholas. I'll be in touch with Jim and if he agrees with me, I'll have him contact you regarding the same. My preference is Monday, 11:00 a.m. That gives everyone a chance to rest up from this incredible inconvenience. We'll all come back refreshed and ready for whatever."

"What if they don't find the jewels by Monday, Gladys? Have you given thought to that? Grace wanted those jewels on during her service."

"Well, they're not going to be buried with her, for Pete's sake! She's dead. It's not going to matter what Grace gets now. Some things she just might have to live with." Gladys thought how silly her last statement was and quickly added, "Or die with." She turned on her heels and marched out of the funeral home.

Nick took a deep breath. That bought some time for his mom. He didn't know how long he could keep up the excuses with Gladys. But Carmen would be here soon. If Gladys was still around, the fur might fly. But knowing his mom, he was confident Carmen Willingham would not back off from what she had planned to do. Not of blood, but the spitting image of the tenacity of Grace. The only one who might unnerve her was Jim Willingham. If Jim was concerned for Carmen's arrival, he kept it to himself.

*   *   *

"INTERVIEW HEADQUARTERS" AT
TURNER'S FUNERAL HOME, OCTOBER 15, 3:30 P.M.

"Madelyn, we meet again. Have a seat." Masters pointed to the chair and took his seat around the desk that had become a familiar setting.

Madelyn sat down. This time, Bryson was in her arms. He grinned at Masters. The detective couldn't help but interact with the contagious smile. Bryson giggled and buried his head in Madelyn's chest.

"You know the routine. You want an attorney?"

"No. Don't need one."

"You might need one more than you think this time. You've been a bad, bad girl, Madelyn. Why did you break?"

"I kept telling your officers that my baby had wet through everything, he stunk to high Heaven, and I needed to get him home. That's all."

"I don't buy it. They brought you supplies. What'd you do with the jewels?"

"I didn't steal the jewels. You've got the wrong person." Madelyn set her jaw and her body became tense. Bryson began to whimper.

"You have to understand how suspicious all this looks, Madelyn. Surely you understand that. Don't you?"

"What I understand has nothing to do with the jewels. I didn't take the jewels. I keep telling you that. There, there. It's okay, Sweetheart." Madelyn stood Bryson in her lap and he started bouncing. He opened his mouth and moved in for a kiss from Mommy.

"What'd you do with the drugs? You guys always have drugs in your place. The boys tell me there was not even a sign of a baggie, a tube, a script, a bong, nothing. C'mon. If you cooperate, you know it's gonna be lighter for you. You won't get out of this one, Girl. Too much at stake here. No one is gonna work this one out in trade for you. Do you get that?" Masters leaned over the desk to lock in on Madelyn's gaze.

Madelyn leaned her head to the right so she could stare Masters down without Bryson's obstruction to her view. She wasn't budging. If he wanted to eyeball her all night, she could handle it. She would not relinquish. Her lips were sealed.

"Have it your way, Madelyn. Who do you want the baby to stay with tonight?"

"You're not taking my baby."

"He can't go to jail with you, I'm afraid."

"You can't put me in jail. You have absolutely nothing on me, and you know it." Madelyn leaned over the desk getting closer to Masters's nose. "Nothing." She settled back into her chair and touched Bryson's nose to playfully reassure him Mama was fine. He bought it. Madelyn, not so much. She knew if Masters could convince a judge for probable cause, she'd be in the clink tonight. She didn't want to be away from Bryson. There was no one she trusted with his care. And Kareem was inept to take care of him. She didn't trust him anyway. She knew it was a matter of time before she would be history to him. Besides, short of flushing thousands of dollars of drugs, which you would think law enforcement would appreciate, she had done nothing wrong. Well, unless the judge considered checking out of this funeral home as jailbreak. But surely that couldn't carry with it an overnight jail stay.

Masters knew Madelyn was right. They had nothing on her. Holding these people hostage for two days without a bona fide order from a judge could be nothing short of negligence. Masters might have to answer for that one. He was glad the Chief would be there beside him to take the heat.

"So, you going home, Madelyn? Is that what you're gonna do?" Masters knew what Kareem was capable of. The domestic violence calls had been more frequent of late. The poor girl barely recovered from one beating before she was getting another. By the time the police got there, there'd be no story. When that got old, they'd haul them both in for booking, only to have them walk within two to four hours. Masters was fairly confident Madelyn had no desire to show up to Grace's funeral with a battered face.

"I don't know. Home, I guess."

"Really? You want to go home and let Kareem discover he's got no drugs? Don't you think he's gonna be a little upset with you, Madelyn, knowing you took off without him from the funeral home. Or, did you tell him you were going to do that so you could hide the jewels and take the heat off him?"

"You're ridiculous." Madelyn rolled her eyes and went back to entertaining Bryson. She could only hope her concern was not as evident as it felt inside. She knew if she went back, Kareem would be waiting. There was no sign of a drug anywhere and he would blame her for leaving the funeral home, not looking at it as protecting herself, and especially him, for that matter, for discarding the drugs. She had to get a plan for where to go, but she couldn't go back there. She wouldn't. This was it with her and Kareem. If she were going to break free, it had to be away from him, as well.

"Well, I have reason to believe you and Kareem teamed it up, Madelyn. He's pretty persuasive over you. Why is that? You don't let anyone push you around. What's he got that attracts you to him?" Masters was condescending in his questioning.

"It's a place to land for a while, that's all. He has no hold on me."

"Well, I mean, we both know he supplies you all the drugs you need. That's been a pretty impressive free ride for you, Madelyn. We're onto you guys. We're close, Madelyn. When we move in, it's going to be bad. Foster care will wind up with your boy there. You'll never see him again. You're going down for a few years. And when we find the jewels, and we will find them, you'll get a nice package added to that."

Madelyn had no idea what Masters was talking about. She didn't know where Kareem got his drugs and didn't care. All she had cared about was that she had them available for her. She felt fidgety and sweaty, but not because of the questioning. Withdrawal was setting in and she knew it was going to be increasingly more difficult to hold it together.

"You could make this easier on yourself, Madelyn. If you tell me some names right now of the mastermind behind Kareem, I could help you out a little bit, maybe take any sentence away and you could be a mommy to your son there. I'm sure you know. Help us out, Madelyn. Your grandma would want that."

"I don't know what you're talking about. I don't run in Kareem's circles. I just live with him. That's all."

Masters shook his head, got up from his chair, and sat on the corner of the desk to close in on Madelyn. "We already know, Madelyn. We know who it is. But we need a witness to bring it down for us. You could be that gal. If you'd just cooperate with us, this could work out better for you. You think on that tonight while you're in jail. I can talk the judge into a warrant for your arrest."

Madelyn felt imposed upon. Masters was scaring her. Whatever he was talking about sounded big. Kareem was a shady character. She'd give him that. But she had nothing to do with his life. She kept his house, washed his clothes, cooked his meals, and had his kid. She had never been involved with the selling end of drugs. Even when folks showed up at the apartment, he always went outside and cut his deals. This explains why Madelyn had felt she was being followed at times. They actually felt she was part of Kareem's underworld.

"Cat gotcha tongue? The jewels, Madelyn? What'd you do with them? If you don't want to talk about the other, we'll talk about the jewels. You've been used, Madelyn. It's as clear as the nose on my face. Kareem has used you to get to your grandma's jewels. Don't you see? Tell us what you did with them before he gets to them. Everybody's gone home. Kareem is on his way. If he knows where you stashed them, they'll be gone before you can get home. Talk to me. This is your grandmother's legacy. Do you want it to end this way, where someone who has no history with her gets them and Heaven only knows what they'll do with them? Is that what you want? These were special to her. You know the significance behind them. Is this how you want it to end for Grace Willingham? Or did you even have an ounce of love in your heart for her?"

Madelyn wanted to run. Her heart was beating out of her chest. This man had no idea what she felt for Granny Grace. No idea at all. How could he know? Did anyone? The moments they shared were special. They were private. No one else intruded in that space and time. She suddenly felt like a river was forging its way from the recesses of her soul. She had not cried in a long time. Madelyn's emotion code had been reset years ago. Numb. Empty. Lifeless. These were the only gauges of feeling that registered with her. She longed to run to Granny Grace's and see her get up from her chair, wearing a big grin of gratitude for her visit and bearing arms full of love, wrapping her up in care and protection.

Bryson began to squirm and let out a groan, then a heartfelt sob. Madelyn realized she had been holding him tight, mimicking Granny Grace's embrace. Bryson had never seen his mama cry, and she was certain her heart had never been as flooded with emotion.

Masters choked back his smug content. This was a big breakthrough. The girl had a heart after all. He was confident he would have his lead to the jewels very soon, and the possible final nail for the coffin to the big sting operation they'd been working on for more than three years.

"I've got to go." Madelyn jumped up and headed for the door.

"Wait a minute. We're not done here."

"This interview is over. If you want me, you'll have to get a warrant. I have to get home," and Madelyn rushed out the door.

"Ricks, get someone on Madelyn Willingham's trail. Now. I'm going to see the judge and get a warrant."

"You have your thief?" Ricks was hopeful.

"I may have to smoke him out through her. But it's a start."

"You got it."

"And, Ricks."

"Yes, sir?"

"Don't lose that girl. She's a sly one, that gal. Do you hear me? Don't lose her. Not for a second."

"I'm on it, Bruce."

Chapter 17

"Nick, I've been lookin' for you everywhere. Where ya been?" Masters was inquisitive and highly interested. He could not assume Nick and Madelyn were not in cahoots somehow. After all, she knew about the funeral home basement. How? Why? Who told her? Besides, they were cousins. He was new in town. And they were the outcasts of the Willingham family. His puzzle pieces were falling together.

"I've been taking care of my funeral home business, Bruce. That's why you relieved me of my duties. Remember?" Nick was a little tongue-in-cheek with his comment, but he intended to let Bruce know he took note of his intentions.

"Yeah, well, I knew you probably had lots of odds and ends to tie up. You've been mighty gracious to let us just take over your place here. Glad to turn it back over to you. Hey, I've really got to run, but I do need to talk with you. You gonna be around for a bit?"

"Hard to say, Bruce. It's been a long two days for me, too, you know. And besides, my mother's in town and I'd like to spend some time with her. I have to get with Jim and Gladys and figure out what they're going to do with Grace. Any luck with your part of the investigation?"

"Not yet. Getting close, though, Nick. Real close."

"Are we going to get the jewels back in time for a funeral tomorrow, if that's what they decide? That's really what I need to know."

"Well, now, you know I can't promise you that, Nick. I'd say if you want to put Grace to rest, you'd best be going on about your business and making those plans. You might just have to finish out the rest of the service without the heirloom at this point."

"That's a shame. But, I'll let the family know. Thanks, Bruce. I'll see you later."

"Yes, you will. I do need to get with you again. I can come back here or you can come down to the station, either way. But don't get away from downtown without me having a few minutes with you today."

"Sure. I'll do my best. I should be here for another hour, but after that, I'm splitting. I need some rest."

"Gotta run. I'll catch up with you later, Nick. I'll run you down somewhere." Masters made peppy steps out of the funeral home and to his commission. He had to go to the judge's house to secure a warrant for Madelyn. If he didn't get someone behind bars for this, the FBI would be dispatched soon. Even if it was the wrong suspect, it would be enough to call them off in order to give him more time to smoke out his criminal. He sat down in his car and took a deep breath. He was exhausted himself. He turned the ignition and drove away. He took a deep breath, leaned back in his cruiser and attempted to unwind. _I'm getting_ *too old for this kind of stuff.*

*　　　*　　　*

Turner's Funeral Home, October 15, 4:01 p.m.

"Mom! It's so good to see you. You look fabulous." Nick gave Carmen a big hug and they held tight for the four-second transfer. He remembered that Grandma Grace always said, "If you don't hug for at least four seconds, your hearts don't have time to connect." It had been a ritual since Nick was a child for the two of them to always make sure they held tight for at least ten.

Carmen brushed Nick's cheek tenderly. "Nick, honey, you're tired. You need some rest. Let's go out to Mom's." Carmen knew her son. He was hollow-eyed and running on steam. It was obvious his stress level was high.

"We will, Mom, after we make some decisions about this funeral. I'd love to go out and just sit on Grandma's porch." Nick's heart got lighter at the contemplation. "What are your thoughts about getting together with Gladys and Jim within the hour? We need to get this ball rolling so we can get word to the media, especially if the funeral will be tomorrow. You know Grandma Grace always wanted to be buried on a Sunday but not be held over for a week to get it done. We can still keep her wishes if we do this tomorrow. I'm going to push Jim and Gladys on that if you're in agreement."

"Sure, I'm open to meeting as soon as possible. And, of course, you and Mom planned out her funeral to the minute detail. If you can honor her wishes, let's do it." Carmen wanted to encourage Nick all she could. She had to admit, however, she felt the stress deep inside her beginning to find its way to the surface after many years.

"Let me take this call real quick. I'll be right back." Nick stepped away from his mom. It gave Carmen a moment to ponder the upcoming event.

It would be the first time she had laid eyes on James since everything had happened. The uneasy feeling would have to be reined in. She had conquered the anger and bitterness inside her. She felt no malice toward him at all. What she sensed inside was more awkwardness of years of separation.

The same was true for Gladys. The two of them had had their share of trouble as well. Her last encounter with Gladys ended in a venomous emotional attack–Gladys being the snake. Gladys was the master of deceit. She had been a very attractive young girl, but had to work at it. Carmen possessed a natural beauty that grew into her exceptionally defined body. Gladys viewed her as competition, not a little sister. Her jealousy of Carmen promulgated into a heart-wrenching battle between Gladys and Grace.

Things changed in the Willingham household when Carmen became a part of the family at six years of age. In Grace's assessment of her adolescent daughter, Gladys, became a child of daily drama. Carmen often wondered if Mom had it to do over again, would she opt to adopt. It must have been challenging to assume the role of mom to a wayward child. Had Grace known the threads of adversity this kind of challenge would weave, would she have risked dividing her family in that regard?

If Carmen allowed it, it could cause her heart to be burdened even today. She had much to be grateful for. She had traveled the road of guilt for an extended season, but with the help of Grace and strength from her Lord, she had not only overcome but had managed to override that stronghold on her life.

Please, Lord, let me be gracious in spirit when I am face to face with my enemies. Will they still be against me today? Or, will time have mended hearts and years matured minds? Let me be all I need to be and more. May I be a reflection of you when I meet them again. Amen.

Carmen walked into the viewing room where Jimmy and Nora were looking at the floral arrangements and greetings from loved ones.

*   *   *

"Mom, are you sure you're up to this?" Nick was well aware of the deliverance in Carmen's life, but he also never intended for them to hurt her ever again. Not on his watch.

"Yes, absolutely, Nick. I'm fine. I really am."

"I'm sorry. Please forgive us. I'm Nick Willingham. And you must be Jimmy, all grown up."

"Hey, Man, it's great to see you again." Jimmy accepted the handshake but pulled Nick in for a brief manly hug.

"Remember me? Nora. I didn't know if we'd ever see you again once you moved to France."

"Il est bon de vous voir, belle dame," and Nick reached and kissed Nora's hand.

"El placer es mío, señor," Nora responded, and then embraced Nick and held on for the full four seconds GG had always encouraged.

"That is extremely adorable," Jimmy threw in his best Zimbabwe English dialect. "I could do a little Shona or Ndebele, but I wouldn't want to show you guys up."

Nick laughed. "You haven't changed, Jimmy. Still a great sense of humor. If you'll excuse me, I need to make a couple of phone calls. Then, I'll take you guys back to see Grace. Why don't you look around in the viewing room at the flowers and tokens of love people have sent. It's a bit overwhelming, but certainly gratifying."

"Uh, yeah, we barely got started. It's amazing how loved she was," Nora noted.

"That's not even the half of it. There's much, much more," Nick shouted back over his shoulder.

The three made their way to view the overindulgence of floral arrangements and expressions of admiration for Grace Carissa Willingham. With as much discomfort as a funeral home brings, there was great peace that accompanied the remembrances inscribed on the cards.

Nick walked into his office for the first time in two days. It looked undisturbed. Without prior knowledge, no one would be mindful of the interviews and interrogations that went on here in an attempt to uncover what people had touted as "The Theft of the Century," "Grandma's Jewels Stolen!," "Funeral Home Heist," and "Crown Jewels Missing from the Dead." The papers all over the country and abroad were covering the extraordinary jewels that had been seen in public on only three previous occasions. It was hot news. Grace was quite the person of interest.

Not that she hadn't been all along. Nick slumped into his chair and chuckled to himself. *So this is what you were talking about. You knew. You knew all along that one of us would go after your prized possessions. You were generous with everything else. You never withheld anything from your family. But these, you wouldn't share. You intrigued the world because of it, too. You sly little fox. These jewels were more than a sacrifice to you. They were your link to love. You were a rare piece of art yourself, Grandma Grace. A wise and shrewd woman. A woman who knew her family intimately. What else will you unfold in your Will? Ashley is the only one who really knows, I guess. And she's not talking.*

"Hey, Jim. Can you hold just a moment? I want to get Gladys on the line so we can conference this." Nick knew it would be best to get the two pinned down at once.

"Gladys, hey, it's Nick. I have Jim on the conference call here. Wanted to see if the two of you possibly could get back down here to the funeral home ASAP so that we could make a final decision about Grace's funeral."

"Well, why do we have to come there? Let's just talk about it on the phone right now. I think Monday or Tuesday is a good time. We're all exhausted. It'd be good to get a day or two of rest before we go through this all over again." Gladys was still pushing her agenda.

"No way, Gladys. I have to get back to my duties. I say let's do it tomorrow and get this thing over with. My goodness, we can't get tied up any more than we have been already. This has been a mess. Tomorrow is as good—" James was interrupted by Gladys's concern.

"But what about the jewels? What if they're—"

"Well, I'm sorry guys. I need you to come here and talk about this. I must insist." Nick had to take charge of the conversation.

"That's nonsense, Nick. We can take care of this right now. There's no reason—" James was insistent.

"Yes, there's plenty of reason. Mom's here. She'd like to be a part of the decision, too."

If Gladys desired to discuss the matter, silence invaded the notion. Nick felt an iciness flow through the landline. This could mean heartache for his mom, and he was already feeling the hair stand up on the nape of his neck.

"Hello? Did I lose you guys? Gladys? Jim?"

"Yeah, I heard you. She hasn't been here for any other decision, Nick. I don't see why she has to—"

"I'm sure you don't, Gladys, but she is one of Grace's children, too. She's come a long way to be here. And as I told you earlier, I do things by the book here. If you could be here within the hour, I'd appreciate it. And so would Carmen."

"You guys don't need me. You can just count my vote. I vote for tomorrow." Jim was politely estranging himself from the reunion.

"Oh, no, you don't, James Willingham. You're not weaseling your way out of this! You will absolutely be there. Give us a time, Nick. I'm not showing up until we're ready to meet. I've seen enough of Turner's to last me for a lifetime." Gladys huffed, but not at the thought of having to return to the funeral home. Her concern evolved around the idea of having to confront Carmen. She had hoped against hope the girl wouldn't show up at Grace's funeral at all. But why she thought Carmen would stay away was beyond her now. Reflecting on the knowledge that her son now owned the funeral home, Gladys felt somewhat foolish in her expectation.

"Good. Glad you guys could agree on this. If you could get here in the next fifteen to twenty minutes, we would still have time to let the media know so they could run it on tonight's news and it could still make the paper. I've taken the liberty to alert them that arrangements could be forthcoming, so they're waiting for my call. All they have to do is insert the date and time. See you both in a few."

Chapter 18

Carmen, Nora, and Jimmy followed Nick to the newly designated area where Grace Willingham rested. They held tight to each other's waists. Nora and Jimmy encircled Carmen and pulled her in closer. The initial viewing for a child of a deceased parent can swallow one's soul. Carmen drew the two youngsters closer to her. Realizing she had visited Grace many times during their prolonged leave of absence in other countries, she considered it might be tougher on them having not seen her for more than five years.

Nora began her inquisition. "Did you prepare her body, Nick? Was that difficult? I mean, how could you even think about embalming a family member? Did you supervise only? Or, did you only work on her face and let your assistants do the rest?"

Jimmy and Carmen looked at Nora as if she had three heads. Did she not realize how uncouth her inquiries sounded? The fact that Nick had to be involved at all in Grace's preparation must have been taxing. The stress of the entire ordeal was stamped on his countenance.

"Nora, let's not go there." Jimmy's was a dual-purposed grimace. The suggestive thought was causing him to entertain nausea, for one. And secondly, his concern for Nick wanted to kick Nora in the fanny for her still-in-character-to-this-day lack of sound judgment.

"It's okay. I'm sure everyone thinks it. Nora's the only one who's bold enough to say it out loud. I've heard all about your curiosity from Grace, Nora. Of course, you had lots of training when we were kids." Nick winked and curled a one-sided Granny Grace-style smile.

"I didn't do the more intimate details. I couldn't bring myself to do that. Besides, they don't advise that sort of thing in mortuary school. But I did work on her face and hands. There wasn't much to do, actually. She had that wardrobe smile of hers. She never dressed without it. It was a permanent fixture. Imagine what the world would be like if we all could wear a smile on our faces regardless of what life was dealing us at any given time? Grace was a life lesson every day she lived."

"I'm so glad you told me that. I would have gone to *my* grave thinking how really weird you are," Nora teased. Everyone laughed. It was a welcome ice-breaker at a solemn moment. Each of them knew it was exactly how Grace Willingham would like for events to materialize surrounding her death.

"Oh, my! She's beautiful!" Carmen felt her knees go weak but held her stance. Nora immediately came unglued at the sight of Grace. Jimmy buried his head on Carmen's shoulder, while Nick offered comfort to Nora.

Nora was sobbing through her words. "She didn't age a bit in the five years I was gone. She was quite the beautiful lady."

"Inside and out, Nora. I loved Grandma's inner beauty most." Jimmy attempted to brush away tears, but his long lashes refused to release their prey. His head was swirling with memories of Grace's infectious smile. His dampened eyes could visualize her anticipation of his visit. She would stand at the storm door as he ran up the stairs breathlessly counting each step until he reached the thirteenth and last one at the top of her grand porch. There stood Grandma Grace, smile in place, with a glass of Grandma's special batch of fruit punch for him and a kiss for his forehead. His mouth watered, crying out for the taste of both one more time.

Nick backed away from the three spectators of Grace Willingham. He situated himself in his professional stance. Two of his close family members stood reminiscing of days gone by and recounting cherished memories of the homeplace Grace made special for the ones she loved. He had already spent his private moments with Grace. During his time, he reflected on his own memorable activities with her. He couldn't help feeling a bit envious, however, of the memories Nora and Jimmy spoke of. He had limited times in the Sugar Shack. He was privileged to hear tales of the apple seasons and could only dream of being a part of those earmarked days. School was always the obstacle. Carmen would never hear of Nick traveling South and missing a week of California school regardless of how much Grandma begged and pleaded. Grace always respected Carmen's judgment and reminded Nick that he must, too. He did enjoy summers at Grace's. It was the highlight of his year. The camping excursions were the feature focus of his stay. His other treasured moments centered around the porch and at the kitchen table with Grace.

"Nick, you remember the summers that GG surprised all of us kids with month-long trips in the RV? She meant we were going to see America before we laid eyes on any part of the rest of the world." Nora beamed at the recall.

Nick moved in closer and relaxed his stance. "I do indeed. It was such a blast. I learned more about the history of our country traveling with Grandma than I was ever exposed to in school, I must say."

"I was in my rebel years then. I was a real jerk." Jimmy sheepishly confessed recalling how Ashley, Nora, and Nick wanted to leave him at the Grand Canyon one year.

"Madelyn was no joy ride either, as I recall. She was always a difficult child. How's she doing anyway?" Nora's question was more out of courtesy than concern. As hard as she tried, Nora and Madelyn never clicked. She knew Madelyn had a hard life at home. But then again, so did she. Nora finally understood what GG had meant when she said, "Life comes down to choices. Make good ones, and your life will reflect it." Nora and Madelyn were on even playing ground. Both had less-than-reputable moms. Both were products of infidelity on Jim's part. Neither had the benefit of his interaction in their lives. Nora was, however, at least acknowledged as his daughter. She had that one over on Madelyn. But when everything came out of the wash, each of them had the love and support of Grace Willingham. Truth be told, none of the five grandkids had the benefit of a father in place. And poor Jimmy and Ashley had no mom either. Grace was the cornerstone of the Willingham family. She was the mom, the dad, and the grandmom to each of them. And the truly amazing thing to Nora was that Grace pulled off each role like a pro.

"We need to be praying for Madelyn right now, Guys. The law is looking at her pretty heavily. She broke out of the funeral home when it was on lockdown. Now, it appears they're trying to pin the theft on her." Nick didn't know any other details, but he was concerned about all the events surrounding Madelyn and her escape.

"Nuh-unh! You've got to be kidding me!" Nora was incensed at the news.

"Oh, Nick, surely she didn't. Why would she do such a thing? Mom would have given them to her rather than her have to steal them." Carmen held her hand over her heart as if it might tumble out of her chest.

"Hold on there, Guys. Let's not find her guilty before we even know she is." Nick came to Madelyn's immediate defense. "They're desperate to find who did this. Gladys is really putting pressure on them. It's been all over the news—local, national, and as of an hour ago, it's now made the international spotlight."

Carmen and Nora flushed with their indignant remarks. Jimmy made no overture of concern.

"You guys have been away for a while. There's a lot of dynamics at play here. I'll try to fill you in later on tonight, but for now, our first and foremost concern is a proper burial for our Lil' Sweetheart here. She deserves a better send-off than what she's been afforded thus far.

"I'll tell you what. Nora, Jimmy, let's step outside and give Mom some alone time with Grace. She needs to do that first so that we can meet with Jim and Gladys to make final arrangements. Then, you guys can come in individually and have some private moments while we meet."

"What! Jim and Gladys and you? Are you all right with that, Carmen? I mean, do you think Gladys still holds anything against you? How are you going to handle Jim? Are you feeling anxious inside? Are you okay being by yourself with them? I mean, I don't know why you three couldn't get along, but apparently there's something there. But if you want someone to be with you, I don't mind to—"

"Nora, I'll be in there with her. She's my mom. I'm not going to let anything get out of control."

"Oh, of course you won't, Nick. I'm sorry. I didn't even think about that. You'll do fine, Carmen. Just fine." Nora patted Carmen on the back, bent down and whispered in her ear, "But, I do wish I could be a fly on the wall."

Jimmy grabbed Nora by the shoulder and prodded her out the door. "Come along, Nora. The more things change, the more they stay the same."

"What's that supposed to mean?"

"You haven't changed a bit. You can ask a million questions in the time most people can even think of—"

The door closed and Carmen stood over Mom Grace. She reached out and touched her hand. It was cold. Not like the warmth she had come to love. Carmen fixed her eyes on the lifeless body of the woman who had pulled her from a life destined to be wrought with pain and injustices. *What was it? What did you see in me that motivated the love in your heart?*

*   *   *

GRACE'S FRONT PORCH,
THIRTY-SEVEN YEARS EARLIER, 2:13 A.M.

"Why did you adopt me, Mom?

"Oh, so you want to hear that story again, do you?" Grace never tired of telling the story. The chronicles of Carmen were rewritten the day she stepped into Grace's world.

"Yes, ma'am. I need to." Carmen not only *needed* to hear the evidence of her worth, she loved to be reminded how God chose her.

"It was very much like the story of King David and how he was chosen to be king. Jesse paraded all his sons in front of Samuel. But Samuel was listening to God and wasn't satisfied with what he saw. He asked if he had any others, so Jesse sent for David who was tending sheep. As soon as Samuel laid eyes upon David, he told Jesse *that* was the son who God had chosen to be king.

"And that's how it happened with you, Little One. I didn't have a choice. I had always wanted three children. But then, I didn't have a husband anymore. So I tried foster-parenting. I kept several children for short periods of time, then, they were sent back to their parents. All of a sudden, there you were. Those big, sparkling brown eyes, your coal black hair, and that forgotten look of life on your face. You didn't give me a chance to say no to God."

"God told you to adopt me?"

"In a sense, yes, He did."

"Did God talk to you?"

"Oh, not in a loud voice, Carmen. God doesn't talk like that.

You have to be still and listen to God. There was a tugging in my heart for you the moment I laid eyes upon you. I loved all the foster children I kept. Don't you think for one minute that I didn't. You were the youngest one I had accepted. And the best part of all, you were being put up for adoption. You were the sweetest little five-year-old cutie I had ever seen. When they brought you to my front door, you seemed full of shame. I looked at you and your eyes were vacant and expressionless. There was hurt buried deep within them, yet surfacing with a plea for help. There was an undeserving sense about you, Carmen. My spirit was pricked right then and there. I had to rescue you from that pain. It became my mission to put the joy back into your little eyes. And you made it very easy. You took to love like a bee takes to pollen. It was the most beautiful thing to be a part of that assignment from God." Grace settled back in her rocker and kept pace with her nocturnal friends. They were the only ones privy to these sorts of private moments on her porch.

"I don't like the dreams I have, Mom. They make me sad. I'm afraid they're going to come back after me. What if they do?"

Grace reached over and stroked Carmen's hand resting on the arm of her special rocker. "I won't let them have you. You're mine now. As long as I'm around, no one is ever going to hurt you like that again, Carmen. That is my promise to you."

Carmen positioned her knees under her chin, pulling her nightgown snug around her ankles. She and Grace had spent many times here when she would be awakened by one of her night dreams. She was too big to sit in Grace's lap now, but she fondly recalled how Mom would cradle her like a baby and rock and sing to her until she fell into peaceful slumber. Would she ever break free of her emotional prison? Mom Grace had introduced her to the One she said could help. "He will rescue you because He delights in you, Carmen." That single assurance created a hunger in Carmen that could not be satiated. She had come to know Grace's God of Impossibles. Grace Willingham was a woman who had been rescued many times herself. Not from the same pit Carmen had been cast into, but a pit is a pit is a pit. At the tender age of fourteen, Carmen had already come to appreciate the different kinds of trenches in which a gal could land.

"Everything will be all right, Carmen. It takes time to get over the kinds of hurt you experienced. You're blessed, you know. You were just shy of six years old when you came into my life. Many young girls endure sexual, physical, and emotional abuse until they marry and leave home. Unfortunately, many are like a magnet and they attract men who use and abuse them. You were spared at a very young age. And now, you have the rest of your life ahead of you to love without fear. You are suffering consequences of someone else's poor choices for your life. That is not your fault. But the choices you make from now on, you will be accountable for. Your purity is now your decision."

*   *   *

Carmen shook her head. "Neither one of us knew what was to come shortly after that, did we, Mom? I knew you were good to your promise. If you had been around, I wouldn't have gotten hurt. My purity should have been my decision. I know you hated it as much as I did. I wanted to tell you when it happened. I really did. But I was afraid you wouldn't love me anymore. Thank you for finding me. Thank you for reminding me it wasn't my fault. But like you said many times, Mom, 'God causes all things to work together for good to those who love Him and are called according to His purpose.' Look at our Nick. Isn't he just something else? What would we have done without him?"

"Mom, I hate to disturb you," Nick interrupted.

"Oh, no, I was just talking about you to Grace."

"I know. I heard. You're partial. Jim and Gladys are here. Are you sure you're ready for this?"

"As ready as I'll ever be. Let me just run to the restroom real quickly. Where am I going for the meeting?"

"The conference room. Take a right for the restroom. Then, take a left out of the restroom, right at the end of the hall, second door on the left. We'll be waiting for you. I'm there for you, Mom. Don't worry. If you want to abort at any given moment, just excuse yourself. I'll take it from there."

"Don't worry about me. I'll be fine, Nick. There's nothing that God and I can't handle together. Plus, I know I have you. You've always been there for me. I appreciate it more than you will ever know. Give me two, and I'll be right in." Carmen stepped into the restroom, locked the door, and hit the floor.

Chapter 19

"You're wanting me to issue a warrant on these puny facts? It's speculation at best. Where's the probable cause? I need a spent casing if not the smoking gun, Masters. What you've presented is nothing. She broke out of the funeral home to go home and get her baby some clean clothes? That's it? You searched the apartment and found nothing. No hot ice, no hype stick, no scripts. Nothing. You have absolutely zilch for me except the desire for a suspect because of the high-profile nature of this jewel case."

Masters knew Judge Rowland wouldn't buy his rationale and would suspect his urgency. But, the only feasible evidence he had was a handful of suspicions and Madelyn's breakout. He decided he might as well come clean. It might just get him what he needed. "With all due respect, Your Honor, I have to get someone cuffed for this. If not, Savannah is gonna be crawlin' with FBI tomorrow mornin'. The Chief just told me it made the *London Evening Standard*. I really would like to see this one through, Judge. I'll be retiring soon, you know. I'd hate to close out my career as the one who let Grace Willingham's jewels get away. We took all the necessary precautions, Your Honor. We had video cameras installed. Someone tampered with the one over Grace's casket. I had men posted. No one saw a thing suspicious. We locked the place down immediately."

"Yeah, I heard." Judge Rowland sounded unimpressed with the decision Masters and Chief Griffin corporately made. "The City might have some repercussions over that poor judgment call yet."

"We suspected somethin' like this might happen. I mean, we're talkin' some high-dolla' jewels, Judge. Did you see those things?" Masters whistled. "I'm talking red-carpet jewels. I set the trap, but there's always a sneaky mouse daring enough to go after the cheese without getting' snared. I just thought I had all my bases covered. I musta slipped up somewhere."

"Yeah, well, the trap was weak. Sounds like an inside job to me, but I don't know, Bruce. You want to talk about some bad press? If we put Grace Willingham's granddaughter in jail for something she didn't do, or you can't prove that she had anything to do with, it's not just your tail on the line. We're all going to take a pounding."

"I know, Your Honor, but you and me, we've been right here a lot throughout the years, with little to no evidence, that is. I always get my man. You know that. I'd be ever so grateful to you if you'd stick your neck out for me on this one, Your Honor. I believe if Madelyn didn't do it, whoever did is gonna surface if we get her behind bars. If Kareem's in on this, she'll spill the beans. She don't want him getting' custody of that boy of hers."

"All right. I'll sign it. But I don't want to, Bruce. I have a bad feeling about this. We can't hold her forever, and if Kareem comes up and posts bail, we won't be able to at all. There's no murder here. It's just a theft. He will post bond for her. You can count on it. And, do we even know the real value? When was the last time they were appraised? There's a lot to consider here, Bruce."

"I'm workin' on the appraisal. Just hold off on an arraignment as long as you can, Judge. I really appreciate this. You won't be sorry. I'll get my thief. You can count on it. And we might crack even more than this case in the process. That's my goal."

"If you don't apprehend them, I suspect somebody will. Every jewelry store and pawn shop all over the world will be looking for these to come their way. What else would anyone do with them? Keep them locked up in a safe forever? Wear them to bed? I mean, someone wants to liquidate them. I'm sure you've encouraged the family to set a reward for their return. That gets people going."

Bruce wanted to crawl in a hole for the little details he had let slip by him. Reward? Appraisal? *Maybe it is time for retirement.*

"Get some rest, Bruce. You look awful."

"Thanks, Judge. I will soon. You'd better get back to your game. Who's winning?"

"The Dawgs, 21 to 7. But that could change, if it hasn't already."

The detective headed back to Turner's Funeral Home in the hopes of talking with Nick Willingham. The young man had some explaining to do. He needed to give Ricks a call and a heads-up about his progress. "Ricks, hey, I got the warrant. Uh, yeah, for Madelyn Willingham. Bring her in and get her booked."

*   *   *

Ashley Willingham's Townhome, October 15, 4:22 p.m.

Ashley stepped out of the shower and threw on her house-coat. She had no idea who could be banging on her door, but the unrelenting nature of the thuds presented quite the urgency. She hurried down the stairs trying to keep her balance as she wrapped her wet blonde tresses in a towel.

"I'm coming, I'm coming." She peeked through her one-way security viewer, then, quickly opened the door.

"Oh, I'm so glad you were home, Ashley. I need a really big favor. You're the only one I can count on. If you say no, I don't know what I'll do. Please help me."

"Calm down, Madelyn. What's wrong? You look like you've seen a ghost. Come on in. I'll get us a glass of tea."

Madelyn had never seen the inside of Ashley's condo. She only knew Ashley lived here. It was an incredible location. She gave a quick glance around the room. Her décor was impeccable. There was a place for everything, and everything was in its place. Madelyn had only dreamed of living a life like this. Ashley was within walking distance of the downtown hub. She was independent. She had already celebrated success in her career. Ashley had it all. But then, she had made the right choices that Granny Grace had always spoken about. Then, again, Ashley had not seen the dour days that were more than familiar to Madelyn.

"Hey, my Baby Boy. You like this place? Yeah, probably not too suitable for the likes of busy little hands like yours." Madelyn nuzzled Bryson's nose and tickled his tummy. Bryson's little hands clasped Madelyn's face and his mouth flew open with delight. Her mommy heart melted into a puddle of sheer joy.

"Here you go, Madelyn. What's going on? I didn't know you knew where I lived. I'm so glad you came, though. Don't take that wrong. Where did you go? They were looking for you everywhere at the funeral home. Why did you leave? What happened?"

"It's complicated, Ashley. I don't know how much you know about me and what all I'm into."

"I'm a lawyer. I hear the scuttlebutt, Madelyn. You hang with some pretty scary people. Your reputation precedes you."

"Ashley, you've got to believe me. I know I've done some rotten things, but I didn't take Granny's jewels. I wouldn't do a thing like that. But, I think that detective is going to have me arrested."

"Bruce Masters? Why do you say that? What does he have on you? Where did you go?"

"I went to my place. I went down in the basement of the funeral home, swiped–I didn't steal them. I planned to take them back–a woman's burial suit from their client wardrobe and some slippers. I threw something over my head and took off home. Something came over me in between there and home. I don't know what it was, Ashley. Maybe Granny's spirit visited me. It was strange. I don't want to do this anymore. I took all of Kareem's drugs and flushed them. Took the–"

"Stop, stop, stop!" Ashley rose from the couch and put her hands over her ears. "Don't tell me anymore, Madelyn. I'm not your counsel and if you tell me something and they question me,

I'll have to tell them what I know. Don't tell me anything else."

Madelyn froze and then melted into the couch. Her eyes filled with tears. She kissed Bryson's head and stroked his cheek. She held him close and began to rock back and forth. "I didn't take those jewels, Ashley. You have to believe me. I only broke out because I wanted a fix, but I didn't even do that. I believe they're going to arrest me because I broke out. That's all they have on me, Ashley. That's all."

"Well, typically they have to have more probable cause than that. I don't think any judge would issue a warrant if they didn't find something incriminating." Ashley put on her most convincing lawyer face in order to calm the extremely shaken Madelyn. She knew Masters was well respected and if he went to Judge Rowland himself, he could persuade him against all odds.

"Can I leave Bryson with you, Ashley? You're the only one I know who I trust with my baby."

In her wildest imaginations, Ashley had not anticipated keeping Bryson would be the favor Madelyn needed. Money, perhaps. But a baby! *What am I going to do with a baby? I am completely clueless with what to do with a baby.*

"I know it's a lot to ask, Ashley. You don't have to worry. I'll get everything over here for him. I'll get—" Madelyn stopped midstream stricken with reality. If she goes to the apartment without Bryson and Kareem is there, she feared the worst of how he would react. She was too keenly aware of what he was capable of. If he didn't dispose of her, he would have someone do it for him.

"What is it, Madelyn? What are you thinking?" Madelyn's fear-ridden face was like reading an open book. "Are you afraid for your life?"

"Please take care of Bryson. I'm going to try to get him some clothes and things from my place, get a pack-and-play so he'll have somewhere to sleep. But if I don't come back, promise me you'll take care of my baby. Promise me, please."

"Madelyn, don't go back there. Don't do it. I'll get Bryson what he needs. You don't have to worry about that. You can stay here with me. Kareem would never suspect you being here."

"I can't put you in that kind of danger, Ashley. I wouldn't do that to you, and I wouldn't do that to Bryson."

"Well, at some point he's going to know I have the baby. We can't stay locked inside my place forever. I have to get him some things. I have a job. Plus, Grandma's funeral is going to be sometime soon. I can't stay in hiding. And neither can you."

Madelyn paced the floor. Life was unfolding before her and it was a repugnant turn of events. As long as she was with Kareem, no one would get hurt but her. There was no doubt in her mind that he would kill her. He had shared stories of what had happened to others who had crossed him. She would be next if she ever saw him again. Bryson would be left at the mercy of a murdering drug lord involved in other surreptitious affairs. She wanted more for her son. Now, that possibility was crumbling before her very eyes. *God, please help me. If You are there, show me that You really care. Granny Grace said You would never forsake me. She told me You would take me at my worst. Hear me now, O, Lord. I'm in a real bind. It's not for me. It's for my son. He doesn't deserve any of this. He's just a baby. Help me find a way out of this, and I will turn my life around. If You protect me, Lord, I will serve You forever. Please, Dear God. Please.*

"I have to go, Ashley. Please, don't let anything happen to

Bryson. Give me your word."

"Madelyn, I don't know how to—"

Madelyn moved closer to her chosen guardian. She stuck out her hand to Ashley, crooking her little finger. Like the mighty rushing wind Grace had spoken about many times, their memories were swept back into childhood to a simpler time in life. "Pinky swear. I need your word, Ashley."

Madelyn stabilized Ashley's wavering thoughts. Ashley crooked her pinky and the two attached themselves to a shared promise. Half-sisters divided socially in lifestyle, morals, and values reunited their kindred hearts fashioned by one common denominator—the legacy of Grace Willingham.

*   *   *

ABERCORN TERRACE APARTMENTS, #14,
SAVANNAH, GEORGIA, OCTOBER 15, 3:35 P.M.

Kareem flipped through his contacts and made the call. "She's gone. Man, I don't know where she is, but when I find her, it ain't gonna be pretty. She's gonna be more than gone."

What do you mean? That's not part of the deal. You can't lose her, Kareem."

"You don't get to tell me those things. This could go down bad for you if she rats us out."

"You said she didn't know anything about me. So now you're telling me she's going to rat us out? I'm clear with Hawk now. I'm settled up. The jewels aren't part of the deal anymore."

"If you think I go down for anything and leave you out of

this, you crazy. If I get busted, you going with me, Man."

"Don't forget who I deal with, Kareem. If you want to live, you'd best think twice before you start implicating anyone else."

"But she wiped out my stash. I have nothing. And she took my money. She's gonna suffer. That's all I gotta say."

"I can get you more where that came from. Don't wig out over that. If she's got those jewels, I want them. They don't go to Hawk."

"You leave that to me. I have my way of getting them out of her."

"Don't kill her, Kareem. Threaten her, rough her up, but don't do her in. There's too much hype over this case. They'll bring you down on this one. I can't help you this time. Play it clean."

"Whatcha mean you can't help me?"

"I can't help you, Kareem. Not this time. It's too risky. I have to go. Don't hurt that girl. Do we have an understanding?"

"Uh." Kareem could only grunt at the command. He didn't take orders from anyone when it came to his women.

"Kareem? Do we have an understanding?"

"I hear ya."

Kareem put his phone back in his pants pocket. He sat down on the couch and waited. He had his scouts out looking for any sign of Madelyn and Bryson. She wouldn't get away, wherever she was headed. He would find her. And when he did, there was no deal. Everyone knew about her drug habit. He'd get the information out of her with Bryson as the lure, then, she would just disappear with her overdose. After all, it was like her Granny always said, "A woman without purpose is like a bird without a song—visibly there, but silently vanishing." *What a shame. Such a beautiful mama, too.*

Chapter 20

"Where you going now, Woman?" Ralph Murphy was in his usual drunken stupor.

"Back to the funeral home, Ralph. I'll be back soon."

"You just came from there. When is this all gonna be over?"

"We have to settle on a time for Mother's funeral. I'll be back in time to get dinner."

"I don't care what you do about dinner. I have my friend here," and he held up his squared-bottle Maker's Mark bourbon and tipped it at Gladys, then poured himself another round. He emptied the bottle and grabbed his new one still donning the distinctive red wax.

Gladys closed the door behind her. *Drink on. You will soon be history, my dear. I have waited a long, long time for this day to come.* She backed out of her drive and all but hit Mr. Pickens on his lawnmower. Her preoccupation for brighter days ahead had her in quite the intoxicated trance herself. She was tired, but she couldn't remember when she hadn't been. Life had been one long, drawn-out drama of exhaustion. If she could turn back the hands of time, she would have worked harder at becoming the woman of excellence Grace modeled for her. She had never known her mother to be caught up in jealousy and envy and malicious conduct. Why did Gladys allow those vices to permeate her character? *Serves me right, Mother. You did your best. I was unwilling to accept your instruction, your model, even your love. I was angry. I wanted my dad, and I blamed you because he wasn't there. If I could do it all over again, you would have died a woman proud of your blood-born daughter. Instead, you had to rely on an adopted daughter to shower your love upon. And I even wrecked that for you.*

Gladys was sure she left skid marks at the intersection of Broad and 37th, slamming on the brakes just before plowing into the back of an SUV. Her anxiety centered on coming face to face with Carmen again. What would she say to Carmen? Better question—what would Carmen say to her? Gladys was not the fireball she used to be. There was a time when she would stand against anyone. Everyone feared her. Now, she feared everyone. She had developed such a terse demeanor that it became the perfect camouflage for her insecurities.

The memory of her role in Carmen's sudden and unannounced departure had haunted her for years. She wasn't sure Carmen was even aware it was all a setup instigated by her sister. It was Gladys's revenge for how Carmen humiliated her in high school. The true accounts of the scenario shamed Gladys even more. Poor Carmen was not even to blame. No child gets to choose the degree of his/her beauty or dowdiness. Carmen was naturally beautiful. She could wear sackcloth and capture the attention of every male within a hundred-mile radius. Gladys was eye-catching, but she spent hours creating her image. In order to enhance her creation, she wore clothes that looked modest enough when she walked out of the house. But by the time she was out of Grace's sight, she was rolling up the waistbands to show less skirt and unbuttoning the top button of her blouse to reveal more skin. She managed to attract the kinds of guys who wanted pleasures in the back seat of a car or against the wall behind the stadium.

Every girl was jealous of Carmen, but every girl didn't have to live with her. The sisterhood exacerbated Gladys's resentment. Gladys found Carmen insufferable. Consequently, she did everything she could to make Carmen's life miserable... anytime Grace wasn't around, of course. When Grace was on board, Gladys was the perfect sister. Grace Willingham, however, was not to be fooled and parsed the truth in her own inimitable manner. She was quick to remind a person, "Anytime you see a red flag, there is usually a bull charging full steam ahead." She had many conversations with Gladys about how she should treat her baby sister. But, the day ultimately arrived when Gladys was done with competing with Carmen.

*   *   *

827 Victory Drive, Grace's front porch, Thirty-seven years prior, 11:05 p.m.

"Have you lost your mind? We have prom in three weeks and you're going to dump me? I don't understand, Kyle. Why are you doing this?"

"I'm sorry, Gladys. I really am, but I just don't—"

"Sorry? That's all you can say—you're sorry? I love you, Kyle, and I thought you loved me. We've made so many plans together. Where is this coming from all of a sudden?"

"I just need a break, Gladys. I think we should date other people, just to make sure we're meant for each other."

"Date other people? We both have dated other people already. Who is she? Last week you were fine with only me. This week you want to date other people? Who is she? I'm not an idiot, Kyle."

"Let's just say we're taking a break for now."

"There is someone else! I knew it! I want to know who she is, and I want to know now. You owe that much to me, Kyle Hardee."

Kyle stuffed his hands deep into his pockets and shuffled his feet. He had wanted to find the nerve to break it off with Gladys for the last three months. He loved the Willingham family. Gladys was a challenge and a bit more controlling than he had in mind for a wife. He did admire the determination and success of Grace, and especially would like to join a family with a rich heritage. But there were two Willingham daughters, and he had been smitten with Carmen for a month of Sundays. He was the best-looking young man this side of the Mississippi. Every girl in school wanted a stab at winning his love. But the strongest character of Kyle Hardee was his integrity. Honesty was his policy. It was instilled in him by his father who had gleaned the quality from his father. He didn't want to compromise that kind of strength by lying to Gladys about there being no one else he was interested in. He held his breath hoping she wouldn't ask that question.

"I'm waiting, Kyle. Answer me. Your silence intrigues me even more. Who is she? You've cheated on me, haven't you?"

"Don't be silly. You know me better than that."

"If you haven't cheated, then, you have your sights on someone. You owe it to me, Kyle. I gave myself to you."

"Don't give me that line, Gladys. You've given yourself to everyone." Kyle was hoping to distract her in order to divert the question.

"Now! I want to know right now, Kyle. Who are you interested in?"

"You know, Gladys, it really isn't any of your business who I'm interested in. I mean, if I am or not. Let's just decide to take a break. Maybe we'll get back together. Maybe not. If we're supposed to be, we'll find our way back to one another."

"If you walk out on me, Kyle Hardee, you'll never get the chance at me again. You can count on that."

"Good-bye, Gladys."

Gladys stood on her porch and watched Kyle's Ermine white '62 Corvette roll down the mile-long stretch. She was devastated. She had known many guys, but Kyle held her heart. She plopped down in her rocker and could not control her tears. She would despise a full moon for the rest of her days. Until this night, she had celebrated the celestial wonder for it introduced a total disregard for the boundaries of time and space.

Grace sat down beside her. "Everything will be all right, honey."

"You don't even know what's wrong, Mother. How do you know if it's going to be all right?" Gladys was not in the mood for her mother's pearls of wisdom tonight. She was hurting and really preferred to bask in her sorrow without being reminded that God fixes everything. *Well, He won't fix this one. And even if He does, I meant what I told Kyle Hardee.*

"You can save your sass for someone who doesn't care about you. But you, young lady, will treat me with respect at all times. Whether you listen to me or not is your choice. But I am your mother and you will show me deference. Do we have an understanding?"

"Yes, ma'am. I'm sorry."

"Thank you." Grace never wasted an opportunity to exercise her authority in the home. She learned as a young mother when Albert was traveling that if she lost the upper hand in her home, she would be in constant battle with her children. While they lived under her roof, they abided by her rules. There was a valued understanding regarding her tenets in the home. She had dreaded the day but knew rebellion would come. It typically does with all children. She particularly expected to encounter inner turmoil from each of her children, even Carmen, due to feeling abandoned by a parent. The season was a difficult time for her, as well, and she had to pull from the strength of the Lord in order to accomplish her commitment to the family He entrusted to her. She would rely on His wisdom and guidance in order to compensate for the loss each was certain to feel.

"I recognize a broken heart, Gladys. Mine has been broken before. When your father left us, I was certain my heart would never heal. But it did. I became stronger realizing I had to face life, because it wasn't going away. I became a fighter because I didn't want to lose any more than life had stolen from me already. I became patient because I would have damaged the hearts of innocent children who had no control over the turns life takes. I became dependent upon God because I wanted to live my life, not die a new death every day. I was confident He loved me enough to see me through the difficult times in life. In time, I fell in love with life again. Time heals almost everything. Give time time."

"Time hurts, Mother. Kyle broke up with me tonight, and it already feels like an eternity. I don't even want to think about tomorrow."

"Then don't. Jesus told us to let tomorrow take care of itself, because today has enough trouble of its own. Don't let this ruin your life, Gladys. There were times the nights trounced on my heart so the days could defeat my zeal. It was tough. I know you will have to learn the lesson yourself. That's true for everyone. But I would encourage you to be patient on God and not to take matters into your own hands. It works best when we let Him drive our lives. I'll be praying for you. Everything *will* be all right, but it is your choice."

*   *   *

Gladys didn't remember getting to her destination, but she was parked outside of Turner's Funeral Home. Her heart was pounding, her palms were clammy, and her breathing anxious. Was it because she would soon meet head-on with Carmen, the one who not only captured the heart of her mother but won the heart of everyone she met, especially Kyle Hardee? Or, perhaps her bewilderment was for the many times she regretted not following the wisdom of her mother. Gladys had rarely done things God's way. Now, she was uncertain of the reception she would get from Carmen. Especially in light of the devious and unconscionable scheme Gladys orchestrated to drive Carmen out of her life forever, all because of forsaken love. She had not factored in how the drama might play out. She never considered how it would affect Grace. She never once had the notion that five years later her deceitfulness would drive her to an emotional meltdown and require a year of confinement in order to decompress. She did learn how to function in life again, but Gladys Faye Willingham had never forgiven herself.

Chapter 21

James Willingham buried his head in his hands. He did not want to go back to the funeral home. His loose ends needed securing. This funeral had more than complicated his life. Now, there was Carmen. He had almost forgotten about the whole sordid ordeal that severed her from the family. He regretted the role he had played in it and had wanted nothing more than to get beyond that part of his past. When he bought her one-way ticket to Los Angeles, it bought him freedom from embarrassment but no peace of mind. Entertaining the idea of searching for her invited endless night terrors, and he would soon dismiss the possibility to right his wrong. Grace's brokenness almost brought him to confession. The woman wore new calluses on her knees during the prayer vigil on behalf of Carmen. All she had was a note from Carmen saying she had to leave and not to worry about her, that "everything would be all right." That note was written at the insistence of James. He threatened her life if she ever contacted the Willinghams again. Grace had all of Georgia and beyond looking for her daughter. Law enforcement, friends and well-meaning church friends tried to convince her that Carmen had finally returned to her roots, but Grace refused to take party to the nonsense. James's act had brought a pain to Grace's face that he had never been witness to. That is, until he saw it in his own face at the news of his Sweet Annie.

He was convinced had he come clean and Grace given him a good lickin' as part of his penance, it would help ease the punishment God was sure to dispense for the wickedness of his transgressions. The words would never be uttered from his mouth, but James would always take personal responsibility for Annie's illness. He was certain God punished him through her, and when he stopped hating himself for what he had done, he might possibly stop being angry at God for taking her life instead of his.

James sat back in his chair and extended his arms to the back of his head. *Ah, Annie. I still miss you. You know I have loved no one since you. You kept me respectable. You turned my life around and upside down all at once. Ours was a romance that extended far beyond our comprehension. We experienced a glorious significance few lovers will ever unveil. You were life to me, my Annie. Once you were gone, everything that mattered vanished.*

James cupped his hands to his face. He had not cleansed his heart of the emotions since Annie's death. His need for release had been pent up for years. He had cried at Annie's funeral, but he'd never repeated the act of grief. He had taken to the bottle instead. He was a happy drinker. He wasn't belligerent or mean. Just happy. It was a good place to be once his heart was buried with his wife. James Albert Willingham II was going through the motions of day-in/day-out living, but there was not a thread of time he enjoyed walking the sod without his Annie beside him.

Why did you take her, God? It was me you really wanted! James raised his fist toward Heaven and shook it furiously at the One he had put his faith in once upon his fairytale time. *Had you left her here, I would still be a good man. I would never have brought more shame to the Willingham name. I would have been the kind of father Ashley and Jimmy needed. I could have made things right with Carmen. Nora and Madelyn would not have been born to know the confusion about family and the indifference of a father.*

James turned his chair and stared out the window at his busy metropolitan city. He sighed. *Savannah. You won't find a town more beautiful than you.* He loved this historic district. He cherished the Spanish-moss-laden garden squares. He prided himself in having helped to restore the old cotton warehouses that stood like giants as a reminder of prosperity in bygone days. He had fought for the preservation of the eighteenth and nineteenth centuries' architectural style that graced the hub of the original city. His feet had strolled the cobblestoned waterfront facing the mellow Savannah River where long-ago pirates had once stirred its waters. Savannah deserved more than he was producing. Savannah deserved integrity.

He continued muddling through seesaw emotions vacillating from rage to calm—angry at God, then himself. There hadn't been a day he hadn't thought about his mom. No one saw fit to oppose his seat at election time, and if they did, defeat was certain. Yet in the public's eye he was viewed as the wicked one when it came to Grace. That community opinion would be dead on target. Whereas most estranged children could cast blame on a parent for the family dynamic, Grace Willingham could never be accused of harsh or unloving treatment to anyone, especially her children.

Why didn't I listen to you, Mama? You were a saint. As much as I showered you with love in my youth, I treated you like dirt for too many years thereafter. I am sorry, Mama. I wish I could tell you now how much I love you. You knew a lot of despicable things I did, but you loved me anyway. Why did you? How could you? I was as unworthy of your love as I am the love of the God you worshiped and adored. If I could turn back time, I'd do life differently. One thing for sure, I would not be wearing the regret of not having spoken to you in three years, four months, two days, seventeen hours and forty-seven minutes. If you could have lived one more day, Mama, just one more day.

James pondered the past. He had been through a difficult season in his adolescence. Starved for the love of a father who should have been in the home, his spirit was full of contempt. He had no father to show him how to see things from a man's point of view. He had no guidance for knowing when to be strong and when to be tender. A father would have coached him on when to stand up for principle, regardless of ensuing consequences. He needed a dad to explain when it was okay for a boy to hurt, to cry, to grieve, and how that was supposed to look. Where was his father? Never there for him.

God, it wasn't Mama's fault. She did everything she could. She tried her best to be both mom and dad. It was never good enough for me, but she was more than adequate. Why couldn't I just let that be enough? It wasn't her fault that life took away the only one she had ever loved any more than it was my fault

Annie could not pull through her cancer. Mama learned to cope with her loss through Your strength. But, oh, no, not me, God. What did I do? I got angry at You. I did it my way. I really did a bang-up job at it, now, didn't I, Lord? I'm in way over my head. Grace told me many times, "The simple truth is all it takes to unscramble the complexities of life." I know she's right, but the truth isn't pretty right now, Lord. Not even You can fix this mess I'm in. There is no way out.

James had silently grieved the loss of the father he had never known. He didn't have to say it out loud. Grace was confident the absence of his dad was the source of his discontent. As pleasant as he was to her as a young boy and even a teen, she knew he would rebel someday. An in-tune mother knows her children intimately. Grace had the pulse of her family. She knew James mourned what he *knew* he missed in a father, and even what he *might* be missing through never having known Albert. She had done everything within her means to make her son feel worthy of love. What she lacked, his precious Annie balanced out. Grace could not have asked for a finer young man after Annie turned his heart to God. Grace had told many mothers of prodigal children: "A godly mother would love to be the recipient of the credit for the salvation of her children, but she never bemoans relinquishing the medal of honor to anyone who might bring them to the place she has devoted her life praying for them to land." Annie was the one who would capture James's heart and bring him to his knees. When she died, James suffered another immense loss in his manhood. Instead of clinging to the Rock, he became a disappointment to himself, Grace, and God.

Grace Willingham was a single mom left to her own devices

to figure out how to cope with life. Through multiple insurmountable obstacles, she never wavered in her faith. She never gave up hope, never ceased praying for what she desired for her children. After Carmen left, Grace took each day in stride. She became familiar but never comfortable in the feeling of permanent separation from one of her children. It was enough to make a lesser woman lose all joy in life. Grace Willingham, however, took to heart the instruction of the Apostle James who admonished Christians to "consider it all joy." She grieved, but it ran amok with courage. Her joy and courage were two ingredients which served her well in dealing with the contentious natures of her adult blood son and daughter.

James, like Gladys, realized Carmen had brought more honor to the Willingham name than they had, and she was the adopted child. For James to admit he felt Carmen had intruded on his time with his mother would have been observed as weak and petty. Gladys was a girl; she was allowed that display. James resented his older sister to this day for devising the shameful scheme to which he had fallen prey. But when he joined in the folly, he surprised himself. His flesh got the best of him. Jason and Tyler were taunting him, and he—

*　　*　　*

"Jim, are you all right?" Gloria had been the Mayor's administrative assistant since he first took office. She was as familiar with his ways as anyone. She wasn't eavesdropping but couldn't help but overhear Jim's anguishing tone. He was in obvious turmoil.

"Oh, yeah, yeah, Gloria. I'm sorry. Just having a moment

here. It's been a long couple of days. I guess I'm just really tired." James rubbed his eyes as if sleep was causing their irritation. "What are you doing here anyway? You're not supposed to be working today."

"I had to get a cell phone number from my computer so I could cancel an appointment for Monday. If there's anything I can do, Jim, you know I'm happy to help. I'm sorry about everything going on with your mom. It's bad enough to suffer the loss. Have they found the jewels yet, or at least a lead?"

"No, I don't think so. I know they're looking at someone now. Not sure what they're going to turn up, if anything."

"When will you resume with the funeral?"

"I'm headed there now, Gloria." Jim glanced at his watch. "Oh, my goodness. I've got to get over there. I just had a few things to take care of here. I'll give you a call as soon as I know something and you can circulate the word about the funeral."

"Get yourself some rest, Jim. You look awful." Gloria watched as Jim left the office. She walked over to the window and watched until James got in his car and drove away. *I'm praying for you, Jim Willingham. I've prayed for you for a long time. You can't run from God forever. I'm taking over where your mama left off. You'll return to your roots, Prodigal Boy. You will return to your roots.*

Chapter 22

"Hey, guys, one of you can go in now. Mom is going to her meeting. You remember how to get there from here? I left it unlocked."

"Oh, yeah, I think we can make it, Nick," Nora assured.

"You go ahead, Nora. The lady is always first. I'll just sit here until you're done. Besides, I'm enjoying reading through all the names of the guest registries. Can you believe how many people have come to see this lady? This is incredible." Jimmy beamed as he opened the numbers of pages that had completely filled two registries, and almost a third. There had been a constant stream of people for the entire event of Grace Willingham's wake. He had missed the entourage, but the imagery was striking him rich. He threw his head back and laid it on the plaid sofa.

You beat all, Grandma. You were quite the woman. What a legacy you built for yourself and have now passed on to your family. What did we do to deserve you? I know you never got over Albert, but your character might not have been the dynamic quality it was except for the adversities you faced without him.

*　　*　　*

Grandma Grace's Front Porch, August 17, Sunday, Five years prior, 6:50 a.m.

Like two lovers parting for a season, the warm evening and cool night's rendezvous was revealed by the morning sun. The dew glistened on the grass as it dried against the gentle breeze. The fog cast a smothering shadow across the dawn's early light as it was pushed aside by the light wind. This was a morning like so many Jimmy had shared on Grace's porch in his rocker.

"Grandma, do you think I'm ready for this tour of duty? This is really a big deal."

"If God has called you, it doesn't matter if you think you're ready. He does."

"I just feel at times I'm really inadequate. I'm still a babe in Christianity."

"But you're on fire, Jimmy Willingham. God needs those set apart for your kind of service to be fervent when you're in battle for His cause. You make sure that you bathe your day in prayer before you place yourself on that battlefield every day. He will equip you in every way you need to be prepared for whatever befalls you."

"What if I'm not cut out for mission work? I feel like this is my calling. I've wanted to go to the mission field since I went on the mission trip you sent me on as punishment for my third late curfew. I never got it out of my system. But what if I'm wrong?"

Grace's chuckle was a pleasing one. "Don't hang your hat on what-ifs. God never wastes an act of disobedience. He'll take a chance on us if we'll give Him the chance to do so. Consider his pursuit of Saul of Tarsus, Jimmy. He was an unlikely candidate to be an Apostle, but look at the impact Paul made on our world then and even still today."

"Yeah, well, he was making a pretty sizable impact when he was persecuting the Christians, Grandma."

"Just goes to show you, Jimmy, God can use the least of these to make an impression upon His Kingdom. I can only imagine the lives you will touch for the Lord in Zimbabwe. Who knows where God will send you from there? Just be ready for an adventure."

"I'm scared, Grandma." Jimmy paused. "There. I said it. I haven't admitted it to a solitary soul until now. But I am scared half out of my wits. Thousands of miles away from the people I'm familiar with, the people I love, my home. This is my comfort zone. I lie in bed now and envision myself looking out at an African sky. Look at what you and I enjoyed this morning watching the sunrise here in Savannah, G-A. I know it's the same sun, the same planet, the same God there as He is here. I get all that. But then, I know only one person in all of Africa and have spent less than six hours with the man. If I stop to think about all those things, it seems a bit insane."

"I'm quite sure it does. But when there's a calling upon your heart to the degree you have it, you would be miserable watching the sunrises here knowing you should be there. You have stored-up memories that no one can ever take from you. Your fear is natural. Of course, the Lord tells us not to be anxious for anything. We are also instructed that God didn't give us that spirit of fear. Instead, He gave us the power of love and self-control. If you're not ready to die for the Lord, then you don't understand the mission He has laid upon your heart."

"I am ready, Grandma, but I don't want to die. Not yet. I mean, when you're a Christian, death is victory. I've heard you repeat that many times. But then, you're not afraid to die at all, are you?"

"No, I'm not, Jimmy. I look forward to that day when I'll be absent in the body and present with the Lord. We should all live to die. But while we're living, there's much work to be done. An awful lot of folks think God's work has been assigned to the preacher, to the missionary, or the chaplain in the military or at the hospitals. They fail to realize that each of us has a distinctive purpose. God has ordained my days with assignments just like He has yours. My gift of service has been different than what yours is now, but I don't know who would have accomplished my service had I decided to shirk my responsibilities as a Christian.

"I'm going to miss you, Jimmy. Everyone will miss you. But there will not be a day that you won't be lifted up in prayer by me. And when I get to Heaven, I'll be checking out who's been assigned guardian watch over you and I'll keep him on his toes." Grace smiled pleasingly and patted Jimmy's hand.

"I'll bet you will, Grandma. I'll just bet you will."

Jimmy and Grace watched the dawn break into a blistering crimson morning sky. The red rubber ball bounced from the ground and secured its appointed position in the east. Jimmy was certain he would never witness as glorious a sight as the Georgia horizon on this celebrated August morn. Should time freeze and allow the sky to roll back so that Jesus would come for His Bride, it would be the perfect setting for such an arrival.

Grace broke through the silence of the thunderous magnificence. "You have your Grandpa's heart, Jimmy Willingham. You're brave like him. Exploration is more than an interest for you. It's a necessity. It was for him, too. You're a lover of people, and they love you. Everyone who knew your Grandpa loved him, and he loved them. Life will always be a challenge, and the quest will be your crown. You reflect Albert's vigor for life and love. But never lose sight of the fact that your feet will follow your chosen paths. Make sure they always walk with God."

"I will Grandma. I'm really going to miss our times together. Thank you for that. I feel honored to be likened to the man you have always loved. That's pretty cool."

Grace reached into the pocket of her housecoat and pulled out her *God's Promises for Your Every Need* book filled with her favorite scripture. Jimmy pondered as to whether he'd ever seen her without it. She opened it to a page and pulled out a folded piece of paper. "I wrote something for you, Jimmy. I want you to have it. It's nothing fancy. It's simply a reminder for how valuable your steps will be as you go through your journeys in life. People will follow you, James Albert Willingham III. You make sure your feet lead them straight to the Cross."

*   *   *

Jimmy pulled the poem out of his wallet. It was worn but still intact. Grandma Grace had been a wanna-be poet. She wrote poems for birthdays and special events, and even rhymed her clues for scavenger hunts and redeeming presents at Christmastime. This one was extra special. He treasured the time, the proletarian talent, the paper, the ink, even the smudge of chocolate in the corner.

My Feet

My feet are mine and they will be
walking the pathway to my destiny.
My feet will take me where I allow,
and stand strong and fierce against the plow.
My feet will follow me around,
and rest upon my chosen ground.
My feet will run and dance and play,
wherever I find myself that day.
My feet will rise to men's applause,
but renew in strength for a greater cause.
And even though they might be lame,
my feet stand battle just the same.
My feet become a pure reflection
of my own permission and direction.
My feet obey, and all will see,
as their prints define my legacy.
My feet will always do their part;
I pray their efforts reflect God's heart.
For when I seek Him in the whole,
my feet will serve me sole to soul.

*   *   *

Jimmy's heart sang as he wept for the last memory he would

have of Grace Carissa Willingham. Her knees would oblige him to Calvary. He had been a mixed-up rebel of a kid, the anger-ridden son of James Albert, II. How could prayer change the path of someone destined to be lost? He didn't quite understand. He hadn't tapped into the power of prayer to the extent Grace Willingham had, but from this day forward, he had every intention of putting more than feet to the ground.

Chapter 23

Nora was in her usual state of query. "If you could tell, would you? You never snitched on a soul. But would you tell us who stole those jewels if you but could? Was it Madelyn? You know she always said you promised them to her. But I know you didn't because you told me I would be the recipient someday. Madelyn has had sticky fingers. We all know that. I just wish she'd waited until I got here so that I could have at least seen them again. You know, I never got to lay eyes on them but once. But why would Madelyn risk that? Well, for that matter, why would anybody risk that, GG? Of course, Lil' Miss Aaassshley could fool us all and be the culprit. That would shock everyone. She always was the perfect little—"

Nora came to an abrupt halt. What was she doing? Standing here wagging her tongue to a corpse, assessing a situation about which she had little to no knowledge! If GG could move, she would probably be taking Nora by the hand and finding a basin and a bar of soap. She did get that punishment once, but that was for swearing. She had never done that around GG again.

Funny how those sorts of acts of discipline tend to stick with a gal. Of course, in today's world that would be labeled as cruel and unjust treatment. That wouldn't have mattered any to Grace Willingham. She was as tough about her discipline as she was tender about her love.

*   *   *

Grandma Grace's Sugar Shack, Late May, Eleven years prior, 3:39 p.m.

"GG, are you busy tomorrow?"

"GG's always busy, Nora. Why do you ask, Sweetheart?" Grace was preparing her first picking of blueberries. She handed Nora a dish towel, colander, and a bucket of berries. The two had stood at the commercial sinks of the Sugar Shack and prepared many fruits and vegetables to stock Grace Willingham's pantry.

"I want to come here and hang out with you. I don't want to go to school tomorrow." Nora was flat. She couldn't help herself.

Grace dried her hands and placed one to Nora's forehead. "Are you planning on being sick tomorrow? You're not feeling feverish today."

"I lost, GG. I wanted to be senior class president next year, but I lost. I tried my hardest to get enough votes, but Cindy got two more votes than I did. I really wanted that title, GG. I could do a much better job than Cindy would. I just know it."

"Well, that might be true, Nora. You're a very capable young lady. So what are you going to do now?"

"What do you mean? There's nothing I can do. I didn't win.

I'll just be a student."

"*Just* a student? Cindy's a student. Can't you get on some committees and work alongside your new class president?"

"I wanted to *be* the president, not work *with* the president, GG. Besides, I'm not in her clique. She's a hoity-toity. I don't fit in."

"Hoity-toities need help, too. Don't be intimidated because you're not part of a circle. You step up and step in and offer help in whatever way you can. Have you considered being the yearbook editor? That would be a fabulous venue for you. You're incredibly creative in that area. I love looking at your scrapbooks you've created. You capture memories on film and then wrap them with your gift of words. You are stellar in your skill. I still believe you should have your own magazine someday."

"That's a hobby, GG. I don't know if I could do the yearbook. Or even that I want to."

"You can do anything you put your mind to, Nora Jean Willingham. Should you become the editor for senior year at school, imagine how eclectic you could make it. It would be the best yearbook Chatham County Schools has ever had. Has the office been taken by anyone yet?"

"No, ma'am. But, I don't know, GG. I had my hopes on class president."

"Why? Why set your hopes on that particular position only?"

"Because, GG, then you're popular. Then you're recognized. If I could have gotten class president, I would have been somebody." Nora grabbed her skirt and pulled it up to her face and twirled around in frustration.

Grace turned off the faucet, dried her hands, and took Nora

by her shoulders. Now the two were getting to the real source of the problem at hand. "Hope that is seen is no hope at all. Who hopes for what they already have? But if we hope for what we do not yet have, we wait for it patiently. Name the book."

"Romans 8." Nora always took it to one level higher. She could have named the verse, too, had she not been in a stubborn mindset.

"Good girl. Nora, popularity here on earth is nothing. The thing you hope for, you already have. You *are* somebody. You don't need the vote of classmates to tell you that. I understand aspirations. I also understand the disappointments of seeing them evaporate. But you can't allow disappointment to disengage you."

"But I prayed about this, GG. You have said thousands of times, 'You have not because you ask not.'"

"Finish it."

Nora glared at Grace not wishing to obey the command.

"I'm waiting."

This was going to be hard for Nora to admit. Why did she have to? GG always pressed and impressed this response. "If it be Your will." Nora hung her head. She couldn't recall adding the tagline to her prayer for the presidency.

"Nora, just because one door has been closed for you doesn't mean God can't use you somewhere else. It might not have been His will for you to be the president of the senior class any more than it was the class's will that you were. But now the burden is upon you. What will Nora Willingham do with her disappointment? It *will* be a defining moment for you. What definition do you want that to be? That is within your will. Now, you can let your *won't* get in the way of your *will* if you'd like. But if you won't do anything else, you will regret it later. It's your call."

GG's logic seemed to always clear confusion. Sensibility was her gift. Grace Willingham was the master of making lemonade out of lemons. Nora knew the pleasure her scrapbooks had brought. It was therapy for her in times of trouble at home, and GG was right—they were pretty remarkable. "So, you think I'd make a really good editor of the yearbook? Could I work in the Sugar Shack and save enough money for a new camera? Do you think I could take a photography class this summer? I could do some pages of a fashion foray and explode with the imagery of the best-to-worst-dressed kids in school. Oh, but I won't predispose the kids' thinking. I'll let them decide for themselves. Do you think I could introduce some culinary ideas? I could even bring kids to the Sugar Shack and—"

Grace laughed as Nora chattered on. She was cranked up to high gear again. She loved the girl's spunk, but she was especially grateful that her negative could be turned to positive in a heartbeat. At least, for the most part. She still had some work to do with Nora's jealousy of Ashley and Madelyn. That insecurity is a difficult one for a woman to overcome, and try as she might, Nora could battle with that one until Jesus comes back. But Grace was confident Nora had a future as a journalist. She also knew she would be a young and aspiring entrepreneur, and she would never settle for living small. It would take some doing, but Grace would guide her for as long as Nora allowed. This one had a mind of her own.

*   *   *

Turner's Funeral Home, October 15, 4:39 p.m.

"It was the best yearbook ever, GG! You were so proud of me. And I was kicking high. It lit up my world and created a monster within me. But look at me now. My very own magazine. In Spain, no less! Who cares if they don't know me in America? You were right, it's not about popularity at all. I wonder where I would be now if I had been the class president? Right here in Savannah? Do you think? Thank you, GG. Thank you for all of your guidance. I'm… happy. Not full of joy yet. I know there's a difference. You stressed and impressed that time and time again, too. I'm looking, though. Sometimes. I really try not to think about it. It's easier just to go through the motions of life, staying busy and keeping to task. If you ignore that you're not content with joy, happiness will sustain you."

Nora's blood ran cold at what she was hearing herself say. That would have been rebutted by Grace Willingham, and she would have set herself up for a good long sermonette at a porch rocking session. *Wish you were here for another one of those, GG. I miss them. You were right, you know. I need to find the joy and not fool myself that I'm satisfied just with the happiness. Would I ever fit in back here in Savannah? Could I be as successful with my work here? Do you think I'm running by being in Spain? I think I would miss it as much as I have missed Savannah.*

Did you hear that? I can't believe I just said that! As much as I have missed Savannah? I have missed Savannah. I have missed you, GG. You were Savannah. My mom was caught up in her husband and their kids. I was shunned. A fifth-wheel in their family of four. My real dad didn't want me because he was

Jim Willingham. My stepdad didn't want to adopt me because I was Jim Willingham's daughter. Ashley was the only one of his girls who got to be proud of wearing his name. Wow! It would be hard to come back here without you, GG. I might have to settle for happiness.

*   *   *

TURNER'S FUNERAL HOME, OCTOBER 15, 4:44 P.M.

"I don't want to rush you, but when you get done, I'll be outside in a front-porch rocker. I need some fresh air."

"No, no, Jimmy. It's fine. I'm good. You come in and I'll get some fresh air." Nora was a bit embarrassed that Jimmy had caught her with her shoes off and legs pulled under her chin, sitting beside the casket. Not a very somber position for someone paying last respects.

"No, I really do need the fresh air, Nora. I'll be there when you're done if you'll come and get me. I'm not sure how long the meeting will last, though, and Nick kind of indicated he would like to close this place down since Grandma is the only *guest* he has for the time being."

"Sure, sure. I'll be done here in just a minute. Thanks, Jimmy."

Nora slipped into her shoes and straightened her comfy dress she had changed into at GG's. She tenderly stroked Grace's hair and face, gliding down her arm and resting her hand on Grace's wedding band. "You wore his ring all those years, GG. You could have wed anyone you wanted. You were beautiful, charming, intelligent, and successful. Yet you stood by your man. I want that kind of love. I will never marry until I feel like I can love with that type of committed heart. I've been close, but not there yet. No one else would ever do for you. That's the kind of love I want. Thank you for modeling that. I love you, GG. I'm really going to miss you."

*   *   *

TURNER'S FUNERAL HOME, OCTOBER 15, 4:50 P.M.

Jimmy knew his time would be limited, but it really was okay with him. He felt conflicted about standing over someone he'd spoken with face to face, less than a week ago, thanks to the glory of electronics. *Now she's not here to talk to any longer. Ever again in this life. Just like that. It was the Apostle James who said, 'What is your life? You are a mist that appears for a little while and then vanishes.'*

"Sorry, Grandma. You know me better than most anyone else, and that would mean you understand I really don't want to be here. At all. Dead bodies give me the heebie-jeebies. Stiff. Cold. Washed-out. I find people paying respects to be highly amusing. 'Oh, she looks so good.' Really? Uh, she's dead. And, 'It looks just like her.' Hello? It is her! Just thought I should come clean with that right up front. Thanks for the indulgence.

"Grandma, I just want to say— No. I just want to tell you— I mean, there are so many things I— It's no use. I really don't know how to do this. This is far too weird. It's more than weird. It's demoralizing. I'm standing here talking to someone who is dead. You can't hear me. Can you? I mean, the Apostle Paul said to be absent from the body is to be present with the Lord." Jimmy raised his hands toward Heaven and directed his gaze upward. "That's where you are right now, Grandma. I can deal with that. I know it's a better place for you. It's what you lived for. I got that. But here, lying in a casket, that's not my Grandma Grace. I mean, it looks like you— Listen to me. It *is* you. Okay, I need to go. This is just too creepy."

Jimmy headed for the door and then walked back to the casket. "I really am going to miss you, Grandma. You will leave a void that none of us will fill individually. But we'll do our best to carry on your legacy. My feet will serve God better because you set them on the right path. I love you, Grace Carissa Willingham. You were one of a kind." A stronger force was in Jimmy's heart than his stomach, and it pulled him up close and personal so that he could kiss Grace on the forehead. "All right, that was *really* weird! I'm outta here."

Chapter 24

Carmen paused at the conference room door. She drew a deep breath and whispered, "I can do all things through Him who gives me strength." She put on her biggest smile, threw back her shoulders, and sucked in her tummy. She turned the handle and reentered a life she had last seen in the rearview mirror of a Greyhound bus.

"Gladys, it's so good to see you." Gladys was seated at the conference table alone. Carmen made her way toward Gladys, extending her arms to embrace her sister. Gladys shrunk away, uncertain of Carmen's intentions. Carmen bent down and hugged the sister who had brought many anxious days to her childhood.

"N-N-N-Nick stepped out for a moment. He'll be right back." Gladys cleared her throat. "It's good to see you, too, Carmen."

"It's been a long time, Gladys. How's Ralph?" Carmen struggled to find a suitable starting point for conversation.

"Ralph is Ralph. I'm sure Mother told you all about us." Gladys was smug and curt. She didn't want to stare at Carmen, but she couldn't help but notice how time seemed to be her best friend forever. She had always been such a beautiful girl. Her beauty had added to the turmoil in Gladys's life. Sharing her mother to an outsider who became an insider practically overnight had been a very difficult transition. She wanted to love Carmen, but she didn't know how. Always desiring a little sister, she found herself torn between including Carmen in her world and making the child's life miserable. Everything Carmen did brought delight to everyone. The jealousy was more than Gladys could pray away. Carmen's eyes were big. Her skin was naturally tan and flawless. Her hair was silky and black. And as she grew, she transformed from perfectly adorable to absolutely striking. She was everything Gladys wanted to be. To compound the dilemma, Carmen was the ideal child. She was polite and grateful, eager to help and willing to work, and always went the second mile when asked to go one. Her personality was pleasant. She seldom cried, and when she did it was because Gladys had taunted her in an undesirable manner. Perfection in Carmen was unacceptable to Gladys. She began devising ways and means to change that image. The quest to taint Carmen had been the beginning of a root of evil within Gladys.

There was iciness in the air, neither woman really knowing how to catch up on thirty-plus years of separation. Carmen sensed immediately that if the mood was going to lighten, it would be left to her to turn it on. *Lord, we can do this. I can't on my own, but I know You will give me the words. This is the opportunity I prayed for. Help me to make the most of this time.*

"Time has really changed us, Gladys. Inside and out. At least for me. I'm glad we have this moment alone. There are some things I've wanted to say to you for a long time. I—"

"Hey, Ladies, sorry I had to make a phone call." Nick was business as usual. He showed no deference to his mother over Gladys, or vice-versa. "We're waiting on Jim, but he's on his way. He got detained at his office, but should be arriving any moment. Can I get you girls anything? Water? Coffee? Soft drink?"

"No, no, Nick. I'm fine. Thank you." Carmen respected Nick's position and played along with addressing the two of them as if they were his clientele rather than his family.

"No, thanks. We shouldn't be here too long, anyway." Gladys was hopeful.

"Oh, I don't think it'll take us long at all. We just, basically, need to decide on a time for– Well, I'll wait on Jim before I go into detail." Nick picked up his phone and sent a text.

*   *   *

The three sat in silence. Gladys picked at her nails. Nick made notes in his daytimer. Carmen looked around the conference room admiring the exquisite décor. Nick had shared with her that he had given Turner's a much-needed overhaul. His art background served him well in his impeccable selections. His goal was to attract a high-end clientele, and from all indications, his plan had worked. He did have a great business head, along with his eye for flair. She had seen his condominium when she would sneak into town, but would not dare be seen in public at the funeral home.

It was dicey enough stowing away at Grace's place when she had the rare opportunity. Carmen found herself dodging bullets as there was an occasional visitor to the homeplace. Like

the personalized rockers, Grace had a my-very-own secret key
hidden for each child, unbeknownst to the others. It was one
of those sacred confidences that made Grace's loved ones feel
extraordinary. Each one felt he or she was the only one who had
exclusive passage into Grace's homeplace anytime day or night.
Carmen never let on to Grace she had discovered that everyone
was equally special. She would have been none the wiser about
the keys had she not been a stowaway and watched from her
bedroom window as each visitor retrieved his or her key. It was
yet another dimension to the creative loving personality of Grace
Willingham. There was always a lesson behind Grace's wiles,
and trust was the attribute she was developing in her kids. If
anything ever went missing, everyone knew Grace would deal
with the matter her way.

*   *   *

Nick glanced at his watch. He was hoping James would get
here in enough time to let the local media outlets know the time
of Grace's funeral, especially if it could happen the next day.
The top of the hour was approaching and he was feeling a little
contentious in his spirit.

"I got here as quickly as I could. Traffic's getting a little
heavier out. All the early diners, I suppose."

Carmen had seen pictures of James. His hardened look was
of little consequence to her, but seeing him in person for the first
time was a bit disarming. He was the one she most dreaded to
see. What came over her was not of her own might. She bolted
from her chair and presented him with the same greeting she

did their sister.

Her move startled Jim. He wasn't sure whether to stand and face his music or duck to avoid her fist. When she hugged her brother as if no ugly history had severed their bond, his heart began to examine his thoughts.

"James, it's been a long time. Too long. You look wonderful. I can't wait to see your Ashley and Madelyn. I've visited with Nora and Jimmy already. You must be very proud of them. They truly are remarkable kids."

"Carmen, I–I– Well, thank you. It's good to see you, too."

"Guys, I hate to break up your reunion, but we are up against the clock here, perhaps." Nick was feeling the pressure of time.

"Up against the clock? Why do you say it that way? We're in no hurry to get Mother in the grave. This has all been very disconcerting, Nick. We can wait another week if we have to. What we need to do is to find those jewels." Gladys showed her testy side.

"Gladys, finding the jewels has nothing to do with getting Mama in the grave. We need to get that behind us. It could be a long time before we track down the thief. I believe we should have the funeral tomorrow. Late in the day would be okay. Is four o'clock too late, Nick?" James was hoping to get back to business on Monday. He had spent too much time away already being on lock-down for two days.

"It is starting to get darker earlier, and I don't know how you guys want to handle the folks who haven't viewed Grace. They were wrapped around the block twice. We only got through roughly two-thirds of the viewers. If you have a processional one-third the size of your viewers, it's going to be a long time before we get to the gravesite. Then, the minister will give a few words and a prayer, and we'll dispense. But you're pushing nightfall. I'd bump it up an hour if I were you."

"Hold on there, you two. I'm not in favor of Mother being laid to rest tomorrow. Why can't we wait until Tuesday, or Monday at the very earliest? But I vote for Tuesday. We're all exhausted. It's been a grueling four days since her death. I'm totally opposed to tomorrow. I won't have it."

"Gladys, you're being unreasonable. You don't have a life. Everyone else does, and we need to get on with it." James was not going to be horse-wrangled by Gladys today. His patience was as thin as a communion wafer, and he would not succumb to her perverse behavior.

Nick cleared his throat. "Well, we do have a third party involved who might want some input. My apologies, Ms. Willingham, for not including you in the original arrangements. But, you're here now and we're anxious to hear your thoughts. What say you?"

Carmen felt a lump in her throat. Not much healing ground had been plowed due to time constraints, but this could undo what little headway she had possibly made. "I appreciate the consideration of being included in this decision. And no apology is necessary, Nick, for the original exclusion. I was indisposed and got here as quickly as I could. The arrangements Gladys and James made were perfectly acceptable.

"I deeply appreciate you two bearing the brunt of Mom's demise and making all of the arrangements. From everything I've heard, it all was handled in an outstanding manner."

James nodded. Gladys tilted her head slightly to the right.

Carmen silently summoned for help. She wanted her words to be deliberately kind but compliantly firm.

"I suppose the issue begs the question: Did Grace have any specific preferences regarding her burial? I mean, I'm sure she didn't consider theft when she was planning her funeral, but did she make any specific requests about a certain day, or if it was raining as opposed to sunshine, anything like that? I haven't seen her funeral requests document."

"Actually, there are certain requests she made. A celebration, no cameras, who would prepare her body, where she would be buried, and what day she would prefer to be buried if the timing was right." Nick was matter of fact.

"And?" Carmen persisted.

"It was Sunday, Carmen. Sunday is when Mother wanted to be buried." Gladys threw up her hands as if she was not buying Carmen's innocent ignorance. She was, after all, the funeral director's mother.

"Yes, Mama always wanted to be buried on The Lord's Day, Gladys. You know that. I know that. Now Carmen knows that. I'd say that settles it." James was short and condescending. He wanted to make the decision and go home.

"It's not my decision. I have no vote in this at all. But I would remind you all that time is ticking away. If we are going to abide by Grace's wishes since technically we can, we really need to make the decision in the next few minutes." Nick realized he was tipping the scales, but he had promised Grace himself that if it was possible, he would do everything he could to make it happen for her to be buried on Sunday.

Gladys stood in objection to his influence. "I realize I'm going to be out-numbered here today, but let it be known that I think it is too soon to give Mother the proper service. Plus, everyone seems to be dismissing that she ... won't ... have ... her ... jewels ... on! I'm assuming that's not bothering either of my siblings, but it does me. Wasn't that one of her requests, to be wearing her jewels at the service?"

"Actually, no, it wasn't, Gladys. I believe the document says that she would only wear them for the duration of the viewing. She wanted them removed and only her wedding ring would be left on during the funeral. From what I understand, she wanted to be remembered for being Grace Carissa Willingham, not the proprietor of coveted jewels."

"Who told you such nonsense? I don't remember seeing that written in the document," Gladys barked.

"He is her grandson and her funeral director, Gladys. I'm sure he's had occasion to have a few conversations with Mom Grace." Carmen was quick to come to the defense of her son. It was one thing for Gladys to be snide to her, quite another for her to be nasty to her son. *Sorry, Lord. I'm trying here, but she can't go there.*

Gladys recoiled her claws and reclaimed her seat. "So, Carmen, it's up to you. You get to break the tie. I realize James is wanting tomorrow. I feel it's too soon. You weren't here for the two-day lockdown. We were only released a couple of hours ago. It's been a very trying time. I know Mother, and she would not want anyone to be pushed into inconvenience simply to fulfill a Sunday burial time. She was far too considerate for such."

Jim drew a deep breath. He despised his sister–oldest sister much of the time. The remainder was left to indifference.

"Carmen, don't pay attention to Gladys. Yes, we've been here and been here and been here. We're all exhausted. That's exactly why we need to get this over with so we can get back to our lives. As long as Mama is in cold storage, it's hanging over our heads. We can't move forward. It's time to put it to rest by putting her to rest once and for all."

Carmen cringed at the insensitive choice of words. Who could dismiss Grace Willingham so effortlessly? She would like nothing better than to spit in James Willingham's tactless face. *I won't, Lord. Okay? But I would really like to. You know my heart and thoughts, so I might as well fess up here and now.*

"Mo— Ms. Willingham, I know this is a difficult decision for you, being pulled with two valid positions, but we only have a few minutes before we will miss the opportunity to make the public aware of Grace's funeral service should you decide for it to take place on Sunday."

Carmen fidgeted. She knew her decision would be unpopular with one of her siblings. This decision was not about Gladys, James, or her. This was about Grace Willingham and the legacy she left behind. Preserving her dignity and honoring her wishes should be central to each of her children. After all, what was lying in state was just a body. Grace was now present with the Lord. What was going on down below regarding what everyone did with her body was insignificant in the scheme of things.

Carmen took a deep breath and laid both hands palm down on the conference table. "I don't mean to offend either of you in the vote I cast in this. James, your reasons are valid. Gladys, likewise. It's true, I haven't been in lockdown here at the funeral home, but I have been in my car since I decided to drive here from Texas where I was on assignment. We're all weary from our own experiences. Jimmy came from Africa. Nora flew in from Spain. We would have loved being here with all of you, but this is life. It takes us in different directions, and we come together for such a time as this."

Gladys and James each felt pangs of guilt for Carmen's explanation of life. Her direction could have been different but for their transgressions toward her. Nick was tapping his fingers obtrusively.

"Let's go forward tomorrow. She deserves the last request we can grant for her."

"Tomorrow it is. If you'll excuse me, I need to make a phone call." Nick grabbed his cell phone and began alerting the scores of media who would be eager to hear the news first. James peered at Gladys with his usual haughty demeanor when he had the upper hand on her schemes. Gladys slung her purse on her shoulder and headed for the door.

"I'm sorry, Gladys. I know this disappoints you. I really do feel we should honor Mom Grace with this."

Gladys was sharp and short. "You did what you felt best, Carmen. Never mind me. We didn't really decide on a time. I'm assuming Nick will take it upon himself to set the designated hour. We'll hear it on the news tonight." Gladys stuck her nose in the air and marched out of the conference room.

James realized he was still seated and did not want to be left alone with Carmen. He jumped up so quickly that he tipped the leather chair over, creating quite the scene. Carmen reached down to help him pick it up, and purposely snared his gaze.

"Thank you, Carmen. I appreciate the consideration, although

I don't think I had a thing to do with your decision."

"You didn't, James. It was purely about Mom."

"Well, I guess we'll see you tomorrow."

"James, could I have a moment with you?"

"Well, I really need to get going, Carmen. Valerie's waiting dinner on me with some friends. I'm really pushed for time." James did not want to broach the story and the regrets surrounding the sordid ordeal that had haunted him for years.

"I only wanted to say to you that I need your forgiveness." Carmen's voice was jittery. She knew the moment would unnerve her, but she had hoped it wouldn't be quite so obvious.

"You need my forgiveness? Are you kidding me? You need my forgiveness? You didn't do anything, Carmen. I did. Gladys did. But, I guess you never knew that she was involved."

"Oh, I pieced it together in my mind. It wasn't hard to figure out. She was the only one who knew where I was and that I would be in a compromising situation."

"I wanted to call you, go get you, bring you home. Mama grieved herself to death over you. I have felt guilty every day since. I can't take it back, but if I could, I would do it in a—"

Carmen grabbed James's wrist, then touched his hand tenderly. "It's okay, James. We don't have to rehash the past. None of us can bring back one second of time. It was a dreadful day. But something really good came of it."

"How could anything good come out of a day like that, Carmen? I mean, I dropped you off with a back-street abortionist with a one-way ticket to California, paid for the abortion, threatened your life if you didn't do what I told you, and left instructions for the driver to take you to the Greyhound station.

And you need my forgiveness?"

"You did what you thought was best at the time. I harbor no malice toward any of you. I forgave all of you many years ago. You really don't have to relive it."

"Those guys were my friends, too. They had football scholarships and whosever child it was, it would have ruined their reputations, their lives. I mean, they could have gone to jail for rape. I could have gone to jail." James contemplated how he had categorized the self-serving comrades. "My friends. I can't even tell you what has happened to either one of my so-called friends today. And I chose them and myself over my sister. What an idiot I was. I don't know what came over me, Carmen. It was a power I had never experienced before, that kind of fleshly desire. I never meant to hurt you. Oh, I can't even say that, Carmen. I knew what those guys were doing was wrong. I just had no intentions of doing that to you. Then, when you came up pregnant, I didn't know what else—"

"Stop, James. Please, don't do this to yourself. It's all okay. It really is. I've overcome and overridden all of that. God makes all things beautiful in His own way."

"I was responsible for an abortion, Carmen. I've had to live with the guilt of taking the life of an unborn—"

"I didn't abort, James. I didn't go through with it. I ran away. I climbed out of the window in the restroom, hid away in an alley for a while, then watched until your driver was distracted, walked back to the car and got in it. He took me to the station. I used the money for the abortion to live until I could get on my feet. I found a great church that helped me find my way. God provided, just like Mom always told us He would."

James's felt wilted from head to toe. "I have had no idea for all this time. I'm quite sure Mama did, though. She never said anything about you not aborting. She never said anything about you having any children at all until Nick arrived on the scene one day. I didn't ask questions. Quite frankly, I didn't care. For that, I'm sorry. He's a fine young man, Carmen. Why didn't Mama just tell me she knew where you were?"

"She wanted to. It was at my insistence that she didn't. And Grace never broke a confidence. We agreed that if you or Gladys came to her, she could share it with you. She repeatedly asked you to sit down and talk with her, James. Had you taken the time to do that, she would have shared an awful lot with you. You avoided your rocking-chair time with Mom."

"I did avoid it. She did try. The last time I saw her, she begged me to sit down and talk. My heart was callous, Carmen. I got in my car and drove away like an idiot. I was going to make it up to her. I was. If she had only lived one more day. Just one more day." James had choked back the tears until the dam finally burst. Carmen rested his head on her shoulder and wrapped her arms around him. It was a moment that Grace would have enjoyed. Her prodigal son's heart was softening.

"It's okay, James. Mom knew your heart. She knew a lot of good covered up the rubble of your life in that soul of yours. She prayed incessantly for you. She wanted nothing more than for you to come to your senses about some of your choices in life. She had more faith in you than you have in yourself. Mama always said, 'The best way to survive a troubled child is to love them tough and tender. Whether they show you they appreciate it or not, they won't forget that you did.' She was right, James.

You haven't forgotten."

"She was something else, Carmen. I was a horrible son, and she deserved better. Now, I can never make that up to her. What have I done? What have I done?"

*   *   *

Nick was looking down at his notes, unaware of what had been transpiring in his absence. "Got it all covered. It'll be in the Sunday paper and on the six- and eleven-o'clock news. So we can—"

James bolted from Carmen's shoulder, startled and embarrassed at the disturbance. He turned from Nick and grabbed his coat, seizing the opportunity to wipe his eyes. "I'm sorry. I have to leave. Valerie is waiting on me. Thank you, Carmen. It's really good to see you. Welcome home.

"Nick, I really appreciate the way you've handled things for Grace's funeral. You've done a very professional job with a lot of personal touches. Grace would be proud of her grandson." He gave Nick a strong gentleman's handshake and walked out the door.

"Did you—" Nick was going to inquire of Carmen what had happened between the two, when James remembered he had one more piece of business.

"Do I have to hear it on the news tonight or can you tell me now? What time is Mama's funeral?"

"I set it for three o'clock. Figured we'd best bump it up an hour. I don't expect nearly as many spectators. Quite frankly, much of the crowd consisted of rubber-neckers. They weren't coming to pay respects to a great woman as much as they were coming to catch a glimpse of the infamous jewels of Grace Willingham. Now that they're not in the picture, we'll have a lighter crowd. See you tomorrow, Jim."

"Thanks, Nick. Carmen. See you tomorrow."

Nick waited till he heard the front door close before he hurled the question to his mom. He was more than curious about the events leading up to what he had witnessed. "Did you tell him?"

"Not everything. Your timing has been a bit rancid today, my son."

"You *are* going to tell, though, aren't you?"

"Oh, yes, the two of them will know every detail. They deserve to know. Grace would want that, too. And we don't want to keep it all to ourselves, now, do we?"

"Oh, brother. This could get very interesting, Mom. Very interesting indeed. Let's go home. I'm exhausted."

"I've got a better idea. Let's go to Grace's."

"That's exactly the home I had in mind."

Chapter 25

The taxi pulled over to the landing of 827 Victory Drive. Madelyn casually exited, not wishing to draw attention to her frenzied state of mind. She began walking down the long drive to Granny's house, a path she had met with enthusiasm each time she came to visit Grace. Floods of memories consumed her presence, but distant sirens interrupted her mental escape and she hastened her steps to move beyond the vision of Victory Drive commuters. She worked her way to the left of the path, darting behind one of the enormous oaks dwarfing her into insignificance. The heavy foliage, evergreens, and palmettos beyond the splendid trees disguised the vastness of the terrain. A soul could get lost on the Willingham property, and that's exactly what she intended to do. For now.

Madelyn's backpack was filled with a few provisions. If she could make Camp W'ham before dark, she could stay there for the night. No one would come looking for her at the camp. She had never brought Kareem to this part of Grace's property. They had explored other areas when Granny was out of town, but not

275

the camp. W'ham was her safe haven.

Madelyn smiled. W'ham. Short, of course, for Willingham, but the kids had affectionately called it "wham." Granny Grace debated it initially, but she put it to vote. The kids won. She came to wholeheartedly agree with the name, however, once she surmised that Camp W'ham, after all, did leave "a forcible impact" upon all who experienced it. She was right.

It was at Camp W'ham where Grace taught her kids to survive on little to no provisions. One meal a day during Boot Camp Week. She educated each one individually in the art of making a fire from rubbing sticks together or catching a strong ray of sunshine. She majored in Fishing 101 and taught not only the basics of how to bait the hook and hold the rod then reel in the fish, the class also entailed the preparation process from cleaning to cooking. If you wanted to eat, you had to graduate from her class. Madelyn recalled how her inhibitions for worms waned after three days of not eating. It was the best fish she'd ever put in her mouth.

Forging her way, Madelyn kept her eyes open for snakes. She did despise those creatures. She got that phobia from Granny herself. The lady never allowed one in her sight for very long. She took care of the creature in one fell swoop but failed to retain much about what brought the critter to its demise. Granny boasted of being afraid of only two species: dead and alive. It was snake-crawling season. Madelyn picked up her pace at the mere thought.

Setting her foot on the cleared path brought relief. It had obviously not been visited in at least a couple of years. There was growth, but the rocks kept it somewhat controlled. The sun was setting, but masked by the growth, dark would settle in fast in the wooded area. It had been a long day. Madelyn wondered how she had gotten from point A to point B in her life. This was not the plan she and Granny Grace had talked about for her as a little girl. Dreaming of a life of total independence and civility was far removed from her mind-set. She had allowed an incident in high school that was beyond her control to preside over her destiny. Had she told Grace about the assault on her womanhood, Grace would have shared her wisdom with Madelyn. She would have known what to do and how to get beyond the hurt and anger Madelyn felt. Together they could have come up with a better plan for her future. Now look at her. Evading the law. Running from Kareem. Hiding away like a desperate criminal. She never intended for her actions to come to this. She never wanted anything more than what was rightfully hers.

Madelyn knew full well it was her defiance that had landed her in this position. Granny had worked with her to bring balance to her impudence and boldness. She didn't want anyone telling her what she could or could not do, at least not anyone who didn't love her. And those, she could count on one finger. Living with mom, she was left to figure out everything on her own and make her own rules. Only at Granny's did she have boundaries. She craved them. Boundaries meant love. Restrictions came with concern. Limits were wrapped in care. Demand for respect found a willingness to give it.

*   *   *

GRACE'S PORCH, ONE YEAR PRIOR, 5:33 A.M.

"Granny, am I going to Hell?"

"Only if you want to, Maddie."

"I can't be good out there. It's too hard. It's easy here with you because you make me want to be good." Madelyn halted her rocker. She needed to hear every word Granny Grace would have to say to her troubled heart.

"You have too much to offer the world to stay locked up in a shell. Besides, God needs your boldness, but He's not going to tolerate your disobedience."

"I try, Granny. I really do. I think about the verses of scripture you taught me. I try to apply them in my life. It's just that I see so much of the world and so little of you. I go to school, then to mom's place, and then I hang around with some real undesirables right now. I know I shouldn't, but no one good wants to be my friend. The only ones who have anything to do with me are the troubled kids. They are, you know, troubled, I mean."

"I know, Maddie. The world is going to Hell in a hand basket. But we still have to learn to live in this world, not be of the world. If I had allowed myself do what the world wanted me to do all these years, I might not be fit for Heaven today. I might never have come to learn a dependency on Christ. You have to be strong, Maddie. It's as easy to say no to evil in your life as it is to say no to the good. That's what you're doing, you know. By saying yes to things you know you shouldn't do, you're saying no to a less troubling life. Doesn't mean if you give your life to Jesus that everything will be a bed of roses. It doesn't work that way at all. It just means when adversities come, you don't have to face them all alone. You've made some poor choices in life in your past five years, Sweetheart. But as hopeless as you may feel, it doesn't mean you can't turn it around today. This is as good a day as any to start living for the Lord."

"I don't think God wants someone like me. I'm damaged goods."

"Damaged? Have you forgotten the story of Rahab and the spies? She was perhaps one of the most unexpected characters that God used to fulfill His plan for mankind. A prostitute. A quick thinker. A convincing liar. A confidante. What saved her life as well as her family's lives? She was familiar with God and recognized Him as the only true God, the God Who was worth risking her life for in order to help Joshua conquer Jericho. She put out her scarlet cord and it saved her life."

"The scarlet cord. It is an amazing story." Madelyn drew a deep sigh. "I wish my mom was a Rahab. Life would've been very different for me."

"Life can still be different for you, Maddie. It's your choice now, Sweetheart. You get to decide how you live. It's not your mama's fault anymore. You can't let your past be your crutch. You'll limp around for the rest of your life if you do. Make your own mark on this world, Maddie. Don't let the world leave its mark on you."

One lone star fell from the sky, streaking boldly as it left its mark for only a scarce moment in time. Madelyn quickly closed her eyes to embroider the image in her mind. She scanned the details of what she had seen. Then, as if finding the pieces to a puzzle, she began to assemble the feelings the vision stirred within her. She was that star falling from a world of stars exactly like her. Where would she land? Who would be there to catch her? Would she leave a mark on the world as she took flight? She desperately needed to rid the world from her life. She felt trapped. Her soul was in lost and found waiting for someone to claim it. *Please, someone rescue me.*

Grace made no mention of the falling star. She wasn't superstitious in the least. But she never missed an opportunity to pray for a need. She knew no greater need at the moment than the soul of this child beside her. That star was for her sweet granddaughter. She silently declared it an omen of the security of Maddie's salvation.

"You brought me out into a spacious place; You rescued me because You delighted in me. Name the book, Maddie."

"Psalm 18:19 and 2 Samuel 22:20."

Grace was more than pleased—books, chapters and verses. "*Are* you going to Hell?"

"Only if I want to, Granny. Only if I want to."

*   *   *

There it was. Camp W'ham. And none too soon. A blanket of darkness had settled beneath the regal Sugar Maples. Beyond their towering splendor, the sky reluctantly was surrendering its daylight vigor. Matchless autumn beauty of brilliant yellow, orange, and red pressed against the sky begging to demonstrate a more beautiful performance tomorrow. Fall was Madelyn's favorite time at W'ham, but nature provided a perfect backdrop and natural landscape for year-round enjoyment. Each season bespoke its unique personality and created an array of memories for Grace's clan.

Madelyn pulled her flashlight out of her backpack. She lifted the guardian of the key, and hundreds of rolly-pollies scampered from underneath the rock to find cover again. The door screamed out in desperate need of oiling. The place was dusty, but it would be a second-hand respite for the night. She lit the oil lamps. It was still a cozy setting. A rustic campsite made out of hand-hewn logs from the property. Madelyn knew how to prime the pump if necessary. It would not only be adequate for this night but perhaps others should her upcoming days dictate. She brushed off the mattress cover, opened the chest, and unzipped the plastic covering protecting the linens for the bed. Leave it to Granny to have things in impeccable order. But then, she always thought of everything.

Madelyn crawled in the middle of the bed and crossed her legs yoga style. She pulled a protein bar and water from her bag. It had been a long time since her coffee and sausage biscuit at Turner's this morning. She placed her Australia snow globe on the nightstand beside her bed after giving it a good shake. Next she retrieved her picture of Bryson, pulled it to her face, and then cradled it to her chest. *Lord, do you delight in me still? Then, rescue me so I can protect my baby.*

Chapter 26

Nick headed straight for the kitchen. It wasn't hunger that lured him there since the three had stopped for dinner after leaving the funeral home. The kitchen was his favorite place in Grace's home. It was the hub of her heart, and the quintessence of her survival as a single mom. Her kitchen *was* the place for mealtime magic. This place of entertainment was the mantra–the very song of her home. Here she kept her finger on the pulse of her loved ones. Grace Willingham served up more love around the kitchen table than most families come to know in a lifetime.

Grace's kitchen was simple. An original Hoosier cabinet complete with flour bin and complementary sideboards were the extent of furnishings apart from the kitchen table and chairs. No fluff. Just basics. The attention-grabber in Grace's kitchen was her collection of fine art. One corner of the kitchen was designated as "Measure of Life." This was where Grace charted life and growth of all the Willingham offspring. Bryson's ultrasound picture was temporarily affixed waiting his first birthday measurement. Masterpieces of her grandchildren bordered the countertops like skirting around a bride's table. Renditions of toddler-to-adolescent creativity revealed progression in expertise. The young artists autographed each creation and waited for Grandma's seal of approval, i.e., tape. Layers of pictures of pink pigs and hairy monsters, starry skies and fairies, skyscrapers and rollercoasters, spiders and lizards, monsters, and dragons were now faded from years of bearing witness to Grace's pride in her children. But perhaps the most significant display and hallmark of creativity was Grace's "Wall of Remembrance." Life-equipping scripture was inscribed on the walls by Grandma's hand. Underneath each verse were dated signatures of her precious little promises who recited the words hidden in their hearts.

Nick broke out a familiar smile, one he wore as a child when he rounded Grandma's counters to inspect his artwork. His mind slipped back in time as he carefully examined his quaint artifacts. Grace had introduced him to an ability that would dominate his passion for the abstract. Her praise was more than dutiful enthusiasm. It was a sincere appreciation for what would eventually become a career for him. She recognized his skills that set the course for his very successful profession as an architectural engineer.

Grace ignited Nick's desire to visit Paris during her "Around the World" adventures. By eighth grade, his trip with Grandma was a toss-up between Italy and France. Historical architecture fascinated him most and harmonized with his love for art. Paris would win the toss. Grace struck a bargain with Nick, and he never lost sight of his dream.

GRANDMA GRACE'S KITCHEN,

Twenty years prior, 8:07 p.m.

"Heads. Paris it is, Grandma. I'm going to Paris for my senior trip."

"Either choice would have been wise. Of course, with a Eurail pass, we can visit Italy for a couple of days, if you wish. But you will love Paris. It's a beautiful city."

"You've been there?"

"Oh, yes. A friend of Albert's lives there. I visit occasionally. They served together in the war."

"A man, Grandma?"

"He's married. He's a friend. We keep in touch." Grace didn't discuss possibilities, or lack thereof, of romantic love with her grandchildren.

"You love art, Nick, but I do believe you have an eye for structural design. You've created some pretty dandy buildings on paper. I'm going to make you a deal. I will send you to college in Paris to study architecture, provided—"

"No way! Are you serious, Grandma? Really?"

"—provided you learn the language in high school, and—"

"I've already signed up for French next year, Grandma! This is too cool."

"Don't interrupt. And with one other caveat."

"What's a caveat?"

"It's a requirement. I want you to do one thing for Grandma, though. And it's a lot to ask of a young aspiring architect."

"Grandma, you're going to send me to Paris to school. I mean, I'll do it. Tell me."

"I will when you're older. You just finished your freshman

year in high school, Nick. It won't be *that* difficult, but it will entail a small sacrifice on your part. I will tell you that I need a year for each year you're in college. That's all I'll say for now. You won't have to make a decision until your senior year. Then, you can consider whether it's Paris or the United States where you'll finish your education. If you say no, you can go to college here and I'll still pay, provided you learn French. You still get to go to Paris on your senior trip, you know. We'll discuss it more when you're older, perhaps the end of your junior year. Then, you can consider it during the summer and let me know at the end of the season. You'll need to make application to your college of choice."

"Okay, Grandma. Whatever it is, I know it'll be an adventure. You're always full of them." Nick hugged Grace. Their bond was special in Nick's eyes, priceless in Grace's.

*   *   *

PARIS, FRANCE, SIXTEEN YEARS PRIOR, LE MEURICE
HOTEL RESTAURANT, 8:07 P.M.

"I can't believe I actually toured the Louvre. It's been an incredible day. I can't thank you enough, Grandma."

"I knew you would love this city, Nick."

"Grandma, remember the caveat?"

"I do."

"Is it time for me to know what it is? I want to come to school in Pairs. I love it here. It's been an awesome ten days. Bits and pieces of my heart are all over this place."

"I understand. It can get in one's system." Grace was about to present a plan for Nick that she wasn't sure how he would accept. She had fervently prayed for guidance, and forgiveness where necessary, regarding the idea. As she presented it, she would carefully examine his face. She didn't want to put undue pressure on him. She would have to be the judge of that based on body language, because he would never say it out loud.

"Nick, you know Benny Fulkerson has had his eye on me for a long time."

"Yeah, he's been sweet on you forever." Nick couldn't help but snicker. Ashley had shared with him the story of the gun.

"Well, he'd like to get his *hands* on me. And that is not going to happen if I have anything to do with it. I like Turner's Funeral Home. They do a fine job. That's where I want to be prepared for burial. But when I die, I don't want the likes of Benny Fulkerson preparing my corpse. You understand what I'm saying?"

Nick found it odd that his grandmother would be addressing this topic with her grandson, but she certainly had his attention.

"I want to propose to you that you finish college in Paris. You might even begin your career here in this very city. Who knows? But when I sense it could be time for me to start making preparations for going Home, I want to call you and ask you to move back to Savannah and buy Turner's. I'll front the money, of course. You won't have to worry about that."

"Won't I need to be a mortician for that?" Nick was smooth as silk. He never missed a heartbeat with his response.

"Or just the owner and have licensed undertakers working with you. And, you're welcome to keep Benny on. I don't want him to lose his job. But he is never to so much as be alone in the same room with my dead body." Grace studied Nick's body language with deliberate concentration. He showed no sign of resistance.

"You don't have to give me your answer now, Nick. You can think about it. But you can never breathe a word of this conversation to anyone ever, as long as I am living."

"I'll do it. It's the least I can do for you, Grandma. Look at all you've done for me."

"Everyone gets a trip, Nick. You're as special as the next one."

"Not the trip, Grandma. Love. You have loved me when you didn't even know me. You spent years looking for Mom and me. And when you found us, you invested your whole being into us. I owe you my life. I'll do it."

"Thank you, Nick. You're the sweetest thing. We don't have to make plans now. We've got a lot of years before I kick off."

"Okay, now that that's settled. What exactly have you been doing in *Bulgari's*? That's a high-end jewelry store, Lady. You have made a visit to your friend every day since we've been here. You got lost for hours today. I guess you thought I wouldn't notice since I was at the Louvre. Are you sure you're not sweet on him?"

"It's a shame not to visit with him while I'm here, Nick, that's all. He's lonely since Monique died."

"Lonely, eh? Something's up with that, Grandma." Nick was taunting her in jest. He wished Grandma would find someone else to love. She had been alone for an awful lot of years. Someone deserved to be the beneficiary of her heart, but Nick wasn't sure that Albert hadn't taken hers with him when he left.

"I am content without a man, Nick. Besides, I've given what's left of my heart to my kids. That's enough for me. I'm blessed."

"I know. And so are we, Grandma. So are we."

*   *   *

CHATHAM COUNTY POLICE DEPARTMENT, OCTOBER 15, 9:12 P.M.

"What do you mean you can't find her? What does Kareem say? Well, keep looking, Ricks. Check the airport, the bus station. Geez! Get more men on this if you have to. I want that girl in jail by morning." Bruce Masters closed his cell phone and stuck it in his pocket. He had hoped to be seeing nothing but the backs of his eyelids by now. Instead, he was seeing stars! How could a girl traveling by foot with a baby out-fox the Savannah Police, Chatham County Sheriff, and the Georgia State Patrol? Bruce had all surrounding counties on all-points alert, as well.

Masters reached into his pocket to grab his phone. "Me again. Have you checked out the Willingham place? Figures. I haven't been able to run down Nick Willingham, and he's not at home. I suspect he might be there with his family. No, no, I'll check the homeplace. You get officers to comb every square inch of the acreage. Maybe she's hiding out there. Oh, rats. The Judge is going to kill me. Yeah, go by and tell him we need a search warrant. As much as the Mayor wants these jewels back, we had better cover our tails."

*   *   *

Masters looked through his contacts to retrieve Ashley Willingham's phone number. "Hey, Ashley, I hate to bother you, Sweetheart. We seem to have misplaced Madelyn. She's split. We're trying to secure a warrant for her arrest, but I need to find out where she is so we can pick her up. Can you help me out with that at all?"

Initially, Ashley was hesitant to answer her phone, but finding out where the investigation was leading would be to her advantage. "Arrest her? Are you sure you can do that, Bruce? You know you were legally outside the boundaries of detaining people. I wasn't going to make a stink because I wanted you to find out who did this if there was a chance. But, I hope you have more probable cause than her leaving the funeral home. I don't know if you'll get a judge to sign something like that." Ashley knew Rowland would cave again to Bruce's wishes, but needed to play the part.

"Ashley, I know it's a long shot, but I believe if we get her behind bars, whoever's in on this with her will come crawling out of the slime pit."

"There you go again, Bruce. You've got her tied to this theft. She's got a baby. What's going to happen to that child if you lock her up? You leave him to the likes of Kareem. I don't like it. But to answer your question, no, I have no idea where Madelyn is. I don't even know where the girl lives. Wish I could help with that."

"All right, Lil' Missy. Sorry to bother you. You get some rest. Long day tomorrow." *That girl can be a thorn in a man's side when she wants to be.*

Ashley didn't lie. She didn't know where Madelyn had gone to. She did know that Bruce was out on a limb with this theft, but to apprehend someone who had nothing to do with it wasn't appropriate. *Madelyn, you'd better not be pulling one over on me, girlfriend. You're a master at deceit. I've been fooled by you more than once growing up. You'd best not let me down.* She stood over Bryson who was sleeping soundly in her bedroom in his new pack-and-play. His angelic face was innocently unaware of the lifestyle his mother was entangled in. He didn't get to choose his parents. Yet whether deserved or not, unless there were radical changes in one or both lives, this precious child would have little to no chance of a healthy emotional or spiritual life. She felt a tinge of remorse for not having been a more positive influence in Madelyn's life.

*   *   *

827 VICTORY DRIVE, OCTOBER 15, 9:50 P.M.

The flashlight provided some source of light. Even had there been a full moon, the soaring trees guarding the path to Camp W'ham blocked its illumination. He hadn't braved the dark in these woods for five years, but when he saw the key hanging on Grandma's Pecky Wood key board, he was urged to come and explore. "This could well be the craziest thing I've ever done. The dark creeps me out as much as dead bodies. I don't want to think about that."

Jimmy turned the key in the door, walked into the cabin, and immediately had the wind knocked out of him. Madelyn gave him a mighty punch to the midsection and it brought him to his knees. She spotlighted his face with her flashlight and breathed a sigh of relief.

"Jimmy? What are you doing here?"

"What are *you* doing here?"

"I asked you first." Madelyn really didn't want to go into her details.

"I ... I really don't know. I felt an urge to come. Maybe it was gas."

"No, you probably did. Jimmy, I'm hiding away. I think the law is after me. Did you hear what happened?" Madelyn spent the next few minutes explaining what brought her to stowaway at Camp W'ham.

"You have to believe me, Jimmy. I don't know anything about Grandma's jewels. It's not me. I have a baby who needs me. I've had my share of trouble, Jimmy, but I didn't do anything this time except get rid of drugs, and they're going to lock me up. I just know it."

"Well, let's not jump to any conclusions. You don't know if—"

"Look, Jimmy! Flashlights are everywhere. They're coming. I told you. Please, Jimmy. Help me. What am I going to do?"

"Look, let's take some of these blankets out of the chest, you climb in, I'll pile some back on top and lay some on the bed. Leave the rest to me. Don't suffocate. And whatever you do, don't sneeze!"

Jimmy grabbed a Bible off the table, climbed on the bed, and began reading by flashlight.

Ricks gave a swift kick with his boot thinking he would have to break a lock. The door flew open easily and Jimmy squealed.

"What, what, what? What's going on here? Who are you?"

"Put your hands up. Now!" Ricks spoke with fierce authority.

"Okay, okay. Can you put that gun down? It kind of freaks

me out."

"What's your name?"

"Jimmy Willingham, grandson of Grace."

"Are you here alone?"

"Yes, sir. I've just been sitting here reading my Bible, just reminiscing about my Grandma. I mean, you do know she died? Didn't know if you'd heard, you know. I–I guess you did, eh?"

"Where's Madelyn?"

"I have no idea what you're talking about. My cousin Madelyn, you mean? I just got in from Africa and I really haven't seen much of anybody yet. Barely got to see Grandma before the funeral home closed tonight. Came back here, just been sitting here … you know … reading about the boys–Matthew, Mark, Luke, and John. I'm a missionary. You probably didn't know that since you don't know me. I'm just brushing up on what I need to tell the natives when I get back."

"Yeah, yeah. Mind if we look around, Jimmy?"

"No, no, not at all. Go ahead. Take your time. How many of you guys are there out there? Look at the flashlights! I mean, seriously? Looks like we're being invaded by alien fireflies. I mean, you kind of scared me half to death, you know. You could've knocked first. Of course, I'm a little jumpy by nature. That probably would've had the same effect, actually."

"Mind if I check under the bed there?"

Jimmy scurried out of the way. Ricks gave a quick glance. He had looked behind counters and in cabinets. Jimmy was silently praying and all the while smiling, *Lord, please don't let him open this chest.*

"All right. What else is beyond here, Jimmy?"

"Woods. More woods. Lots and lots of...woods. That's pretty much it. Woods."

"Excuse me a minute." Ricks engaged his handheld two-way radio. "Yeah, she's not here, Bruce. We've scoured these woods. She'd be crazy or awfully brave to be out here at night, or even in the daytime, especially with a baby. I think she's long gone." Ricks was yelling over the two-way.

"You're probably right. It's a spooky place for a baby at night," Bruce responded. "

"It's scary for anybody," Ricks responded.

"Hey, let's use cell instead of two-ways. People scan these things, you know. I'll be turning mine off. You can catch me by cell. Yeah, I know, they can scan those, too. Get out of there and get back to the streets and continue searching."

"10-4. And, the search warrant is on its way. Should be coming at you just anytime now." Ricks signed off.

827 Victory Drive, October 15, 9:54 p.m.

"Someone is coming. Do you think that's Ashley?" Carmen was hoping she would join the rocking party on the porch.

"I called her and she's not coming. She's apparently tied up with another commitment. She'll see us at the funeral home tomorrow."

"Did you let Madelyn know about the services?"

"Goes straight to voicemail. I don't have Kareem's number. Hopefully, she'll hear it on the news or see it in the paper. Other than that, Nora, I don't know how to get word to her. I have no idea where her mom lives, what her number is, nor do I want *that* information. But, honestly, with Madelyn on the run, we need to lay low with our contact. No telling who will be listening in. I left her a voicemail. Hopefully she'll get it. That's all we can do." Nick realized their visitor was driving a squad car. "I'll talk to them. You girls sit tight."

*   *   *

"Nick, hate to bother you so late. You didn't call me this afternoon. We were supposed to have a little chitchat." Masters might not have intended to sound irritated, but his tone suggested he was.

"Oh, yeah, I totally forgot. It's been a few really long days. Sorry, it slipped my mind."

"Do you have a minute? I won't keep you long."

"Sure. I guess. We can go inside if you like. Can I get you some coffee?" Nick offered Masters a chair in the sitting room. Nora and Carmen strained to overhear the conversation.

"No, no, I'll be up all night if I drink that stuff. Been meanin' to ask you, and I don't think we discussed this. Some undertakers don't fasten jewelry, like necklaces and bracelets to the body. They just position them, if you will, because it's easier to hand them to the family at the end of the service and before the body's laid to rest. What's your typical practice?"

"We typically don't fasten, but given the novelty of these jewels and that we were going to such lengths for security, I did clasp the necklace and bracelet."

"Okay, good. Good. It would've been difficult for someone to remove them seems like. What kind of clasp was it?"

"A slide-in with a hinged secure lock. Not really that difficult, actually. Grace said it would have been her choice of clasp, as well."

"I see. You know, Nick, when I joined the force umpteen years ago, I made it a point to know entrances and exits to buildings. I never knew until today that Turner's had a basement."

"Oh, yeah. It's our overflow storage area. We keep our surplus items down there mostly. Seldom if ever used as an exit, really."

"Well, I guess you know it was today?"

Nick offered no response. He sat curiously to see where Bruce was going with his line of questioning.

"I'm really curious, Nick. About a couple of things, actually. Number one, why didn't you tell me about the basement when we were setting up cameras? To law enforcement, that's a pretty important piece of information, especially when they're setting up surveillance."

"I guess I never thought it was of significance. It was off limits to the public from the outside, as well as the inside. Only staff can get down there."

"Is that right? Is Madelyn on payroll at Turner's?" Nick stared back at Bruce. "Cat got your tongue, Nick? How did Madelyn gain access to the basement? How did she even know there was a basement down there? I guess I didn't realize the two of you were so…tight."

"I think you're jumping to a lot of conclusions there, Bruce. You know I helped you most of the day. I have no idea how Madelyn knew there was a basement, nor how she gained entrance."

"You sure did, Nick, you helped out. A lot. Until you were relieved, of course, which was just before Madelyn left the premises."

Nick rose to his feet and stepped over to the door. "Look, Bruce, I don't know what you're implying, but I think we're going to end this conversation. If you want to talk to me any further, you get in touch with my attorney."

"Have you seen Madelyn? We are looking for her, you know. We have reason to suspect she's involved with the theft of your Grandma's jewels. And strangely enough, she's vanished. Baby and all. Would you mind if I looked around for her?"

"You have a search warrant?"

"My men are getting one from the Judge now, Nick."

"Good night, Bruce." Nick opened the door and escorted Masters to his car. The look on Nick's face piqued the girls' curiosity, but even Carmen dared not interfere.

Masters's taillights dimmed before anyone found courage to speak. Nick broke the silence. "They're looking for Madelyn. Nothing to be alarmed about."

"Madelyn? Still? They really think she did it. I knew it! I knew she did it. She's always had sticky fingers? Is she here? Now? Or, do they even know where she is? Have they checked with her deadbeat boyfriend? I do still have friends in this town, and they keep me posted. GG certainly never said anything about the trouble that followed her. Will they arrest her when they find her? What if she's gone and we never see the jewels again?"

"Nora, listen to yourself. You're accusing Madelyn and you have no more proof than they do that she took anything. Let's not get carried away just yet." Nick excused himself and went in to collect his thoughts.

Carmen knew Nick needed a moment. She would give him

some time, then slip away from Nora to find out what was really troubling him. He could fool some, but not his mom. An unsettling feeling swept over her. *They think Nick had something to do with this. O, Lord, please. It can't be.*

Chapter 27

Gladys chased her sleeping pill with wine. She was fully prepared for a more fitful night than the usual given that her thoughts were consumed with Carmen.

Carmen had something she needed to say to her. Gladys's heart altered its rhythm at the thought. She was not the same girl Carmen knew thirty years ago. Life had changed her. She cowered from confrontation. In her better days, she created it. Her nerves were wrecked. Of all the mistakes she could account for in her life, Ralph was the biggest. He had unraveled her dreams and annihilated her will. In an effort to seek revenge on Kyle Hardee, she seduced Ralph Murphy and convinced him to put a two-carat diamond on her finger. She got in head over heels, and before she could undo her misfortune, she was walking down the aisle. She had not slept with Ralph since the honeymoon. He disgusted her. Contrary to rumor, her barrenness was by choice, not an anatomical displacement. No sex, no baby. Imagine that. Her misery bought her the company of a host of emotionally distraught friends at a treatment center in Jacksonville. After her doctors deemed her stable enough to return to society, life felt insensible.

Her disordered mind was of her own doing. Gladys would have abandoned her dastardly plan against Carmen had she realized the toll it would take on her entire family. She never meant for James to become involved to the extent he did. Any hope she had for reestablishing a relationship with Grace had been ambushed by guilt. Her plan to quash public adoration for Carmen served only to deny her serenity.

*   *   *

827 VICTORY DRIVE,
THIRTY-FIVE YEARS PRIOR, 2:20 P.M.

"Hey, guys, come in here." Gladys motioned for Taylor and Jason. She had taken possession of the family room the entire day. Now that she was to be a high school senior, she had more than earned the right to occupy a designated territory. After all, when Grace wasn't around, she was the mistress of the home. No one dared disturb her solitude. She was sitting in the middle of the floor manicuring her fingers and toes. Her extremely cutoff shorts concealed very little of her long, shapely legs. Her magazines were scattered around her on the floor. Her scissors and glue were beside them where she had cut out pictures and articles that interested her most. She carefully disguised her collection of selections in composition notebooks labeled "Projects." Gladys had always had a hankering to keep abreast of the latest gossip about celebrities and their hottest fashions in *Cosmopolitan* and *Vogue*. It was where she learned to adapt her clothing once she distanced herself from her mother's eye for modesty. She loved the freedom of bringing the magazines out in the open when her mother was out of town. Otherwise, Grace would have never tolerated Gladys's favorite ones that took a more liberal approach with a young girl's sexuality. When Grace was home, Gladys had to endure the more wholesome magazines like *Good Housekeeping* and *Woman's Day*. Even though she was now eighteen and old enough to make those decisions for herself, Grace held her to the same standards for living. Her motto was, "My house, my rules." Until Gladys could get out of the household once and for all, she would be left with no choice but to sneak around and try and hide her disobedience. If Jimmy or Carmen either one snitched, they knew firsthand the consequences would not be worth the enjoyment of ratting her out.

Gladys's influence had rubbed off on James. Her brother was, likewise, getting bolder about taking liberties. That is, as long as Grace wasn't around. She would have never tolerated her children crossing any boundaries she had set. They decided "what Mama didn't know wouldn't hurt her." Carmen wanted no part in "disappointing Mom." Gladys had been fed up with Carmen's little walking-the-straight-and-narrow ways for quite a while. The girl was literally too good to be true. It was time Carmen dabbled in mischief, even if it wasn't at her own invitation.

Grace didn't like James's choice of friends this year. Taylor and Jason had stirred a rebellious spirit within her son that challenged Grace's ire. After her initial meeting, she had forbidden James to bring them to her home again. Since she was on one of her mystery excursions, James offered them free rein of the house and amenities. Plans were to drink and be merry at Camp W'ham. They'd clean up the place, discard the beer cans, and Grace would be none the wiser. He knew the rules. Each of them did. When Grace was not home, no one was allowed on the premises. She agreed not to have her friend come in and babysit them now that they were older. There was a trust a parent expected from children who had been reared to understand respect for authority. James was in a season of throwing caution to the wind. The risk was worth any consequences of getting caught.

"If you guys hurry, you could catch Carmen down at the swimming hole. I'm sure she's lonely, if you know what I mean." Gladys taunted them.

"Jim's in the shower. Tell us where it is and we'll head on down there and keep the little lady company." Taylor nudged Jason. He was definitely in. Gladys obliged with copious directions, and the two set foot to path.

"Where did Taylor and Jason go?"

"Keeping Carmen company at the swimming hole. They said to meet them down there."

James couldn't believe what he was seeing. He didn't scream at them. He never tried to make them stop. He only stood there with eyes wider than mouth taking in what he had only viewed in his girlie magazines locked in his safe away from his mama's eyes. He had never seen a real nude body before, and Carmen... well, she was way more blessed than he'd ever detected beneath her modest attire.

"Come on in, the water's fine." Jason was holding Carmen's mouth so she couldn't scream while Taylor was pawing over her body. "It's my turn next, then you can have her," he yelled. "Come on, Jim, whatcha waiting on?"

James didn't understand the fleshly power that possessed him, but the next thing he remembered was raping Carmen himself. When everything was over, Carmen was heaped in a fetal position weeping and shaking. Taylor zipped his pants and reached in his pocket. He opened a switchblade and walked toward Carmen.

"Taylor, what are you doing? Are you crazy?" James grabbed his arm.

Taylor brushed his hand away and held up his finger. "Sssh."

"You don't look happy, honey. You'll be fine in a minute." He patted Carmen on the back. "Here's the deal, Sweetheart. You so much as tell a soul about what went on here today and you will never live to tell another." He took the knife and held it at Carmen's throat. "Nod your head if you're in agreement."

Carmen spit in his face and Taylor retaliated with a slap across hers. He pressed the knife to her cheek. "You want to keep this little face beautiful? You keep your tongue silent. Do ... we ... have ... an ... understanding? You can nod if you agree."

Carmen nodded gently not wanting the knife to penetrate her skin. Taylor released her and began walking away. She gathered her legs around her nakedness and began rocking back and forth. The three boys headed to the camp. James glanced back over his shoulder. His remorseful look was never noticed by Carmen. Her head was buried between her knees. Taylor slapped him on the back. "Man, you've got quite a spread here. You've been holding out on us."

Echoes of laughter and wailing met with calamity at the treetops. Until this day, Camp W'ham had been witness to a righteous history. Like a hovering fog, the secret transgression would congregate in the hearts of Gladys and James by night and linger until defused by the morning light.

*   *   *

Gladys screamed out in her night terror. Like every night for the past thirty years, she would be deprived of a peaceful sleep. She could have avoided the night taunts had she stayed in her room and not been audience to the distasteful scene. Like a debauched coward, she veiled herself behind a tree as her preconceived drama played out before her eyes. The anticipated satisfaction of dethroning Carmen in the eyes of her peers had felt shameful instead. She never thought about the long-term effects. Carmen running away, Mother's anguish over losing her, James becoming her enemy... it was more than she could assimilate, so her mind took a hiatus. Tranquility might have been restored had she confessed to Grace. Her mother tried to liberate her, but Gladys feared the wrath of God for her foul deeds more than the dread of telling Grace. Contrary to what she had been taught by her mother and preachers, Gladys couldn't seem to convince herself that God would absolve her sin. Why would He when she couldn't even forgive herself?

*   *   *

CARMEN'S BEDROOM,
THIRTY-FIVE YEARS PRIOR, 8:23 P.M.

"I know I've been preoccupied with the search for Carmen, but I am very concerned about you. Talk to me, Sweetheart. Tell me what I can do to make things better. You haven't eaten for days. You can't go on like this." Grace brushed the hair from Gladys's eyes. They were hollow. She was apparently disturbed, but Grace surmised she was being swallowed up by grief. She had not left Carmen's room the entire two weeks since Carmen ran away. But no one else knew what had taken place at the swimming hole that day besides those involved. After the big stir in town about her sudden disappearance, Taylor and Jason had informed James of Gladys's involvement and sent word to her that if they went down, she would go with them. Consequently, the two siblings took a vow of silence. She was none too sure that she could live up to her end of the deal.

"We'll find Carmen." Grace pulled Gladys close, and for a moment, Gladys found her voice.

"How does God punish people who are mean, Mother?"

"That's up to God. We know He's a forgiving God. He made provisions for sin through Christ."

"Is being mean a sin?"

"It's not how God would have us live. He encourages kindness, brotherly love, self-control, and a gentle spirit."

"I was mean to Carmen, Mother."

"There were times you were jealous, but we dealt with those issues. You apologized. We prayed about things. Did you ask forgiveness with a sincere heart?"

Gladys picked at the chenille bedspread and stared blankly into space.

"Repentance demands sincerity. That's why Jesus told the

woman caught in adultery, 'Now, go and sin no more.' When we repent of a sin, we have to step out of that lifestyle. If we repeat our sinful acts, were we really sincere about our remorse? One thing for sure, we can't fool God. He knows our heart."

"I hurt Carmen, Mother. I wasn't a good sister."

"Don't worry yourself over what you did in the past, Gladys. If this is why you're depressed, you have to understand that Carmen forgave you, God forgave you, but you have to forgive yourself, too."

"I don't know how to do that. It turns and churns in my head constantly. I was mean to Carmen. Now she's gone and it's all because of me." Gladys's tears were uncontrollable. She tried to talk but couldn't swallow the lump in her throat. Grace held her for the longest time. Her arms were comforting. It was the first time Gladys had allowed her mother to extend tenderness to her since her intense dislike for Carmen had manifest shortly after the adoption.

Hate was a forbidden word in the Willingham home. Surely Gladys had not reached that extreme, but the responsibility she shared for what happened to Carmen found nourishment from the source. Fear invaded her very soul for the consequences accompanying that kind of sin. Her voice retreated to the depths of her sinister soul and locked the door behind it. She would keep the secret buried. To reveal it now would only serve to hurt her mother more deeply. For now, Gladys would incur her deserved pain. The only solace she found was as long as she was hurting, she wasn't hurting anyone else.

*   *   *

Gladys buried her hands in her face. "You should have just said what you wanted to say to me today, Carmen. Why couldn't you have stayed away? Why did you come back? To torture me? What happened to you didn't change you one bit, but it wrecked my life."

Gladys reached for her prescription bottle. She needed to get rest somehow. Perhaps a second one would knock her out for the remainder of the night. She had a funeral to attend tomorrow. After that, she would proceed with her plans for a better life.

*   *   *

BAY STREET, SAVANNAH, GEORGIA, OCTOBER 15, 10:03 P.M.

Tourists began to busy the streets of Savannah after an eventful Friday night shopping on Broughton and partying on River. Seldom was the city quiet during daylight hours, even on Sundays. With the revitalization of Savannah, it had become a melting pot of varied attractions.

The jewels were secured at the base of the third tree at the second block of Emmet Park which was sandwiched between Bay Street and Factors Walk. Luckily, the early morning rain didn't last long, but wisdom dictated to check out the location for any sign of disturbance. It was risky with many eyes about, but a bigger risk to have someone discover the hidden treasure.

The umbrella dropped exactly on the spot that needed a closer inspection. *Ah, there you are.* A tug on the rope would give the peace-of-mind answer. *Nice. Still good and tight.* A quick stirring of the leaves to camouflage the jeweled site drew no attention from passersby.

You'll soon be coming home with me, little jewels. You're safe for now. I'll be back later. We'll give it an appropriate mourning period, then, I'll rescue you once and for all.

*   *   *

LILLY'S BAR, POOLER, GEORGIA,
OCTOBER 15, 10:48 P.M.

James had been staring at his shot glass since half past ten. He had no taste for what he came here for. He hadn't been able to stay home another minute. Valerie was intolerable. The girl had griped and badgered him constantly since Grace's death. All he had heard since he walked in the door tonight was her whiney, shrill voice asking, "How much do you think the jewels are worth?" He could only say he didn't know so many ways. After that, her conjecturing of their value would have to suffice. For the time being, they were worth nothing, because they were in someone else's hands.

But, Valerie's irritating voice was not the overriding one in his head tonight. He could not shake free of Carmen's gentle, kind, forgiving tone. How was it possible for a heart to forgive such an egregious sin? While technically it was not exactly incestuous, on its face it was certainly suggestive of incest. This is the kind of absolution Grace said her God possessed. James had battled his guilt of Carmen's disaster privately, but harbored his anger of Annie's death openly. He couldn't get forgiveness from God as long as he continued to wrangle with forgiving himself day in and day out. Tormenting demons had occupied his soul. James found it easier to distance himself from God. Alcohol, women, and gambling became his satiating substitutes. Until some five hours ago, at least. His taste for escape was momentarily curbed.

*　　　*　　　*

TWO MONTHS AFTER ANNIE'S FUNERAL, JAMES WILLINGHAM'S LIVING ROOM, 10:37 A.M.

"James, I'm not going to stand by and watch you get deeper into the pit of depression and dependency without voicing my strong disapproval."

"Flash for Grace: I'm a grown man. I don't need Mama's approval anymore."

Grace picked up the half-emptied whiskey bottle, stepped into the mud bath, and poured it down the drain.

"There's more where that came from. It's not going to work." Jim held up a full bottle of Jack Daniels and tipped it at Grace.

"It's not even noon, James. You're going to become dependent on alcohol and you'll be of no value to anyone. You could lose your job. And your children. I won't allow them to live with you under these conditions."

"Well, Mama, I figure you can just pray for your God to fix it. You think He can fix anything. But He didn't fix Annie, did He? What kind of God could let a woman as sweet as Annie get cancer, and then let her die? That's a little confusing to me."

"God isn't the author of confusion. Satan is. And confusion leads to defeat."

"Well, I have another flash for the lady. I've already lost the game! I got crushed, trounced, annihilated. He took my team. I'm toast. And, He took my heart… but left the pain." Jim poured himself another round and gulped it down.

"You don't get to quit in life, James. I know. I've been there. Don't you think I have a sense for how difficult it is to live without the person you love more than life itself? It's hard. I'll be the first to admit that. But you can't quit. You have responsibilities."

"Yeah, well, we all can't have the strength and perseverance of the famous Grace Carissa Willingham." Jim's tone had grown from loud to condescending.

"You can draw from the same source I did, James Willingham. You are the only one who can change your will in this. God's not going to force His love, comfort, or peace on you. But He can save you from yourself if you allow it."

"Well, He'd have His hands full with my sin."

"James, grace is always—"

"Greater than sin. Yeah, yeah, got it. I can quote them all still. My name's on your kitchen wall. Remember?" He laid his head back on his chair and closed his eyes. "You can leave, Mama. I don't feel like any more company right now."

"You have a choice, James. You can stay angry at God for Annie's illness and death, or you can thank Him for the time you had with her and what the two of you created together. That's what she would want for you." Grace's voice had been tender and patient, but she knew the safety and protection of the children had to be firmly broached.

"If you continue on this path, mark my word, James, I will take these children out of your custody. They will not grow up bearing witness to objectionable behavior. They're young, James. They're not able to take care of themselves if you're passed out drunk on the couch. I won't allow it. Not on my watch. These children lost their mother. They don't need to lose their father, too."

"Good-bye, Grace."

*   *   *

I just couldn't tell you that I believed God was punishing me for what I did to Carmen. And it cost Annie her life. I know you would have explained to me that God doesn't work that way. I was going to let you talk me through that after all these years. That's why I had come to your house that morning. The Coroner said you hadn't been gone long at all. Your body was still warm. If I had just gotten up an hour earlier, or you could have held on just one more day, I could have righted a wrong I'd kept from you for so long. It wasn't your fault. I wouldn't let you in because I knew I thought it would hurt you beyond unconditional love. Now I have one more regret to add to the laundry list. I was going to confess it all. Why? I don't know. But I do know that I'm really tired of being a fraud.

James pushed the glass away. It was time he started to get his life in order. He had bigger bears than alcohol to skin, but it was time to come clean for the sake of his children who despised him. He didn't know what that timeline entailed, but as Grace had drilled into him many times, "Time is in His hands, not ours."

Chapter 28

Bruce Masters rolled up to the Victory Drive manor. He intended to search Grace Willingham's place himself for Madelyn. He had a hunch she was still in town. There's no way she would miss Grace's funeral. Officers were watching Kareem. If he was behind the theft, he and his hooligans would smoke her out. The poor girl would probably rather the law find her than Kareem. He had two reasons to track her—the jewels and his only boy child. If Kareem wasn't in with her, then Nick was the next obvious. It's possible the girl could have found the basement on her own; he would acknowledge that. But questioning Nick met with strong resistance and that caught his attention. Masters had experienced walls of defense before, and there was typically a reason for taking cover behind the walls. Of course, after interviewing the Willinghams, there was good reason to suspect most of them.

"Where's your warrant, Bruce?"

Masters handed Nick the warrant to search the premises signed by Judge Rowland. Nick stepped aside and allowed the detective entrance. Masters and two deputies combed through the house. Every nook and cranny was explored. Upstairs, downstairs, and even the wrap-around porch.

"Satisfied? Haven't seen or spoken to Madelyn, Bruce. There must've been a hundred officers on this property looking for her. I think you need to be searching elsewhere. We do have a funeral tomorrow. It's been a couple of very long days and everyone's tired." Nick respected the law, but there had to be boundaries at some point. He knew they were pushing their luck with unlawful detention of numerous citizens for more than twenty-four hours. It was Grandma's jewels they were trying to recover, but he deduced they had no concrete proof for their investigation.

"Could I check your cell phone, Nick?"

"Uh, okay." Nick put in his password and handed his phone to Masters.

"I'll just look over your shoulder. I'm not used to those fancy phones. Do you have Madelyn's number in your contacts?"

"No, but I did call her."

"Do you know which number it is? Look at your recent calls."

"Not sure I would recognize it, but I have a sense for what time it was."

"Read me off all the numbers you have there of the calls you made after twelve noon yesterday, if you would, including the ones that have contact names. Slowly. I'm writing them down."

Nick read him the numbers, many of which included media. He found the exercise senseless, but thought cooperation was wise. "I believe the one with fifteen seconds is where I attempted to contact Madelyn and left her a voicemail that Grandma's funeral was at three. Then, I hung up."

"Where'd you get her number?"

"Hmm, good question. Where did I get her number? It's probably on the list of family members at the office. Sorry. I'm tired. Best I can tell you tonight."

"Thanks, Nick. If you see her, you need to let us know. We have a warrant for her arrest."

"Seriously? You have proof that Madelyn took the jewels?"

"We have reason to believe that since she's the only one who broke out after being in lockdown."

"Without authority. You know you didn't have the right to do that, and if any citizen wanted to challenge you on that, they bloody well could, Bruce."

"You're touchy when it comes to Madelyn, eh, Nick?"

"Good night, Detective."

*   *   *

827 VICTORY DRIVE, OCTOBER 15, 11:12 P.M.

"Nick, there's another car. Who would it be this time?" Nora was visiting with Carmen on the porch. Nick was making a fresh pot of coffee.

"Oh, great. I don't know, Nora, but I'll be right out."

"Ashley? Is that you?" Nora ran down the stairs to help her with whatever it was she was struggling with. "When did you have a baby? GG didn't say a word about that last time I talked to her. I didn't even know you were seeing anybody. You look great to have just had—"

"Nora, sshhh! He's sleeping. And he's not mine. This is

Madelyn's baby." Ashley handled the baby carrier awkwardly. She had no idea how Madelyn dragged this heavy thing around everywhere.

"What are you doing with Madelyn's baby? Where is she? The law is looking for her. They've been here off and on all night. Do you know where she is? They think she stole Grandma's jewels. Well, we know she's always had sticky fingers. She couldn't keep her—"

"Nora, chill. Let's not jump to any conclusions about Madelyn. She may not be involved in this at all. Let's go inside. Grab that diaper bag, would you?"

"Ashley? Is that really you? I'm Carmen. It's so nice to meet you." Carmen gave Ashley a genuine hug, and the sincerity was exchanged.

"I'm so glad you made it safely. I've wanted to meet you since Nick arrived in town, but I know you stay busy with the Child Recovery Center. It's really amazing what you've done for abandoned children. Grandma was very proud of your accomplishments."

Nick didn't give Carmen a chance to respond to Ashley's greeting. "Ashley, what are you doing with Madelyn's baby? Do you know where she is?"

"No, I really don't, Nick. She knocked on my door, told me she couldn't trust anyone else with him, and she thought the law would be looking for her. Sounds like she was right." Ashley continued to keep the volume of her voice low so as not to wake the baby.

"Yeah, they're pressing hard. What do you think? Did she do it?" Nick wanted to find out if Ashley knew anything at all. But she could keep a stone face if she had to. Unless she was willing to say, you'd never know it by her body language.

"I don't think she did, Nick. I really don't. She was very convincing. I think I have a good read on people, but Madelyn's a colorful character. So, she could be lying through her teeth for all I know. I'd like to give her the benefit of the doubt. Plus, Bryson doesn't deserve being dragged around.

"Kareem will fight you over this baby if he finds out you're in charge." Nick could see this working up to be a really tangled web. And he didn't want trouble with Kareem at Grace's home nor the funeral parlor.

"I've already made arrangements for someone to keep him during the funeral. I don't want any disturbance there. I knew you guys were here, and it's not often that we get to be together. Wish it wasn't for this occasion, but I did want to visit. I went and bought some baby products since he came with nothing but the clothes on his back, dumped them at home, and I came right on out here. It took me awhile. I'm a novice at this baby stuff."

Carmen had made Bryson a makeshift bed on the floor. They grabbed cups of coffee and made their way to the rockers. Ashley and Nora shared bits and pieces of life. Carmen talked about her passion for her business and talked about a couple of remarkable success stories. Nick was quietly giving thought to the day's events, as well as the upcoming funeral. He was hoping it would come together and be the celebration Grace had requested.

"Oh, no, here we go again. Is that another cop?" Nora tapped Nick encouraging him to take care of things for the girls.

Nick walked to the edge of the porch. "Who's there? Answer me. Who are you?"

Madelyn whispered, unsure of who might be around. "Nick, it's me. And Jimmy."

"Madelyn?" Nick raced down the stairs. Everyone jumped to their feet in disbelief.

"Did you see how many cops were on the property? There were scads of them out there. I was so glad that I decided to visit the camp. I was a great decoy, actually. I kind of saved the day. I guess that would make me a hero of sorts." Jimmy was kidding, but did feel a bit puffed up for throwing them off her trail.

"You were a lifesaver, Jimmy. He thinks fast on his feet," Madelyn praised.

"I think the same way off of them, thank you very much," and Jimmy laughed at himself.

"Guys, what are you going to do now?" Nick needed to know Madelyn's intentions.

"Guys? I'm not being tracked by the law. She is. I'm staying here," Jimmy quickly interjected.

"Ashley? Where's Bryson?" Madelyn charged up the stairs. "Did someone take him? Tell me, please. Where's my baby?"

"Madelyn, it's okay. He's fine. He's inside asleep. Calm down." Ashley had forgotten she would be concerned about her baby. Of course, she would be.

"Everything is going to be all right, Maddie." Carmen walked over and held her for the familiar four-second squeeze. Madelyn's heart melted. No one had called her Maddie except Granny Grace. Nor had she been hugged with the kind of genuine touch of Granny. Tonight she needed the two more than she had realized.

Carmen assumed the motherly role of the grandkids of

Grace Willingham and ordered them to their rockers to take five minutes to catch their breath. "We don't get opportunities like this often. God is in control of this situation, Maddie. You relax. I really think they're gone for the night. Tomorrow might be a different story for you. They're going to be watching for you at the funeral. The best we can hope for is that they'll let you sit through the service before they do anything. We'll see what we can do, if necessary."

"Why do they want to arrest me? I haven't done anything. Guys, you all have to believe me. I didn't take Granny's jewels. I promise you. I didn't. You do believe me, don't you?"

Nick was the first to speak up. "No one's doubting you, Madelyn. I think we all have to keep our heads. You do need to get an attorney lined up. And, I don't think it's a good idea for Ashley to be the one." Nora didn't necessarily want to be lumped into the category of no one doubting, but she kept the button on her lip.

"Agreed," Ashley said.

"I don't have the money for an attorney, Nick."

"We'll worry about that later." Nick would call his local attorney in the morning and let him be prepared to defend her.

"The State will appoint you one, Madelyn. But, with something this big, you might want to let Nick help you if he can. I'm going to try and keep my nose clean on this one. I have to practice in this town." Ashley was thinking of conflict of interest. If Masters talked about aiding and abetting, her career life could become complicated in an instant. She would make some calls to some of her attorney comrades if necessary, but she would take Nick's lead. He exuded confidence, and she trusted his judgment.

"Guys, let's slow down a bit. Let's not talk about that aspect of our lives anymore tonight. Let's just enjoy one another. It's been a difficult day for all of us. Besides, some of you haven't seen one another in years. I haven't met any of you until now. I mean, of course, other than Nick. And, Maddie, I'm Carmen. I should have introduced myself pre-hug, but it's a pleasure to meet you. Mom talked so much about you, I feel as though I know you. She loved you dearly." Carmen's advice was exactly what everyone wanted and needed to hear.

Madelyn's eyes filled with tears, but they didn't wash away her fears. Everyone agreed they would sit on Grace's porch and reminisce about the collection of memories around the home-place. Jimmy started with his tales of Grandma, followed by Nora. Each had baskets full of memories. Some tales brought them to laughter, others to tears. The night wore on, midnight, one, two, three o'clock. Fresh pots of coffee and snacks were consumed in Grace's memorable kitchen. Hilarity conflicted with tears until they arrived at a satisfying truce. Each of them recited memory verses and added a new date beside their name for each one they could deliver flawlessly. They flipped through the faded skirted artwork and compared levels of skill. Carmen assumed Grace's role as they added their final mark to Grace's "Measure of Life" growth chart. Madelyn was touched to see Bryson's assigned spot. When Grace was with them, everyone's birthday met with assessing physical growth as well as sharing the spiritual growth they experienced during the year. Meeting with tradition, Carmen quizzed each Willingham grandchild for an update. If God allowed Grace to listen, she would have boasted of their increase in understanding since the last report. Madelyn's was a recent revelation, ostensibly initiated by the loss of Grace. Nora was struggling, an obvious fence-straddler. She would need cushioning with prayer, and although timid in her request, her appeal was encouraging. Jimmy was on fire for the Lord and his zeal was comically adorable. Ashley's heart still mirrored the heart of Grace. Her compassionate firmness was a tenacity God would use in extraordinary ways. Nick surprised his mother with the depth of his gift of discernment. He was a take-charge man. He credited his business head to Grace, as well as his desire to preserve the faith. Positive reports, but sprinkled within each update was some weakness in the flesh. It was a bitter spring mix tossed with weaknesses in anger, codependency, bitterness, envy, and sensuality. They had been well-tutored by Grace. Each knew in order to overcome limitations, the first step was admission, the next to seek prayer from a good warrior. Bryson slept like all babies deserve—peaceful and safe.

"Let's watch the sunrise on the porch, guys." Carmen commandeered the troops in fine Grace Willingham style. Madelyn had actually forgotten that her well-being was in peril. She had relaxed and melded into a familial feeling. She couldn't recall a time she had felt as accepted by the youngster Willinghams. It was a sense of contentment she had scarcely known her entire tumultuous life. She could get used to the idea of belonging.

*   *   *

GRANDMA GRACE'S HOMEPLACE,
OCTOBER 15, 4:53 A.M.

"We are going to be zombies at the funeral. I can't believe

we've stayed up all night." Nick knew his day was going to be somewhat frantic, and that he might regret not having crashed for a couple of hours at least. But they were all young enough to work through it, and Carmen tough enough.

"I want to hear the story about Albert. I've only heard it once."

"We all have only heard it once, Nora. Grandma told each one of us the same way at the same age." Ashley wanted to make sure Nora didn't feel excluded from anything. She had always had the tendency to feel a bit slighted.

"So you girls heard it at the same place as we did? Wow, that's weird." Jimmy had never really considered that Grandma wouldn't make a distinction with the girls and the boys.

"No, it's not weird. It's Grandma." Ashley was quick to correct him.

"Carmen, you tell it. You seem the likely candidate."

"You think so, Maddie?" Everyone agreed and encouraged her to tell the story of the man who stole the heart of Grace Carissa Willingham and left her to face the world alone with kids. Her perseverance was a huge part of her enigmatic legacy. Grace had made the best of a really bad situation for which she credited to the God she served.

Chapter 29

It was late. Too late to go calling on anyone, but Bruce Masters had to get some answers tonight. He knew Ashley would be the last to know where Madelyn might be, but he was hoping she might be able to give him some much-needed insight about Nick. Something about that man troubled him clear down to his size 13 sole.

He rang the doorbell, knocked, then banged on the door. Still no sign of disturbance from inside. *Surely she's home. Where would that girl be this late at night with her grandmother's funeral tomorrow?* He felt a little intrusive shining his flashlight in her window, but he was in his uniform. Duty prevailed.

"Well, what do we have here, Lil' Miss Ashley? Are those baby items on your floor there? You little stinker. You didn't even so much as let on when I called you earlier. I guess I didn't ask you all the right questions. You're a smart one for sure. You might not know where Madelyn is, but you certainly were caught by surprise to acquire her baby. Interesting. Very interesting. You

Willinghams. There's a lot more to you all than you let on to folks. I guess blood really is thicker than water."

*   *   *

EAST SAVANNAH CHRISTIAN CHURCH PARKING LOT,
OCTOBER 16, 4:25 A.M.

James Willingham pulled again and again on the church doors. *What happened to the day when church doors could be left unlocked? People have reasons to go in and pray. People, that's why. People like the ones I'm tangled up with, at least. That's enough reason to keep everything locked tight.*

James had been in the parking lot of East Savannah Christian since leaving the bar. When he finally got nerve enough to go in, the church was locked tight. He sat in his car and stared at the church's impressive steeple. At an appointed time today in this church, the preacher would speak words about Grace's affluent and bountiful life. He had been away from this church for many years. Grace, however, had been a strong pillar. James couldn't come and sit in a pew week after week bearing his guilt, being angry at God, at least, not in the same building with his mom. He was fine at his church. He was a big name with a big position, and no one questioned his lifestyle. Ever. They wanted his money too badly, he supposed. Why else would Christians allow immorality, drunkenness, and questionable integrity to infuse a service where they were worshipping God? He could throw back his shoulders, hold his head high, and walk away from a sermon only to return to his godless lifestyle. He would have never been able to pull that off with Grace Willingham among the membership.

Today's clarity could have offered better judgment years ago. In hindsight, it would have been prudent for him to remain involved at East Savannah. Grace had taught him about the consequences of poor decisions. Had he made the right choice and stayed, he would not have been entrapped in a gambling ring and in more debt than he could possibly pay back in a lifetime, especially on his salary. Winning streaks tempted him to roll the dice again and again instead of paying the debt down while he was ahead. Losers are the most gullible in believing winning streaks will last. At the end of many nights, James found himself in a bottomless grave of insurmountable debt. It was a dead-end street. That indebtedness led him to Kareem. Now, he was enmeshed with a drug lord and had compromised his integrity, position, the town he loved, his family legacy, and possibly his freedom.

Valerie was his only floatation device. She had managed to amass a small fortune from her career as a trophy wife for her one-foot-in-the-grave victims. James was her youngest husband, and he was no spring chicken. He wasn't sure how secure he felt in that knowledge, but the prospect of dying soon seemed more plausible to him than ever. She had been generous initially and tapped into her funds when he needed to balance debts. That generosity accompanied a promissory note as well as a promise of Grace's fortune in the form of *Honey, whatever I get is yours.* Her curiosity as to the net value of Grace Willingham could never be satisfied. Truth was, no one knew her worth. She kept her business to herself. Valerie had her eye on the jewels and the property. Had she been privy to the knowledge that James had been excised from Grace's Will, she would have been long gone, and his creditors would have dumped him in the Savannah River. Their eyes were on the novel jewels, as well. James had feared for Grace's safety on more than one occasion. Valerie was his salvation once she set her gold-digger sights on him and loosened her purse strings.

James recalled his desperate moments when he searched for Grace's hideaway for her prize jewels. He felt relief amidst his shame. Had he found them, he might never be having this moment of true confessions about his state of peace. Had Grace been privy to all his high jinx, she would have been disappointed, but mostly broken-hearted. *Maybe it's best I didn't talk to you, Mama. Maybe God knew exactly when to call you home. Your heart didn't deserve to experience any more disappointment from your only son.*

James looked out his window, turning his eyes away from the church. He had some hard-core soul-searching to do. How would he break free from this noose? There wasn't much hope without a pot of gold, and his rainbow was nowhere to be seen. The plans he entertained to create the financial means for escape were less than honorable. There was no more rolling the dice now. His house of cards had fallen. *Why didn't I listen to you, Mama? You never gave up trying to get me to see the error of my ways. But that doesn't change a thing now, because I didn't listen to you! I heard you, but I simply ignored your wisdom.*

James hit the dashboard with his hands, then grabbed the steering wheel and banged his head repeatedly hoping if he struck it hard enough, he might wake up from his nightmare. His torment was futile frustration. He vacillated from anger to humility, from frustration to deprivation. To sum up his state of mind this moment, James was a broken man. *This is exactly what Mama prayed for me all these years—brokenness. She loved me wisely.*

I ignored her foolishly.

*   *   *

THE MAYOR'S OFFICE, NINE YEARS PRIOR, 10:15 A.M.

"Did you have an appointment, Mama? I have someone else coming in I believe. I can check with Gloria, but I'm pretty sure someone else is scheduled. I can't afford to run behind today. I have too many irons in the fire."

"Susan Chambers is scheduled. That would be me. I figured I'd have to get in by way of disguise if I was going to see my son."

"What do you need, Grace?" James busied himself in paperwork. When Grace called on him, he would have to endure the harangue, make a few comments, or not, and she'd be on her way. The woman was relentless in her efforts to win her son's soul back from Satan.

"I'm concerned about you, James. You've ignored your children. They scarcely know you. Jimmy needs you so badly. He's become quite the rebel these days. Reminds me a lot of you in your rebellious years, only not nearly as distressed. His insolence stems from much of the same source as yours—he needs a dad in his life. You didn't have a choice. Your dad was gone. He doesn't have a choice either, but his dad lives in the same town. You can't tell me you want Jimmy growing up like you with a heart full of anger and resentment for what he's been denied during the critical years emerging into manhood. With Ashley, you've at least acknowledged paternity. She hangs onto every look you give her, every touch, but she longs for much more. She needs a daddy who will dance with her, who will protect her, who will teach her how a man should respect a woman, and who won't embarrass her with his lifestyle. Nora and Madelyn have never experienced acceptance from you at all. You fathered those girls, regardless of the lack of sound judgment involved. It's not those girls' faults their mothers were not someone you loved, no more than it's Jimmy's and Ashley's fault that Annie was someone you did."

James's heart and mind stopped, but his hands continued to shuffle papers in an attempt to send the message to Grace that she wasn't fazing him. He didn't know how to make things right with his kids. There would be so much explaining that he knew he would fail miserably. If Grace knew how deeply involved he was in unbecoming lifestyles, she would understand why he would distance himself from his children. They deserved a better man. With her in control of their lives, he knew they would get the guidance they needed. He did receive direction. He simply made poor choices in friends one school year. After he stepped off God's chosen path, he never got secure footing again. When the event with Carmen occurred, it was too late. He couldn't turn back. How could a man who would do a thing so despicable to his sister—not a blood sister, thank goodness, but his sister nonetheless, or anyone for that matter—how could he be trusted to rear godly children? James wanted to make Annie proud. If God wasn't punishing him through Annie, James doled out the punishment himself. He felt responsible for Annie's death. He didn't deserve anything as wonderful as the children for whom she sacrificed her life.

Grace interrupted his thoughts. "I want to ask you, Son. Do you blame yourself for Annie? Is there something that gnaws at you about that?"

There! She did it again. How does she read my thoughts? Is a mother that intimate with her child? Is she so intimate with God that He would whisper the secrets of my soul to her?

"I've always detected that you blamed yourself for her death, that you feel somehow you deserved to lose her. What is it, James? Talk to me. I want to help you step out of your prison. It keeps you hostage. You and Gladys have demons that haunt you. I can't lay my finger on it, but they are torturing you both. Had I not been obedient in my walk with the Lord and done my very best to give you both godly guidance, I might blame myself. I won't allow that to rob me of my peace. I did my best. I wasn't perfect by any stretch, but I did my best. God knows it, I know it, and that settles it. But if you feel I failed you in some way, then, I need your forgiveness."

The truth held hostage at the bottom of his soul was screaming for release, but the demon that guarded it denied it pardon. It would be the opportune time for James to come clean with his mom, restore the relationship he missed desperately, and step in and become the dad he knew he could be. His tongue was on lockdown. His voice was lost at sea. The words slipped back into his soul's abyss and might never be as close to claiming freedom again.

"You're conflicted, James. You appear prideful, but I believe it's a front. The Bible tells us that God opposes the proud but shows favor to the humble. That pride is forbidding you to do what's right. Humble yourself, James. There is nothing that God won't forgive. The same is true for me. God's love is like that of a parent's—unconditional. But He does expect repentance.

"It's never too late, James. You don't get to turn back the hands of time, but you can make an impact for the time you have left. God knows all our quirks and foibles, but He loves us just the way we are. It's left up to each of us to discover the beauty and the duty of His love."

James stopped shuffling papers but couldn't bring himself to look at his mom. Grace took her purse and headed for the door. She turned the handle, looked back at James for one last effort. The words she spoke resound still today from the walls that bore witness to their legitimacy. "There's a godly man trapped inside you, James Albert Willingham II. Set him free and live."

*   *   *

"Father, please forgive me. I have sinned against You. I have littered the landscape of my life! I have discredited a good woman's name. But I am in so deep in wrongdoing that I'm not sure even You can fix it. If you are half the God Mama put her trust in, then I surrender to you. I'll confess to everything. But, please, Lord, give me strength, show me mercy, and grant me time to make things right with my children."

James recalled one winter coming downstairs at one o'clock in the morning. Grace was in the living area but not in her usual praying position.

"Are you talking to God, Mama?"

"No. Tonight I'm listening to see what He has to say to me."

So James sat silently without contemplation, waiting on God's counsel. Time had no value. No urgency. He couldn't remember a time when he witnessed the night's tranquility bridge the gap between darkness and light and welcome the new dawn.

Chapter 30

South of Gaston was located this side of Hell. No one respectable would be seen on the streets of this locale. Those kinds of folks had exited when the gangs moved in. Abandonment was stamped at every route. Businesses flaunted boarded-up windows, iron bars, chains, and graffiti. Warehouses long since abandoned were decorated with broken panes by idle hands of unsupervised youthful boys waiting for induction into one of the raucous gangs. There were no sounds of children playing in the streets. People used caution entering and exiting their cars when going about daily life. The elderly residents lived in fear of being looted and/or physically harmed.

Every city has its own South of Gaston where crime plagues the area. Savannah was no different. The law frequented this neighborhood, but only upon demand. The stench that assaulted the district was produced from more than urine and heaps of garbage. The smell of death lingered from one fatality to another. When undesirable business needed to be handled beyond the eyes of the law, back alleys harbored secrets of the "hows" and "whos," and divulged only remnants of the "whats" that remained.

Kareem had been summoned by Hawk, The Boss. No one begged off an appointment with him. A man could run but couldn't hide from the influence Hawk mounted. Kareem was barely able to stand waiting to face the meaning behind his order for a meeting. His legs felt as weak as water and could falter at any given moment. There were few men he feared, and he would soon be face to face with one.

*   *   *

"What's up with you, Reem? You can't keep up with a woman? You're pathetic." The sinister gentleman was escorted to the alley in a black extended-stretch limo with four bodyguards. His zoot-style suit was an exaggerated '40s fashion, flashing a loosely-fit jacket with padded shoulders and high-waisted tapered pants. The featured Rolex watch dangled from his waist below his right knee. His stoic face was ready for answers.

"Hawk, I don't know. She split on me, man. Didn't say nothin'. Wet my drugs. Wiped me out and took my bread. I'll get her. Don't worry."

"Does she have the jewels?" Hawk didn't care for excuses. They portrayed a man as weak and insignificant. He was a bottom-line man.

"I don't know. She told me she didn't snag 'em, but she lies like a dog. I'd've wasted her a long time ago except for the jewels. If she ran, she has them." Kareem was scrambling to give Hawk answers that would satisfy.

"If I don't get my jewels, Reem, you pay. I mean, you know it has to go down like that, don't you? It's the law of the street. It's Hawk law."

"Boss, I can't help it that she split on me. She took off from the funeral home and didn't say a thing to me. I haven't seen her since. I've got eyes out for her. Give me some time."

Hawk held up his index finger to hush Kareem. He wasn't interested in excuses. "You have 'til midnight... tonight. That's it."

"Come on, Hawk. Give me some more time than that. Give me at least forty-eight hours."

"The ol' woman's being put down today at three. If the girl's in town, she'll show for that. Don't let her get away from you. Bring her to me. I'll take it from there. Twelve tonight at Montgomery. With or without the girl. Don't disappoint me, 'Reem."

"But I need—"

Two of the escorts walked up to Kareem. One held him while the other encouraged him not to question Hawk's edict. Kareem was left heaving in the alley as Hawk's stretch rolled out of sight. His delivery of Madelyn would be a challenge. But if he wanted to live, he had to entreat the help of insiders to make it happen. As soon as he could walk and breathe at the same time, he would get a plan together. She could go down, but he wasn't ready. Nor was he ready to take on the responsibility of a son, but his mother would take in another child until Bryson was old enough to take care of himself. Then he could hang with his dad. It would be an experience. He could get used to the company.

*　　*　　*

GLADYS FAYE WILLINGHAM-MURPHY'S HOME,
OCTOBER 16, 4:16 A.M.

Gladys's attempts at sleep were futile. Two sleeping pills in a night's time chased with a glass of wine should have knocked her off her socks by now. She had paced the floor. Tried to read a book. Opened the refrigerator and indulged in not one but two pieces of death-by-chocolate cheesecake to appease her angst. The television brought no comfort. She had been tormented for hours. Fear had taken her hostage for the night.

What exactly was it that Carmen had wanted to say to her for a long time? This was it—her moment of reckoning. Gladys would now have to face her sins. She had allowed her jealousy to completely reign in her life. From reign to ruin. That had been the fate that followed.

She threw the covers from her legs and sat on the side of her bed. She pressed her face in her hands, wringing at her eyes. *I will be a sight for sore eyes tomorrow, Mother. I'm just a mess. Didn't I throw away everything you taught us your whole life? I not only cluttered up my life, but I wreaked havoc with James's and Carmen's. Who knows how it has affected Jason and Tyler all these years? Neither was a shining citizen, but they didn't need that deed added to their plate of cruelties.*

What have I done? Why didn't I tell you, Mother? I should have confessed to you. That would have made it easier to confess to God. I was so afraid that you would love me less. You should have, but knowing your heart, you would have made things better somehow. I have lived my whole life regretting what I did, because

it was unforgiveable. To know I caused you pain over a child you
saved from a horrible past by giving her another past to overcome,
I am undeserving of forgiveness, from you or the Lord.

Gladys's agony was incessant. She had pushed the replay button in her head many times in early morning fits of unrest to hear the comforting words her mother had spoken years ago.

*   *   *

EAST COAST COUNSELING CENTER, FEBRUARY 3, TWENTY-TWO YEARS PRIOR, 3:10 P.M.

Grace Willingham had visited Gladys in Jacksonville every weekend family was allowed to call on their loved ones. It was a beautiful facility with flower gardens to meander about the grounds and enjoy the open space. The administration area was welcoming and warmly contemporary. Beyond the sane world, however, the atmosphere was sterile and institutional. Furnishings were straight-line, box-type firmly-padded sofas and chairs. No fluff was afforded for pleasing the eye. Safety was of utmost priority. Residents who were not blessed with visitation stared aimlessly or wandered from group to group hopeful for an invitation to join in the conversation.

Gladys had come to East Coast eight months ago to the day. She had been on Grace's top-priority prayer inventory for the past eight years. She had noticed a decline in her daughter's fire for life after Carmen had left home. To a mother's intuition, Gladys acted as though Carmen's departure was somehow her fault. Despite repeated inquiries by Grace, Gladys never revealed a word that would lead her to suspect anything other than the sibling rivalry Grace had dealt with appropriately. But Grace had a strong hunch there was something more than her unhappiness in marriage that kept Gladys depraved in spirit.

Grace was never convinced Ralph was the one for Gladys. Try and tell that to a young girl who has her eyes set on wedding bells. She wanted a wedding and would have no part of hearing what Grace had to say about marrying your best friend and being romantically attracted to your spouse for a lifetime. Grace knew the look of love. It was far removed from Gladys's face when she looked at Ralph.

Discontentment had settled into Gladys's heart. Nothing Grace might say changed her unoccupied, cold, lifeless sentiment that sheltered her heart. A mother can narrowly endure watching one of her very own living days without purpose, devoid of joy and lacking peace. It was as though Gladys was an abandoned child, one who had not experienced a loving touch, an encouraging word, or an expression of acceptance. She had been bathed in all the balms of harmony a child could need to be assured of unconditional love. Yet Gladys's eyes reflected only a lost, contemptuous gaze.

"Gladys, I hope you know how special you have always been. You are my joy. I remember when I first held you. I knew God had blessed me in a way that I never dreamed possible. I only thought I knew how to love until you. Your dad had taught me much about that strange phenomenon. But when you were born, you extended those boundaries for both of us. You were his prize. The harmony the two of you created was amazing to witness. You have always been loved and always will be. Nothing you could possibly do will ever change that in my heart. I'm sure I could speak for your father in that regard, as well.

"Imagine how much we have loved you. Now, multiply that times millions more and you will not yet measure God's love for you. It is truly immeasurable. You can't be too contemptible for Him when you ask His forgiveness. You won't have to be tormented in your mind. It belonged to Him once before. Give it back to Him. Make your peace with God and you will find your peace within."

*   *   *

Peace within. That was music to Gladys's ears. She had known very little peace for many years. Despising the man she shared a home with. Spewing venom from her mouth when words escaped. Conniving to find a way to secure Grace's possessions for her own had become her obsession. Now, the reality was she was unsure of her inheritance. She was convinced Grace told her what she wanted to hear about her inheritance for fear she would find her way back to East Coast. Whether Grace trusted her to be mentally stable enough to assign her any portion of inheritance remained to be seen. Gladys had driven herself more than mad trying to unravel the mystery. She had gone to the extent of entreating Ashley to disclose bequeaths in Grace's Will. She insisted on knowing whether her mother had left her financially comfortable. Ashley was incensed that Gladys would ask her to compromise her code of ethics and asked her aunt to leave. When Gladys became uncontrollable and started going through papers on Ashley's desk and rifling through file cabinets, it initiated a 911 call. She suffered further embarrassment when the police came to escort her from the office. Things had been quite tense between the niece and aunt since that day. Gladys was grateful that Ashley never shared the disturbance with her mother. At least, if she had, Grace did not divulge it. Either way, Gladys was relieved for not having to explain her desperation to Grace Willingham.

The invitation to peace lay on her nightstand. It had been there since Grace had given the Bible to Gladys when she was receiving care at East Coast. She never opened it at the center. Nor would she open it at home until several years later. On her most frantic sleepless nights, she had found great comfort from its pages. Familiar verses she had memorized as a child would surface as a reminder of her fortified roots. It was comforting to know her heart had cherished them enough to safeguard their impression.

Today the mother she distantly adored would be laid to rest. She would never be able to share the words she had swallowed in Carmen's room more than three decades ago. Carmen's departure closed the door on that possibility for release, yet it would not free her from the obligation of continuing to carry the yoke. Now that Grace was gone and Carmen had reappeared, she would be denied the opportunity to bury the burden once and for all.

I don't know what you have to say to me today, Carmen, but say what you will. Don't spare me any ill will. Annihilate this soul. Humiliate me like I humiliated you. Then, when I move on, I can go forward without the encumbrance of your presence entangling me. I am tired. Exhausted. You have won, Carmen. Gladys threw herself back on her bed, arms out to the side and laughed out loud. *You are the winner of a battle in which you were unaware of being a participant.*

Lord, what's wrong with me? What am I missing inside me that makes me such a contemptible person? Show me, God. Reveal it to me. I need to know. I need peace.

Gladys straightened herself in her bed, laid her head on her pillow, tossed the covers over her legs, and closed her eyes in her first peaceful rest. Her Bible remained in its undisturbed position with its invitation to peace, and patiently awaiting her RSVP.

*   *   *

17905 LOCKLEAR PLACE, JAMES WILLINGHAM'S DRIVEWAY, OCTOBER 16, 7:47 A.M.

Sunday morning had stepped into place on time. The day was ordained for greatness. Not only because Grace would find closure to this life, but that James would find a new way to live. The night had brought a revelation of clarity. The events that unfolded from this moment on were questionable. He would take one hour at a time. But until Grace Carissa Willingham was in the ground, he would focus on stepping into the role of son and father.

His phone alerted him of numerous messages. There had been seven missed calls from Kareem and two from Ricks. He engaged his voicemails, curious to see what either would have to say.

"Hey, Jim, it's Ricks. We haven't found her yet. Still looking. If she's in town, we suspect she'll be at the funeral tomorrow.

Let me know how you need me to handle her. Take her to jail or take her out. I can pull off either."

"Uh, yo, just like you to get lost when the heat's on. Hawk ain't happy. He wants answers. I'm not going down on this thing. I can't protect her, so you need to figure out how you gonna get those jewels to him. He's dead serious. I may be next, but you'll be after me if we don't deliver." Kareem was more than irritated.

Jim deleted both messages. He looked over his shoulder, put the key in the door, and wished he had cleared out his side of the garage so he could have parked inside. He knew how Hawk's people worked. He and Valerie would drive her Lexus to the funeral today. Just in case.

Chapter 31

"Don't tell that story until I get back." Madelyn rose gently so as not to disturb Bryson. She handed him to Carmen, and he nuzzled cozily against her bosom. "I'm going to get another cup of coffee before the sunrise. Anybody else want one?" Everyone else followed. "Want one, Carmen?"

"No, thanks, Maddie. I'm good just holding this little angel." Carmen gingerly touched Bryson's nose and stroked his brows. He was a beautiful child. She knew one of Grace's wishes was to hold her great-grandchild before she died. She wanted to pray over his life while looking at his face. Carmen cupped her right hand around his head. She would do the honors on behalf of Grace.

"Dear Lord, You are the Author of Life. You have ordained this baby's days just as You have made plans for each one of Your children. This little boy is a special one, Lord. He's going to need extra care and attention from You. Shelter him from the evils of this world. He's already been exposed to much more in his formative years than any child should be in a lifetime. Place

Your hedge of protection around him, Father. Secure his days. Go before him and prepare a better life for him. Place a burden in his mother's heart to break the chain of dysfunction in her life. Cause her to remember her roots, those nurtured by Your servant Grace. She was a woman familiar with Your ways, and she taught us how to walk in Your path of righteousness. May the seeds planted in his mother's life transfer to this sweet gift of joy. May all who are a part of his life be acceptable examples for him to emulate. May those who cause him to stumble seek repentance for their wicked ways. These things I ask in Your precious Son's Holy and Awesome name—Jesus. Amen."

There, Mom Grace. That was for you. You would have said it much more eloquently, but his life has been prayed for now. I promise I will pick up where you left off and pray for your children every day.

Carmen leaned her head against the rocker. Her thoughts revisited her small California economy-size apartment. It was all a single mom could afford, but it had all the makings of home—love. She and Nick were happy. Nick never seemed to mind that he wore Goodwill clothes, played with second-hand toys, and ate skimpy meals day in and day out. Her home was a place of love and acceptance. Nick never wanted for attention, instruction, or time. While he was at school, Carmen worked. At night she ironed for her church girlfriends. Their husbands wore wonderful starched shirts every Sunday. It was a skill her mom had taught her. Grace would stand for hours and remove wrinkles from clothing and linens. From the first piece to the last in her piles of fabrics, Grace performed her task with masterful precision and devoted pride.

Carmen traced her memory to the knock on her door that would change everything in life for her and her son.

*   *   *

16374 Sandusky Trail, Los Angeles, Twenty-Nine Years Prior, 6:20 P.M.

"I'll get the door, Mommy." Before Carmen could stop him, Nick had unlocked the deadbolt and turned the handle to the door. Nick had never done that before. He knew he was forbidden to open the door for anyone, regardless if he recognized the voice. What possessed him to do so that day was Heaven's hallowed secret. She grabbed for the dish towel to dry her hands and darted for the door.

"Well, hello there. What's your name?"

"I'm Nick. Nicholas Albert Willingham."

"You do the name much justice, Nicholas Albert. I'm Grace Willingham, your grandmother." Grace stuck out her hand and gave the young boy a hearty, firm shake.

Carmen had stopped cold in her tracks, not because Grace was the last person she expected to see at her door, but because Grace was the only person she had wanted to see there for almost seven years.

"Well, are you going to stand there like you've seen a ghost, or are you going to invite me in so we can properly hug and love on one another before I have to get out of here?"

Carmen ran to Grace and the two embraced for much longer than her four-second rule. Little Nick watched the two ladies in bewilderment. He was attempting to process what a grandmother might be. Other children had spoken of having a Grandma, Granny, Nana, and even a Mimi. He had grown to accept the fact that a family member bearing such a title might be absent in his life, just like his father had been. He had been "somewhat adopted," was how his mother had put it, by a few of the women and men in the church. They called themselves a Substitute Dad or "Sugar-gate" Grandma, in a five-year-old's vernacular, but it wasn't the same as having a for-real one. Now the young boy would be able to put a face to the imaginary one he had pictured when his mother shared stories of Grandma Grace.

"How did you find me, Mom? I wanted to call and talk to you. I did call you several times, but when I heard your voice, I couldn't bring myself to say anything."

"I suspected it might be you. It cost me a small fortune, Child, but I ran you down. I had the folks at the Greyhound station searching all the tickets that were purchased a week before, of, and after you disappeared. I've been looking forever and a day in every city where a ticket was bought. But, I started in the churches. I figured if you had nowhere to go, it's the first place you would land. It's what I taught you, you know, to depend on the Lord. I uttered miles of prayers that wherever you were, you would find a good church home. I'm proud you did. God led you there. I just had to find you in His time."

Grace knelt down to level herself with Little Nick. "So, you're a mighty fine little fellow. How old are you, Nicholas Albert Willingham? No, don't tell me. Let me guess. Five?"

"Tomorrow is my birthday. I'll be six."

"Well, I'm just in time for the party. What a lucky grandmother I am!"

"I'm not having a party, but you can stay. Mama's going to make me a cake."

"Well, we'll make our own party, Nicholas Albert. It's not every day a handsome boy turns six years old."

Nick grinned from ear to ear. He liked this lady already. She spoke with a kind and genuine voice. Mama always told him that children and dogs could spot sincere people and that adults should take lessons from them. He wasn't sure how she might react, but he couldn't contain the compulsion to hug her. He threw his eager arms around her neck and she came toppling down on her fanny. Grace giggled and fell with her back against the floor, and she and Nicholas Albert Willingham set in motion a prevailing bond that would bridge the ordinary familial link to that of a trusting liaison. Little did either realize the trust they initiated would mature to that of a confidante for preparation of the most decisive event in a person's life—death.

Carmen wouldn't share with Grace the details of why she left. Not initially. It would be many visits later that she acquainted her with the sordid saga. The story came only after Grace gave her declaration that not a word would be mentioned to nor charges ever brought against the parties involved. Carmen had forgiven and put everything behind her. The joy Nick had brought into her life was the good that God made out of a horrible deed at Satan's hands. She wanted no part of altering people's lives in order to bring about justice. Carmen prayed for each of them to hit upon their own convicting moment. She had stepped out of her emotional prison forever, and she was indebted to Grace for handing her the key.

Keeping her promise to Carmen would become one of the most difficult things with which Grace had ever been tasked. She would witness the passing of Annie become the failure of James. She now realized that James struggled with Annie's death because he felt it was God's punishment for what he had inflicted upon Carmen. Likewise, she came to understand why Gladys would be tormented by demons that set up camp in her head, robbing her of peace and much needed rest. Her regret would manifest itself into a mental disturbance, and unless she confessed, she would forever be hostage to her own undoing.

It was Carmen who comforted Grace to let it be. "Trust me, Mom. I am intimate with God in this matter. In His perfect time, there will be a day that I can tell them face to face that I forgive them. You may or may not be here to witness that, but please trust me when I tell you everything will be all right."

Grace's face blushed as she broke out in a solaced grin. Carmen had clung to every teachable moment and then some. The lessons Carmen embraced were the same instructions Grace had imparted to Gladys and James. She was their mother. She absolutely wanted the best for them. Of course, she would love to tell them it's not as bad as they think. But she knew Carmen was right. She had trusted in the Lord for guidance. Now Grace would have no other recourse but to trust that God's way had directed Carmen's decision.

*　　*　　*

CHATHAM COUNTY SHERIFF'S DEPARTMENT,
OCTOBER 16, 6:07 A.M.

Bruce Masters winced at the sip of his coffee. Burning his lips and the tip of his tongue was not how he wanted to begin his Sunday morning. He'd rather be home in bed and getting up just in time to make it to the Bible school hour. He rarely missed church these days, but today would have to be an exception.

Masters had combed through the list of guests who had paid respects to Grace Willingham. He only recognized about a tenth of the names. He had been through every surveillance tape himself. Everything was right on queue until someone tampered with the camera. Who would have had access to the camera? No one even knew the cameras existed except Nick and the other employees. His interviews of the employees turned up nothing suspicious. The fingerprinting had proven unsuccessful. Whoever interfered with the surveillance either stole the jewels or was in league with someone else. Madelyn and Kareem were a likely team, but Nick was becoming a stronger candidate for the crime. It made perfect sense. Everything pointed back to him.

The man had only been in town for five years. Why would a grandson of a woman not show his face until he waltzes into town to buy a funeral home for a million dollars? What kind of man of tender youth has that kind of money anyway? It didn't add up. He was too helpful. *What a fool I've been! You are a sly one, Young Mr. Willingham. I will bring you down. You won't get away with this. Madelyn may be involved, but you're the ring leader. I'd stake my life on it!*

Bruce slammed his hand down on his desk and grabbed his cup of coffee. He glanced at his watch. *Too early to wake everyone. I'll swing back by the Willingham place and just shake Nick up one more time. Nothing I can do yet. He's got to pull off his grandmother's funeral this afternoon.* "I'll be watching your every move after the funeral, buddy. You're not getting out of this town with those jewels. Not while I'm in charge."

*   *   *

PARKING LOT OF OGLETHORPE SQUARE
OFF ABERCORN, 6:10 A.M.

"Where have y'all been looking? She's somewhere in this city." Kareem snapped at Jahron in frustration. The hours were ticking away. He needed to find Madelyn before the funeral preferably, but definitely no later than eleven tonight.

"Kareem, I don't know where she went. I don't know where your woman would hang out. You da one married to her, not me."

"Don't get smart with me, Jahron. I ain't got time or patience for your nonsense. Have you been to the ol' lady's place?

"Uh, no. You should probably be doin' that yo'self. They wouldn't think nothin' of you going. Word on the street says this is a high-profile case, Kareem. We do somethin' stupid, we're goin' down for this one."

"Get outta here, Jahron. Now. Keep looking. Everywhere. Don't stop till midnight. And you call me the minute you spot her, wherever that is."

"We done been up all night, Kareem. We need to crash out, man."

"You can sleep after midnight. I want that girl."

Jahron spun off, leaving a trail of rubber smoking in Kareem's worried face. If Madelyn didn't show up soon, there'd be nothing left of his pretty-boy face. He hadn't really considered her grandma's house. He figured that would be the place for everyone else to hang. But with all the acreage there, it's possible Madelyn would be hiding in the woods and the cops just didn't know where to look.

Kareem began assessing a plan. He would round up a group of walkers, take them with him, and they would scour the area for any signs of Madelyn. He would try to get close enough to the house to see if he could spot her through the windows. If she was there and the opportunity presented itself, he'd move in and take her. If not, he'd follow her to the funeral and, of course, sit beside his live-in and mother of his child. It was, after all, an expected position for the occasion.

Chapter 32

"The story, Carmen. This is the perfect occasion to relive the story of James Albert Willingham, Senior." Madelyn had not relented in her thirst for the ancient tale.

"And you probably know the better version, too." Jimmy had never compared stories, but just assumed it had to be filled with more details each time it was passed down.

"The better version? Is there more than one?" Ashley was curious. "Every time Grandma Grace relayed the story to me, it was always the same."

"Yeah, I'm not so sure there was another version. Maybe just a different place she told it each time. Where did you hear the story first, Jimmy?" Nick's interest was piqued. He would never forget when she shared it with him.

"At the cemetery. Didn't everyone? The place scared the heebie-jeebies out of me! I have a phobia of dead bodies, and Grandma took me right in the middle of them that day. It was a blessing she was a great storyteller, because I was a fidgety thing, constantly looking over my shoulder for something to come up out of the ground."

"You're ridiculous, Jimmy. It was lunchtime when she shared the story. Everyone knows ghosts and goblins come out at night. She didn't take you out there at midnight." Madelyn rolled her eyes at the absurdity of such a comment. "Did she?"

"No, it was broad daylight, Madelyn. I just don't like those kinds of things. I always told Grandma I wanted to be a doctor, and she kept telling me I probably should think about another line of work, like missions. She was right. I think she pegged us all, didn't she? Ashley, the lawyer. Nora, the journalist. Madelyn, the—" Jimmy wasn't sure how to proceed.

"Teacher." Madelyn dropped her head and lifted it again quickly. "But, guys, I'm going to be one. I promise. It's what I love to do. I have a real gift for instruction. And, hear this. I'm going to Sydney someday. Oh, no!"

"What, Maddie? What's wrong?"

"I just remembered I left my snow globe at Camp W'ham, Carmen. That's all. I'll run back down and get it when it gets lighter. And after the story."

"And, Nick, what about you? Did Grandma get your career right?"

"Yeah, she did, Jimmy. She always knew I would be an architect."

"What! She knew you *would* be an architect? I thought you were a mortician. I don't understand. I'm a little confused on that one, Nick. I guess I've been out of the loop." Madelyn was not familiar with Nick's comings and goings.

"Yeah, well, it's a long story. We'll save that one for another time. Mom, you tell us the story of Grandpa Albert."

"Wait, wait, I have to know. Did Granny tell everyone the story the first time at the cemetery?" Madelyn returned to her curiosity.

"It's where I first heard it, Madelyn," Ashley voted.

"Me, too," chimed Nora.

Nick confessed that he had heard the story first in California, but Grace promised him the story at the gravesite on his first visit to Savannah. And as she had done with each of her other grandchildren, she and Nick set out to the Bonaventure Cemetery with a picnic lunch, a blanket, and flowers. Luckily, the gravesite rested underneath the sprawled-out branches of a mighty oak that provided shade from the noonday sun. For two hours, Grace Willingham resigned her position as grandmother and assumed her role as wife as she shared the adventure of life *for* death surrounding the love of her existence—James Albert Willingham, the First. Her captive audience of one dared not breathe heavily for fear he or she might miss a single word of the legendary tale. Mesmerized by the adventure, eyes and ears were attentive to Grace as she spilled forth with pride and propriety the account of the fallen hero of the Willingham legacy.

"So... the story, Carmen. Please." Madelyn's persistence was echoed by the others. All the wishes in the world would not place Granny in her chair, but her need to hear the beginning of her roots was more than compelling. This time her heart would listen differently.

"But I want to hear the version I heard. Hey, I have an idea. We could grab a blanket and go the cemetery. Did I just say that? I did. That came out of my mouth."

"Why not, Jimmy! That's a great idea. Let's do it. It would

be perfect. If we hurry, we could get there before sunrise."

"Really, Ashley, I was just kidding. I mean, forget I said that. Really."

"I'll grab the blankets," Madelyn announced.

"No, I'll grab the blankets and flashlights, Madelyn. You get the baby's things and a bottle made up just in case. Let's scurry guys. We have a really big day ahead of us." Carmen's heavy eyes were a reminder that she was not nearly as young as these kids.

"I-I-I really was just joking about this idea, guys. We're good right here on the porch. I mean, a cemetery at dawn, I'm not so sure— Hello?" Jimmy looked around and realized he was standing on the porch alone talking to the columns.

One by one the Willingham clan piled into Nick's SUV. If they were to make it to Bonaventure Cemetery before sunrise, they had to hustle.

*　　　*　　　*

827 Victory Drive, the Willingham Estate,
October 16, 6:27 a.m.

The lights were glowing from Grace Willingham's place. *Guess I'm not too early after all.* Masters pulled into the drive slowly and turned off his lights before approaching the house. *Fewer vehicles than last night. Looks like it's Nick that's gone. Just my luck!*

Masters exited his car and walked up to the porch. He tapped lightly on the door hoping to gain the attention of whoever was up but not disturb the entire household. He tapped a little harder, then, crescendoed into a loud bang. He rang the doorbell and still no response. He jiggled the handle to no avail. He walked around the immense porch and peered in through the windows. A pallet of quilts on the floor, a bib, and a chew toy? *Well, well, well, what have we here? Looks like we got a baby on board.*

Where could everybody be this time of the mornin'? "I'll just sit right here and enjoy the sunrise until you all get back. Surprise! It will be a real sunrise surprise for Nick and Madelyn."

Bruce Masters examined the parade of personalized rocking chairs. He had not experienced the pleasure of visiting Grace Willingham's homeplace. She was a peaceable citizen. He never had cause to be in her neck of the woods when he was on patrol. He considered the legacy she had amassed in her life. He was familiar with her story of survival. Grace was a legend in her own time. Now that Grace was gone, unfortunately, her children's characters would begin to quickly eradicate the greatness she steadfastly worked to achieve.

Out of respect, Masters passed up Grace's chair. Quite frankly, he wasn't sure he could fill such a lofty throne. He initially chose James's chair and passed on that one when he noticed the accumulation of the dusty black film. He swiped his finger across Gladys's rocker and his assessment made the decision easier. He cozied himself in Nick's chair. He felt a sudden childlike sensation and chortled at the thought of his Goldilocks choice.

Masters began rocking in cadence to a silencing of the crickets. Dawn would break soon. He looked around at Grace's property. *The Sugar Shack? Apparently where Grace created those masterpiece recipes that got her rich. How many acres does this woman own? She did this singlehandedly. One woman. Everyone who knew her loved her. What was it you had, Grace Willingham, that the rest of us are missin'?*

Bruce turned his reflection on his own legacy. What would he leave behind for his children and grandchildren? His entire life had been dedicated to preserving the law of the land. He had had hands-on time with plenty of criminals, had put many of them behind bars, and brought justice and closure to families when no amount of comfort could lessen their pain. But what would his family say about him? Would they boast of the time he gave the community when he deprived his family of the same commodity? Would they applaud his record of cracking every case assigned to him, or recall that he never helped them solve a single problem … in math equations or in life issues? Would they praise his tenacity for ferreting out the truth when he had spent most of his adult years overlooking the real Truth? For sure they wouldn't remember him for his tenderness or compassion, because he couldn't recall a single occasion where he extended it. God bless his wife. She had been the spiritual provider, the financier, the mom and the substitute dad in the home. It was little wonder why her eyes had lost their luster.

Fatigue weighed heavy upon Bruce Masters. He wiped his eyes, and then looked at his fingers in disbelief. Were these tears? He couldn't remember the last time he had cried. Not since he'd become a man, for certain. He hadn't even shed a tear at his parents' funerals. As close as he was to his brother, no tears had spilled forth at his tragic death at twenty-four. Was his heart completely callous? Is this what law enforcement had brought him to? The system had taken a sensitive, sympathetic and affectionate young boy and applied layers upon layers of veneer until nothing could penetrate the walls of his heart. The stirring within the depths of Masters's soul was somewhat unnerving to him. He struggled to focus on matters at hand, but he was drawn again to the spotlight of his absent family legacy. He had worked more diligently at creating that legacy in his career. He suddenly realized that a detective's heritage would be worth absolutely nothing five minutes after retirement. The uneasiness making its way from within continued to force its departure by way of his eyes. He grabbed for a handkerchief, then realized he hadn't carried one for years.

*   *   *

827 VICTORY DRIVE, CAMP W'HAM, OCTOBER 16, 7:23 A.M.

Kareem and his gang of explorers had stumbled upon the clearing in the middle of the Willingham acreage. The swimming hole, the campsite, and the cozy cottage in the woods had never been introduced to Kareem by Madelyn. He believed by design.

"Bingo! She's here." Kareem picked up the snow globe and gave it a quick shake. "You're never going to see Sydney, this side of Hell!" He threw the globe across the room, and Madelyn's dream splattered and dripped slowly down the grain of the yellow pine door.

"Look in every nook and cranny in this place. If she has the jewels, they're here. It'll be light before long. We'll look under the rocks and search for fresh-turned soil. If we don't find them, she will. Or she'll wish she had them."

Kareem's boys ransacked the little cottage, tearing up cushions, ripping into pictures, overturning tables and lamps. Morning broke and they began looking for signs of disturbed ground, turning over rocks and looking inside rotted tree trunks and stumps.

"There's a trail out here, Kareem. Probably leads to the house. You want us to go get her?"

"No, Blake, she'll be back here. I know that girl. She loved that globe. We'll just make ourselves at home in this place. I'm gonna catch a wink or two right here. If she doesn't come in an hour, wake me up and we'll head up to the house. Maybe hide out in the Sugar Shack. Gotcha, Girl. I gotcha."

Chapter 33

"I wish the sun would go ahead and rise. This gives me the creeps." Jimmy tried to stay in the middle of the group, but inevitably he would lag behind and then scramble to catch up again.

"Stop it. No, you don't, Jimmy. We want to tell the story and then watch the sun rise. It's a new tradition for the Willingham family. Grandma would love this!" Ashley was excited at the mere thought of interjecting a fresh ritual as part of their heritage—Sunday morning celebrating Sunrise Love. It was Grace's favorite time of the day, and especially at Easter. Jesus was the Sunrise Love that she lived for.

"We're almost there. How are you doing, Baby Bryson?" Carmen tickled his chin and the baby responded to the brief attention. He was on his first big adventure with his extended family.

Nick pointed to the gravesite. "Here we go. Be careful. The grave has been dug and is only covered with—"

"Oh, no! Jimmy, Jimmy! Are you all right?" Nora didn't know whether to laugh or panic, but seeing Jimmy one second and him gone the next was like something off of *America's Fun-niest Home Videos.*

"Get me out of here! Nick! Get me out of here now! Helllppppp!" Jimmy was clawing at the sides of the freshly-dug grave, frantically trying to escape. The girls couldn't hold it back. Carmen and Madelyn were bent over double laughing at poor Jimmy. Ashley and Nora had fallen to their knees at the side-splitting mishap.

Nick popped on his professional courtesy hat and rushed over to aid Jimmy. He shined the flashlight in the dark abyss to locate Jimmy and offer his hand in rescue. Once he caught sight of Jimmy's face, his amusement at the image released his pent-up laughter and weakened his grip. Jimmy fell back in again, and the drama lingered for another round of an attempt at freeing Jimmy from his phobic peril.

"Come on, Nick. Get me out of here, please. Get me out now!" Jimmy's pleas courted despair. Hysteria was at bay, but he couldn't hold it back much longer. Nick eventually composed himself and mustered up the strength to pull Jimmy to freedom. Jimmy brushed off his clothes and tried to ignore the laughter that continued to echo from headstone to headstone in all of Bonaventure Cemetery.

"Jimmy, are you all right, honey?" Carmen's sincerity broke through her stifled laughter. Everyone was genuinely concerned, but hilarity had invaded their mourning. And for that Carmen was grateful. Anticipating what Nick was announcing immediately prior to the calamity wasn't settling well in her spirit. Later that day they would place her mother in that grave covered with the artificial turf. She found comfort in the fact that if by chance

God had allowed Grace to observe what was taking place, she had dragged a host of angels to witness the comical sight as well.

"You just couldn't let Grandma have first dibs at that, now, could you, Jimmy?" Nora burst into laughter again. Nick straightened up the turf covering, placed it over the site, and steered everyone toward the Albert side of the dual plots. They threw blankets down and gathered around Grandpa James Albert Willingham's headstone. The inscription read: "Husband, Father, Hero. His death bought life."

"Jimmy, I can just about bet you that Grace didn't vary one iota from the details each time she told this story. The many times she relayed it to me were practically verbatim from one account to the next. I'll do my best to replicate the great storyteller's description of the events. If any of you want to chime in if I miss a pertinent detail, feel free. The story belongs to each of us, you know."

Carmen took a deep breath, then closed her eyes and began to impersonate the enjoyable Grace rhythm of storytelling. "The mind is a fascinating machine. At a single command one can return to a remember-when moment. I can picture myself once again—a little girl with big, bold, eager brown eyes staring into the face of Grace Willingham at this very spot I'm sitting today. Mom Grace tenderly brushed away collected debris from Albert's headstone left by winds and rains. She would intentionally drag out the occasion. First clean, followed by talking about life, and then we would eat, saving dessert for later. Grace always had a way of whetting the appetites of the participants of her memory-maker events. But this time at the cemetery was different. The occasion was a watermark of the Willingham family. With the unveiling of the story of Albert, there would be questions to be consumed along with her specialty sweet course before heading home."

Everyone followed Carmen's lead. Their eyes closed in unison, and one by one, each captured the memory of their individual set-apart day with Grandma Grace for the momentous occasion of unveiling the mystery behind and her undying love for Grandpa Albert.

*   *   *

BONAVENTURE CEMETERY,
FORTY-TWO YEARS EARLIER, NOONDAY

"Your father was a highly-decorated Sergeant Major in the US Army. Here are some of his medals—Purple Heart, a Meritorious Service Medal, Distinguished Service Medal, and Silver Star. Oh, and his Good Conduct commendation, as well as his WWII Army of Occupation and Victory Medals."

"Wow, Mom, he won all these?"

"No, he *earned* all these, Sweetheart. It's not competition in the military. It's for his service and bravery. And these two are my favorite. This one is the Soldier's Medal. It's the highest honor a soldier can receive for an act of valor in a non-combat situation. And this one is the Medal of Honor. Only a few people have received such a prestigious medal, and about half were awarded to those who served in the Civil War. This one is the highest military honor a soldier can receive. It's awarded for acts of personal valor above and beyond the call of duty. The

President of the United States presents this medal at the White House. I was the recipient on Albert's behalf."

"You went to the White House? You saw the President? Who was the President then, Mom?"

"Well, Truman was President when Albert died, but Eisenhower was the one who presented the medal to me. He had just been sworn into office, and Albert's medal was among the first he presented to families of fallen soldiers."

"Did he die in battle?"

"No, he died in an act of bravery above and beyond the call of duty, Carmen. I can only paint the picture for you because of a friend who was with him, one of his comrades who served beside him."

"Who is that man? Did that man get hurt?"

"They weren't involved in the War at the moment. And, no, it was just my sweet Albert who got hurt. His name is Benton, David Alexander Benton. He lives in Paris now. He met his wife in his travels and settled with her. He's a jeweler."

"Wow, Paris. That sounds wonderful. But I want to go to Italy."

"And you shall, my dear. You shall. And while we are there, we will visit Paris, just for you, and I'll introduce you to Sergeant Benton."

"So what happened, Mom? If they weren't at war, how did Daddy die?"

"They were on a four-day leave. They had been in heavy combat and were granted a short leave of absence. Your dad and Sergeant Benton went to London. Imagine how exciting it must have been to arrive there in June during the long-celebrated

Trooping the Colour ceremony."

"What's Tripping the Color, Mom?"

"No, darling, *Trooping the Colour.*" Even though Queen Elizabeth's birthday is in April, tradition has been, dating back as far as 1820, to host a fabulous military parade so that all of London can celebrate The Queen's special day in pleasing weather. So she is assigned a new birthday in June. It takes place at St. James's Park on what's called Horse Guards Parade. It's quite the military pomp and pageantry. Oh, your dad and Sergeant Benton were most impressed at the ceremonial dress of the British military. They had to be extremely polished and spiffy because The Queen conducts her inspection of the troops from the Household Division. Then, when she's done, she leads the troops down The Mall to Buckingham Palace, one of London's most famous landmarks."

"I've learned about Buckingham Palace in school, Mom. The soldiers stand there for hours without moving until they have the changing of the guards. No one can make them smile. Hmm. I think I could. I'd like to try that someday."

"Oh, Carmen, you bring a smile to everyone's face." Grace touched the tip of her nose and mussed her hair.

"Oh, it's a fine occasion indeed, Carmen. The Queen salutes her soldiers and then guns are fired in Green Park and at the Tower of London in response to her approval. When all this has taken place, The Queen joins the other members of the Royal Family on the balcony to watch the fly-past of the Royal Air Force. It is a remarkable sight to behold for it is the mother of all formations. It was the most magnificent moment I have ever experienced."

"Can I see it someday, too, Mom?"

"I'm sure we could make that happen, Carmen. You were not yet a part of our family. Gladys, James, and I had a special invitation from Queen Elizabeth to be a part of the celebration. It was a difficult thing to do, but once I got there and experienced the awe of the event, I felt Albert's spirit invade my sorrow, and he swept it away from me forever. He died a hero. I couldn't allow my sadness to deprive him of that honor. I had my time of mourning, and now I have my time of anticipation of joining him someday in Heaven. It's a joy to be the widow of such a fine man."

"So who killed our daddy? And why would he do such a horrible thing? Did he know we needed him?" Carmen's eyes filled with regret. She had never met Daddy Albert, but she loved him nonetheless. He was alive in her heart and mind. She cherished every story Mom Grace had shared about their brief years together. Her heart was convinced she would have adored him as much as she did her sweet mother. At the same time, she wondered if had Albert not died, would she have been needed as the compensation to fill the void in Grace's heart. God does work in mysterious ways. She suddenly felt as blessed as any ten-year-old girl could possibly feel.

"Albert and Benton were on The Mall, the road between Trafalgar Square and Buckingham Palace, right where The Queen parades. They were near the grandstand seating area. You have to ask very early for your free ticket to be seated. Otherwise, you stand along the streets, which is a very acceptable view, as well, but a bit exhausting."

"Well, he didn't know he was going, though, or I'm sure he

would have ordered a ticket."

"Smart girl. Exactly. Your father was a man of order and deliberation.

"The clock on the Horse Guards Building struck eleven in the morning, and the Royal Procession arrived. Queen Elizabeth accepted the Royal Salute, and then led her troops to Buckingham. It was an enormous parade. More than fourteen hundred soldiers, some two hundred horses, and four hundred musicians marched along while The Queen grand-marshaled in her horse-drawn carriage. Two hours later, at precisely one o'clock p.m., she made her appearance on the balcony awaiting the fly-past. The crowd was cheering, the planes were approaching, and all eyes were now on the brilliant blue sky.

"Albert was always an observant man. He would frustrate himself over my tunnel-vision disposition. I assured him I was not conceited. I was merely a woman who minded her own business and took care of it expediently, for there was much to do in a day's time. But Albert was a vigilant soul. Never met a stranger, and never let one out of his sight. Benton was officially off duty. He'll tell you that himself. I'm not criticizing. He was captured by the moment. But your dad was examining the crowd. He was prompted to look to his right about thirty feet away. Through a crowd of people, it might as well have been a hundred yards. His eyes zeroed in on a man standing on a milk crate. He blended in with the children who sat atop their father's shoulders in order to watch the events. He began moving closer to the man, weaving his way through the crowd, not meaning to be rude. He was never rude. But whatever he observed prompted urgency in his response.

"Benton relates that he heard women screaming and the crowd dispelling. He looked around for your father, and he was nowhere to be seen. He pushed against the grain of the fleeting crowd and there he saw Albert in physical struggle with a gentleman. He had almost made it to the scene to assist Albert when he heard the gun discharge. The man rolled Albert aside and tried to flee. Sergeant Benton stopped him until the authorities could come and arrest him.

"The planes were flying over during the scuffle. The noise had escalated so loudly that no one was aware anything had happened, except the few people in proximity of the crime. Your father saved Queen Elizabeth's life. She had only been in power since February of that same year. It was her first official birthday celebration as The Queen of England. But it would not be her last. His death bought her life."

"Wow! Daddy was a real hero. I never knew. I don't like that man, Mom."

"He was a nefarious soul, Carmen."

"What does that mean?"

Grace realized she had spoken unkindly about a man she knew nothing at all about. She had always wanted to visit him in prison but not when her children were with her. On her trip alone, she learned he had hung himself in his cell. She regretted never having shared forgiveness and the message of Christ before he died, and she vowed that she wouldn't miss other opportunities. Ever. Having spoken out of character, she immediately corrected her mistake. "Forgive me, Lord. It's not a word you should care to know, Carmen. I pray you never meet such fate."

*   *   *

Carmen paused. Not for lack of continuing a beautiful story, but for her understanding of the meaning of that word. She had indeed fallen to such fate at the wicked, despicable, and immoral act of the very children that these two precious people created. What force of evil can drive the goodness out of a soul? The blood children of this godly couple had felt trapped by misspent best-laid plans. If they had studied the comings-and-goings of their parents, they would have realized there is always an escape hatch.

"Mom, you okay?" Nick was all too familiar with Carmen's discerning face. His mind had conjured up the same conjecture regarding Gladys and James. How did they turn out so differently from the adopted child of Grace Willingham? Same upbringing, same solid roots, but actually possessing the same incredible DNA of Grace and Albert. Some things in life would remain a mystery.

"Yeah, yeah, I'm fine. How did I do, guys?"

"You were incredible, Carmen!" Madelyn was blubbery and Bryson began to whimper not understanding why Mama was crying. "It's okay, Baby B. Mama's fine. She's just a blubbering silly girl." She pulled Bryson to her and hugged until he giggled, satisfied that Mama was safe. The story held more meaning for her now than ever before. A man who would protect a woman rather than abuse her was foreign to her. She wanted someone to love her that way—the obvious love Grace held for the man who stole her heart. The woman harbored no ill will but only adulation for the way he lived and died. Madelyn had never known love like that. Today was the first day of the best of her life, to maneuver a quote of a wise old lady. She smiled and turned toward the eastern sky to welcome her new day dawning.

Ashley faced the fresh day feeling numb. She had been the one of all the grands who checked in regularly on Grace. She didn't have a social life; it centered on her visits with Grandma. She liked it that way. Her law practice kept her busy. She was focused on her cases. But when she needed a reprieve, it was cucumber lemonade or apple pie and hot English tea and a dose of Grace that ticked off her tension like a wound-up clock. When she was in law school, pushing herself to get out more quickly, she could hear Grandma encourage her to slow down or she would miss the fragrance of the roses. Ashley reminded Grace if she made time for pleasure, she would never get out of law school. She would never forget Grace's response: "Time is only as short as the distance it takes to get there." It was that wisdom that prompted Ashley to enjoy what time she had with the one who had invested much of her life into loving her children. Marriage could wait. Grace would be shortening her distance to get to Heaven day by day. Ashley had no regrets for her time with Grace.

Jimmy stared off into space. Dawn was just a moment away. He returned his thoughts to his mission field and the two weeks that Grace had spent with him in Zimbabwe. She wanted to see firsthand what God had set about for him to accomplish there. She was a magnet for people starving to be loved, even across the oceans. He wanted a piece of that character, a bit of her charm, compassion, and consideration. He wanted a lot more of the courage of Albert. He aspired to be that kind of man to a wife half the measure of Grace. His children would know tenderness and time with their father. Jimmy would not repeat the history of James but rather pick up where Albert's had abruptly ended.

Nora was quickened in her spirit. She looked at the horizon and shook her head. *What would drive a man to sacrifice his life for someone in another country? Why would he risk his life and leave behind the gem of a wife and two children he had waiting at home for his return? I will never understand the profundity of valuing another's life more than you would your own. Why would anyone die for another person? For his wife, sure. His children, of course. But for someone he didn't even know? Nonsense. Would anyone ever die for me? What kind of man would do such an act of service?* "I know, I know, GG. Jesus. You told me that story."

"I'm sorry, Nora, did you say something?"

"Oh, no, Carmen. Just talking to myself."

Nick had positioned himself along with the others, focusing on the breadth of daybreak. He would love to satisfy his need to confess. It was a poignant opportunity. Hearts would be more receptive. Or would they? He had never kept anything from his mother. He prayed she would understand. The lessons Grace had taught him and the prospects that had availed themselves to his favor, he simply couldn't pass them up. He would be forever grateful for the kindness and generosity of a woman who didn't have to love him. But not only had she loved him, she had trusted him. She trusted him like she had trusted no man since Albert. And Benton. *I really wanted to make you proud, Grandma Grace. I'm sorry it had to go down like this. But at least you get to be buried on a Sunday. You really wanted that. Touché.*

*   *   *

BONAVENTURE CEMETERY, OCTOBER 15, 7:29 A.M.

The group of six-plus-one rose to their feet. Baby Bryson was quieted by the stillness as if he sensed he was involved in a Hallmark feature. No one dared disturb the peacefulness of this Sunday morning. It was the pronouncement of a legacy that was defined in each of their hearts. The legacy created by two people who had vowed to one another a commitment that would never be severed. The heritage passed down to each of them was rich in composition. In hushed vows, they individually pondered the responsibility each bore in preserving the genuineness of the woman they would gather to honor later this Lord's Day, and then lay to rest where they were standing.

Indeed, today would begin a new tradition for the Willinghams – a sunrise visit at Bonaventure. Each of them envisioned countless future mornings in this place as they would anticipate the sun's salutation in the eastern sky, and equally as many awaiting its farewell in the west. The ceremony wouldn't match the pomp and circumstance surrounding the *Trooping the Colour* salute to The Queen, but the queen they saluted deserved more. God had ordered her parade. Specially designed for Grace Carissa Willingham. The sunrise was more brilliant and masterful than any eye had ever seen. The reds were more explosive, the oranges more fiery, and the blues and grays were brushed with perfection for the ideal blend of a "Welcome home, thou good and faithful servant" celebration of a *new birth* day.

Chapter 34

Darkness tried to hide, but at 7:29 the sun advanced with authority and rendered the day anew. The Earth delighted at the salutations from the whippoorwills, mourning doves, robins and sparrows. Two blue jays flirted with one another, cautiously darting from the lowest branches of the shady Sycamore trees scattered throughout Grace Willingham's wooded front yard. The fattened squirrels climbed down the trunks of their tree homes and greeted the morning with eagerness, ready to store up for the upcoming meager season. A chipmunk scurried past the Stone of Remembrance marking the life of Annie Willingham, pausing as if to pay respects to her legacy of kindness.

That was a sweet woman, too, thought Masters. He could not remember ever enjoying a serene sunrise. He had been awake for many, but his eyes were always fixed on criminals' early-morn activities.

He wished his sweet Glenna were with him to sense the atmosphere of Grace's homeplace. He could only dream of a place like this. Salaries for service-oriented people have always been grossly below decent wages for the numbers of hours spent. Glenna was content, though. She never complained if she was dissatisfied. She was a woman who had supported her man. If she only knew…should she ever be privy to some of his less-than-honorable actions throughout their forty-one years together, she might not be around to celebrate their forty-second anniversary. He shuttered at the thought.

Bruce had recently surrendered his life to the Lord. Glenna had been praying for years for his decision. Patient. Waiting. Living the example. Despite their longevity in marriage, Bruce felt like he was on his honeymoon since his baptism. He was a different man. He had finally plugged into his marriage. For the first time since he joined the force, he counted himself as a married man. He had his wedding band enlarged so it would slide on his finger. He had taken it off about thirty years prior. His Glenna deserved more, and he intended to make up for lost time as soon as he retired. A good woman is a priceless commodity, and she was the salt-of-the-earth kind.

Yep, I'd like to see us in a place like this, Glenna. But wherever we are, you make home the grandest place on earth. Bruce's impatience was waking up with the animals. He wandered around the property, peering in at the Sugar Shack. Then he peeked through the backdoor glass to the kitchen. His eyes weren't what they used to be, but it looked as though someone had written on Grace's walls. Squinting more clearly defined that it was scripture that was written there and what looked like kids' names underneath. "Hmm, Wall of Remembrance? How clever. Measure of Life? I'll have to pass those ideas on to Glenna. This kitchen was obviously the heart of your home. Everything they said about you is true,

Miss Gracie. You were a woman of purpose."

Bruce circled the wrap-around porch, feeling somewhat intrusive but too inquisitive to be polite. The mosaic tile tea table was inviting. His Glenna would love it. He previewed the family pictures setting on the wicker table in front of the settee. *Nice-looking bunch of kids Grace had.*

A handwritten framed piece caught his attention. "Wow, the ol' gal was a poet, too."

The Colors of Rain

I love the colors of rain.

I love to watch the craters its drops leave on the breadth of a lake;

to hear it strike between the leaves on the trees;

to listen to it splatter on the wooden porch in harmony with my swing;

to get lost in the sounds of thunder applauding its arrival;

to glimpse the lightning as though the very fire of God

has collided with the dirtiness invading His Creation;

to smell the freshness of Earth after He has cleansed its impurities.

But mostly, I love the laziness that settles in my bones

from the lull of life being silenced for a brief moment in time.

Cherish the thought!

History has long ago left its mark since that feeling,

yet it feels afresh, like yesterday, or even just now.

Life is rich with the rain.

Without it, our very souls would dry up and

the barrenness would be too much to defeat.

Thank you, God, for the magnificence of the rain.

It paints life anew with each color.

*   *   *

"Hmm. Not bad, Grace. Not bad."

Bruce marveled at the order of life this one woman had established. Furnishings were nothing fancy, save for a few pieces she obviously acquired from her travels. But modest for a woman of impeccable taste and a hefty account. Clean, quaint, essential. The cushion on the floor beside a chair exhibited obvious signs of prayerful indentations.

It caused him to wonder where Glenna did her praying. He knew she did. Her Bible would be open with highlighters and pens. She had notes and dates and underscores of scripture that she said "spoke to her." On every page, mind you. He didn't quite understand how she found that much depth from a book she had been reading for years. She said every time she read a verse, it spoke differently to her. It was an area he was struggling in still. But the devotions they were doing together were helping immensely. He hadn't quite gotten up the nerve to pray out loud with her, but that was his goal for the year. He thought he would surprise her at Christmas and have the mealtime prayer. He had been practicing silently over his lunch meals. He didn't want to stumble and embarrass her or the kids, let alone himself.

Bruce settled back into Nick's rocker and glanced at his watch. He didn't know how much longer he could wait, but surely this crew would be back soon. He patted his stomach trying to settle the beast inside. He hadn't been kind to its nutrition the past few days, and it was rearing its ugly head this morning. A nice plate of scrambled eggs with cheese and a good bowl of Southern-style grits would be mighty appetizing. Perhaps tomorrow when the funeral was behind everyone, he would pop in at Millie's Café. If he played his cards right, he might even talk Glenna into being late for work and joining him. He cherished the thought.

*   *   *

CAMP W'HAM, OCTOBER 16, 8:08 A.M.

"We're splitting, Kareem. We got things to do, man. I gotta get my mama to work." Blake didn't dare leave without first seeking permission.

"Then go on. I'm waiting here on Madelyn. Keep your phone on. And keep your eyes open, just in case."

"She ain't at the house. We went down the trail. Nobody's home. But, there's a County Mountie there. Been snooping around. He's waiting, too. Just saying."

"Masters! That complicates things." Kareem sat up on the edge of the cot. He stretched and rubbed his eyes and then tried to shake the cobwebs from his head. He needed a plan and he needed one quickly. What he didn't need was trouble with the law, at least until he got his hands on Madelyn.

Masters would not take Madelyn. She'd find a way out if she was with the family. The girl was too cunning to be apprehended. She had out-foxed Kareem more times than he wanted to tolerate, but she was too important to his plans to get rid of. If she could evade him, Masters wouldn't get her either. She would come back for that ridiculous globe. It was special to her. Her dreams were wrapped up in that silly pent-up facsimile of Australia. Why, the girl had never been outside of Savannah, Georgia. At least, that he knew of. She had ridden to Rincon once, just eighteen miles north. And she had visions of Australia. The closest she'd ever get would be staring at the snow globe. She went berserk on Kareem once when he took it from her and held it over his head. The girl could throw a punch he never knew she had in her. Brought him to his knees. She paid for it once he caught his breath, but she got her globe. He was glad he didn't bust it to pieces then, because today he was, well, kind of holding the ace she was after. *Little does she know her hand is about to fold.*

Kareem dialed Jim's number again. It was unlike Jim not to call back within the hour. That man didn't want to be on the wrong side of Hawk either. But he didn't want Madelyn hurt. It put Kareem between the proverbial rock and the hard place. If Jim had any kind of relationship with his daughter, he could have possibly convinced her to get the jewels to him. The web being spun here would snare the lot of them. All he knew was he wanted to wake up tomorrow. If he hadn't brought the gang here, no one would know where he was. He could have hidden from Hawk until he concocted another plan. That wasn't feasible, so it was back to plan A. Regardless of how long it took, he wasn't leaving without Madelyn.

Hawk would be merciless. Whether Madelyn had the jewels or not, he would hurt her. He would inflict pain until she gave them up. Once she did, she'd be floating down the river. If she truly didn't have the jewels, she was still wasted. Either way, today would be the last day Madelyn Joy Willingham would have to enjoy his son. By midnight, all bets were off for the granddaughter of Grace Willingham.

*　　*　　*

17905 Locklear Place, Savannah, Georgia
October 16, 8:05 a.m.

"You could have called me, Jim. You didn't. I texted you. I called you. No response. You didn't come in all night. A man who's up to no good is one who doesn't check in with his wife. I demand to know where you were." Valerie had been in a fit of rage since James walked in the door. As soon as he entered, she threw a wine glass at him. He barely dodged the thing. All he needed was a cut face for a funeral. Of all nights for Valerie not to take sleeping pills, she had decided to wait up for him and discuss the jewels.

"Valerie, I told you where I was. If you don't believe me, then you don't believe me. I can't change that for you. I don't have an alibi. You can call down at Lilly's Bar and ask the bartender. I sat there for hours and didn't touch my drink. That's all they can vouch for. I left there and went to East Savannah Christian Church and sat in the parking lot. Then, I drove home. That's it. Nothing more. Nothing less."

"And I don't believe you. You took the jewels somewhere, Jim. You drove them to a remote location. I wish I knew what the odometer registered on your car. At least I'd know how far you'd driven. I've been furious! Furious, Jim!"

"Valerie, I don't have the jewels."

"Of course you don't. You've hidden them somewhere. It took you all night to do it. So while I didn't have anything to do but wait on a call from my husband, I sat and calculated how much you owe me, Sweetheart. Here's your tab. You can either pay me the money you owe me, or you'll be telling me what you did with the jewels."

"This is crazy, Valerie. You're not listening to me." James struggled to keep his composure. Any man would struggle if his wife handed him a financial accounting of an indebtedness of $500,780.13.

"What's it going to be, Jim, honey? Are you going to ante up or you going to tell me what you did with the jewels last night?"

"Valerie, can we discuss this after the funeral? I mean, I'm burying my mother today. I'd like to go to her church this morning. After that, we can hash all this out. I promise."

"*You* go to Grace's church? And you can honestly stand here and tell me that you are going to pull the I'm-burying-my-mother-today card. Pahleeessse! You hadn't spoken to that woman in more than three years, Jim. All you have talked about is how much she's worth and how great it's going to be when we get our hands on that money and how valuable those jewels are. Don't stand there and act like the fair-haired child who's broken-hearted over Mama dying."

"That's enough, Valerie. You don't know what you're talking about. We'll settle this after the funeral."

"We'll settle it now, Jim Willingham. I want my money and I'm outta here."

"Not now, Valerie, please. Just give me time to get through today. I've got to get ready for church. I need to be in service this morning before the funeral this afternoon."

Valerie rushed Jim, jumped on his back and began beating him on the head and neck. Jim grabbed her arms and flipped her to the side in an attempt to restrain her. Valerie was unrelenting. She and Jim had been in scuffles before. He was always more combative and gave her a really good fight. Instead, he would continue to grab her wrists and keep her from striking him.

"Valerie, Valerie, stop this, Sweetheart. Please. Stop." He grabbed Valerie and pulled her to him and just held onto her. She squirmed but quickly relinquished her desire to continue. There was an unfamiliar tenderness that Jim displayed. Perhaps he *was* upset over his mother's passing. He *could* have been dealing with a bit of remorse for the graven silence between the two. Valerie wanted to believe him, but she'd caught him in lies before. Why should she believe him now? But if she ever intended to get her hands on those jewels, she couldn't leave him. Not yet.

Jim stood holding Valerie, swaying back and forth. Valerie would have loved to be able to read his thoughts. As uncomfortable as the moment was, she felt iciness melting away from her heart. No man had ever held her like this, not even Jim. What was different? Where was this coming from? Should she be frightened? Yes. No. She hoped not. She wasn't going to disturb the moment. Whatever he felt, the feeling transferred to her as tranquility. She enjoyed this new sensation. The hopes of returning to this place again would attach itself to her heart.

"You want to go to church with me, Valerie? I'd love to have you be with me."

"Uh, sure, I guess. It's a big church."

"It'll be all right. I know my way around."

*   *   *

Gladys Faye Willingham-Murphy's home, October 16, 9:20 a.m.

Gladys set Ralph's breakfast plate in front of him and went back to get his cup of coffee. Ralph pushed the plate away. "I don't want eggs this morning. I want oatmeal."

"Then fix it yourself, Ralph. I don't have time to cook you anything else." Gladys was more curt than usual. It had been a long night, and if he knew what was good for him, Ralph didn't want to cross the line with her. Not today.

"Where have you been so early today?"

"I had to go out and get some eggs, Ralph. If I'd known you didn't want any, I could have saved myself a trip. Okay?" If she thought he was concerned the least bit for her, she would tell him about her fitful night. Gladys really had no one to confide in. No friends. Only gossipers who would call to stir things up, because they knew she was a pipeline of information, and she stirred up stink better than anyone in these parts. She would have enjoyed being friends with Ralph. He was a genuine kind of guy who carried on a wonderful conversation. She could have fallen in love with him had she not been adamant about using him in settling of scores.

"Well, what's wrong with you today?" Ralph asked in his usual unconcerned manner. He had learned not to care long ago. He had adored Gladys since elementary school. His wildest of dreams never envisioned marrying her. He fantasized plenty of times about her. He had vowed to himself if she would just let him love her, he would never ask her for what every boy wanted from her. He would wait until their honeymoon for that. Her womanhood deserved respect, and she was worthy of unchained love.

He was the joke of the school. Regardless of the progression of years–elementary, middle and high school, he remained the rejected boy. No one befriended him. No one respected him. Not a soul knew he existed. Until Gladys pursued him. Oddest thing. Why Grace Willingham's daughter would invite the likes of Ralph Murphy–the poorest and oddest boy in all of Chatham County–into her life was beyond everyone's comprehension, and especially Ralph's. Poor in material wealth, but blessed with a loving home. Ralph's dad and mom never treated him as odd, only his classmates. Johnny Blanton started it all in the first grade. He circulated the rumor that Ralph was poor and odd. The reputation stuck with him. It's funny how you begin believing the lie yourself. Grace Willingham had once told him, "If you buy the lie, you never search for the truth." He bought it hook, line and sinker, and he sunk to the depths of humility. It was meekness to a fault.

But he did love Gladys. And she allowed it, but only once. He poured his heart out over her, and she never remembered a thing. She was drunk their wedding night. She announced to him the morning after that he would have never touched her had she not been drunk and she would not drink around him anymore. Ralph Murphy had only courted rejection for years, but that day he married it.

Gladys did pills. Ralph did the bottle. It became his closest and only friend. The bottle was his lover and companion. It was faithful to him. It allowed him to escape his miserable existence. He crawled inside its safe haven during his most virile years. It understood his needs and never argued with him. The bottle brought him comfort and stroked his ego. It made him feel like a man and empowered him to say and do things he might not have the courage to without the encouragement it provided. He had wanted to abandon it many times and pursue the woman of his dreams. But would the bottle take him back if he met with rebuff again from Gladys? It was a risk Ralph wasn't willing to take.

"I'm going to East Savannah today, Ralph. If you want to come, you can. I would rather have you there than here at home to drink. Mother's funeral is at three at the church. Please don't come if you are drinking. It would mean a lot to me if you were sober just for today."

Ralph would hang onto those few words—"mean a lot to me." He could do many things that would mean a lot to her if she would grant him rite of passage to her heart. He reminded himself once again that he didn't care. He pulled his plate of eggs back to his reach, picked up his fork and began to eat. Gladys swayed past him close enough to brush his arm. He had not felt her skin in many years. He pulled the keychain flask out of his pocket. He only drank when he needed to drown the thought of touching his wife. Lucky for him those only came along about twenty hours out of a day's time.

Chapter 35

"Nick, is someone on the porch?" Carmen stretched her neck to get a better look at the lone figure rocking and reading the Sunday paper.

"Yep. We've got company. Masters is back." Nick backed off the gas to detain their arrival. He gave a quick glance in the rear-view mirror to see if Madelyn had heard him. The four had been chatterboxes on the drive home. If anyone stopped talking, sleep would overcome them. She and Ashley were entertaining Bryson.

Carmen lowered her voice to not create a sense of panic. "Nick, what are we going to do about Madelyn? That's who he's here for. You know that."

"He's likely not leaving without somebody in cuffs."

"I'm going to talk to him. I believe we can persuade him not to do anything until after the funeral. It's too insensitive. The town would be in an uproar. Can you imagine what the media would do with a story like this? Chatham County Sheriff's Department Denies Granddaughter Right to Attend Prominent Grandmother's Funeral." Carmen's mind was churning.

"It's worth a try, Mom. But, Masters is dead set on getting his criminal. I don't know, but I suspect he's close to retirement and this is about as big a case as the man has ever encountered. At least, the coverage aspect. I mean, it does have the international spotlight, you know. But, hey, go for it. If anybody can convince him, you can."

Nick wanted to prepare Madelyn and the others for their surprise guest. "Hey, guys, I need your attention real quick. Madelyn, Bruce Masters is here."

"Oh, Nick. No. He wants me." Madelyn began trembling. Her face was stricken with fear. Bryson immediately zeroed in on her body language and began to cry. His little arms reached for her neck as if he knew that when Mom was this tense, something bad was sure to occur. "Oh, it's okay, Baby B. It's okay." Madelyn took him from his car seat."

"Here, Madelyn, you think he'll come to me?" Ashley tried to free Bryson's grip to no avail. He raised a fuss immediately.

"Ashley, don't upset him. Just listen. Let me tell you what we'll do. Mom is going to try and talk to Masters, see if she can convince him to put this off until after the funeral. In the meantime, I'll get in touch with my attorney."

"Nick, I don't want to go to jail. I didn't do anything. I'm innocent. Why is he doing this?" Madelyn could be hysterical with little encouragement.

"Everything is going to be all right, Maddie. You let me handle this. I'm going to talk to him. Surely the man has a heart." Carmen was silently praying for strength, wisdom and for God to cause the detective to have a spirit of understanding. She was confident he would come through. She knew what God could do.

"Madelyn, I believe in Mom. If anybody can convince him, she can. But listen, we're going to have a backup plan, just in case."

"I like a plan B," Nora declared.

"Madelyn, do you have a lollipop?"

"Oh, yeah. In my emergency kit."

"Give it to Ashley. Ashley, bribe Bryson as soon as we get out of the car. Offer him anything to distract him. Make him come to you. But Madelyn, you stay close behind and play with him. Take him to the back of the house, Ashley, as soon as you can. Madelyn you stay close at hand. Nora, you're a talker. If he balks on this, you ask him a gazillion questions, get him involved in answering you. Madelyn, you and Jimmy sneak around the porch, get lost in the Sugar Shack. Or in the woods. That's probably the better place."

"I need to go down to Camp W'ham and get my snow globe, anyway. I can hide there if I have to." Madelyn's anxiousness had her face and neck beet red. For the past several hours, she was introduced to a world of carefree love. She had fallen into a sense of belonging. Suddenly, her own reality was slapping her out of a beautiful dream. Then, there was Kareem. Too many harsh certainties awaited her back in the real world of Madelyn Joy Willingham. If today was going to be the beginning of the best of her life, things had to turn around.

"Jimmy, you go with her. Don't let her go alone. She needs someone."

"Aye-aye, Nick. Can do." Jimmy gave a lively salute. He deepened his voice and tried to add levity to a seemingly indefinite moment. "It will be my pleasure to escort the lady to a bolt-hole refuge away from any dangers that lurk amongst us here."

"You're hilarious, Jimmy. You make me laugh. Thanks. I really needed that." Madelyn was grateful for his witty diversion.

"Are we all on the same page? Everybody's cool?" Nick checked the rearview mirror for puzzled looks. Everyone gave a united thumbs-up response.

"Okay, I want you guys to get out of the car laughing, talking, acting normal. Just relax. Madelyn, you stick close to me or Mom. Be calm. And don't say a single word. Nothing. You got it?"

"What if he asks me a question? Do I just ignore him? Won't that incriminate me?"

"I'll let him know your attorney has advised you to remain silent. No worries, Madelyn. Just stay calm. And you and Jimmy know the plan. We're good, guys. We're good. Grandma Grace taught us to be warriors when necessary. Let's do it with Grace."

"I've backed us up with prayer already. It wouldn't hurt for you all to say your own." Carmen bore the likeness of Grace.

*　　*　　*

BAY STREET, SAVANNAH, GEORGIA,
OCTOBER 16, 8:01 A.M.

Emmet Park was quiet. One lone person on the park bench sat quietly eating a breakfast sandwich from Goose Feathers Café. It was a beautiful day to walk along the streets of Savannah. The sunrise had been delightfully rich. *Befitting, one might say, to have red splattered across the sky all for the love of Grace. After all, she wouldn't be adorned with her beautiful jewels. Tsk-tsk.*

Seems a shame. Somewhat, at least. For yonder is the tree which holds the root which secures the rope which ties the box which houses the jewels which will soon be mine. A chuckle emerged to break the silence of the morning.

A few early-morning risers would amble past the park bench. Most took the shortcuts from the hotels to the breakfast dining choices. The fall morning was slightly brisk. Winter would be coming soon. But for the coastal winds blowing in occasionally, winters were pleasant this far South. By midmorning, it would feel like late summer again.

"Good morning. It's a beautiful day." Less hungry strangers would engage in conversation easily in this town. Savannah infused an ambiance of affability. The charming anachronistic trolleys would soon clang along the streets, inviting tour-takers to view the wonders of her 19th-century architectural edifices. Cameras would customize memories complete with the olden natural backdrops which had found favor in establishing roots in a city that engendered such charm. By day she was breathtaking, by night Savannah was enthralling.

"I shall miss you, Sweet Savannah. This turn in life will take me away from here forever. But a gracious lady you are for granting to me such a splendid memory of today's events. A toast to Savannah and the rich treasures she holds." The coffee cup tipped a spill and a gentle hand brushed away its debris from the park bench.

*   *   *

827 Victory Drive, October 16, 8:45 a.m.

"Bruce, back so soon?" Nick's sarcastic salutation met with a glare from Masters. He had always respected Nick, but Nick was beginning to turn the tide with any admiration he formerly held.

Masters noticed Ashley tiptoeing to the front door with Madelyn's baby. "Well, good mornin', Ashley. You been holdin' out on me there, Lil' Missy. Noticed you had a nice setup for a baby at your place as early as last evenin'. You failed to mention that when I talked to you. I guess that might be considered as an oversight on your part. Or could be mistaken for aidin' and abettin'. Just sayin'." Ashley gave no response. She opened the door and took Baby Bryson inside away from the encounter. She knew if Masters desired, he could mar her impeccable reputation for law and justice. She would consider that when the time came. Jesus and Grandma had taught her there was no need to worry about tomorrow when today had enough troubles of its own.

Bruce directed his attention to the issue at hand. "I'm really not here to see you, Nick. Although, there are a few concerns I'd like to go over with you later." But, I believe you guys are aware that we have a warrant for Miss Madelyn's arrest, and I just need to take her with me, and then I'll be on my way and let you kind folks get back to your business. I believe you got a busy day ahead of you."

"Detective, I'm Carmen Willingham, Grace's daughter."

Bruce took his hat off like a true Southern gentleman and stuck out his hand for a friendly shake. "Bruce Masters, ma'am. It's a real pleasure to meet you. And you're?"

"Nora Willingham, sir."

"Jimmy." Jimmy reached for Masters's hand and attempted to

hide his grimace when the detective squeezed more firmly than expected.

"You're Grace's long-distance family, I understand. Been needin' to talk to you folks, too. But we'll save that until after the funeral. I'd ask that you don't leave town until you make sure that happens."

"Why would you want—" Nick put his finger to his lips to hush Nora's objection.

"I'm truly sorry about your loss. Miss Grace was an awfully fine lady. She won the hearts of all Savannahians. Now, you're the daughter—"

"That was adopted, yes. I'm from California. I'm Nick's mother."

"Yes, ma'am. It's good to have you in town, but hate it's under these circumstances. When'd you get into town?"

"I got here the day the funeral was originally scheduled. Nick told me the funeral home was on lockdown, so I came on to Mom's place."

"That would've been just yesterday. Seems like a week to a lot of us. So less than twenty-four hours. I see. First time you've been to Savannah?"

"Oh, no, actually, it's not, Detective. I've been here many times since I left. Of course, I grew up here, as well. I suppose you would know that, though."

"Well, I mean, obviously you did. I guess you got married and left Savannah, did you?"

"It's a long story, Detective. We'll have to chat sometime. We all really need to get ready for Mom's funeral. We'll need to be there early, of course."

"Yes, ma'am, I understand. Well, I just need to secure Madelyn here and we'll be getting' outta y'all's way.

"I see you're married, Detective. How long?" Carmen remembered Mom Grace's modus operandi in dealing with people. She always prayed first, asked questions next, and then carefully edited her words before speaking them.

"Soon to be forty-two years. Her name's Glenna."

"Beautiful name. Any children?"

"We have three. Two boys and a girl. Two grandchildren, one of each."

"They're pretty special to you, I'll bet, Detective?"

"Oh, yes, ma'am. There's nothin' quite like those grand young'uns to turn your heart inside out."

"What do they call Glenna?"

"Mimi. She's a Mimi. I'm Papa."

"I'll bet those kids love you both to death."

"Well, they love her to death for sure. She spoils them rotten. She lights up their worlds, and they keep us young. Yes, ma'am."

"Detective, I understand you have a job to do. I respect your position, as does everyone here. But surely even the authorities would not deprive this sweet girl of the opportunity to attend her grandmother's funeral. I firmly believe—"

"Ma'am, I—"

"Please, Detective Masters, hear me out, and then, I'll let you have your say."

Masters typically didn't follow orders from parties involved in an apprehension. Whether he was taken by her stunning beauty or her commanding performance, he could tell she could be quite the persuasive woman.

"I firmly believe that Madelyn has committed no crime so severe that you would deprive her of attending her beloved grandmother's funeral. Grace Willingham was practically the only family this child had. Certainly, she was the only parental figure in her life. You're well aware of the circumstances surrounding the unfortunate events, sir, I'm quite sure.

"But, a funeral service is something you can never bring back. No one can capture the moments, or recount what the minister says, nor give justice to the songs that will be lifted up, much less relate the bountiful prayers that are offered. No one will ever be able to convey the kind of celebration that will be experienced in honoring a lady of the caliber of Grace Willingham.

"There won't be cameras. Mom's wishes. The media will cover the occasion as best they can. But even if Madelyn could watch a video, she would lose the personal involvement of the emotions of a very significant event for a beloved family member. The comforting condolences from friends and community people can't possibly be shared with Madelyn. She will be dispossessed of feeling a necessary attachment to her family.

"The Willingham family has a rich heritage, Detective Masters. Ours is a family of staunch faith and abiding love for not only our Lord and Savior but for one another. Despite the estrangements this family has known throughout the years, there is a common thread that runs through each of us. That thread has instilled in us a strong appreciation for family and gratefulness for the values she injected in our lives because of how she loved us. If you believe you can duplicate the events surrounding such an impressive occasion in a granddaughter's life, then we will step aside and allow you to take Madelyn with you. We won't interfere. But I implore you, sir, to search your heart, the heart of a grandfather. Imagine the burden that would press down upon you if one of your grandchildren was forbidden to attend their Mimi's funeral. If you can justify an act of this magnitude by the evidence you have, then, please, by all means, take her with you. Take her now. But go about your business quickly, sir, because we have a funeral to attend."

All eyes were on Bruce Masters. Even had he not had the last couple of hours to reflect on where real life and family values connect, he would be hard pressed to deny Madelyn the privilege of attending Grace's funeral. He lifted his head up from its shameful position and saw the faces of the people Grace Willingham had poured her heart and soul into. Nick's mother was right. He didn't have enough evidence to put Madelyn in jail at all, much less to keep her there during her grandmother's funeral.

No one moved a muscle, not even Baby B and Ashley who had blended in the background when she joined the rest of the family. Only a closer inspection would have given an accurate indication of life in their still bodies. Breathing had been momentarily paused. Bruce removed his hat, tipped it, and retrieved the warrant from its inside rim. He looked at Madelyn. Her face was fearfully hopeful. He placed the warrant in her hand, cupped his hands to hers, and assisted her in putting the warrant asunder.

He tipped his hat at Carmen and politely said, "Ma'am," then turned to walk down the thirteen steps of Grace's porch. Madelyn stared in disbelief at the two halves of the warrant that would have separated her from the warmth of familial ties. Each of them stood in silent awe as they watched the taillights of his enforcement vehicle wind down the long trek making its way to Victory Drive.

Chapter 36

"Pastor Webster, it's good to see you." James extended an admirable handshake.

"Mayor James, Valerie, it's a privilege to have you with us this morning. It's been too long."

"Yes, it has, Pastor, it has. I assume Mama had her usual seat. Grace hadn't switched it on us, had she?" There was light-heartedness in James's voice when he spoke of his mother that Martin Webster had not detected in many years.

"Same seat, Mayor. You make yourselves at home. Visit our Koffee Korner if you'd like and just do some meetin' and greetin'. I'm sure there are many folks who would like to express their sympathy for your loss." Martin pointed the way to their coffee exchange. He couldn't recall James having been to church since their renovations and the addition of their quaint café.

"Oh, James, I'm sorry, could I stop you just a moment. With everything that happened, I didn't have an opportunity to speak with you or Gladys regarding anything you would have me say about Grace at the service today. My message is done, but I can certainly interject a story, a personality feature, something along those lines. Anything special you would like for me to say?"

James thought for a moment. There were so many strong one-liners his mama articulated that he didn't know which ones to choose from to share with Pastor Webster. He had given much thought to several of them over the recent days' events. He had surprised himself with his recall of her life-lessons wisdom. "Mama always had an answer for every adversity someone might be going through, regardless of how big or small. Some were more profound than others, Pastor. But she was never at a loss for words."

"You won't get an argument from me on that, James."

"I remember a couple she shared with me." Valerie had James's attention. He wondered when she had the opportunity to be around Grace, because as far as he could remember, she had not been there with him when he visited his mama. Grace's words eased off her tongue. "'Only open transparency reveals invisible behavior.'" That one really stuck with me. And I remember another one, but it kind of ticked me off, to be quite honest with you. I guess we *are* in a place where we should be truthful, right, Pastor?"

James held his breath. He never knew what Valerie was going to say, but one could bet it would be at the most inopportune time.

"She said, 'When money sits on the throne of the heart, it can ruin the kingdom that it rules.' I think she might have been judging me a little bit, Pastor." Valerie retreated to her highest-pitched Southern drawl mixed with a flirtatious timidity.

"Oh, Grace never judged, Valerie. She left those kinds of

things to the Lord. But she was a woman who would plant a seed and then pray that it would find fertile soil." Pastor Webster didn't want to miss the chance to plant his own kernel. He had learned in his tenured ministry that some seeds lay dormant until a bit of fertilizer was applied.

James pressed his lips together firmly, drawing in the corners of his mouth to keep from breaking into a big grin at Valerie's double-take. She was processing. It would settle with her sooner than later and when it did, James prayed it would penetrate her need rather than incite her untimely senses. He stepped in before she could make a curt comeback.

"Grace didn't choose her target, Pastor. If you gave cause to necessitate her wisdom, it landed in your lap. Then, it was your call from there." James spoke with the authority of experience. The images in his mind were cinemagraphic. Numerous times his mama had brought to the surface one of his shortcomings, not in an offensive way, but in a proverbial sense. "Valerie, Mama said to me things like, 'Temptation is only appealing at your invitation,' and 'My won't interferes when my will isn't God's.'"

"Now, that's a good one," Martin took note.

"'The simple Truth–with a capital T–is all it takes to unscramble the complexities of life.'" James was on a roll. He hadn't recited these for years. His wellspring of appreciation for his mama's nurturing had found a crevice in his heart. "Then there's 'It's often at wits' end one finds a new beginning,' and 'A dad who gives his time is a dad who wins the heart.' That one rocks my world right now. I'd be the first to admit it."

Pastor Webster was enjoying what was taking place. *If Grace were alive, she would reiterate her pearl of wisdom that "Patience*

*is a virtue that comes equipped with a timeline not in my control."
One can never dismiss the power of prayer and instruction in a
child's life. Even the prodigals draw from its strength when least
expected.*

"But one of my favorites of her corniest sayings was, 'When
the *ships* are down, THE Anchor holds.' That was a staple in our
home. I can see Mama setting food on the table at dinnertime and
listening to our woes from the school day. She'd come out with
that line, and we'd all join in at the end. Then, we'd join hands
and pray over the meal."

James hadn't felt this kind of warmth in his soul for years of
seasons. What kind of fog had he been lost in? Carmen had no
idea what her forgiveness had done for him. Had he held tight
to the teachings of Grace, he wouldn't have spent his life creating
messes for a lot of people who didn't deserve it. He had some
making up to do, but he first had to remedy some urgent issues.
Where that road would lead him, he was uncertain. And quite
frankly, it frightened him to death. But he had to start somewhere,
and his parking lot encounter here at East Savannah had been a
real eye-opener for him.

"Pastor Webster, do you mind if I come in to see you tomorrow or sometime this week? I'd love to sit down with you and
sort out some things."

"That would be great, James. I have an open-door policy.
No need for an appointment. Just drop by at your convenience.
Friday is my family day, though, just in case you've forgotten
my routine."

"It could be a long visit. I'm just warning you. Mama always
told me 'When life crumbles at your feet, your ultimate concern

should be the foundation you laid to catch the pieces.' I think I need to do some damage control. God probably wishes He'd cut me from another mold." James couldn't look the preacher in the eyes with that confession. He lowered his head and stared at the floor.

Martin took James's elbow and raised his arm to receive a hardy handshake. He then placed his left hand on James's shoulder. Their eyes met. "Well, James, to quote a very wise woman we both knew very well, 'God doesn't make mistakes. He leaves those to us.' I'll be looking for you tomorrow. Hope you enjoy the service. And if you think of anything else you need for me as far as the services for Grace this afternoon, here's my card. My cell number is on there. God bless you both. Valerie, you take care. Thanks for coming today."

"Are you going Jesus on me, Jim?" Astonished at the sensitivity James was displaying, Valerie needed to know where his behavior was leading. The only thing she could surmise was that grief, intertwined with the remorse of estrangement, must have been bearing down upon him. Until now, Jim had shown such little compassion for anything, and especially his mother. He seemed to be unaffected in the slightest at Grace's passing. In fact, the only discussion between James and Valerie Willingham had been the upcoming inheritance. If Valerie were truthful, she would have to admit that she had been discussing it. Jim had been mostly removed from the conversations. She hadn't considered that odd. Suddenly, she wasn't so sure. *What was he up to? He didn't come home last night? When I accused him of suspicious behavior, he went tender on me. No outrage. No cursing or yelling. Now, he's all mushy about his mom. What gives? How does one make a distinction between unsettling and pleasing?* Jim's new demeanor was a mixed bag for Valerie, and an introduction to fresh, raw emotion. What she was experiencing with him was working into a very attractive, enticing proposition. Tenderness. Compassion. Even cheerfulness. There was calmness she could honestly say she had never witnessed in Jim before. But the woman inside could long for a man like that.

"I've had Jesus, Val. I've simply had Him locked away for a very long time. Let's go find a seat, and then we can meet people. I'm sure they'll be happy to see the First Lady of the fairest city on God's green planet."

There it was again. The feeling she very much enjoyed less than twenty-four hours earlier. *Be still, my heart. A girl could really get used to this.* Valerie cozied up to Jim, interlocking arms. He had never called her Val before. Ever.

*   *   *

EAST SAVANNAH CHRISTIAN CHURCH,
EARLY SERVICE, OCTOBER 16, 9:29 A.M.

Gladys and Ralph situated themselves in the back of the church. Since Ralph had come with her, she wanted to remain less noticeable. Arriving in time for services to begin kept mingling to a minimum. Ralph waited for Gladys to be seated first, but Gladys motioned for him to enter the pew. She was unconcerned about appropriate chivalrous etiquette. She wanted the aisle seat and she would have it no other way.

It had been awhile since she had been in her home church.

No one seemed to really mind that she was MIA. At least, no one ever called to let her know she was missed. The preacher did, but then, he didn't really count. After all, everyone knew it *was* his job to keep tabs on the flock. She thought of all his personal handwritten letters she and Ralph continued to receive inviting them to return "home." *Who does things like that anymore?* She looked at the size of the congregation. The numbers had increased considerably since her last visit. She reconsidered her casual dismissal of his gesture of thoughtfulness. *A demanding job, and yet he cares enough for two less-than-desirable back-slidden members.* She swallowed her self-pity and struck a new admiration for Pastor Webster.

The worship songs sounded familiar, even though more contemporary. The music should have been foreign to her repertoire of gospel favorites, but she welcomed the acquaintance. *Of course! These are songs Grace played at home.* Ahead of her time and among the saints, her mother was one who embraced stepping aside and allowing innovation for the sake of growing the Kingdom. Grace would have never tolerated compromise of the Word, however. That is why she got along so well with Pastor Webster. He divided the scripture and left no stone unturned. She would have called his hand in a heartbeat had he stepped outside of scriptural boundaries. After all, she was intimately familiar with the Gospel. He stayed inside the lines, and she had stayed true to the ministry at East Savannah Christian because he did. Grace was not one to cause dissension. She encouraged her peers to not only accept but to appreciate the young leadership. After all, they were the future leaders of the church, the community, and our nation. Her idea was to keep them true to the Word, but give them latitude in worship style. She was certain God was pleased they showed up to praise Him. That was more than she could say for the ones who stayed home because they were mad at the church for their style of music. Grace Willingham wasn't about to be that kind of rebel in His Kingdom.

How did the preacher know the questions Gladys posed to God early this morning? Most ministers write their sermons before they present it Sunday morning. Was it the same sermon he preached last night? She didn't want to squirm. It would be too obvious. The fit was tight, almost choking the life out of her. Life? Could one assign such a label to her existence?

*   *   *

PASTOR MARTIN WEBSTER,

EXCERPT FROM SERMON, OCTOBER 16, 10:03 A.M.

"We find in 2 Peter 1:5-7 these words: 'For this very reason, make every effort to add to your faith goodness; and to goodness, knowledge; and to knowledge, self-control; and to self-control, perseverance; and to perseverance, godliness; and to godliness, brotherly kindness; and to brotherly kindness, love.'

"Love is kind. What a great quality to permeate a home. Kindness. One would think that this quality would be automatic in a family setting. The people within a family unit love and care for one another. They share life on a very close, intimate level. Basically, nothing is hidden in the home. Oh, there may be concealed passwords, secrets, et cetera, but for the most part, everyone in a family knows an awful lot about each family member.

Could it be that this familiar knowledge is a barrier to genuine kindness in the home? It irritates some folks to know that others are aware of how they really are, minus some of the secrets they keep to themselves. The show that is put on outside the walls is just that—a façade, a theatrical-type illusion of something that looks real but isn't.

"Authentic! Now, that's a special word. *Webster* says it means to be real, genuine, reliable, dependable, true, or valid. How sad it is when family members can't be simply authentic. I believe it takes less effort to be kind than to be rude. Kindness must begin within a person's heart. Whatever the reasons for unkind words or behavior, it simply isn't that difficult to be genuinely kind.

"I suppose one could ask: Why in the world are people unkind to someone they love? Why is it difficult for a father or mother who brought life into the world to be kind to that offspring? It is a mystery to me, and I will readily admit, it is not easily understood by anyone. Perhaps it is a matter of the heart. Or, could it be the head? Whatever the source of unkindness, kindness is still a godly virtue.

"God demonstrated His kindness to Israel. In Hosea 11:4 we read, 'I led them with cords of human kindness, with ties of love; I lifted the yoke from their neck and bent down to feed them.' The writer here describes God showing, quote/unquote, human kindness to the nation of Israel. He led them with ties of love. God did not pull them with ropes like cattle. He drew them along, if you will.

"That's what God can do in our lives. He is willing to draw us into becoming a better and kinder person. Peter follows his words in the above-mentioned scripture by outlining the costs if we do not add these virtues to our faith. In 2 Peter 1:9, the author writes, 'But if anyone does not have them, he is near-sighted and blind, and has forgotten that he has been cleansed from his past sins.' It's like forgetting who we are … or who we are supposed to be.

"Is it possible that we forget we are Jesus people? Do we forget from where we have come? We were lost, blind, without hope, far away from God and eternity, but in Christ we are a new creature! A new creature is a *kind* creature. Not just a show or a display of insincere kindness, but an authentic and genuine spirit of gentleness, compassion, thoughtfulness, and benevolence. All those components and more should be evident in our lives. We are now to be a kind person because we can't forget to Whom we belong."

*   *   *

Ralph had forgotten how to be kind. It was buried beneath the booze. His roots grew from kindness seeds. His parents epitomized all the attributes of kindness. If he could get rid of his habit, he believed he could bring Gladys out of her depression. Misery had attached itself to her years ago. He should have forced her to get help before she melted down. He blamed himself for that. He was angry because of being deprived of sexual and emotional intimacy. Those should automatically accompany the marriage license. The only way he had to punish her was to drink himself into oblivion and become helpless around a home where he was unwanted. The preacher was right. He had forgotten to Whom he belonged. Tomorrow would be a turning point for him. It would begin with the preacher and then progress to finding an Alcoholics Anonymous to attend. Gladys deserved to know some sense of decency from her husband. Whether she ever loved him or not, he could show Jesus to her by how he lived.

Ralph turned his head away from Gladys and wiped away his tears. The preacher was calling for first-time commitment or rededication. To rededicate was exactly what he needed to do. But, he didn't want to embarrass Gladys. She would be mortified. Her mother was going to be buried today. The circumstances surrounding Grace's death had been a disturbing ordeal for her this past week. He didn't want to add to her stress. She might end up back at East Coast. But could this kind of urgency of the soul be put off until a more convenient time? Ralph's throat was tight. His chest felt as though it would explode if he didn't breathe normally, but his heart was beating ninety to nothing.

Pastor Webster continued his plea. "Folks, I don't like to belabor the invitation to Christ. I believe if the Holy Spirit is pressing you to move, you know it. But, God won't let me go today until we sing one more verse of *Just as I Am.* Just as you are, He will take you now. You don't have to worry about who you are, where you are, or how you got there. He is the God of Impossibles, and He sees the possible in you. In the words of our beloved Grace Willingham, 'This could be the first day of the best of your life.' Will you come? God is waiting. This time, He's waiting for you."

Ralph pushed Gladys aside. His winged feet made their way to the front with ease. He was a mush-mess by the time he reached Pastor Webster. He turned to face the crowd. He had never seen, let alone stood before so many people gathered in one place before. He wasn't one for crowds. Yet here he stood, staring at thousands of friends and strangers in the face and blubbering uncontrollably. The preacher spoke to him privately first, inquiring as to whether he had been baptized and asking him to come in for a visit sometime during the week. Then, before God and countless witnesses, he took Ralph's good confession.

After he finished, Ralph inquired in a quivering voice, "Could I say something, Pastor?"

"Sure," although Martin was a bit hesitant. The odor of alcohol was evident. But then, who was he to judge a man's heart?

Ralph took a moment to compose himself. Larger churches aren't very receptive to allow spontaneous remarks from people coming down the aisle. But Ralph would have shouted it from the rooftop if forced to. He took the microphone and stood tall and confident as he addressed the crowd. Gladys was seated on the last row, right center aisle. His focus drew her in as though she was only two feet from his vision.

"I have failed God, my wife, my family, and my community. I *am* the kind man Pastor Webster spoke of today, but I have held that kind man under the waters of 'Jack Daniels' Lake' for a lot of years. That man is coming up for air today. I have caused my wife to stumble, and I apologize for that, Gladys. Today's rededication is just the beginning. Watch me grow, because now I know to Whom I belong."

The crowd roared with applause and gave a standing ovation. Ralph handed the microphone back to Pastor Webster and walked back down the aisle. "Ralph, we'd love to have you stay here and let people encourage you."

Ralph turned and replied from the aisle, "I'll be glad to have some of that, Preacher, but they can do that back here. I'll be with my wife."

"Absolutely, Ralph. God bless you." Pastor Webster dismissed the service and gave his usual shout-out, "Y'all love and hug on somebody before you get out of here."

*   *   *

DRIVING HOME, OCTOBER 16, 10:45 A.M.

"What did you think of Ralph's announcement today?" Valerie wanted to be embarrassed for Jim, but Ralph's message was so heartfelt that it glossed over any humiliation for the Willingham family. She and Jim were headed for home after early church to change into funeral attire.

"It took a lot of courage to do what Ralph did. I meant what I said to him. I have a different respect for the man. I hope it will give my sister cause for pause. She's lived a tormented life, too."

"Why? What's wrong with her? She had the world by the tail with a mother like Grace. Both of you did. Was it just because your dad died that you both were so bitter?"

"His death had a lot to do with it, Val. But, it's complicated. I'll try and explain it all someday. Maybe. I'm not sure you would love me anymore if I shared my sordid past with you."

A piqued interest cast a strange look. She wasn't sure she needed to know. Or wanted to. "Jim, people judge others for their past. Once you get a reputation for any misdeed, it's like people never let it go. Not outside the church, or inside. I tried this church once. The people hurt me terribly. They judged my heart. They didn't know anything about me, only what they heard other people say. I left the church and went so far away from God that I did things I never thought I was capable of doing. If I judged your speck, I'd have to let you critique my plank. Let's just not either of us go there. Can we just love each other for who we are now?"

"Done deal, my Lady. Done deal. But, Val, I need to be honest with you about some things. There are things that you may not have a clear picture of about your husband. Neither of us have given the other the best of ourselves. I'm going to square with you tonight after the funeral. After that, you can make up your mind if you want to stay. If you do, we'll make a go of this thing called marriage."

Valerie reached over and took Jim's hand. The two rode home in silence. She silently contemplated the events of the last twelve hours. There was a shift in the layers of life for the Willinghams. She was caught in the fault line of a legacy she didn't fully understand. She was keenly aware, however, that Grace Willingham laid the foundation on the solid Rock. The Legend behind her greatness was apparently enough to sustain any stressors life presented.

Valerie turned her head away from Jim and looked out the passenger window. Her eyes caught glimpse of Bennett's Jewelers on King's Way. It's just like Satan to distract. Valerie withdrew her hand from Jim's and placed it in her lap. *But who has those jewels?*

Chapter 37

"Aunt Carmen, that was a stellar performance! I can't thank you enough." Madelyn had melted into her front porch rocker. The tension of the last few days had culminated into complete exhaustion. She was unfamiliar with escaping from the law short of Kareem's strings. He had some connection with the authorities in town. She just didn't know the *who* that trickled down to. Without Kareem, she could be none too sure what her fate would be standing before any judge, especially with the influence of her dad, the illustrious Mayor Jim Willingham, who hated her. Now that Kareem was going to be out of her life, at least as much as possible with a child involved, she was thrilled she had Carmen on her side. She would have been on her way to jail had it not been for her aunt's sincere persuasion.

"You rocked out, Carmen! I would have given anything to have had my digital recorder. This is going to make a terrific story." Nora had been keeping copious notes of some occurrences less obvious to the average observer. It's what a journalist does. She was the best at bringing controversial issues to an increased interest by posing what-if questions and/or planting seeds of supposition.

Ashley's admiration for Carmen had deepened in this short firsthand exposure. Grandma Grace had painted an excellent picture of Carmen's character. Ashley was a bit dubious regarding how much the sweet mother realized her daughter's unity in spirit mirroring her own, but Carmen had erased the doubt. Ashley felt a tinge of jealousy, for she had held that lofty position of likeness to Grace for as long as she could recall. She quickly dismissed such a thought and felt ashamed for her weakness. In Grandma Grace style, she turned the negative to a noble positive: she found comfort in the idea of an ongoing model of the affable demeanor of Grace Willingham to emulate. Who would have supposed that character would filter into the personality of the adopted offspring of the Willingham family? It validated her notion that people are truly products of their environment. Carmen's family origin could have colored her much differently. But when introduced to a new lifestyle, she readily adapted.

Ashley was more familiar with Carmen's childhood background because she was the grandchild who relished the significance of family history. She spent many fascinating weekends with Grace begging stories and uncovering the complete history of the Willingham ancestry. If Grace ever tired of recounting family memories, it was never evident. The two spent countless hours uncovering eclectic stories, visiting cemeteries, and snooping through the National Archives registry. Ashley was compiling a booklet which she hoped to present to each family member soon.

"Could I take you back to Africa with me? I know a few natives who could stand one of your come-to-Jesus talks."

Remorseful for not being more inquisitive about his estranged aunt, Jimmy was captivated by Carmen's ability to persuade. This was the alienated daughter Grandma would visit when she would leave Ashley and him with Melissa Fitzgerald. He cringed at the thought of Melissa. He had put her unpleasant demeanor out of his mind until now. He found her to be a grouch when Grace wasn't around. He wouldn't dare speak unkindly to Grandma about her friend because he knew the trip was important for her. Not to mention Grandma never spoke unkindly of a soul. He followed her lead. He did ask to go with her, however. He always wanted to visit California and see for himself what intrigued her, especially once Cousin Nick was introduced into the family. Jimmy had been outnumbered by the girls long enough. His pleas met reservation. Grace had her reasons. Jimmy respected them. He always suspected there was a murky story behind the elusive aunt, but none had surfaced. Today, he was feeling—a bit very comfortable with her binding emergence. It was as though Carmen would become the new stability for this group of young adults. The idea ambushed his concerns he had on the plane regarding their family becoming disconnected for lack of a strong principal. With Carmen's reentry, he could lay those fears aside.

"Mom's a brutal persuader. She's one of the most diplomatic emissaries I know. You might not like her bold, diplomatic approach, but you walk away thinking it was the nicest scolding you ever received." Nick was proud of his mom for how she handled Masters. He had fully expected him to pull a warrant out for his own arrest after the funeral. He wouldn't be foolish enough to arrest before. Masters wanted someone behind bars for the theft. Nick conjectured Masters felt that getting Madelyn there might be his only way to smoke out the bandit. As far as Nick was concerned, Masters was tracking the wrong bear.

"Thanks. All of you. It really wasn't my victory, but God's. Now, we have a lot to do today. The funeral is at East Savannah at three, but we will need to be there much earlier than that. Ashley, I'm sure you'll be going to your place to get ready. That is, unless you brought clothes here?"

"Oh, I came prepared." That was no surprise to any of the Willingham clan. Ashley was always equipped. She was a great traveling partner. She was the one at all times outfitted with what someone else always left behind.

"I'm the only one that will have to go home, Mom. But, honestly, I need to get to the funeral home as soon as possible."

"What time should we be there, Nick? Do we have time to hear the story about Grandma's jewels? I was hoping you would have told it at the cemetery, Carmen. It's been a long time since I've heard it. I'm writing some memoirs and would love to have it refreshed. Will you? Pleeeaaassseee." Nora folded her hands and gestured a knee-plead. It was a replica of a childhood execution of persuasion the grandkids used on Grace.

"I'm not sure we have time for that, Nora? It's a little after nine. I don't know about you guys, but I need some breakfast. Soon. Then, there are four women and one guy to get ready. What do you think, Son? Do we have time?"

"You guys go for it. I think you have plenty of time for that one. I'm going to scoot and get dressed, tend to business at Turner's, then get the body and florals in place. I'll see you at the church no later than noon. The family will have a special time with Grandma before the final public viewing at one. The place will start filling up as soon as we open the doors, and you'll need to receive as many of the guests as you can. Eat a hearty breakfast because this promises to be a very long day. There will be a light snack there for you if you need a bite before the services at three. East Savannah has graciously offered to provide food tonight. We can all congregate back here at Grace's for a nice dinner. But, guys, we are all whacked. Let's agree to call it an early night. We can visit more tomorrow. Sound good?"

Unity at the suggestion of sleep was immediate. "Madelyn, you take care of Bryson's needs. Ashley, can you give me a hand in the kitchen? Nora, you and Jimmy get your showers out of the way. While the baby's down for his morning nap, the rest of us can get ready."

"It's a plan I like," and Jimmy ran upstairs.

"The story?" Nora inquired.

"Around the breakfast table. Let's move it." Carmen clapped her hands and ordered up the day. She smiled as she walked toward the kitchen. *I learned from the best how to get a plan first, and then to light a fire under the executors. Thanks, Mom."*

*   *   *

GLADYS FAYE WILLINGHAM-MURPHY'S HOME, OCTOBER 16, 11:20 A.M.

"You haven't spoken a word to me since church, Gladys. I'm sorry if I embarrassed you." Ralph felt peace in his heart. He had abandoned the idea of harmony between the two of them three decades ago. While Gladys was preparing lunch, he had poured

Joyce Oglesby

all of his whiskey down the drain and thrown his reserve flasks in the garbage. He had made a vow not only to Gladys, but more importantly to God. There was a new day coming for this side of her Willingham legacy. If he had been her hindrance to freedom from depression, he would alleviate his biggest issue–his addiction to alcohol. There were many wrinkles to iron out of the fabric of his life. Those would come later. He loved her still. He had always loved her. But in the process of making a mess of himself, he had brought an abundance of heartache upon Gladys, as well.

"You didn't embarrass me, Ralph. I'm proud for your decision. It's something you've needed to do for a long time. But if you did that for me, you did it for the wrong reason. Self-improvement is basically what it says–for one's self. It's laudable. I am proud for you."

"But are you proud *of* me, Gladys?" Ralph needed to hear one positive word of approval from Gladys. He needed her to be as kind to him as she was to a mere stranger. It's wasn't much to ask. To share a home, a name and a life with a woman who respected his manhood had been nothing more than a rhetorical dream for him. Any young man rejected by male and female peers would have consumed the idea of attention from an eager personality like Gladys. Ralph's life desire was to work the land. It was the skill he knew best. It was his passion. But a greater passion was to be loved and accepted, to have a wife with which to share his dreams, and children he could toss up in the air and develop a trust that he would never let go of their hands. He was a good provider. That is, until the last five years. His need for booze had gotten him fired from his long-time job just before he was eligible for retirement. It was a good thing he had saved money.

What he had was enough to sustain Gladys. He thought of all the hard-earned dollars he had squandered on alcohol. He would have amassed a fortune had he been a man of honor. Marriage was supposed to be different.

Ralph's father had loved an amazing woman. Her support and encouragement of his father was commendable. She was well aware of the kind of heart it took to love a man. She had warned Ralph about trying to please a woman like Gladys. "Grace Willingham is a fine woman, Ralph, but Gladys has not honored her mother with her lifestyle. I hear things. It's important to me what happens to you. I know relationships have been difficult, practically non-existent for you. But there is time, Ralph. Don't rush into something for the sake of experiencing it. Love is a difficult thing to dismiss once it grabs hold of your heart. But love becomes even more complex when the heart that loves is rejected by the one who grabs it. I've seen it in her eyes, Son. She doesn't love you the way you deserve to be loved. I don't know what it is, but I believe she's using you. Find out why, and you'll find out how to release the hold she has on you."

His mother always had his back. He should have trusted her instinct, but his heart wouldn't. It was dying a slow death from the disorder of emotional deprivation. Its remission was short-lived. He was grateful neither of his parents was around to see what he had become. It was their demise six months apart that was an overwhelming obstacle for Ralph. When they were alive, at least he had someone to talk to. Theirs was a world he could get lost in. He worked factory by day, farm by night and weekends. He drank a lot, but it never got in the way of productivity. He was trapped in a world of silent torment. Walls were voices of disappointment. Darkness a veil of regret. Isolation had become his life-long companion.

His question was ignored. Gladys was preoccupied with having to be confronted by Carmen. She knew it was not likely she would escape the ordeal. But when it was over, it would be behind her and she would be happy to have it in her rearview mirror than have it coming at her like a head-on collision. "I have to get ready for the funeral, Ralph. Nick left a voicemail during church. We need to be at East Savannah by twelve."

Ralph picked up his roll. His hands were trembling as he applied the butter. It promised to be a long afternoon, but the night would be his ultimate challenge of the day. He had to keep his mind strong. If he allowed Gladys's indifference to affect him, he would lose the war in the end. Today's battlefield was just the beginning. Tomorrow, AA would present a different mêlée.

Gladys didn't want to answer Ralph. She had annihilated his life over a selfish motive. It not only destroyed Ralph, but it set a self-destruct device within Gladys. The appointed time was undisclosed. Her only hope of disarming it was Grace's inheritance. She would not allow a time of rededication to thwart her plans. Ralph's only control in the marriage was his money. It wasn't a fortune. He never concealed it from her. She simply was never a signatory on the account after their honeymoon. He doled it out to her monthly. It was get-by money for household expenses with a couple hundred for extras. She had not been approved for disability. Denied three times. She was capable of working. She wasn't crazy, nor disabled physically, but she went for it after her extended stay at East Coast. Gladys immersed herself in a fairytale pretentious world, content to believe she was somebody of consequence. Fully aware that people were knowledgeable of the unhappy state of her life, she imagined they lacked such truth. She walked away from every social event leaving the participants to their snickers and gossip.

The attorney had informed the siblings that reading the Will could take as much as a week, maybe longer. Technically, the hold-up would entail waiting on a certified copy of the death certificate before the Judge would sign off on the order to officially probate the document. The sooner the better, as far as Gladys was concerned. Once she had all of her business in order, she was as good as G-O-N-E. Ralph would need to be self-sufficient, so his rededication was a good thing for him. Her plans were to leave in the night and place a note in Ralph's breakfast plate. *How's that for an appetizing meal, Ralphie?* She would serve him divorce papers three days after she left town. Her attorney would represent her in her absence. When she didn't show up in court, the judge would grant him the divorce and Ralph would keep everything. She wanted nothing from home anyway. Only enough clothes to get her by. The remainder could go to Goodwill. If Ralph was stronger by the time she made her exit, it meant one less issue to add to her life of compunction.

This was a mindset for Gladys. A new life was something she had needed desperately more than thirty years ago. She had planned this new life for many years, and Tuscany had been waiting on her patiently. Gladys was cloaked in determination. She opened her bureau drawer and unfolded the worn-out travel brochure. Hugging it to her breast, she longed to twitch her nose and be there. Or just ask Scotty to beam her up. Perhaps call

Aladdin for a magic carpet ride. Her ticket would be purchased as soon as she received the go-ahead. She didn't want to wait another day, but protocol and lack of funds dictated it. *Tuscany, you will soon introduce me to the freedom I have searched for forever.*

Chapter 38

W as it a spell? Was it conviction? The answer was not readily available. The ride to his headquarters was silent. Bruce Masters had walked away from the person of interest that he had half of the law enforcement this side of the Mississippi looking for. He had torn up the warrant he finagled out of Judge Rowland. It was an opportunity for him to possibly crack one of the highest-profile cases of his career. The Chief would have his head! For the life of him, he could not explain what had come over him. But the lady was right. Mayor Willingham's forgotten sister was dead on target. Madelyn deserved to mourn like all her other grandchildren. He didn't have anything he could legally pin on the girl. He only had hunches. Gut feelings are not enough to deprive a young girl of attending the funeral of her grandmother, her one true guardian parent. The Bruce Masters he knew six months ago would have slapped the cuffs on that girl and scoffed in the face of wiles. Bruce was on the heavier side of the Lord than the law these days.

Now what? Where does this leave me, Lord? A fine mess I

*have myself in here. I'm really needing your help. Is it Nick? I
have the strongest of suspicions it is. But what if it's not and I'm
spending the chase after him while I let the real thief get away?
Is it Gladys? Should I be leaning more heavily to her? Or Jim?
They're tarnished Willinghams. Oh, my. Carmen? Do you think
that's how Nick is involved? That's why he would— Bingo! Makes
perfect sense. Conveniently, she wasn't in town to pull off the
theft. It is kind of odd that a daughter of the deceased wouldn't
ride into town until the scheduled day-of. That way, she couldn't
have been a suspect!*

Bruce slammed his hand on his desk. Why hadn't he seen it
before? "A girl with a slick tongue like hers, she probably talked
her way out of the cookie jar as a kid! I can't ask the Judge for
another warrant. That'll never fly. I'm watching you, Nick Willingham. And I'll be watching that beautiful mom of yours, too.
The forgotten sister. Man! Why didn't I think of that sooner? Oh,
Carmen, Carmen. You've been estranged for years. You weren't
near and dear like your brother and sister. Maybe you felt you
were the left-out child. You have the motive. As much as any of
the others, I'd say. "

Bruce kicked the edge of his desk and sent himself and his
swivel chair flying back to the wall. He folded his leg over his
knee and stared off into space. This was a tough one. The familial tenor of this theft was compelling, the personalities complex.
He had been over and over in his mind. Sleep had evaded him
since the theft. If the family had an ounce of the character Grace
Willingham possessed, the issue at hand wouldn't be as complicated. The possibilities were limited. Not a huge family. At least
not yet. Gladys with no children. Jim and Carmen had them all.

Madelyn and Ashley were two extremes. The other two of the grandchildren, Masters knew next to nothing about except they lived in other countries from what he understood. But when he linked the fragmented clues together on paper, it all pointed back to Nick. From what he witnessed at Grace Willingham's home-place, Grace devoted her life to her family. This kind of stink in the woodpile would taint the legacy she built single-handedly. He would prefer his investigation point anywhere else besides one of her family members, but nothing was turning up to direct him otherwise.

He picked up his schematic and gave it another look. All the puzzle pieces fit.

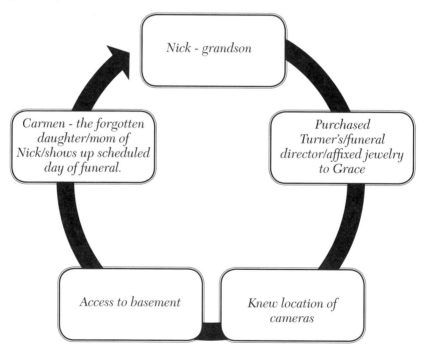

Bruce's timing was off, that's all. He should have waited until the funeral was over, and then apprehended Madelyn after the graveside services. He wished now he still had his warrant for Madelyn. She was still his most viable smoke bomb. Nick continued to be very protective of her, and now Carmen. He did take note of that. It would have been interesting to see how the arrest would have played out. *Masters, you're smarter than this. What were you thinking?* He would attend the funeral today and be astutely vigilant. He would prepare his team to do the same.

Masters stood and gazed out his window for what seemed an eternity. He needed to dig deeper into his gut than he had. He had looked at this case from every angle he had to work with, which wasn't much. He didn't want the Feds involved, but it was looking grim at this point of the investigation. He knew the Chief would want a report first thing tomorrow. He bowed his head and closed his eyes. He had been trying to do this sort of thing more often lately. Today, it felt like the only thing he had left to do. *"Lord, these past six months I've been trying to honor You with my life for a change. Things have been differ-ent, because I am different. I sure would appreciate it if You'd look down on me with some favor here in the next twenty-four. I could use some of that. Thank you, Lord. Amen."*

Masters took his phone from his pocket. "Ricks, I need men posted at all points at East Savannah Christian today. Uh, no, I didn't get the girl. Want you to keep your eyes open for Kareem and any contact he and Madelyn have with anyone. Also, Nick Willingham. Keep close eyes on him and his mom. You can't miss her. She's a beauty. Probably in her early fifties. Looks thirty. She'll be sitting on the front row with The Mayor and his sister. Don't touch any of them. Have heavy surveillance at the Willingham property tonight. Once they get in, no one out of that place that you don't follow. You got it? We'll give it the night and be over there first thing tomorrow. I want to know about anything and everything that looks suspicious in the slightest."

*   *   *

827 VICTORY DRIVE, OCTOBER 16, 9:33 A.M.

Jimmy leaned back in his chair and rubbed his tummy. "That was delicious. I am stuffed. I have eaten scrappily since I've been here. Of course, scrappy here is better than scrappy in Zimbabwe."

"I'm sure it is. You'll have to share some of your stories with us. Probably tomorrow, though. And, gee, thanks. Ashley and I just threw it together."

"You did most of the throwing, Aunt Carmen. You have the speed of Grace in the kitchen."

"Okay, the story. Am I the only one who wants to hear about how GG got her jewels?" There was a plea in Nora's voice for some encouragement from the others as she slapped her hands flatly against the table and bounced up and down in her seat.

"I think we have time. I'm an easy fix. I mean, I have rainbow hair. You don't have to do much with that." Everyone laughed, which encouraged Baby Bryson to mimic.

"I never tire of hearing that story. It's like a fairytale." Ashley, like Carmen, had heard the story from Grace, her Aunt Gladys, and during a visit of Grandma's long-time friend, Kathy Sueberger, who actually gave the most colorful rendition.

"Let me do the honors, Ashley. Once upon a time a beautiful queen in a far-away land picked up her cell phone and dialed—"

"That's okay, Jimmy. I'll do the honors. Here, you chew on this," and Carmen stuffed a cinnamon roll in Jimmy's mouth. Carmen reached to grab the treasure box of memoirs Grace had filled with treasures of Albert. His commendations and medals had been taken out and shadow-boxed years ago, but a few things remained tucked inside this musty box. "It's also only second-hand for me, so it may lose some of its illustrative flavor. As you recall, I came after Daddy Albert's demise so I missed all the pomp and circumstance." Carmen reflected on how sad it was that Gladys wasn't conducting this tribute today. She was the only one really old enough to remember the Royal affair.

*   *   *

1432 Armstead Place, Savannah, Georgia, June 15, 1952, 6:00 a.m.

"Grace wiped the sleep from her eyes and slipped into her robe and house shoes. She turned on the kitchen light to begin her morning routine. She had not slept well. It was unusual for her to have a night of fitful unrest. She wasn't necessarily burdened by anything and couldn't place her finger on why the night had been robbed. Her intuition was leaving her restless even this morning. She had gone to her knees twice in the night. She missed Albert, like always, but she left matters beyond her control in the hands of the Lord. Whatever it was, God had it under control by now, but lack of a proper night's rest would leave her spent by the ends of her day.

This was Albert's and Grace's first home. Quaint, but rich with shades of Grace. The couple and their four-year-old daughter had moved in two months after the announcement of expecting their second child, James. She drew water from the pump and prepared the percolator for a rejuvenating cup of coffee. She would stir together a batch of fresh blueberry muffins for her and Kathy Sueberger to enjoy. Her neighbor and close friend had a morning ritual of praying together for their husbands and all troops involved in the War. She went through her ceremonial lighting of the stove. It was a stubborn blessing, but she had learned to manage it without speaking to it unkindly. She was extinguishing her match when she heard a knock at the front door. It would be too early for Kathy, as dawn was just shy of rising. Grace's heart froze in time with her feet. She placed her hand on the edge of the stovetop to steady herself. A visitor this early in the day could mean only one thing.

She was familiar with the protocol. The military was inundated with notifications to loved ones of fallen soldiers. It was their policy to inform loved ones within four hours of receiving word of a death but only between 0600 and 2200 hours each day. Even when a soldier's spouse might be expecting a visitor, a knock on the door gave her cause for pause. This War has seen more casualties than anyone ever cared to admit. With the increasing numbers of deaths, families were notified by telegram only. When available, the telegrams were accompanied with more dignity and compassion.

Distinction all such heroes deserve greeted Grace at the same threshold Albert had carried her across four years prior. The Class A uniformed soldier accompanied the Chaplain and Medic with a Western Union Telegram in hand. Another messenger remained in the vehicle for security should Albert's loved one react in a violent manner.

"Mrs. Albert Willingham?" The young officer stood at stoic attention.

Grace's heart was bleeding all over her robe. It had burst through her chest and was beating a path to hide underneath her bed until life ebbed away. The floodgates behind her eyes were forced open as though the rushing waterfalls of the great Niagara powered them. Her hands trembled as she took the Telegram. Her knees were suddenly magnetized and drawn by a greater force to the floor than any prayer had commanded.

"The United States Army joins in your tremendous loss, Mrs. Willingham." The Chaplain squatted to fulfill his assigned responsibility. He placed one hand on her back and the other touched her hands which cupped her face. His voice was soft and appeasing, but no level of comfort penetrated through the confusion ringing in her head. The two men stood tall and rigid for a respectable time. The Medic inquired as to anything he might provide to assist her through her initial moments of grief. The encounter was brief. Grace dismissed them like shooing away flies from Sunday dinner. They drove away to deliver news to the next victims of a cruel War.

"Mommy, are you okay? Mommy, Mommy. Mommy! No! It's Daddy! It's my Daddy!" Gladys ran to Grace with little James running behind and crying. He was too young to know why he should be brought to tears, but Gladys, at the tender age of seven, was profoundly aware that little girls and boys lost their daddies on the battlefield. The scene of her strong and spirited mother dissolved into a pool of tears spelled fatherless to her.

Kathy Sueberger had arrived and found the family in a state of mourning. The door was open and she let herself in. The Western Union Message was laying on the floor near the door. Tear stains decorated the memo and the damp spot on the hardwood revealed its underlying intent. Desiring to affirm her dreaded knowledge, Kathy reached for the note and read what she silently prayed she would never receive:

 # WESTERN UNION

CLASS OF SERVICE	SYMBOLS
This is a full-rate Telegram or Cable-gram unless its deferred character is defined by a suitable symbol above or preceding the address.	DL-Day Letter NL-Night Letter LT-Int'l Letter Telegram VLT-Int'l Victory Ltr.

```
THE SECRETARY OF WAR ASKS THAT I EXTEND HIS
DEEPEST SYMPATHY IN THE LOSS OF YOUR HUSBAND
SERGEANT MAJOR JAMES ALBERT WILLINGHAM SR.
PERIOD REPORT JUST RECEIVED STATES HE DIED
IN LONDON ENGLAND ON 14 JUNE 1952 AS THE
RESULT OF A HEROIC ACT ABOVE AND BEYOND THE
CALL OF DUTY PERIOD CONFIRMING LETTERS FOLLOWS
JONATHAN M DONAHUE
ACTING ADJUTANT GENERAL OF THE ARMY
```

Kathy began ordering up the home that Grace so adequately managed. Today this widow needed to think of none of her responsibilities as a mother. She required and deserved time to grieve her lover. Kathy could only dream of the kind of relationship this special couple shared. He adored her. She held him in highest esteem. Their love was incomparable. He was tender and patient with Grace. She was kind and doting of Albert. The loss would burrow an abyss in her heart that would be filled only with a love superior to that of man. Grace Carissa Willingham would never oblige another here on Earth to experience the kind of love she exchanged with her Albert. Her faith would get her beyond this valley and into a greener pasture. No one could befriend Grace and not realize two things about the woman: God was in control of her life, and she was committed to only one man for a lifetime. It would surprise Kathy Sueberger if Grace Willingham ever remarried, but she would be willing to bet her life it wouldn't happen.

Grace offered no resistance to Kathy's commands that she allow her to take care of things. Sorrow stricken, she retreated to her bedroom. Her door was closed and her friend respected her privacy. Kathy took charge of the kids and fed them breakfast, then kept them entertained in an attempt to distract their precious hearts and minds from thoughts of their father. Little James had spent a small portion of time with the man. He would grow up without vivid recollection of how much his father adored his son. Gladys would be carefree for a while, and then suddenly reminded of the tenderness of her prince charming, she would break out into a disconcerting wail. Little James didn't understand, but seeing his always happy sister cry evoked troubling shrieks from the little fellow as well. Kathy's big bosom provided comfort and safety for their bewildering times.

Only two hours after Grace had learned of Albert's death, the phone rang. Kathy wondered who would know so soon, and how. Grace admonished her not to make any announcement just yet. "Give us the morning to mourn in private," was her request. "Then, we'll call the minister and the paper. Kathy hoped that the party lines would not pick up to eavesdrop on the conversation. Even with the glorious new dial-up phones, lines had to be shared.

"Hello?"

"Mrs. Willingham? This is the operator. We have a call for you from England."

"This is not Mrs. Willingham. This is her friend. May I help you?" Kathy's palms became sweaty immediately and her brow formed drops of moisture.

"The party wishes to speak with Mrs. Willingham, please."

"May I tell her who's calling?"

A voice of strong British brogue joined the conversation. "Please tell the lady of the home that Her Majesty, Queen Elizabeth requests the pleasure of conversing with her."

Kathy's clammy feeling intensified. "Uh, just one moment. I'll–I'll get her for you." Kathy laid the phone down quietly, shushed the kids and scurried them into Gladys's bedroom. "Gladys, you take care of Little James for a few minutes. Keep him quiet, whatever it takes. There's a very important phone call for your mother. Can you do that for Miss Kathy?"

"Who is it, Miss Kathy? Is it a General?" Gladys looked wide-eyed at the obvious nervous excitement Kathy was displaying.

"Oh, no, Gladys, honey. It's not a General. It's The Queen of England!"

"What? A queen is calling my mommy? James, a queen is

on the phone, a real queen!" Gladys got James excited and the
two began squealing and jumping and acting like little ... excited
children. Kathy shushed them again and closed the door.

She knocked on Grace's bedroom door and received no
answer. She knocked again. Still no answer. *She's probably
asleep, but she would never forgive me if I didn't wake her.* She
turned the handle and barged into the room. "Grace, Grace—
Oh, I do apologize."

Grace was kneeling beside a padded wrought-iron bench.
She never looked up from the business she was conducting. Her
head was bowed and her hands were folded and laid upon the
bench as if to cradle the heaviness of her burden. She continued
praying.

Kathy tiptoed closer and whispered, "Grace, I don't mean
to disturb you, Hon, but you have an important phone call."
There was silence. Grace raised her head but remained in
position. "Grace, it's–it's The Queen. You know, Elizabeth,
Her Majesty, Your Highness, as in Royalty. It's The Queen of
England! She's–she's on the phone. As in right this minute!"
Kathy's voice elevated the more excited she became, but never
to its normal tone. She was standing on holy ground and was
feeling a bit intimidated because of her interruption.

"Tell The Queen I'm indisposed."

"Grace, I mean, it's The Queen. Of England. As in London.
Really. It's *The* Queen."

Grace was kind but deliberate. "Tell The Queen I'm speaking with God. She'll understand her place."

Kathy melted into the crevices of the hardwood floor and
slithered back out to the phone to address the caller. "I apolo-

gize for the delay, Ma'am. Grace–Mrs. Willingham is currently indisposed. Could I take a message for Your Majesty?"

"Would the party wish to speak to—"

"Kathy, Kathy Sueberger. I'm her friend. More like a sister to her."

"Would the party wish to speak to Ms. Kathy Sueberger, a friend of Mrs. Willingham?"

"Yes, by all means. It will be quite satisfactory."

"You are connected. Go ahead, please."

"My name is Harriett Ainsworth. I'm Queen Elizabeth's aide. Your Majesty wishes to express not only her condolences but her deepest heartfelt appreciation for the heroic act of valor on the part of Young Sergeant Major Albert Willingham at yesterday's celebration of *Trooping the Colour* here in London."

Kathy moved the receiver from her ear and gave it a strange look, *Tooping the who?* She quickly reengaged in the conversation. "I will be happy to speak to Your Majesty on behalf of Mrs. Willingham." Kathy thought if she could come this close to talking to The Queen of England herself, she wasn't about to pass up the opportunity. *I mean, let's face it, it's not every day one has this opportunity. Forgive me, Albert.*

"The Queen would prefer to speak to Mrs. Willingham. I will relay her message. If you would be so kind as to pass the information along, The Queen would be appreciative indeed."

"Oh, yes, ma'am. I'll be happy to give her the message." Kathy was chagrinned but kept her disappointment to herself. Gladys tugged at her apron. She was standing beside Kathy with Little James straddling her hip. He was chewing on a piece of homemade taffy Grace had made from cane sugar and the goody was running down his elbows. That would keep him occupied in order for Gladys to hear the conversation up close and personal. Kathy held the phone lower and divided the distance between the two inquisitive heads.

"Her Majesty's Royal Air Force has requested of your Government to take special attention of this remarkable young hero. Your War Department has agreed to the arrangement but will send their own representation to assist us. The Queen herself will be accompanying the flight with Young Willingham aboard. When she arrives, she requests the honor of meeting Mrs. Willingham personally. She further requests that Mrs. Willingham allow The Queen to take care of any expenses of the funeral above and beyond what might be covered by your military provisions. In addition, she invites Mrs. Willingham to view Bonaventure Cemetery and select the necessary cemetery plots of her choice, as many as she needs to accommodate her family's future needs.

"Excuse me, please. Give me one second here." Kathy handed the phone to Gladys to hold. She grabbed and pen and furiously began writing down the instructions of Ms. Ainsworth. "That's Bonaventure Cemetery. Yes, ma'am. Got it."

"With the permission of Mrs. Willingham, of course, the RAF Red Arrows—"

"Whoa, whoa, whoa. What's that? RAF Red Arrows?"

"The Royal Air Force unit that performed at her Queen's Trooping the Colour will perform a fly-past at the graveside services in honor of the Sergeant Major. Her Majesty would consider it a supreme honor to remain for two days following the services in order for the two ladies to become properly acquainted. The Queen will contact Mrs. Willingham as soon as they land at Hunter Army Airfield in Savannah, Georgia."

"Land at Hunter. Got it."

"Do I need to repeat anything?"

"No, ma'am. You guys are bringing the body, accompanied by some of our soldiers. The Queen wants to meet personally with Grace–Mrs. Willingham. She's to pick out cemetery plots, several of them at Bonaventure. Does The Queen know how expe— Never mind. Some airplanes are going to fly over the gravesite, if Grace allows it. And Your Majesty wants to stick around a couple of days and get to know Grace–Mrs. Willingham. Got it."

"Please don't forget to express our deepest condolences. He is truly a hero of great valor. Thank you. We will be in touch. Goodbye, Mrs. Sueberger."

*   *   *

Okay, hold it. I've heard this before, but never asked. Seriously, Grandma did not just dig the fact that The Queen called her?" Jimmy was shaking his head in disbelief.

"I'm with you Jimmy. I find it hard to believe that GG didn't jump up and rush to the phone. She just stayed right where she was and didn't move. Not even for The Queen of England!" Nora laid her palm to her forehead. The drama she flashed was more real than she wanted everyone to realize.

"She was talking to God, Nora. He trumps The Queen." Ashley's response was immediate and condescending in pointing out Nora's gross oversight. Her response to Nora could–should have been different. It did feel very disrespectful to Grandma Grace. She wasn't even in the ground yet, and Ashley had not seen her half-sister for five years. The competitive edge appeared to have remained somewhat intact between the two girls despite their maturation and professional definitions. Their teenage civil feud had brought frustration to Grace. Her discouragement was due, in large part, to the fact that no amount of discussion, confession or contrition moved either beyond the rivalry.

"The more things change, the more they stay the same. I wasn't the only one who was in disbelief, Ashley. I mean, you can talk to God anytime. It's not every day you get to talk to The Queen of England. I think God would have understood." Nora rolled her eyes and turned her attention back to her aunt.

"If you two don't stop this, I'm putting you in the time-out corner. Grandma would have." Jimmy attempted to lighten the mood.

"Not so. Granny would have taken them to the porch for a good rocker talk," Madelyn surmised. "Don't mind your aunts, Bryson. They really do love each other."

Carmen ignored the snipping. It reminded her of Gladys when she was growing up in this very household. She pulled another document from Mom Grace's treasure box of memorabilia. "This is the follow-up letter that Mom received after the telegram."

THE WAR DEPARTMENT
THE ADJUTANT GENERAL'S OFFICE
WASHINGTON 25, DC

AGPC-G 13 Willingham, James Albert, Sr.
15 June 1952
Mrs. Grace C. Willingham
1432 Armstead Place
Savannah GA

Dear Mrs. Willingham:

It is with deepest regret that I must write to you to confirm my telegram of 14 June 1952, in which it was my sad duty to inform you of the death of your husband, Sergeant Major James Albert Willingham, Sr.

A message from the Royal Air Force in London, England has been received in this office which states that your husband died at approximately 1:00 p.m. on 14 June 1952 at a ceremony honoring Her Majesty. The report further reveals that at the time of your husband's death, he was acting in a manner above and beyond the call of duty.

I understand that added stress lies in the failure to receive additional information concerning the details surrounding your husband's death. Please be assured in the event additional details are revealed to me regarding Sergeant Major Willingham's death, it will be communicated to you promptly.

I sincerely regret this message must bring deep sorrow into your home. My deepest sympathy and heartfelt prayers will be with you in your time of bereavement.

Sincerely,
MARK J. KROSMAN
Major General,
Acting Adjutant General,
US Army

"Wow. That had to be really hard on Granny. I can't imagine how broken her heart must have been." Madelyn kissed the top of Bryson's head. He was the only love she could compare to the love Grace held for Albert.

"Carmen, you're amazing! You really do have GG's gift for story-telling. So, finish it. Tell us the rest." Nora folded her hands and pleaded, realizing they were tight on time.

"We can't, guys. Look at the time. We have to get going to the church. Let's reserve the rest of the story until tonight. It'll be a nice nightcap, and then we can turn in for the night." Carmen clapped her hands in commanding style, and the troops scattered to their assigned positions. She began to clear the dishes. Nora and Jimmy took them away.

Jimmy grabbed Carmen's shoulders from behind and began escorting her from the kitchen. "We can handle this. You … go get dressed. That's an order." Carmen laughed but obeyed. There was much to do, and she wanted to get to the church early. She felt a strong burden to clear the air with Gladys before the funeral services began. The conversation had been a long time coming. *God, grant me strength, wisdom and calmness. Again.*

Chapter 39

EAST SAVANNAH CHRISTIAN CHURCH,
OCTOBER 16, 11:42 A.M.

The hearse and limousines were parked in convoy style beneath the elaborate portico outlined by massive pillars symbolic of strength in numbers. The family members of Grace Carissa Willingham would soon situate themselves inside the limos, follow the hearse carrying the body of their loved one, and be escorted to the gravesite. Nick and his Turner's crew worked diligently to place the floral arrangements, shrubs and trees that were given in memory of Grace. Time had been shortened due to church services, but his crew came through. Grace had requested that monies spent be donated to a children's home in California, and multitudes of people honored that request as well as sending flowers. Surprisingly, the cut flowers had fared well with two extra and unexpected days of wear and tear. The church was spacious and made their job easier to display the acts of kindness and generosity for a woman who had in some small or big way impacted lives in a superlative manner.

James and Valerie were the first members of the family to

arrive. Valerie was arrayed in mourning attire, and had the good sense and sensibility to downplay her usual sensuous style. Her mood was surreal. A degree of respect attended her sentiment for her mother-in-law. An aura of oddity accompanied that title. In the years she had been married to Jim, she had never been to Grace's house while she was present. Her only occasions to lay eyes upon Grace's simple home were when she and Jim searched the home for his mother's jewels. For the first time, she suddenly felt very criminal in their actions. She would soon be witnessing the closing of the book of Grace Willingham's life, and Valerie robbed rather than anticipatory of some impending inheritance. Judging from the demonstration of affection people in this community and even internationally had exhibited, Grace would have been someone who could have added a new dimension to Valerie's life. Had she been the supportive wife which complements the job description, Jim would not be struggling with regret surrounding the death of his mother today. He was a stubborn man, apparently acquired from the hero father whom he never knew. But being the kind of wife who genuinely regarded the heart of a spouse rather than the size of his estate was removed from Valerie's aspiration. She admired Grace Willingham because she could love only one man. So much so that she was willing to live a life without the financial support of a man. That was a concept that puzzled Valerie. As far as Valerie's love life, the kind of fairytale love that Grace enjoyed was nothing more than a fanciful mental image, something Valerie had read about in romance books and seen in movies. But to know someone firsthand who had lived that kind of love redefined the ability to do so as more likely than not.

She recalled a chance meeting with Grace at a local department store. She invited her for lunch and the two sat and conversed until half past three. There were several catch phrases Valerie had banked in her notables mental compartment. She learned quickly that Grace was a direct and transparent woman. Valerie was taken aback when Grace posed the piercing question.

*   *   *

FANFLEEZIE'S, TWO YEARS PRIOR, 3:17 P.M.

"Do you know why you love James, Valerie?"

"Why do I love him?"

"Yes, what are the why's behind your love for your husband, slash, my son?"

"I think he's a good leader for our city." Valerie was looking for a politically correct reason to lead off with her response to such an imposing question. Her hope was to disguise her lack of a better one for the moment.

"Some people would take issue with you on that reasoning. James can be a very poor judge of character at times. Because of that, the media goes after him. Once the media gets hold of a story, it becomes their own, to twist, to embellish, then to portray as they deem suitable for the purposes behind their intention. It's not always necessarily a lie. It is, however, often not the entire truth. How do you take the public criticism of James, whether deserved or not?"

Valerie was reluctant to answer. She felt her face flush and her blood begin to heat up. Was Jim's mother speaking about her when she characterized him as a poor judge of character? Could she be referring to the media's capitalizing on her ill-spoken comments? Jim had already laid down parameters regarding her loose tongue to journalists. She would address the issue exactly as her mother-in-law asked it. She would stick to Jim and make it all about him. If she began feeling uncomfortable, she would excuse herself and lay claim to a forgotten civic meeting.

"I like how he handles himself, Ms. Willingham. He puts a good spin on things and sidesteps the curve balls they throw at him. I mean, it does place a lot of stress on him. And when he's stressed, I have learned to keep my distance." Valerie remembered the encounter she and Jim had as recent as the night before. It would be awhile before he would be coming back to her bed. She didn't know what he was involved in at work, but his mood had been incorrigible for days. Until he could lighten up, he could sleep alone.

"But what is it about James's heart that you love, Valerie? Aside from his career, what do you find attractive about our James?"

Valerie struggled to give the lady one redeeming quality surrounding the heart of her son. A mother needs to hear those things a spouse admires about her offspring. Her time with Jim had not been spent examining the character of the man she married. She had been assessing his monetary worth. His accounts fluctuated drastically. She had surmised he was involved in gambling. As long as he won occasionally, she would continue to float his losses. She had put up with some real codgers in her brief years. Jim was her youngest betrothal and also took pleasure in holding the title of her longest running matrimonial partner.

Each of her belated husbands had died of natural causes. Their sudden deaths typically drew suspicion from family members, but investigation revealed no indication of anything menacing. Their hearts just couldn't take the pace of the lively lifestyle Valerie had introduced into their ancient worlds. But each could boast of one last glorious fling before leaving this ol' world.

Valerie reined in her smile and once again drew her attention to Grace. The lady had waited patiently for an answer as to why Valerie loved her son. She was grateful Jim's mom wasn't a mind reader. Or then again, was she?

"A heart never hears the song it doesn't dance to." Grace leaned forward, then drank a good measure of her sweet Georgia iced tea.

"I'm sorry? What was that?"

"You were thinking of others just now, not James. You don't have a heart for my James yet. You don't dance to his beat."

"How did you—"

"I've never seen that kind of smile directed to or about James. Although, I don't think that was a beam of contentment or love. That appeared more like a smile of conquest. When you love a man, Valerie, there's an endearment for which you can't disguise. Within the depths of that man lie a thousand seas of reasons for why your world revolves around him. And they don't come equipped with dollar signs. He can be financially the most modest of all men. It wouldn't matter if he worked with a shovel in a pigs' wallow. You would find his brawn enchanting. His smell would be enthralling. His sweat beguiling. His hands would invite you to caress them, and then to caress you. As you stood and watched him labor, your thoughts would be of the memories you made as lovers the night before. No other man would compare to his likeness. Not now. Not ever. That kind of love knows no next of kin. It is unique to the selection of a power far greater than what we consider within our control. The sort of love I speak of is perpetual. It is truly a love till death do you part only to reunite in eternity."

"You really loved your husband, didn't you, Miss Grace? Is that why you never remarried?" Valerie was tender in her question, but the sudden intrigue overpowered the gentleness.

"My heart not only heard the song Albert and I danced to, it wrote the lyrics. Valerie, James is a good man. He has flaws. All of us do. He's made mistakes. He'll make more. But deep down inside of him is a man like my Albert. He is his father's son. I've seen so many qualities develop in James that mirror his dad's. James has been hurt. And, he's angry at God because of it. When he learns to depend on God again, he'll discover He has loved Him all along. James will renew his friendship with God. And when he does, he will learn to forgive himself. Be ready for that man, Valerie. He is going to make a great husband, father, and follower of Christ. I may not live to see that day, but you will. I'm confident of that. Find out what is inside that heart of his. Therein lies your treasure. It is pure gold, and you're not going to care that it won't spend."

With that, Grace excused herself. She bent down and gave Valerie a warm and heartfelt hug, then kissed her on her forehead. She grabbed her purse and ambled to her car. Her gait was poised and graceful. She was a beautiful elderly woman, but simple. No fluff. No designer clothes or regalia to enhance her charm. This woman's beauty emanated from within. For a moment Valerie envisioned how that beauty might reveal itself through her. Did she possess an ounce of the kind of loveliness that spilled forth from Grace Willingham? It was Grace's inner beauty that captured her attention. The thoughtful depths of love as Grace described them sounded ethereal. Valerie's world was unfamiliar with anyone who had loved like that. The idea was enticing at a lofty level. The notion left her wondering what attaining that kind of romance might expect from her.

Valerie leaned forward and propped her elbows on the table impolitely. She didn't care. She was caught up in a notion of love and elegance and Grace. Could she manage loving anyone with that kind of passion? Could she ever know commitment to the degree that Grace had devoted to a man who was nothing more than dust and a memory? She snapped to her senses and ran her hands down her form-fitted dress and corrected her posture. She was none too sure that was the sort of stock with which could maintain her lifestyle.

*   *   *

EAST SAVANNAH CHRISTIAN CHURCH,
OCTOBER 16, 11:52 A.M.

James Willingham pulled his phone from his pocket. There was continuous vibration. He was receiving texts and voicemails from Ricks and Kareem. He looked around the auditorium full of flowers. He paced himself as he read the cards attached to the floral arrangements. "We will miss your grace, Grace! Love, Don, Jane, and boys." "You were never a diamond in the rough.

You have always been a gem! Regards, Dr. David and Susan." "Celebrating your new life and your reunion with Albert. We love you. Janie and John." "Thank you for years of patronage and wonderful PR, Your forever friend, Carrie Melden." "Thank you for teaching me about Jesus when I was seven, and then my children when they were seven. We love you! Sam and Ginny, Lynn, Max, Tommy, Sean, Michelle, Tori, Taylor, and Susie Finley." "I'll always remember your kindness, Grace. You taught me how to pass it on. Heather, Todd, and Gang." "Your heart for Jesus showed me how to be a God-seeker and love my family. What a friend! Mary P." "Thank you for giving me a reason to live! Chris Chandler." "You fed my family when I couldn't, but served us the Bread of Life, too. Thank you! The Alfords." "Your example lives on! Anne Admore."

James continued reading heartfelt dictums of Grace's character and deeds on this Earth. The condolences ranged from abbreviated comments to lengthy discourses of his mother's impact upon the lives of people and businesses. The arrangements were as assorted as the written expressions of gratitude and love. His mother was an esteemed lady. The legacy she had amassed in her eighty-seven years of life were more than remarkable. Her life was a testament to her Lord and Savior that she honored with every breath she drew. James's emotions were a comingling of pride and peace. The peace that Grace had exhibited not only to her family but to her friends and community was a heritage to which he aspired—perhaps for the very first time in the real sense of the word. Growing up familiar with the Gospel and the guidance of a godly parent offered this false sense of security that somehow his ticket to Heaven had been punched by Grace. A transformation was happening inside him. He was well aware. A longing for a personal relationship with the Friend to Whom his mother had devoted her life had suddenly become attractive and imperative. His ticket to Heaven would indeed be punched by grace, only wearing a different face.

The identifying cards of praise and adoration seemed endless. A few of the more commanding displays were centrally located in the foyer of the church and arranged in garden setting, complete with an exquisite fountain. The display would be a permanent fixture within East Savannah Christian, compliments of Queen Elizabeth II. The crew selected for the installation had worked expediently to accomplish the end results. The Palace had only learned of her demise after the jewels had been heisted. The work was professional and a splendid enhancement to the church. "In Memory of Albert and Grace Willingham, a royal couple who gave significance to life, and to whom I owe mine, Queen Elizabeth II."

A beautiful park bench had been placed in the garden scene. It was hand-carved by a French artist. The plaque attached was from an acquaintance of Grace's unfamiliar to James. He did recall his mother speaking of a gentleman jeweler who was a comrade of Albert's. His recollection was the gentleman was with his dad when he was killed. "In loving memory of Grace Willingham, a woman of prodigious worth. *Bulgari's*" Beside the bench was a lavishly-full Ficus tree. The hand-painted plaque was staked at the base of the tree. "In honor of Albert and Grace Willingham. All who knew them loved them. David Benton, and my beloved Monique." *Benton. Benton. The name sounds familiar.* Jim was irritated he hadn't paid more attention to details of Albert and

Grace's friends.

"A penny for your thoughts." Valerie tossed a coin into the fountain and reached for James's hand. They embraced each other's waistlines and pulled in closer as though they had been a couple who had celebrated love.

"My mother was a loved woman, Val. Have you read all of the words of praise? How did I miss this about her? It's as though I've been blinded by life, or at least my pursuit of it. I believe there was a time I appreciated her worth and the value she brought to life. When did I lose sight of the foundation she laid? I've made some pretty bad choices along the way. I'm not sure I can undo some of the things I've neglected. But I promise you, Val, if you'll stand by me, I will make you proud to be my wife." Jim's voice quivered and his bottom jaw trembled. If he spoke another word, his composure would erupt and spill at the site of this memorial for his mother and father.

Is this the man Grace saw within her son? Could she have been a prophetess as well? Were these the qualities buried within James's heart that she spoke of at Fanfleezie's–this tender, remorseful, tenacious spirit? Valerie didn't feel at all confident in how to handle her heart. It had never reacted in the manner she had experienced in the last several hours. She had no idea what had come over James, but at this point, she was fairly certain whatever it was, it was viral.

Footsteps interrupted their privacy. Gladys and Ralph joined them at the memorial garden. "Gladys, Ralph. This is quite impressive, isn't it?" Gladys immediately took notice that James was not speaking to her in his usual brusque tone. "We were a lucky lot of kids, Gladys. All three of us." James reached out his arm and placed it gingerly across the shoulders of Gladys and rubbed her upper arm with his fingertips.

Gladys lost her will for defense. She didn't feel threatened at all. She hadn't seen this tender side of James since the Carmen incident. The slumbering attachment to her brother began to stir deep within. Her heart attempted to make the connection but short-circuited. "If you say so, James." James removed his arm.

"Ralph, I appreciated what you had to say this morning. It touched me. It took a lot of courage for you to get up in front of all those people and talk about your sin." Valerie's intentions, while sincere, fell on the ears a bit sideways.

"I know a lot of sinners who could have done the same thing, Valerie." Gladys responded with a terse tenor attached.

"Thank you, Valerie. I seek your prayers." Ralph appreciated the recognition. It was soothing to hear from a family member.

"Why don't we find Nick and see what he has in mind for us as far as receiving guests." James didn't want to spoil the moment any more than it had been. Dispelling any further opportunity for biting words seemed prudent. "We'll be right back, Gladys." James reached for Ralph's hand, then pulled him in for a man hug. "Proud of you, buddy. I really am." Ralph's countenance revived instantly, and James walked away realizing the importance of encouragement. A little bit of Grace had occupied his spirit.

*   *   *

827 VICTORY DRIVE, OCTOBER 16, 11:18 A.M.

Carmen looked at the time on her cell phone, then gave a

yell upstairs. "Are you guys almost ready? We probably need to pick up the pace. Nick wants us at the church no later than noon. Need to move it."

Ashley and Madelyn were getting Bryson's bag together with snacks and a few quiet toys to keep him occupied. Funerals don't dictate patience and flexibility for small children and babies. They expect to stay on some semblance of schedule. "I can't thank you enough, Ashley, for what you did yesterday. If I compromised you in any way, I won't ever forgive myself." Madelyn's genuineness was brimming with regret for involving her half-sister.

"Don't worry about it, Madelyn. We're sisters. You needed help. It all turned out for the best. At least so far. We'll see where it takes us tomorrow. Bruce Masters doesn't scare me any. He'd have to prove that you did something wrong before he could involve me in any sort of aiding and abetting offense. Let's just concentrate on what is really important for now. Grandma Grace deserves our best hearts today, not a heart that is burdened. Everything will be all right. You'll see." Ashley gave a hug to Madelyn. Her tattooed arms sprang from her side, and Madelyn reciprocated the love. It was the first time Ashley had verbally acknowledged her as a sister. At least within Madelyn's earshot. The picture might be considered by some as bizarre. It was a representation of two extreme worlds of beauty–refinement and rough-hewn.

"Coming!" Nora took one last glance in the mirror. Despite exhaustion, her countenance reflected energy and radiance. She turned to join the others downstairs when another thought flashed in her head. She grabbed her pen and made some bullet-point entries in her journal:

- *Quintessentially, family's best chance of survival— mom and dad. Both serve equally important roles;*
- *Lacking one or both can strangle the life out of potential;*
- *Great legacy always anchored to one;*
- *In times of adversity, the anchor holds;*
- *Becoming increasingly aware that family is more an attitude of the heart.*

"Well, la-di-dah. Don't you look smashing! Allow me." Jimmy offered his arm to escort Nora and they promenaded down the stairs.

"Jimmy, do you mind if I use your vehicle and meet you guys there?"

"Oh, Madelyn, I can't. It's a rental. You know I would otherwise."

"Same with me, Madelyn. Sorry." Nora was glad she asked Jimmy first.

"You can use mine. It's not a rental. But we can all ride together since Nick isn't here. Why would you come later?

"I need to go down to Camp W'ham. I left something there that I need." Madelyn remembered her snow globe and backpack at the campsite. The globe was special to her. She wanted to take it to the funeral and just hold it during the services. It was her reminder of a promise to Granny and better days ahead.

"Oh, Maddie, can it wait, sweetheart? That's quite the hike down to W'ham. You'll miss some really special time with the family. It's time you won't ever have again. You can't bring back moments like we're about to experience. Is it that important?"

"It really is, Aunt Carmen." Madelyn was torn, but in her mind the special time with Granny would include shaking the globe one last time and promising to fulfill a dream they had spoken of together.

"Whatever you think, Maddie. I just don't want you looking back with any regrets of what you might have missed out on with the family. That's all. But, Ashley is the only one with the non-rental. The rest of us can get into mine. We'll see you there." Carmen didn't feel comfortable with Madelyn's decision, but she couldn't place her finger on the gut reasoning behind it.

"I'll take the baby, but we'll have to transfer the car seat." Ashley realized Bryson would slow Madelyn's pace.

"I'm a lot of trouble, I know. I'm sorry, guys. I really am. But thank you, Ashley, for taking Bryson. I'd need another shower by the time I hauled that brute there and back." Madelyn laughed but inside she was feeling a bit anxious. She had not felt her usual angst for hours and was settling in to feeling peace. "I'll see if I can crank the four-wheeler. That would speed things up for me."

"Good idea. Here are my keys. We'll see you there. Come on, Baby B. You're going with Aunt Ashley." Bryson whimpered for Mommy but had become comfortably trusting of Ashley and transitioned without protest.

"All right. Load up, guys. Jimmy, grab the car seat. Let's move it." Carmen clapped her hands to enforce the command.

Madelyn rushed back to the kitchen to get the ATV key from the keyboard. *So many keys, such little time.* Madelyn hurriedly read through the labels on the keys. "Sugar Shack, W'ham, Front Door, Kitchen Door, Garage, Desk, Post Office, Lockbox, Ford, Chevy, bingo! Four-wheeler." She grabbed the key and turned the handle to the kitchen door. Her heart raced. *What will I miss? I'll miss time with family. A promise to Granny now is pointless. It has to be a promise to me. I can do that without a globe.* "I know if anyone understands, you do, Granny. I can take the globe to the cemetery and we can have a chat then."

Madelyn returned the key to its proper place and raced to the front door to see if she could catch the others. Jimmy was still struggling with the car seat. "It's okay, Jimmy. Leave it there. Everyone get in Ashley's car and let's head to the church."

Applause and kudos thundered. Baby Bryson clapped his hands in glee, as well. Carmen breathed a sigh of relief. Her uneasiness had not settled until Madelyn was in the car safe and sound with the rest of the family. She didn't understand the urging she had, but was grateful for the peace that surpassed it.

Chapter 40

EAST SAVANNAH CHRISTIAN CHURCH,
OCTOBER 16, 11:49 A.M.

Carmen and the rest of the group walked into the foyer of East Savannah Christian. Gladys had separated from Ralph looking at the fountain exhibition. This was the moment Carmen had prayed for silently while en route to the church—to find Gladys alone. *Kids. They make our world turn, and they can stop it at their command, too.* "Would you guys excuse me? I'll join you shortly."

"I want to see that fountain first. Nick told us they were doing this." Nora began walking toward the garden memorial. Carmen grabbed her arm firmly and stopped her in stride. "Please, Nora. Would you mind waiting on that just a bit? I really need a moment of privacy."

"Oh, well, sure, Carmen. I guess." The tenseness in Carmen's expression alerted Nora's radar. She would love to be a fly on the wall for whatever was about to happen in the foyer of this church. She would try to hang close to earshot range in order to find out what the rift really was between these two siblings.

Ashley was more keenly aware than any of the grandchildren of the estrangement between Carmen and her brother and sister, although Grandma Grace had never shared the reasons behind it. She took Carmen's hand and squeezed it tightly. "I'll be praying that God will give you the perfect words. And I'll be praying that Gladys has a spirit of understanding as you deliver them."

Her intention, while noble, seized Carmen's curiosity as to whether Ashley knew anything about the conflict between the children of Grace. If she did, where would she have learned the story? Nonetheless, prayers were appreciated. She certainly needed them. But her objective had been to execute a carefully laid-out plan she had patiently anticipated for decades. The time was now. To her knowledge, no one knew the story other than Grace, Nick, and herself. Time would reveal Ashley's knowledge, if any. For now, she would not concern herself about that matter. She had enough to consider.

Ashley took the lead and headed into the sanctuary. The others fell in line behind her, except for Nora, who dallied a bit. Madelyn took note and went back, taking Nora by the hand and leading her away from the eavesdropping distance she had positioned herself. All eyes were on the number of floral arrangements that had accumulated overnight, but their interest couldn't help but be on the summit at the fountain. Madelyn and Jimmy were no less intrigued than the others. Their childhood memories, like Ashley's and Nora's, were familiar with the void of Carmen and Nick, the long-distance relatives. Nick was the late-arrival addition who Grandma Grace seemed to be as familiar with as the rest of her grandchildren. Carmen was the phantom mother of Nick who never visited Savannah, Georgia with her son–at least as far as they were aware. Whereas they might not get to witness the occurrence, everyone had an assurance that Carmen would somehow bridge the gap of decades of separation. They had observed her trait for conciliation with Bruce Masters. If anyone could summon peace, Carmen Willingham was capable of negotiating a pact.

Gladys's heart was racing a mile a minute. She could scarcely breathe. She had seen Carmen and the kids come in and was already feeling despair. Her strongest hope was Carmen would ignore her presence and proceed with the others into the sanctuary. She raised her eyes searching for a way to sidestep the soon-to-be intrusion. The ladies' restroom was to her left. She turned to take a step toward her escape route, but it was too late.

"Gladys, I was hoping to have a moment with you before the services. I'm so glad I saw you here. Did you get some rest last night? Nick said it's really been a very taxing ordeal that you guys have been through." Carmen attempted to put Gladys at ease. Gladys's splotchy neck was like a neon sign flashing "panic."

"Carmen, you frightened me. I–I didn't see you there." Gladys turned her head from side to side avoiding eye contact with Carmen. Her nervous nature could have been comical to Carmen had she not held so much pity in her heart for Gladys's state of emotional well-being. Mom Grace had been burdened for her daughter's mental stability for many years. As a result, Carmen had been praying for Gladys without ceasing. Even though her sister had changed Carmen's world through a malicious act of jealousy, taking delight in this moment of truth would not be characteristic of a woman of God. Her mother had taught Carmen better, and she intended to honor that instruction.

"Gladys, I need your forgiveness." Carmen recognized the full value in that statement. She appreciated how it broke down all defenses to accept the blame as though you owned all the fault. She had considered her approach years before as to how she would handle Gladys and James. _What will it profit to rehash who did what to whom? How can healing come to the present when not a second of history can be recalled? After all, that's exactly what Christ did on the cross. He knew no sin, yet took on the sins of the world. He accepted everyone's blame._

The words she was hearing mystified Gladys. Carmen needed _her_ forgiveness? Gladys had been prepared for a battle. For years she had rehearsed catty comments over and over in her mind. She knew she would need harsh words to strike back at Carmen because she expected the worst. Suddenly, she felt walls crumbling around her heart. Her defenses were rifling for an explanation for this sound of retreat stirring within her.

"I should have never left home and not gotten in touch with you, Gladys. I harbored some ill feelings against you, and for that I apologize. You didn't deserve it. We have allowed so much time to pass between us. I need my sister. I am sorry that I didn't listen to Mom Grace and just show up at your door years ago. I stifled the urge to do that. I know it was the Holy Spirit urging me to make things right with you. So, I need your forgiveness."

"Mother knew? All this time and Mother knew? She didn't say a word, yet she loved me anyway." Gladys felt her knees weaken. She tried to steady herself and reached out only to grab thin air. Carmen extended her hand in order to steady Gladys. It was the first meaningful physical contact the two sisters had shared for longer than Carmen had been gone from Savannah.

Carmen couldn't remember when Gladys had touched her even while she was still in the home. She had longed for Gladys to sit and brush her hair like she did the first year she came into the Willingham home. Gladys had been a real sister to Carmen until jealousy went to seed in her heart.

"Carmen, how can you say that? Do you know what I did?"

"I do, Gladys. I know everything. But it doesn't matter. None of it matters."

"I–I really don't know what to say, Carmen. I'm sorry. Please forgive me." The tears streaming down Gladys's cheek felt different than the stinging ones for which she had become accustomed. Gladys couldn't grasp how a person's heart could be as merciful as Carmen was demonstrating. She had every right to hate Gladys, and her hatred should have been immortal. Isolation was the consequence of Gladys's cruelty. She had been a quarrelsome individual only because of her dissatisfaction with herself. Pinpointing when she traded contentment for torment eluded Gladys. But suddenly, her heart had been laid open and years of pent-up guilt, pain, bitterness, and resentment spilled forth. She envisioned the ground opening at her feet and swallowing up her caldron of misery.

"That happened many years ago, Gladys. But, I do need you to know something you never allowed me to tell you. I turned down Kyle's invitation to the prom. I told him I could never consider dating him because my loyalty was to my sister. It still is, Gladys. Let's not miss any more time together than we have already." Carmen reached out slowly to hug her sister. She was uncertain if Gladys was ready to return the affection, but the opportunity was ripe.

The moment was more awkward than Gladys could have imagined. Her propensity to extend affection in any manner had long since abandoned her. Ralph was a living testament to the cold blood that coursed through her veins. Carmen's grip would not wane. Thirty years of a detached bond was miraculously reconnecting. There was a pull on Gladys's arms. The same force that swallowed up her repressed emotions attempted to restrain her means to restoration. She struggled, feeling the weightiness of the decision to step out of the prison long disguised as her friend. Inch by inch her arms closed the gap of distance she had contrived for the Willingham family.

Carmen patiently postponed any attempt to disengage. She could feel the intensity within Gladys. Her icy veneer was melting away. The initial hesitation would soon be a forgotten memory. Their next encounter would be easier for her. The two reunited girls would soon be greeting as if the past was only filled with today. As she held Gladys, a tinge of regret crept in. *Was it Your plan or mine to wait until this time to forgive? Why did I place the burden on Grace not to tell and to let it happen on this timeline? Mom and I both hoped that James and Gladys would confess to her on their own. But, did I run ahead of You, or fall behind? Had I done this sooner, would life have been better for James and Gladys … and Grace? Or, would it have made an impact then? Lord, forgive me if I lost sight of Your will in this plan. I felt comfortable in my trust in You and I stayed the course. Now, please add Your blessings to the restoration of our family. I am prepared to face whatever happens next.*

*   *   *

CAMP W'HAM, OCTOBER 16, 12:00 NOON

Kareem's phone had only seven percent battery left, but he needed to take the call. "Yo, whazup, Ricks?"

"She's here. She came in with all the others. She has the baby." Ricks had walked away from his post and out of earshot of other officers.

"I got no battery. Tell Mayor South of Gaston midnight." Kareem hung up the phone and dialed Jahron.

"Where you been? Yo' girl is at the church. You comin'?" Jahron was ready to be relieved of his command.

"I told ya I'm staying here. Too many eyes. She'll be back. I know her. I got no battery and I'm hungry. Send Tyrone with a charged phone and food. And I need transportation outta here once she comes, so leave me a car at the back where we came in." Kareem laid down on the bed to try to rest. He knew Madelyn would be detained for a few hours. The boys would wake him when they got there. He had entertained rummaging through the house while they were at the funeral, but Madelyn would not be foolish enough to hide the jewels at Grace's. The jewels might be on the property, but Madelyn was not one for doing the obvious. She was a girl of more deliberate intention.

EAST SAVANNAH CHRISTIAN CHURCH,
SANCTUARY, OCTOBER 16, 12:07 P.M.

James Willingham stood near the casket where his mother's body lay at rest. Nick had greeted him and Valerie. "I want you to know, Nick, that I feel you've done an outstanding job considering all the events surrounding Mama's wake. You've handled yourself admirably under extreme duress. I've been highly impressed with you." James had taken Nick's hand to shake and was cupping his left hand on top of the firm grip the two men held.

"I appreciate that, James. I really do. It's been difficult to assume both roles–grandson and director. But, I want you to understand, and I'll let Gladys and Mom know as well, I'll be assuming my station in the chair as family at the funeral. Matt, my assistant, is very capable of handling the service." Nick had agreed to everything Grace contrived for her funeral, but he was adamant that he would not abdicate his grandson position as pall-bearer or to be seated with the family. Grace stubbornly objected insisting that he regard her as anyone else, she was nothing more than ordinary. Nick had seldom, if ever, seen his grandmother's desire to be set apart as special in any manner, but he detected a very smug approval when he maintained his adamant decision.

"I'm sure Mama would have it no other way, Nick. I'm very proud to call you my nephew. You're a fine young man indeed." James surprised himself when he acted upon his urge to hug Nick. It felt very comfortable to embrace him, and that surprised him even more.

Nick's posture was a bit rigid. Initially his arms hung stiff by his side, but he managed to bring them up and give a gentle-man's pat to the back of a man he knew everything and nothing at all about. The embrace from James Willingham was even more unexpected than the accolades that had fallen on his ears. He was quite certain James didn't realize the full gravity of his kind gestures. His only regret was that his mother was not in the auditorium to witness it firsthand herself. Grace was likely dancing a jig in Heaven at the very moment. He was unsure how all of the logistics worked, but Nick was certain that whatever representative God chose had conveyed the message loud and clear somehow.

The moment was interrupted by the sound of giddy youngsters oohhing and aahhing over the numerous and exquisite arrangements on display. James recognized an opportunity he had asked for in his early-morning parking lot experience. He excused himself and began walking toward Nora.

"Nora, it's great to see you." James's greeting was timidly awkward.

"James. It's good to see you." Nora stuck out her hand to receive a handshake. Any business James would have with her would be simply that–business.

"Could I have a moment of your time?"

"Sure." Nora was counting the fact that this was his second sentence at one given encounter to be a plus in and of itself. Nora walked away from the others.

Ashley's radar immediately began receiving signals of a reconciliatory effort on the part of her dad. Whereas she would love to witness healing on the part of James, she could feel a tinge of jealousy nipping at her heels. She would love to be rid of the vicious vice that kept her from being the young woman Grandma thought she had the potential to become. She wrestled with that imperfection in her life more than any other.

James and Nora walked away and situated themselves in a pew midway of the right center aisle. "You have no reason to respect me, Nora. Not as a man, and definitely not as a father. I need your forgiveness. I've been very wrong by you. Not only you, but all my children. I need to let you know to the best of my ability and availability, you can count on me to be involved in your life in the future. That is, if you'll allow it?" James's statement was fashioned more in question form that an assumption.

"I–I really don't know quite what to say, James. I mean, I guess we can try it and see how it works. You know I don't live here now." Nora assumed he was aware of her adventure in Spain, but he didn't bother to come to her college graduation celebration. She could only assume he hadn't inquired as to her career choices. She felt safe in her supposition.

"I know you've been in Spain, Nora. I know you have your own magazine company. I have several of your issues." Nora's surprise was a telltale to James. "Apparently you don't keep up with your subscribers." James grinned, realizing the absurdity of such a comment, but hoping to bring levity to her apprehension of his intentions.

"You do?" Nora was genuinely surprised. "I'm sorry. I had no idea. Cool."

"You're a rock star, lady. I'm very proud of you and your accomplishments. I'm sure Grace was responsible in some way for setting you on the right career path." James grinned content in the knowledge that Grace Willingham was amazing at her perception for the future. "So, what do you say? It's awfully late in life, I understand, to begin again, but since we never really did begin at all, can we give it a shot?"

Nora shrugged her shoulders and gave a doubtful look, but managed to muster a response. "I'm game if you are. But, long-distance relationships are tough, you know."

"I know it's going to be more of a challenge. But, let's give ourselves time to warm up to one another and catch up with each other's lives. How's that for starters?" James was continuing to astound his good senses with the ease at which his words spilled forth. *God, whatever it is you're doing, please keep it up. I had no idea I had this kind of passion for anything. Family has been the void I've had in my life, and yet I've had it all along. What a fool I have been.*

Several sets of eyes had been on the father-daughter pair. No one knew better than Nora, yet everyone was keenly aware of the estrangement that comprised the history between them. None. The stark realization was that there was a dormant assertion of relation of the tightest knit—that of parent and child. James wanted nothing to do with his daughter born of an affair with his best friend's wife. Nora had long since recused herself as being the illegitimate daughter of James Albert Willingham II. She proudly proclaimed kinship to Grace. That association came wrapped in love and acceptance. It was far easier to deny the need for a man in her life than it was for Nora to deal with the demons in her head. They were the fiends that whispered thoughts of devalue and worthlessness in vile attempt to derail her future. Grace Willingham would breathe life into her spirit again. She was the one who introduced Nora to self-worth and self-preservation. She was very familiar with the story of how GG stepped in and helped Nellie regain confidence after her attempt at suicide. She took her mother into her home and nursed her back to health. Had it not been for the compassionate heart of her GG, Nora would have never been born. GG was well aware that Nora possessed a lot of Nellie's spirit—a wishy-washy kind of love for the

Lord. Nora's mom had even likened herself to a milk-and-honey Christian. She went through the motions, but God was more of a convenient name-drop than a steadfast hope in her life.

Nora would be the first to admit that she had wavered a bit from Grace's teachings. Her mother's influence caught her in a quandary when facing off with the instructions of GG. Nora's confusion regarding God's position in her life, while understandable, met with no acceptance by Grace Willingham. Nellie's reasoning for flagrancy regarding her faith had never been discussed. As for Nora, hers involved trust. If she surrendered her will and heart to God, how would she survive a disappointment if He abandoned her? After all, that's what men did time and time again in her life. She had been rejected by her father and five stepdads that followed him.

Now, here she sat with the man she had always wanted to be her prince charming. Did she really want him now? Had the need for his attention been abandoned by her in the same fashion as he had abandoned her years before? When did it abscond? *How odd. I didn't even realize it was gone. I feel kind of cold toward him. Not angry. Not bitter. Just cold.* A rocker visit came crashing into Nora's thoughts. It was a pearl of wisdom from GG that Nora had never forgotten. Nora had spent hours querying GG about truth and trust of God and men. The young girl questioned if she would ever be able to yield her heart to either. The uncertainty had no more left her lips when GG told her, "Even the obscure takes on clarity when the mind is receptive to endorse it."

Nora could not control what came over her. Her sudden compulsion to embrace her father was more than she could stifle. She reached over and hugged James Willingham. She swallowed hard to get the lump out of her throat and back down where it belonged. She was moved, but she certainly didn't want to cry in front of this stranger dad of hers.

"I take it that's a yes?" James said as he heartily returned the hug.

"Yes, it's a yes," Nora responded.

"Well, are you going to introduce me to this beautiful girl or not? It's okay. I'll do it. Hi, I'm Valerie, Jim's wife. And you're?"

"I'm Nora Willingham. It's a pleasure to meet you." Nora stood up to greet Valerie. *I'm sure you're not going to want me to call you "Mom."* I've heard about you. GG told me James had married again."

"Valerie, this is my daughter. She's beautiful, isn't she? And she's a journalist. Has her own magazine in Spain. She's fared well, this gal. I'm very proud of her. Quite a few accomplishments. She has several meritorious awards for her writing. Her magazine has won national and even international awards. She's done well for herself."

Nora could have been bowled over with a feather. She could be none too sure, but she felt her heart bubbling. It was the strangest sensation she'd ever known. *Is this pride? Is it acceptance? Is it the end of rejection? It's unbelievable is what it is! This man has kept up with me, and, obviously, not through GG.*

"Well, aren't you the special one! Let me touch you." Valerie was not condescending in the least. Her sincerity spewed forth, and she leaned in and hugged Nora as though they had been life-long friends. The two young women didn't go to the same schools in Savannah, but Nora was well aware that Valerie was one of Madelyn's classmates. She was young. Too young for her dad.

"You girls stand here and chat. I'm going to step over here for just a second." Jim moved away from the two talkative women and walked over to Madelyn. She, too, had taken a keen interest in the conversation he was having with Nora and wondered if she might be his next target. She was right.

"Hey, little fella, how ya' doin'? He's a fine boy, Madelyn." James rubbed his hand back and forth and then patted Bryson on the back.

"His name's Bryson," Madelyn responded rather curtly.

"I'm sorry, I should have known that. He's my grandson, and I hope to be a better grandfather than I have been a father, Maddie." James didn't know how else to engage in his reason for broaching her any other way but straightforward. It always seemed to work for his mother.

"You haven't earned the right to call me Maddie. Only Granny could do that, because she loved me like no one else ever has." Madelyn looked straight on at James initially, and then, repulsed by looking at his face, turned her eyes away from him to finish her comment.

"Look at me. I'm standing before you a broken man. You have every right to be angry at me, to despise me, even to hate me."

"Hate isn't something Granny Grace allowed." Madelyn quickly took herself back to the roots of the strong Willingham legacy that she had welcomed back into her life since Grace's demise.

"You're right, she wouldn't let us do that. And for that, I'm grateful because I'm ahead of the game that I'm so far behind in. I don't deserve to be standing in the same room with you, Madelyn Joy Willingham. I'm unworthy to be called your father.

But I want more than that. I want to be your dad. God willing and your permission, I pray I live long enough to make up for the years I have spent so foolishly. I should have been there for you, and I wasn't. I simply forgot Whose I was. I've been reminded, and I'm pressing forward starting today. Will you give me a chance, Madelyn? Can we have lunch next week? I want to find out who you are, where you are in your life, and what your plans are from here. What do you say? I really need your forgiveness. For real, for serious, for positive."

Madelyn's emotions stopped on a dime. Those words pierced her heart. That was her catch-phrase as a child. *Did you really just say that? How did "you" know that? Seriously, did you really remember, and if so, why? Why would you hang onto that all these years? Could it be that you really cared for me all this time?*

Madelyn turned her gaze back to James. His face was tender and patient. His terse business-like, unscrupulous demeanor had morphed into a semblance of civility and trustworthiness. But then, an attribute like trust was one for which Madelyn had lost all faith. Had it not been for Granny Grace, there would not have been a soul on the face of the earth that would have introduced her to the concept of truth. As desperate as she was for a familial link now that Grace was gone, she would guard her heart for a while. A relationship between a father and daughter, she could only suppose, would have to be nurtured. Especially beginning this late in a child's life. History is a difficult thing to relive, even in stories. If a relationship could be cultivated, it would begin with the present forward. But James Willingham was right—it would be God's will and her call.

"Forgiveness never works with only one party. There must

be a beneficiary to accept its reward." That's what Grace used to tell me when I talked with her about forgiving James for not being a father to me. You're always right, Granny. You never led me wrong.

"You don't have to make up your mind today, Madelyn. I totally understand. You have a lot of reason to be angry and—"

"I'll be free on Wednesday. Noon. At Fanfleezie's. Granny loved that place."

"Thank you, Madelyn. It's a start. I think if we both know it'll be awkward at first, we'll be fine. Let's just take it slow and go from there." James wrapped his arms around Bryson and Madelyn and kissed them both on the forehead. Madelyn didn't return either, but his words lingered on her heart. She watched him walk away, and tears welled up in her eyes. *If you could see us now, Granny, you would love this. It's what you lived your life to see, and it took your death to make it come to be.*

"Jimmy, how's Zimbabwe? I hear all the kids think you're King David. Apparently you've killed a giant or two there." James reached out his hand and slipped the other one around his son's neck to embrace him. Jimmy hadn't felt his father's touch in many years. His reservation was noticeable.

"I don't know about slaying any giants, but I have killed a few wooly buggars over there. How are you doing, Dad?" Jimmy was more staccato in his inquiry."

"How long are you in town for, Son?"

"It's kind of open-ended right now. I haven't really had time to think about it much, to be honest." Jimmy scuffed his feet on the floor, kicking at a thread in the carpet. To say the moment was awkward would be putting it mildly. The last encounter he and his dad had was less than pleasant. It resulted in a shoving match, and Jimmy had brought his fist to his face. James had caught his arm before it landed in his eye. *"Don't ever raise your fist to me again, Son. It'll be the last thing you ever do." My father threatened my life. How am I supposed to be standing here talking to a man as heartless as that?*

"Listen, Jimmy, you and I had some rough years. It was all my fault. I hope you understand that. I have acted like a horse's patoot. I don't deserve the privilege of being your father, but I am. You can't change that. But one thing I can change is our relationship from this day forward. Will you give me another chance, Son? I really need your forgiveness." James had his left hand on Jimmy's shoulder and his right one on his forearm. His gaze was front-on hoping to lock in the clemency needed to become a liaison in his son's life.

"Dad, it's as much my fault as—"

"Jimmy, it's not. You were the child. All you ever wanted from me was what you deserved–my time and attention. I was too self-absorbed to consider the damage that I was inflicting upon my own flesh and blood. Let's start from here in order to get there. Can we do that, Son? Will you give me a chance?"

"Uh, sure. Africa's a long way for you to come for a visit, though." Jimmy chuckled attempting to lighten the moment, for himself, at least.

"I think the climate would suit me well. It might take a little doing for me to get there, but don't count me out. Okay? Lunch soon?" James's calendar was going to be crowded this week if he set aside time for four kids and a preacher. The City of Savannah could wait. His family had to be a priority for the first time in many years.

"Why not come by Grandma's tonight? We're going to be hanging out for a little while, anyway. I heard it's going to be a lights-out-early night after a long day's events, but we could sit on the porch like we used to do with Grandma. What d'ya say?" Jimmy could envision a talk-in-the-dark moment with his dad to clear the air. *What better place to start over than on Grandma Grace's front porch?*

"We're all pretty busted after the last few days, but we'll see what we can do. You have a cell phone number where I can reach you?" James took his cell phone from his pocket and pulled up the contacts menu. His son's number was there, but he wanted to make sure it hadn't changed in the past several years.

Jimmy recited his number. No changes were necessary. The mellow thought that settled in when he realized his dad still knew how to contact him was trumped by the reminder that he hadn't. Jimmy produced a counterfeit grin of approval.

"You want my number?" James inquired?

"Oh, oh, sure. Yeah. Right. Let me get my phone here." Jimmy felt in all pockets and realized he didn't have his phone with him. No one from the States ever called but Ashley and Grandma Grace, and he had been with Ashley. His phone was home alone.

"Didn't bring it? Here you go. My card. It has all my information on there. You call me, day or night, anytime you need me. I'm available, Son. I'll drop what I'm doing. I promise."

"Okay, sure. Sir. Dad." The terminology felt strange—a term of endearment that should have been accompanied with respect, but there was none. Jimmy would admit, however, that it took a big man to do what his dad had just done. Apparently, he was making his rounds. He had witnessed an exchange between James and Nora and then Madelyn. He suspected Ashley would be his next stop, although Ashley had the edge on all the children, or so it seemed.

"Ashley, Sweetheart, how are you?" James gave Ashley a hug, and she reciprocated rather pensively. Everyone assumed she and her dad had a solid relationship, but it was far from the truth. She had heard rumblings around the courthouse about "the Mayor sporting questionable company." She could ill afford to be pulled into a circle of his shady reputation. She had mapped out a course for her career. She had worked hard to attain a favorable standing in the legal arena. She had compassion for her father, wanted to honor him as such, but she was unwilling to allow her good character to be tarnished by any affiliation with him. He had stopped calling her for lunch outings more than two years prior. While she missed it and felt a slight sense of betrayal, she had to keep her distance.

"Hey, Daddy. I'm good. How's Valerie?" Ashley really didn't care, but she knew all the social graces and exercised them when necessary.

"She's good. You guys can visit in a moment. Ashley, I need to see you next week sometime. First thing. Some things I need to talk with you about and settle up with you and kind of prepare you for."

Ashley read multiple issues into his untimely announcement. *Talk with me about? Settle up with me? Prepare me for? What have you done, Daddy? What have you done?*

"Hey, hey, don't you go to worrying there, little lady. Everything will be all right. Okay? James took his hand and lifted

Ashley's chin. "I don't want you concerning yourself for me. I just need to talk with you. Okay?"

"Okay, Daddy. You scare me when you say those things." Ashley's heart was already anxious. She sensed a battle of some sort, but what could it be? His new-found acquaintances or something else? *The Will. Of course! He's going to ask me about Grandma's Will. That's exactly why he's being so sugary sweet. Doggone your hide, James Albert Willingham. You're a sly one. Well, it won't do you any good. I'm not telling you anything until the Will is probated and it's read to everyone. That's the way Grace wanted it, and that's the way it will be.*

"Val. Hey, Val, come over here and speak to Ashley. She's inquiring about you." James motioned for Valerie and she excused herself from Nora reluctantly. The two were chattier than James had expected. That could be good, or that could be bad. Nora could ask more questions in two minutes that a team of attorneys could in an hour's worth of depositions.

"Valerie, you remember Ashley? You girls catch up a minute, and I'm going to walk over and speak to Carmen, It'll soon be time for us to gather up as a family and say good-bye to Mama one last time." James took his arms around the two girls' waists and pulled them in closer. There would be no depth to the conversation. Compliments on each other's attire and small talk about the outpouring of love from the community would be the extent of their discussion.

"Carmen, you look great. I know Nick wants to see us here in just a minute, but I had to steal a moment with you. Hey, listen, I just wanted to thank you for yesterday. You have no idea how you impacted my life. I spent a long night with just me and The

Lord. I'm turning my life around thanks to you. There are going to be some tough days ahead for me, a lot of things I'm not proud of and my family won't be either, but I'm not living for the world anymore, Carmen. I want you to know you set me free from an emotional prison, and I'll be forever grateful. If God can change your life and take away anger and bitterness and hatred for what I did to you, He can change anybody, and that includes the likes of me. Thank you. I owe you my life."

Carmen's cheeks were a constant flow of teardrops. "This is what Mom always wanted, James. She wanted to see us reunited."

"I wish she could have, Carmen. I feel horrible about—"

"Oh, don't you think for a second she doesn't know. I believe she does. I believe she's rejoicing over the healing right now. If her death was what it took to make this happen, she would have died a long time ago." Carmen laughed at the tongue-in-cheek comment, but she knew in her heart of hearts that Grace would have gladly given up life for any of her children. "Everything is on God's timeline, James. We can't second-guess how He works all things for the good of those who love Him."

"Hey, let's go over and talk to Ralph. He looks pretty forsaken there. You've never gotten to know him, other than school, have you?" James took Carmen's hand and led her to the pew where Ralph was seated all alone. The two stood and talked to him and attempted to bring him into the fold of the family. James shared with Carmen Ralph's rededication story, and the three stood at the end of the pew talking and encouraging one another.

Gladys entered the auditorium and stopped at the back. She had been hiding out in the ladies' restroom in the children's unit, too nervous to come out. She had been processing the forgiveness

moment that Carmen had surprised her with. Carmen seemed
to hold no malice in her heart, no resentment, no hostility, or
even bitterness. How does someone step out of those kinds of
vices and into a state of complete calm? How can anyone who is
traumatized to the degree that she was, not once but twice in her
lifetime by people she loved and trusted, lead a perfectly normal
and productive life? Why didn't it destroy her? What did she
possess within her that could cause her not only to overcome but
to override the obstacles facing her in the aftermath? Gladys felt
faint at heart, not because Carmen had been victorious, but that
she had failed to capture the big picture of what her mother was
attempting to teach each one of her children.

*Look at them. Everyone talking, acting like one big, happy
and in-love family. What has happened here? Ralph is laughing.
I haven't seen him laugh in years. Carmen is brushing shoulders
with James. How? Why? What? Who? God, it can only be you.*

Gladys straightened her skirt and fluffed her hair. She threw
her head back, her chin up, and she frolicked down the aisle in
a gait that was befitting a prude. She wouldn't allow herself to
be swallowed up in a moment of pretense. The angry spirits
that tormented her conjured up thoughts that raced through her
mind as she made the long trek from the back of the church.
*After the funeral is done and the business is all taken care of, this
camaraderie will all be over. It will not be fair to anyone. They
will all feel cold. And used. What good is a moment of happiness
anyway? It only begs for more. And when it can't be attained,
the heart is left to bleed and gasp for the life it knew once before.
Before? Before when? I knew that life once. Why did I let it end?*

EAST SAVANNAH CHRISTIAN CHURCH PARKING LOT,
OCTOBER 16, 12:40 P.M.

Off-duty security officers gathered to monitor traffic conges-
tion and parking. This was the usual crew that managed parking for Sunday services and special events for East Savannah
Christian Church. The on-duty uniformed officers had assumed
their appointed posts to stand vigil outside the entranceways of
the church. The doors would not open for public viewing for
another forty-five minutes, but people were already forming lines
at the entrance. Many of them had stayed behind after the last
morning service. Ricks was in charge of assigning positions. He
did a mental checklist of officers to make certain he didn't miss
an ingress. He knew Masters would be arriving shortly, but he
had some business he had to take care of. He needed to see to it
right away. He didn't need Masters complicating things for him
at this point. He motioned for Sergeant Benefield.

"Benefield, I need you to watch my post as well. Can you
do that? Just for ten minutes or maybe less? I need to go relieve
myself."

"Gotcha covered." Benefield stepped back to the middle of
the two checkpoints. A big crowd was beginning to accumulate,
and soon it would be difficult to be on guard at one point, much
less two.

Ricks opened the door to the sanctuary where he knew the
family would be. The Mayor was with the family and they had
assembled around Grace Willingham's casket. They had joined
hands, their heads were bowed, and the pastor was having prayer
with them. Ricks took steps to the front. With each step he took,

his shoes squeaked and echoed through the empty auditorium. He slowed his pace, but the squeaks obnoxiously resounded. One by one, heads turned and eyes opened to see who was "sneaking" into the private family moment. When Jim's eye met Ricks's, his heart felt laden with the life he had vowed to abandon. He gave a firm shake of his head, sending Ricks a message to retreat. It was a terribly inappropriate time to be intruding. Jim understood, however, that his disregard of their text messages for the past several hours was likely alarming his former comrades.

Ricks stopped his infernal squeaking, but he didn't retreat. He would wait out the prayer and speak to Jim. It was imperative that Jim was aware of the Gaston meeting tonight. Ricks understood consequences of not delivering weighty messages. He had been eyewitness to the damage of the heavy hands of Boss's assistants. Those men were the kind you didn't want to tangle with, armed or not.

The prayer ended and Jim excused himself. He walked over to Ricks and leaned in closer to address the issue at hand. "Keep your voice down. What do you need?" Jim was more curt than his usual self. Ricks was somewhat startled by it, but brushed it off as a family intrusion.

"You haven't been answering my texts. What's up with that?" Ricks's tone bore a slight annoyance but evoked no response from Jim. "Meeting. Gaston. Midnight." Ricks was short and succinct.

"Can't make it tonight. I'll be with family. I'm sure he'll understand."

"Not a good idea, Mayor. He specifically requested you." Ricks didn't want to be held responsible in any way for the Mayor's no-show.

"Not happening, Ricks. Not tonight. If you'll excuse me, I need to get back to my family." Jim turned and walked back, shaking the hands of Pastor Webster. Ricks stood in amazement and concern at the response from Jim Willingham. This was not going to go down pretty tonight if Jim failed to show. No one said no to Boss. It just didn't happen. There were plenty of rumors about the low-down of his torture chamber. If only half of the stories were true, it was enough to keep one obligated to Boss until death. As for Ricks, he wanted that to happen by a more natural cause.

* * *

EAST SAVANNAH CHRISTIAN,
FAMILY VIEWING, 12:45 P.M.

"She looks so naked without the jewels." Gladys dabbed her nose as she stood viewing her mother for the last few moments.

"I don't think 'naked' is perhaps the appropriate word, Gladys, but I certainly understand what you mean. Her décolleté deserved to have them there. But she's still the priceless lady with or without them." Carmen was tender with Gladys. She rested her arm gently across her shoulders, stroking her arm and offering comfort.

"I never got to see GG wear them. Ever. That's really not fair." Nora pouted her nose in the air in her spoiled little girl fashion.

"That's not true, Nora. I'm sure Grandma placed them on her neck to show you how they looked. She probably did you like she did the rest of us girls—let you actually put them on yourself just to get the feel of the weight." Ashley was none too sure of the last statement. Why she would reveal that to the rest of the family was something she had declared she wouldn't do. For all she knew, perhaps Grandma had only allowed her to try them on for size. After all, the jewels were to be bequeathed to her."

"Well, that doesn't count, Ashley. I wanted to see them on GG for more than just a moment. I wanted to gaze at them for a long time and get caught up in their beauty. I recall them. They were exquisite. But now, I'm of the age that I could really appreciate a woman's best friend, and lots of them, mixed with splashes of brilliant red luminance." Nora was more than dramatic in her descriptive deprivation for the experience. But knowing that GG intended for her to have the jewels appeased her disquieted disposition. She had every confidence in the recovery of the missing pieces of gemstones.

Jimmy, Nick and even Ralph were uncertain how to respond to the avaricious nature of the three women's comments. Ralph had not been around the Willinghams enough to stake any claim into civility between the younger family members, especially. He had not been successful in bringing peace between him and his wife. He certainly wasn't about to interfere into matters he didn't understand. Jimmy and Nick, however, were both keenly aware of the value of the missing pieces from Grace's wardrobe, but neither were exactly sure how to interpret the ill-timing of the eagerness in the girls' voices. These two vipers had been at each other's throats since they had been introduced as next of kin. But the inappropriateness of standing over the casket of the very lady who mediated their jealous rants was objectionable at best.

James and Valerie cut their eyes toward one another but didn't move a muscle. There were many things James would love to have said out loud, as would Valerie, but neither felt they had earned the right to correct any behavior within the Willingham clan. They had certainly been two of the naughtiest in the bunch. James knew his mischief went far beyond the comprehension of even his wife. The disgrace he would bring upon the family was yet to be discovered but would soon be forthcoming.

Madelyn, who never minded speaking her piece, had a slight hesitation. She had finally bonded with this family. Would she dare run the risk of disrupting the unity she had acquired? *How would Granny handle this? What would she say? She would certainly be diplomatically wise. Surely you can pull up something! Think Maddie, think.* Baby Bryson could feel the tension mounting inside his mom. He began to stir and whimper. Madelyn gently patted his back and kissed his fuzzy-top head. "I like to remember what Granny said about her jewels when I asked her why she didn't wear them. She told me, 'It's not how we wear our wealth, but rather, how we reveal it.' I kind of like her without them. This is how we saw Grace all the time. She didn't have to wear The Queen's jewels to reveal her worth. It spilled from her heart every day."

A kind of a hush swept across each of Grace Willingham's loved ones. Madelyn's reminder reckoned with the spirits of misaligned mourning and embraced a victory with those who were at a loss for words. Madelyn settled down into her shoes again, not realizing how she had tensed her way loose from their fit. A pleasing accolade welled up inside her. She knew she had in some way brought a smile to Granny Grace's face. She had felt the sensation many times as a child when she recited a memory verse or said something profoundly simple that pleased Grace. The warmth that enveloped her then had escaped from the dungeons of her cold heart. She had been void of feelings like this for such an extended season that it was like a Lazarus moment for her. Resurrected goodness was gushing from the springs of her soul. She longed to have one moment with Granny to tell her how grateful she was for the life lessons.

"We're all a mess!" Valerie walked over to the table, grabbed the box of Kleenex, and passed it around to the ladies. James, Jimmy, Nick and Ralph each took one, as well. Not another word was spoken out loud, but individuals' thoughts were churning memories of bygone days. They stood motionless until five minutes before time for public viewing. No one stepped aside and gave privacy to any one family member. Instead, all were gathered around the casket, looking down on what remained of the most remarkable woman they had ever known. And she was theirs, in whole and in part. In life and in death, she would remain in their hearts. Bejeweled or not, her beauty shone, not through her deceased body, but through the lives of those standing around her who had managed to capture the true value and worth of Grace Carissa Willingham.

Chapter 41

Rarely had East Savannah Christian Church's services seen the crowds of people who were marching into its building. Every seat was filled in the lower and balcony levels. People stood with backs pressed against the walls. Gentlemen were like popping corn in a hot kettle with their kind gestures. It all began with one man and his son who allowed a lady and her small children to be seated. Others followed their lead, and then assumed their traded positions along the walls devoid of provisions for additional seating. The lobby areas, café, and classrooms were brimming with onlookers desiring to view the service on the flat-screen monitors. Many would have stayed home had the service been televised. Additionally, the place was covered with cops! On the grounds and inside the building were uniformed officers of Chatham and surrounding counties, as well as the Georgia State Patrol who had joined forces to provide adequate coverage for the event. Vans bearing the logo from media venues across the nation and beyond filled and overflowed the designated area at the accommodation of

Chief Griffin. However, none were allowed inside with cameras. The live feed would not capture a memorial of the service to be reproduced in any way, as per Grace's wishes. Many journalists joined the services for firsthand accounts of the memorial to such a prestigious lady. Nick's eyes zeroed in on Bruce Masters in a suit and tie. He was among the men standing against the wall. His position was by design, not because he gave up a seat. Bruce had made certain to secure a place in the auditorium that would afford him a full view of the Willingham family. Nick made no mention of his presence to the others, but silently hoped Madelyn would not notice him so that she could relax and enjoy being with her family. Grace's wish was for her funeral to be a celebration, not a spectacle. Her owner-and-director-of-Turner's-Funeral-Home grandson had intended to honor that request but was learning the limitations of his control.

The final open-casket viewing for the public was laboriously intense. The family members smiled and shook hands with folks expressing ever-so-brief condolences for their tremendous loss. A fine-tuned ear could detect the mumblings and mutterings of all who were curious about the recovery of the legendary jewels once belonging to Queen Elizabeth II. Only a brazen few would inquire, but all such inquiries were reserved for Ashley, James, and Gladys. The townspeople were familiar with the more prominent relatives of Grace. They mused at Nick's family position being out of the familiar setting of funeral director. No one was quite sure what to say to Madelyn. Her rainbow-colored hair, tattoos and piercings were a sore-thumb sidebar commentary to be reserved for on-the-ride-home gossip. Carmen, Jimmy and Nora were the unfamiliar faces that gave people a pastime puzzle to solve while they waited for the service to begin.

Madelyn was grateful for Bryson's afternoon nap. She realized she had been under close surveillance since stepping out of the car at East Savannah. She was well aware that Detective Masters had positioned himself against the wall to her immediate left. Carmen and Nick had warned her to stick with the crowd and not to exit the auditorium if she could avoid it. When Bryson needed changing, Ashley was assigned to the task. Madelyn was more concerned about Kareem showing up than she was the law but had kept her apprehension to herself. There was no need to worry the family with her past-life exposure. She knew Kareem would appear when least expected, but for now, she felt safe and would redirect her anxious thoughts.

Pastor Webster stepped up to the podium, and the background filler music ceased. He stood with a big smile and welcoming eyes as the buzz of voices throughout the auditorium eventually subsided. The massive room was as still as the slumbering night. Everyone's ears waited as if anticipating permission to breathe and stir with signs of life. Martin Webster invited them to bow their heads for a time of prayer.

"Father, We are assembled again today–Your Day–to bring You more praise, honor and glory. We do so because we have come to celebrate the life and death, and then, life anew of Grace Carissa Willingham. She was truly one of Your most trusted warriors, and today, Grace sits at the feet of her Master. She lived to serve You, Lord Jesus, and she died to live with You forever. We don't have to tell *You* what a testimony her life was. You are fully aware of every word she spoke, every deed she spent, and every life she changed. Those she touched, she transformed because, as we all know, when Grace had the opportunity, and even sometimes when opportunity wasn't quite ready for Grace, she introduced folks to the power and love of You, our Almighty Lord and Savior. Grace Carissa Willingham was a rare gem. In our minds, she was one of a kind. In her mind, she was ordinary. Grace knew her secret to a blessed life consisted of nothing more than each of us have the capacity to possess. Lord, as we celebrate Grace's life today, may all who have ears to hear understand exactly what it was that made this lady special. Those of us who knew her best are well aware that Grace would enjoy nothing more than to put the focus on You, for You were indeed and now continue to be the embodiment of her life. Thank you, Lord, for all of Your creation, but among Your finest we celebrate today the life and death of Grace Carissa Willingham. Amen."

Tears retreated as East Savannah Christian Church's band followed the "Amen" with a resounding blast of praise and worship. Screens lighted words of a familiar praise song inviting people to join in and raise their voices in harmony to Casting Crown's version of "My Savior Loves, My Savior Lives." Grace fell in love with MercyMe along with the rest of the world when the hit single "I Can Only Imagine" crossed the charts. Alex Shaw rendered a solo performance of the popular song. The celebration continued with Michael W. Smith's "Ancient Words strong and true, changing me and changing you," followed by his version of "You Are Holy." Voices shouted the lyrics within the song of "You're my Prince of Peace, and I will live my life for You" in honor of the lady who truly did. The panorama of worship ended with perhaps the most befitting of songs led by James Albert Willingham III. Jimmy's rendition of "Amazing Grace, how sweet the sound, that saved a wretch like me" bore special meaning because Grace Willingham captured the essence of the meaning of the word. She understood the merits of grace and how unworthy she was to possess it. And because of its priceless nature, a gift free to all, she generously presented the Giver to everyone so that they could be as rich and blessed as she had been.

Grace's wish was that no one would give eulogies about her. The emphasis was to be aimed at the purpose of a person's existence–that of praising and serving God. The order she had planned was prayer, worship, and ending with a sermon for the living. She had shared with Pastor Webster the Sunday before her passing, "Now, remember, Preacher, you preach to the living. You don't have to worry about me. I'll be better off than you guys down here."

The family's hearts and countenance were lifted. Grace's strategically-planned send-off had worked its charm. The reflection upon The Creator had fashioned the perfect celebratory spirit. Grace herself had been intimately familiar with the kind of peace that songs of praise would kindle within a soul. The entire audience was relaxed and in accord with her deliberate intent to distract them from being filled with sorrow regarding the very thing she had lived to die for–heading home. Even Nick had completely disengaged from the business surrounding the logistics of a funeral process. For the first time since Grandma Grace's departure from this world, he was completely allowing himself to be a family member and enmeshed in the pages of the Willingham legacy.

"Amazing Grace how sweet… the lady!" were the first words spoken as Pastor Webster stepped up to the podium. "Folks, we are gathered here to pay respect to and remember fondly Grace Carissa Willingham. Grace lived an amazing life. If Grace had allowed us—" There was a rumbling of chuckles from the audience. "Yes, if Grace had allowed us the opportunity to share testimonies, this funeral would be stretched out for another several days. But, you and I know what Grace would say about that: 'Don't waste God's time on me. I'm good to go!'" There was enchanting laughter from the crowd. "Grace Willingham would encourage us to spend our time talking about the one thing that really has lasting value.

"It's no secret that Grace lies before us today without the novel jewels adorning her. And while she was appreciative of those famous jewels and the sacrifice that brought them to her, each of us who had the pleasure of knowing Grace Willingham intimately knew exactly where her real treasure lay. She was one of the most decent, wise, loving, and Christ-like people to have lived on this ol' earth. Life didn't happen to Grace Willingham. Grace Willingham happened to life!

"It was Grace who was first to help the down-and-out. It was Grace who instilled wholesome, godly values in her family members, friends, and yes, even and especially strangers. It was Grace who almost singlehandedly filled our church full to overflowing with new converts. It was Grace who lived with a certain tenacity that defied the odds. Why was she abundantly successful at doing these things? Grace Willingham put time into people. Take a good look around you at the people in whom she invested. And you are only a tip of the iceberg.

"Yes, many are here today because of the colorful life of Grace Carissa Willingham. But truth be told, you are mostly here because she lived for Jesus. Don't take me wrong. Grace didn't count herself any different that you and me. In fact, she would be like the Apostle Paul: 'Consider myself the chief sinner.'

"Grace Willingham requested that I remind you today that Jesus loves you. She said tell them all, 'Don't weep for me, but rejoice for I am with my Lord.' She wanted her headed-home day to be a time of worship and revival, and a time of decision. But I suppose that that's what every funeral is. Let us consider what it means to be created by God, and then, saved through Jesus. In Genesis Chapter 1 we read how God *spoke* the world into existence–the sun, moon, stars, the earth, the animals, vegetation, and the oceans. Everything. He spoke, and it was. But visualize with me the Almighty God Himself kneeling, and with His hands scooping up the dirt He had spoken into existence. Then, as Genesis 2:7 reads, '... the Lord God *formed* the man from the dust of the ground ...' God formed man. He shaped us, molded us, and made us in His image. And then, God did for man what He didn't do for all the other living creatures. He *breathed* into his nostrils the very breath of life, and man became a living being, or 'soul' as the Kings James version records it.

"Grace and us–you and me are different from all other creatures. We have a living soul. All of us will live forever! But don't think for a moment that all of us will live forever in Heaven. It's not automatic. Because of sin, God gave us G.R.A.C.E.–God's Riches At Christ's Expense. Grace Willingham knew this. That's exactly why she made it her life's ambition to get *you* in the Lord and into Heaven!"

Pastor Webster went through a brief oration of the Plan of Salvation in accordance with Grace's wishes. He concluded by saying, "Now friends, that's what Grace would want you to celebrate today. She believed it. She claimed it. She lived it. She would not want anyone to be troubled about the missing jewels and cause you to forget or ignore how Grace lived and why she lived so well. Her life invites you to know Who she knew, for you to live for Whom she lived for, and for you to head home along with her when your time is up.

"Let us pray: Heavenly Father, we come to you with thanksgiving for Grace Willingham and her life of love and giving. We thank you most of all for Her Savior, Jesus who will take those who belong to Him to Grace's new home in glory. We need your comfort and your peace in this time of mourning, understanding that we do not mourn like those without hope. Rather, we mourn as those who have experienced hope in the life of Grace Carissa Willingham. Help us, Father, to accept the things she spoke and lived. Give us courage and honesty to follow Your Word, Your Will, and Your Way. In the name of Jesus, our Lord, Amen."

No one could be saddened at the death of Grace Willingham. She would be missed. There would be a void in her family, the community, and at East Savannah Christian Church. But her legacy would live on for generations to come. Each family member was given a red poppy to toss in the casket. It had been Grace's favorite flower since her initial visit to Europe, and Nick had special-ordered them for the occasion. It wasn't Grace's request. She would have never been so presumptuous to think herself worthy of the extravagance, and would have vehemently objected to the cost. Although she had managed to grow some wild ones in her back yard area, October was not their season. Nick felt it a special privilege to do the honors. She looked lovelier than ever with the delicate flowers scattered about her beautiful cream pearl-studded suit. After all, the color matched her ruby red lips and fire-engine red toenails that were peeping out at the end of the casket lining. Although no one would see the painted-up toenails, it was another of Grace's requests that Nick honored.

Surprisingly, there were no tears–a Grace wish but not among her requests. She was well aware the things she could dictate and those she couldn't. Gladys and Ralph stepped up first, and Gladys patted Grace's hands. James and Valerie tossed in their poppies, and James gave Grace the thumbs up. After that, everyone joined in the thumbs-up salute until all family had paraded past. At that time, the casket was closed, and Matt, Nick's assistant, addressed the guests as the family exited the church to prepare for the ride to the gravesite.

"Ladies and Gentleman, the family of Grace Willingham would like to thank you for your attendance today. Please under-stand that, at the request of Grace Willingham, the graveside service will be a private ceremony. The Willinghams would like to invite you, however, to participate in Grace's headed-home cel-ebration as you exit the building. The family members will hand you a red balloon if you would like to participate. It was Grace's wish that you say a prayer for someone who needs lifted up to the Lord. Then, as soon as you clear the portico area, you may let your balloon go. If you came as a family unit, it was Grace's desire that you pray together as a family, and then in unison let your balloons go. Again, thank you for your participation and attendance."

*   *   *

"This is the coolest thing I've ever seen," Nora squealed with delight. "I hope someone is taking pictures. This will be a delightful addition to my magazine."

"Really? Have you seen the media? Pictures, videos! This story will be plastered all over local, state and national news, Nora. You won't have any trouble getting pictures." Ashley smiled as she looked around at the swarming broadcasters with their studio cameras set to capture whatever they could of Grace's memorial service. There would be a heartwarming story evolving as cameras would soon capture a blue sky covered with a crimson reminder of the saving grace of Jesus. Ashley knew immediately that was the precise message Grace wanted to send to the world. She prayed they each were wise enough to figure out its apparent intent.

The triumphant exercise came off without a hitch. The vans full of balloons were emptied as employees of the florists supplied balloons to the hands of family members. The crowd was patient and thoughtful as they gave careful consideration of who they would pray for before releasing their balloons. Those waiting to go through the lines tossed coins into the memorial fountain and offered an additional prayer instead of the traditional wish. The sky was bejeweled with red appeals for grace. It was a moment that adults would endear and children would recall with attention to detail. If it might impress even one soul to be anchored to interest, then Grace Willingham would have accomplished what she set out to do—introduce another soul to Christ.

The parking lot emptied. Media attempted to approach the family, but the security hired by East Savannah had been well versed regarding keeping them at a distance and respecting the family's privacy. The news anchors were instructed to call the family members the following day for any additional comments they would like to gather. The journalists who attended the service would collaborate with their respective networks and complete whatever story they wished to air on the evening and late-night news.

The three grandsons and three family friends poised themselves as pallbearers and placed the coffin inside the hearse. Several floral arrangements were selected to be placed at the cemetery plot. Family members situated themselves inside the limousines, and the journey to Bonaventure Cemetery began. Bruce Masters got in his car. He had lingered behind after releasing his balloon and praying for his family. He would respect the family's wishes of a private graveside ceremony. Whereas he wouldn't be an obvious part of the funeral procession, he would follow at a respectable distance. Once inside Bonaventure, he would park out of sight and watch their every move.

FUNERAL PROCESSION TO BONAVENTURE CEMETERY, OCTOBER 16, 4:55 P.M.

"I had no idea Grandma was so loved." Jimmy sat in a solemn state of startled contentment. "I guess I just thought her world revolved around us. Did you see all the people she touched in her life? That was absolutely incredible!"

"When did she have time to impact all of them? She was always working, making jelly and cookies and sewing and going on trips. Seriously, I'm stunted, too, Jimmy." Madelyn brushed back Bryson's fuzzy hair. "You were such a good boy, little fella. Mommy was so proud of you."

"Grandma was the busiest most available woman I've ever known. I think it kept her young and beautiful. It was never a surprise to me to run into her anytime I was downtown or out shopping or even at the grocery store. Sometimes she didn't see me. I just passed her on the road or saw her get in her car. But no grass grew under her feet." Ashley was caught up in moments racing through her mind of the encounters she was sharing.

"She brought me lunch at the funeral home many times. If it was a light day, we'd sit in the conference room and eat. If I was busy, she'd kiss me and head out. Thing was, she was always carrying someone else a meal, too. Grace would say, 'Well, I made a meal for Ellen today. She's been under the weather for a little while. Thought I might as well throw in a few more beans for my Nick.' We were all blessed by her." Nick closed his eyes and envisioned the special times he and Grace shared over lunch.

"She was just the bomb! If I could be half the lady she was, I'd have life figured out. But then, that would mean I'd have to love to that degree. I haven't loved anyone as much as she did, let alone a church full of people." Nora spoke before she thought. All eyes were focused on her, and they seemed to look at her with pity. "What? What did I say? Why are you guys looking at me like that? I haven't. I don't think I have the capacity to love like that. What do you want me to say?"

"You forgot about yourself." Ashley was quick to come back at Nora, but immediately felt pierced in her spirit for calling her out.

"Ouch. I think. What does that mean?" Nora inquired.

"She means you haven't loved anyone except yourself," Jimmy

retorted. He felt equally as sorry that he had to explain the meaning behind Ashley's comment. But, he felt it only fair that Nora should be aware of how others perceive her.

Nick intercepted the mood with dignity and a touch of professionalism hoping to steer the tension in another direction. He could see the wounded look in Nora's face. He was aware, however, that it probably hurt worse because of the truth embedded in the observation. Most people are acutely aware of their own flaws. "Hey, guys, tell you what. Let's focus on Grandma Grace. The next part of the loss process is typically the most difficult time for the family. If I failed to prepare you for this, you'll have to forgive me. I've been a bit sidetracked, if not totally derailed, on this one. Seriously, this part can be tough simply because the finality of this side of life hits people really hardest at the gravesite. Let's keep in mind that Grandma is in a better place. Her body was a temple on loan from God. The important thing is what she left behind for her family is priceless. Each of us have something unique, something extremely valuable that we will always remember about Grace. If you can understand that she impacted your life in a really unique way, then a part of Grandma will remain with you forever. No one or nothing, not even death, can take that away. It's yours. It's personal. It's heritage. It's likely the single most important aspect to any family—roots. Grandma Grace is our family's beginning. Now it's up to each of us to bring honor to what she began." Nick reached with both hands and tickled Bryson's sides, and in a playful voice he lightened the mood, "And that includes you, Big Man." Bryson giggled with delight for the attention. He was ready for a more lighthearted spirit.

The limo transporting the children of Grace Willingham had

enjoyed less conversation. Gladys and Ralph sat across from James, Valerie, and Carmen. Gladys's gaze vacillated from the right-window scenery to her lap where she rested her folded hands. Ralph sat to her left sitting on one trembling hand and looking at his other resting on his leg. His thoughts were a mess. *How can I console my wife when she doesn't want me to touch her? She has to be hurting. This was her mother, and her only peaceful link to family. If she would only let me love her, I could. I would. I do.*

"It was a beautiful service. Don't you think, Jim?" Valerie moved in closer to her husband and took his hand and kissed it. Jim took note of her attentive tenderness. Valerie was the sort of girl who expected attention but never initiated it. His heart was feeling a tug of something he hadn't recognized in her before. He could be mistaken about what a blessing truly might be, but James Albert Willingham was beginning to look at small tokens of kindness through the lens of great wealth.

"I was blown away from the start to the finish. I expected to hear dirge and come out feeling sad and even depressed. I don't feel that way at all. I'm not sure if that's good or not, but it sure feels better than the gloom I anticipated." James was thoughtful in his comments, and was none too certain how everyone else would consider his opinion.

"Then Mom did exactly what she planned, James. This is how she wanted us to feel. Don't you see? Her leaving us is only temporary. She knew that. 'You are here and you want to get there.' Do you remember her saying that, Gladys? She told us that our whole lives." Carmen was exuberant in her recollection of Grace's wisdom, and hoping to give Gladys a glimpse of the comfort she and James were feeling.

Gladys sat quiet for a few seconds. No one knew if she would respond or not, but their tongues were spellbound as though silence would reign forever unless Gladys broke its curse. Gladys kept her eyes focused on the window, yet shattered the hush with a soft voice. "Mother was so calculated in life. There was such order about her character. Her days were orchestrated with detail, yet she never allowed schedules to dictate where she was needed most. She lived getting from here to there. She conquered more of the here-to-theres than the three of us together will in our lifetimes. I dizzy myself trying to imagine how I might could ever fall into her shoes. I don't believe there is enough time left for me to grow into them."

Ralph picked up his trembling right hand and placed his arm around Gladys's shoulder. He patted her gently, then tightened his grip at the top of her arm and gave her a tight squeeze. With her face turned away, he couldn't appreciate the smile that shaped her lips. He was left to believe there was no response to his attempt at comfort.

"Those are beautiful thoughts of Mom, Gladys. Thank you for reminding us of that part of her nature." Carmen was pleased to witness the tender depth to Gladys. *Did you hear that, Mom Grace? She's still there. Down deep inside, your Gladys is still the wonderful daughter you knew she could be. I'll keep praying. It'll happen yet.*

No one spoke another word. The remaining ride was tranquil. No tension could be detected. The balm of forgiveness had been applied and the healing had begun. They were a family once again. Grace would not live to witness the long-awaited restoration, but her death had initiated it. The hearse pulled into Bonaventure Cemetery. Martin Webster read Psalm 23, and Grace was laid to rest.

Chapter 42

827 VICTORY DRIVE, GRANDMA GRACE'S KITCHEN,
OCTOBER 16, 6:57 P.M.

The Willinghams pushed away from the table with moans begging for relief. Southern style dishes prepared by loving hands had been enjoyed, for some a bit too much, but the hospitality appreciated by all. It had been a long day on the heels of a longer week. Everyone was present—James and Valerie, and even Gladys and Ralph. It was a setting that had never taken place while Grace was alive. Save for Bryson, she had had the pleasure of everyone's company in her home, but never in unison.

As for Ralph, it had been many years since he had been to Grace's homeplace. She had visited him and brought him meals during Gladys's stay at East Coast. Gladys, however, had made her trips to Grace's without even so much an opportunity for him to reject an invitation.

James and Valerie melded into the relaxed family setting. James's botched visits with his mama appeared to have been whitewashed from his memory. He shared stories of fond remembrances he enjoyed as a teenager and young adult. His mention of Annie didn't have the same bittersweet sting when he spoke her name. Ashley and Jimmy cherished the stories they were hearing for the first time. Valerie was not threatened in the least, and even laughed and queried James for more detail.

To everyone's surprise, Gladys shared a comical tale of her girlhood that left everyone laughing so hard there were tears streaming down the faces of the women and clouding the eyes of the men. Gladys had not laughed so heartily in many years. The new introduction to her face muscles made them ache badly enough she had to massage them as she brushed away her tears. Ralph was touching her more frequently, although guarding his affection.

"Okay, so now that Aunt Gladys is here, it's a wonderful time to share the story of The Queen's visit. Right, guys?" Nora was not going to allow the moment to be dismantled. The exhausting day's events were sure to beckon for early dismissal of the night.

"Me? Why me?" Gladys looked surprised that Nora would suggest her as the narrator of such a remarkable highlight of Grace's life.

"That's my fault," Carmen admitted. "I told them at breakfast this morning that you were the only one who had any visual recollection of the ceremony. James was too young, I wasn't part of the family yet, and no one could tell it quite like you."

Breakfast? You spoke kindly of me before breakfast? But that was before you forgave me. The thought struck rich in Gladys's spirit to know the possibility of this moment had been spoken of by Carmen before their fountain encounter at the church.

"Come on, Aunt Gladys. You have to tell it." Jimmy's plea interrupted Gladys's thoughts.

"Pleeeeease," Madelyn folded her hands and placed them under her chin in true begging style.

"We insist, Aunt Gladys. You're the most popular candidate." Ashley reached over and patted her hand and then gave a gentle rub.

"Well, I have never heard a Willingham tell the story. I'd love to hear your version, Gladys." Ralph's desire was that Gladys would recognize the pleasing twinkle in his eye.

Gladys blushed. Many moons had come and gone since anyone had looked at her with that sense of pride, had begged for her to speak, or made her feel special in any way. She felt giddy inside, almost warm and tingly. A semblance of life was sprouting from her cold and abandoned heart. "Uncle! Uncle! You're about to break my arm from twisting it." Gladys laughed at her resemblance of a joke. "But, let's take a rest break first. Be back here in five."

Everyone exited the kitchen except for Nick and Carmen. The two of them began clearing the table. Both relished an opportunity to talk. Nick brought a stack of dishes to the sink where Carmen was preparing them for the dishwasher. He leaned in and lowered his voice not to be overheard by anyone. "So, when are you telling him, Mom? Or, would you rather I did?"

"Oh, no, Son! This has to be on me. It's not your burden. I'm not sure how it will go over with him, or any of the family for that matter. This is going to rock everyone's world, Nick. I hate to spoil the atmosphere that has been created here. Are you prepared to leave if it turns really sour? Are your plans still to return to France? And if so, how soon?"

"Oh, yes, I'm going back home. Abrielle has patiently waited on me. I love her, Mom. I want to marry her and have a family of my own. I have a buyer for the funeral home. It's a Canadian conglomerate who's buying out funeral homes across America. Part of the agreement is that they would like for me to run the place for at least five years. I talked them into two, but I haven't promised that. If they want it badly enough, they'll let Matt take over. He's more than capable .And Turner's is a colossal buy. They'd be foolish not to make the investment." Nick was more than confident with his head for business.

"Tonight. Be praying for me. I have to come clean tonight, Nick. If things get out of hand, we'll figure it out from there. If I have to, I can leave tomorrow."

"Well, I've prepared my attorney for the worst. He knows everything. He'll protect us however he needs to. He's the best there is in these parts." Nick didn't want his mom to be concerned for anything. She had protected him for many years. It had been his turn for the past several. She would always be honored by him, and never forgotten. Grandma Grace had hammered that home to him as God's only commandment with a promise. "I'll be close by tonight, Mom. Just know that if he loses control, I'm here."

"You're amazing, Nick. What did I ever do to deserve you?" Carmen turned and gave Nick a big hug.

"I love you, Mom. You're the amazing one."

James walked in the kitchen. He stopped at the doorway and savored the mother-son relationship. For the first time tonight, his heart felt weighty. *I need that, Lord. I haven't realized what it was missing in my life. Well, other than You. But will You help me, Lord? Help me find a way to earn the approval of my children.*

"Hey, James. Time to get started again?" Carmen felt a tinge of anxiousness. She had been controlled and comfortable with everything else. But her news could change everything. Forever. "We were just clearing the table for round two. We'll hear the story, then have a little dessert and—"

"Remember, Mom. We're all exhausted. We need an early turn-in night." Nick didn't want to interfere with Carmen's plans, but to put a limit on the night was definitely in order.

"But, Nick, I think we'd all agree that it wouldn't be right to not have a moment in the rockers after dessert. Maybe five or ten minutes. What d'ya say?" James had declared in his mind he would not leave without a Grace-time rock. He wanted Valerie to have that experience.

"Absolutely, James." Carmen agreed and gave a wink to Nick.

"I'm overruled. As usual." Nick laughed and settled down in his chair.

"Nick, you're quite the business person. I've admired you from a distance since you've been here. You've taken Turner's and turned it into the most respectable provider for end-of-life planning this side of the Mississippi. I'm proud to call you part of my family, Nick. I really am." James gave Nick an approving pat on the back.

"Thanks, James. That really means a lot to me." *I hope you feel the same tomorrow, James Albert Willingham II. I hope you feel the same tomorrow.*

One by one the crowd gathered around Grace's kitchen table. Bryson was tucked in his make-shift bed for the night. It had been a long day for the little tyke. Madelyn was relieved in a deserving mom's way. She could give her undivided attention to the story. After Gladys had finished, she would make her way to Camp W'ham. She couldn't get her mind off of her Sydney snow globe. Now that Granny was gone for good, she wanted it before she settled in for the night.

827 Victory Drive, Camp W'ham, October 16, 7:07 p.m.

"Where y'all been? I'm starved to death." Tyrone had waked up Kareem, and he was as grizzly as a bear. "Did you leave a car for me at the back entrance?"

"Yeah, and it's full of gas. Can we go now?" Tyrone was obviously irritated.

"What's yo big hurry? Go up to the ol' lady's house and see who's there. Follow that trail. It'll take you right there. If you see anybody coming, bring her to me. If not, come back and tell me if you see my woman." Kareem ripped into the wrapper of his burger and started stuffing his mouth with sustenance. His stomach had been alerting him since midday of its empty status.

"Man, I'm give out, Reem. That's a haul down here through them woods," Tyrone objected.

"I didn't ask you if you would," Kareem barked through his overflowing mouth.

Tyrone and his motley crew of two started up the trail. It was a good ten-minute hike. Grace's porch was lighted. They walked toward the Sugar Shack and saw the family gathering at the table. Tyrone moved in for a closer look for Madelyn in the crowd. He spotted her hair and pulled back. That was all the evidence he needed for a report to Kareem. Then, he could head home. He was tired of catering to Kareem's needs for one day.

827 VICTORY DRIVE, GRACE'S KITCHEN TABLE, 7:17 P.M.

"So where do I need to pick up?" Gladys was as giddy as a school girl.

"GG had gotten the call from The Queen, but she wouldn't talk to her. She knows she's coming, but could kind of care less." Nora added her touch of flavor to the story.

"Grandma was in mourning. She had just lost the love of her life. I think her focus was more on the loss, Nora," Ashley defended.

"Relax. I'm just hyping up the story a little. It's okay. Okay?" Nora's irritation from Ashley's comment in the limousine was still gurgling inside. She was not going to tolerate any further impertinence from her.

Gladys gave a shrug and cut her eyes at Carmen for the go-ahead. "Kathy Sueberger has written down The Queen's instructions. That's where we left off. Elizabeth is coming to Savannah," Carmen prompted.

Gladys picked up without breaking stride. "Well, Kathy Sueberger was the most helpful friend. Mom was in a very, shall we say meditative state. She was mourning the loss of Daddy. I was young, but old enough to understand the finality of death. James, you were too young to know why you were crying. You just cried. A lot. But, Kathy was a godsend. Kathy kept my mind off of sorrow and kept me busy and entertained. She allowed Mother to play the role of the mourning widow while she took care of everything. She cleaned—"

"Do you think GG would have done it any differently, though? I'm sorry to interrupt, Aunt Gladys. But really, don't you think GG would have mourned regardless and simply let the house take care of itself? I mean, that's the kind of gal she was, right?"

"Yes, she was, Nora. Mother loved her Albert. Nothing else was that important to her at the time, other than James and me. Where was I? Oh, yeah. Kathy operated at high-level energy. She cleaned the house from stem to stern and got the yard in pristine order. It was a quaint home we lived in then, but Mother's yard was an explosion of color anytime the weather allowed it. It was a pleasant summer that year, almost like it anticipated The Queen's visit. So, Mother's roses and even her azaleas were in full bloom, and her winter series camellias were splendid. She and I had been in the garden only a couple of days before Daddy's death planting and sprucing up the place. It was always our special project to plant additional tulips and hyacinth bulbs to enjoy in the spring. Mother loved the tulips because of their stately grace and streamlined majesty. She loved the hyacinths for their robust smell, beautiful colors, and their reminder of warmer days ahead. Once we were finished with the bulbs, we prepared the ground to receive an array of pansies and groom the hardy, colorful heather and the coral bells with their vibrant purple leaves. I'm sorry. I can get lost in insignificant details."

"I love the detail, Gladys. Please don't stop," Nora encouraged.

"Okay, if I bore you, let me know. You won't hurt my feelings. Much." Gladys laughed at herself again. Carmen and Jim enjoyed watching their sister step out of her closed-tight box. "The Commanding General sent word encouraging us to have The Queen's visit at the base and they would take care of all expenses. Mother would not hear of it. It was a private affair, and she intended to keep it that way. Well, at least as much as she could control it. Besides, she would have never crushed Kathy Sueberger's dream to be in charge of the gala. The day of the funeral arrived, and I remember there were lots of people gathered on the street and even the front lawn, despite the efforts to keep it isolated from the public. Of course, media was there to a much more limited degree than we witnessed today, but a marked presence nonetheless. At Kathy's request, the military had set up a beautiful white tent earlier that morning. Even though the tea was scheduled for the day following the funeral, Kathy wanted to get as much done ahead of time as possible. Sturdy white wooden columns with full-bodied Queen Anne ferns setting atop lined the processional aisle and bordered the four corners of the tent.

"Kathy had an extraordinary eye for flair. I can remember her grandstanding a beautiful Southern table. A white linen tablecloth draped the round table and puddled on the ground. A brink pink brushed silk table runner gave a breathtaking splash of background color for the floral satin fabric delicately arranged in the center. Amidst the folds of the floral satin set a striking bouquet of pink camellias picked from Mother's garden. They were arranged in an impressive Waterford vase. It was Kathy's grandmother's vase. It dated back to the 1800's when George and William Penrose began the original crystal production with their exquisite flint glass. Complementing the vase were two antique Sheffield twenty-inch silver candlesticks. It was an original Fenton design with remarkable decorative detail. Another heirloom of

Kathy Sueberger's. Her Southern family had an Irish descent and were immensely wealthy. The girl knew how to entertain. Her husband went on to become a two-star general, so her skills were most beneficial. And best of all, she loved our Grace.

"The table was set for Afternoon Tea, which by English tradition is held at four o'clock. It was graced with Kathy's grandmother's china, British-made but imported from France. Kathy showed me the export marks on the bottom. She knew they dated after the 1860's because the markings were printed. The lady was well-versed in the formalities of fineries.

"There was a small meal–again prepared by Kathy–consisting of fresh-baked pumpkin scones served with cream and jam, and thinly-sliced cucumber sandwiches. Of course, with no crust. Kathy said that was a no-no. Her homemade pastries were to die for! It was the perfect meal. And, naturally, she went to great lengths to select the perfect teas fit for royalty."

"How in the world do you remember all those details, Aunt Gladys? I've never heard this rendition of the story before." Nora, along with the others, sat mesmerized by Gladys's account of detail. Carmen closed her eyes visualizing Gladys as a young girl acting out the pomp and circumstance for Mom Grace and her guests. It was quite the delightful production that left everyone charmed, even Gladys.

"Some things just really stuck with me. I can remember desperately trying to focus on anything but the death of my daddy." Gladys's eyes smarted. She pressed her teeth to her bottom lip to stifle the urge to cry. She was her daddy's little girl, and she had never stopped missing the need to be a princess. She felt Ralph's hand on her leg. He patted her gently as if he understood the source of her pain.

Gladys regained her composure and continued. "We knew when The Queen and her entourage had arrived. A messenger came the afternoon prior to the funeral to tell Mother that The Queen would be in attendance and was greatly anticipating the next day's Afternoon Tea. Within the hour, Harriett Ainsworth called to encourage Mother to allow Queen Elizabeth to host the tea at the Savannah Hilton where Elizabeth was staying. Kathy answered the phone and dug in her heels. Mother's friend wanted to show off her Southern social graces, and she wasn't budging. I'll never forget the way she handled that phone call. She was quite the character. When Harriett called, Kathy had already calculated what she would say."

"Don't tell me she was rude. My heart can't stand it." Nora theatrically baulked.

Gladys held up a finger as if to dispel Nora's objection. "Kathy answered the phone, and," Gladys put on her best Southern drawl to capture the personality of Kathy Sueberger, 'Well, if it's not Miss Harriett. Grace is much obliged for the kindness extended, but if Queen Elizabeth wants to personally meet with Mrs. Willingham, the pleasure of The Queen's company is requested at the late Albert Willingham's home the day after his funeral. If it's all the same to Your Majesty, that is. I mean, Mrs. Willingham, Albert's *widow,* doesn't want to miss the honor of meeting with The Highness–Our Highness–Your Highness, or–well, you know. Well, it's a simple request. Seems so little to ask, considering the sacrifice and all.' I remember Kathy cringing, closing her eyes, crossing fingers on both hands and her legs as she held the phone and her breath waiting for Harriett Ainsworth's response. Mother was in a meeting with her church minister, the military chaplain, and the new undertaker in town–Richard Turner. According to how Grace told the story, she knew nothing about the notion of the *stipulation* of that meeting. It was Kathy who controlled the situation and contrived the idea. Mother didn't mind, though. She said Kathy had earned the right to have the tea wherever she wanted. It was the only way she had to adequately thank her, so she was happy to have her show off her Southern charm. And who could say no when you put it that way?"

Gladys drank a sip of sweet tea, took a deep breath, and continued the story. "Oh, my goodness, the funeral was an impressive one, even to a seven-year-old girl. The US Army wasn't going to be understated by British military. Hunter Army Airfield arranged a fly-by before and after the Royal Air Force executed their fly-past. The twenty-one gun salute by the dress-blue soldiers was followed by the British National seven-gun salute of the regal red-uniformed military. The Queen herself delivered a brief eulogy of Daddy's bravery, followed by a four-star general, who presented Mother with one of the medals for valor. That's when he announced she would receive the other medals at the Whitehouse. I recall feeling a measure of guilt for the excitement attached to a trip to Washington, D.C. and an opportunity to meet the President of the United States. But Mother sat devoid of star-struck emotion. I was young. As I grew older and considered what had taken place, I compared it to waking up to celebrate your twenty-first birthday and being told you have cancer on the same day. The pastor closed with prayer, and the funeral ended with the U.S. and the British Armed Forces each firing three volleys of cannons over the casket. I can still feel the ringing in my ears even now. Do you remember that James?" Gladys thought perhaps even a three-year-old boy might recall something as majestic as cannons.

"I wish I did, Gladys. I really wish I did," James sighed.

"I'm sorry, James. Anyway, the day was long, and the night brought rest for everyone. That is, of course, except for Kathy Sueberger. She was scurrying to take care of last-minute details. She kept me busy the crux of the day with minor details that to a child were a really big deal. James, you were at Kathy's house with her mom who had *conveniently* come into town for a visit."

"I couldn't tell you a thing about the whole hoopdelah, Gladys. I was damaged for life because I was denied the experience." James placed his hand over his heart and laughed, and the others joined. "But I did meet The Queen. I have a picture to prove it."

"Nuh-huh! That's so cool, Dad. I've never seen it," Jimmy chagrinned.

And neither have I." Ashely folded her arms as though she had a better stake at the chance of having the experienced shared with her.

As if scripted, all heads immediately turned to Gladys in unison, and she continued. "The appointed hour came, and the red carpet was rolled out for her. Literally. Red carpet. The Queen was escorted down the aisle and seated at the table. There they were–Mother and Queen Elizabeth side by side. The circle consisted of Harriett Ainsworth, who sat at Queen Elizabeth's left, then Kathy Sueberger to Harriett's left. Next to Kathy was her mother, Paige Geoff. Kathy's daughter and my best friend, Lauralee, was next in the lineup by me, who was seated on the other side of Mother. Of course, we were on our very best behavior. It was a delightful affair. Mother was very pleasant but obviously still mourning Daddy. We enjoyed tea and delicacies. And then, it happened."

"Okay, here it is. This is the part I love the most." Nora clapped her hands in staccato rhythm, pulled her tanned legs up in the chair, tucked them against her chest and propped her chin on top of her knees. The anticipation of the next part of the story made her antsy in her chair.

"Yes, Elizabeth had on *the* jewels that day. They were the same ones she had worn on her birthday celebration when Daddy saved her life. I remember her taking Mother's hand and saying, "No part of me deserved what your brave husband sacrificed. His valor was so much a part of him that he could not separate it from his better reasons to live. What a noble and rare character trait he possessed. But when he saved my life, a part of yours was extinguished. If I live to be one hundred and forty years old, I would never be able to express my gratitude. If you will allow me to offer a reflection of the day he showed unmerited favor to me, it would delight my heart and somehow appease my soul. These jewels'— and The Queen took her hand and softly ran them across the diamonds and rubies in her necklace—'that I wear today were given to me by my husband for my birthday celebration that day. We both would consider it the highest of honors should brave Major Willingham's wife wear them as a reminder of his undying love for you. You were the one he spoke of last. I'm sure his fellow comrade Sergeant Benton has shared that with you.' Of course, Sergeant Benton had not yet shared that with Mother. He came to Savannah shortly after the war was over to talk to Grace personally. They have been friends ever since. The story goes that he fell in love with a French maiden and settled in Paris. Mother made several trips to France to visit, and he and his wife visited here a time or two." Gladys paused.

"Well, you can't stop there, Aunt Gladys. What happened next?" Jimmy leaned up on his elbows eager to hear the conclusion. "What did Grandpa say?"

"Oh, that part? Okay. Sergeant Benton said that Daddy's last words were, 'Tell Grace my heart is hers forever.' Benton had tears in his eyes when he told us. He said he'd never known a man to love his family the way Daddy loved us. The Sergeant said he felt as if he knew Mother because Daddy spoke of her incessantly. He also told us Daddy introduced him to the Lord, and that he was indebted to him forever. He told Mother if there was ever anything he could do for her, to please let him know. He was a really kind man. That's about all I remember about him." Gladys pushed her chair from the table.

"Wait a minute. Where are you going? You can't stop now. Take us back to the tea." Nora wanted every detail revealed.

"I will, missy. I'm just getting a refill of tea myself." Gladys chuckled at Nora's persistence. The young girl reminded her a lot of herself when she was younger and excited for life to unfold. She pushed the lever on the refrigerator for ice and thought, *When did I lose my luster for life, Lord? Will I find it again in Tuscany?* The thought injected a familiar heaviness in her spirit. Today had reintroduced her to the comfort companion she had known once upon a time. Life was happening again. Her heart felt full. She felt needed. Included in something bigger than her. Why did it take her mother's death to turn life back on? Or was it that her guilt had found pardon? She glanced back at Carmen. The family was chitchatting among themselves. Ice began spilling around her feet and she fumbled to pick it up and discard it in the sink. She poured her tea and took her seat again.

"Okay, so finish. We're almost there, but I have to hear it." Nora repositioned and scrunched up her legs under her chin again.

"Yeah, there's really not much left, Nora. Mother was gracious to Queen Elizabeth, but she rejected the jewels. 'Your jewels won't bring Albert back, and why he died had no price tag attached.' Well, Her Royal Majesty was speechless. I don't believe she had considered that Mother would reject her *token* of appreciation. The Queen was silent for what seemed an eternity. No one else spoke either. And Kathy Sueberger was silently going nuts! Finally, The Queen responded to Mother. 'But, Grace, you can do with the jewels what you want. If you would like, I can give you— Well, I won't suggest such as I am certain it would offend your honor. Madam, with all due respect, I *need* to bestow upon you some manner of my appreciation, as well as that of my family. As special as the sentiment of these jewels are, Prince Phillip and I find the sentiment attached lies deeper within your heart than ours.' Then, she took Mother's hand and pulled it up to her face, rested the top of her hand on her cheek, and pleaded. 'Please release me from this burden.' Mother's tears flowed freely and she nodded her head. Queen Elizabeth unfastened her necklace, got up from the table, and walked around to Mother. She draped the jewels around Mother's beautiful neck and fastened the clasp. Then, she took her bracelet and did the same. She took off her earrings, opened Mother's hand, laid them in her palm, and gently closed their two hands around the jewels. Then The Queen said, 'A part of Albert dwells in these, Grace Willingham. Each time you wear them, you will remember when the two of you loved.' She bent down and kissed Mother on her forehead.

"Her Majesty sat down again and they shared another hour of conversation. She invited us to England at her expense to be her honored guests. I know you remember that trip, James, because Mother waited until you were older to go," Gladys reminded him.

"I do recall more pieces than bits of that. It was pretty awesome for a little kid," James confessed.

"Awesome? That's radical! Do you think she would invite the family now?" Jimmy jested but his undertones were serious.

"Mother was radiate as she sat there all bejeweled talking to *Elizabeth* as if they were sisters. Like a paper cut to the soul, Mother instantly realized there was a greater need in The Queen than the crater in her own heart. It was as if the very hand of God had reached down and pulled her out of her cloud of mourning and brought closure to the sting of the death of Daddy. It wasn't the jewels that returned Grace Willingham to life. It was her act of selflessness. Mother understood in order to complete Albert's sacrifice that she, too, had to die to herself. Albert paid the price for The Queen's life. Now Mother would let her live it without obligation."

Gladys realized she had been staring at the table. When she looked up, everyone was sitting staring down as well. Tears glistened on eyelashes as others were caught in tissues.

Jimmy was the first to break the thought-provoking moment. "Aunt Gladys, you not only personified the picture of Grandpa and Grandma, you just gave us a glorious analogy of Christ.

Our roots don't begin nor do they end with Albert and Grace. Our roots began in their hearts with their love for Him. I'm–I'm awestruck. Thank you. That was beautiful."

Ralph swallowed the lump in his throat. His rededication was still fresh in his mind, and his bent for the bottle was tormenting him. He recognized what love could do to people. He looked at Gladys with a longing that was desperate to be discovered. Carmen took note and uttered a silent prayer for his yearning to be blessed. Not just for his sake, but for the sake of Gladys. She needed it as urgently as Ralph.

Valerie blew her nose and cleared her throat to speak. "I've never heard anything as beautiful. I was like you, Ralph. I had never heard the story except through the rumor mill. I'd like to say to everyone here that I love being a part of this family. I have never known this kind of bond. You all have a remarkable heritage. Jim and I want to do our part to help keep it going. I hope you'll give us that chance."

"Val, I couldn't have said it better." James took Valerie's hand and kissed it.

"Of course we'll give you the chance. We all have the task ahead of us to keep the Willingham name a strong family of character. None of us are perfect. But we have the legacy of Albert and Grace to be our guide for how we should live." Carmen choked her way through the last line and couldn't go on. Her emotions had surfaced in a big way. She dreaded the next phase of the whole heritage bit. She wondered if it would be better for the family if that part of the mystery never unfolded.

Nick came to his mother's rescue. "Guys, it's been a really long week. Some of us didn't sleep last night at all. As for me, I need rest. Can we call it a night and agree to get together another time?

"I think we need to discuss the missing jewels. I mean, we can't just not. Can we?" Nora felt it her obligation to bring up the obvious.

"Let's don't go there tonight. None of us can solve that mystery. Certainly not right now." Ashley could see a discussion about the jewels being a lengthy and messy ordeal.

"Agreed. But I do have one last request for the day." James didn't want the night to end without executing his plan. "Could all of us, just for old time's sake, gather on the porch for a rocker session? Ralph, I don't know if you've ever sat in your rocker. If you're like Val, you haven't. It's time. Let's just take ten minutes and sit and rock. Could we do that?"

"Love the idea, Dad!" Jimmy clapped his hands and headed for the front porch.

"I don't mind, but afterwards I have to go down to Camp W'ham and get my snow globe." Madelyn was insistent.

"Can't it wait till tomorrow, Maddie? I mean, it's so late." Carmen didn't like the idea of her going down in the dark. She had an unsettling feeling she couldn't quite put her finger on.

"I can't, Aunt Carmen. It's important. I know you probably think I'm silly, but I have to."

Jimmy stopped at the kitchen door and appeased the situation. "I'll go down with you, Madelyn. I need the exercise, and it's practically a full moon. I don't like you walking alone either, not when a capable man like myself is around."

"So that settles that. Ten minutes on the porch. Madelyn and Jimmy get the globe. Lights out. Tomorrow, around three right here. Can everyone make that happen? Ashley? James?" Nick was again taking charge and ordering up business.

"Works for me," Ashley agreed.

"And I'll make it work," James conceded.

The family pulled rockers in close but leaving enough room to rock. Once they sat and the rhythm began, their voices ceased. They watched the twinkling fireflies, listened to the night creatures yap in choral clatter, and recalled Grace-filled moments where she had offered each of them pieces of her selfless heart.

Chapter 43

Ten minutes. No one lingered. The out-of-towners would stay at the homeplace and the others would return to their homes. Carmen would listen for Bryson while Jimmy and Madelyn went to retrieve the Sydney snow globe.

Ashley and the Murphys were eager to leave. Jim and Valerie tarried. Carmen was grateful for their sluggish exit. Nick excused himself insisting that he would clean the kitchen so his mother could get some rest. Then, he'd be on his way home. Nora offered to help him.

"James, could I have a word with you, please? It'll only take a moment. I promise I won't detain you long." Carmen's heart was doing flip-flops. She was certain if he looked closely enough, even in the dim lights, he would have seen the pounding of her pulse beneath her gold cross pendant.

"Sure. I don't mind." James was amenable to her request.

"Do you need me to step inside?" Valerie was curious, but wanted to be polite.

"Well, you know, I hadn't thought about that aspect, to be quite honest, Valerie. I don't know." Carmen gulped. She wasn't sure if James would want Valerie to hear this discussion at all.

James squirmed with an uneasiness. If Carmen was going to mention the past, he had not shared that with Valerie, and wasn't sure he ever would, quite frankly. "Do you mind, Val? Why don't you visit with Nick and Nora in the kitchen. Thanks, Sweetheart. You're a love."

"I'll just help them clean up. We'll find plenty to chat about. Let me know when you're ready." Valerie kissed James on the cheek and turned to leave. She opened the door to step inside, then looked up at James and Carmen who were situating themselves in their rockers. *You two have a past. I don't know what it is, but there is serious business to settle. Could it have something to do with the missing jewels, perhaps? Is this where you really were last night?* Valerie closed the door reluctantly. The business between the siblings would remain a mystery to her. At least for now.

827 VICTORY DRIVE, GRACE'S SHED, 8:51 P.M.

"Do you think this thing still cranks?" Jimmy took the four-wheeler key from Madelyn and climbed aboard

"Only one way to find out, Jimmy." Madelyn moved in close behind her driver. "We used to fit better on this thing."

"Yeah, seems like you grew up," Jimmy laughed.

Jimmy put the key in the ignition. She cranked up like a charm. Neither of them realized that Grace had ridden it herself the week of her death. She was checking on the status of her small apple orchard.

Madelyn shouted so that Jimmy could hear her voice over the engine. "It shouldn't take us long on the four-wheeler. We'll be there and back in a jiffy. I really appreciate your coming. I know you're exhausted. I could've come alone. These woods don't scare me."

"You've always been fearless, Madelyn. It's part of what makes you so attractive." Jimmy wanted to encourage her. His assumption that she never got told of her beauty was dead on target.

"Me? Attractive? Have you really looked at my hair and artwork, Jimmy?"

"The outward is not what makes a woman beautiful, Madelyn. It's the inner beauty that is most appealing to a man's heart. What do you think of your character? Are you confident in who you are?" Jimmy was hoping to leave her with some probing questions to cause her to think of where she wanted to go from here in order to get there, as Grandma used to encourage.

"I haven't done much to be proud of, Jimmy. In fact, there's a lot that I've done that goes against everything Granny taught us. I'm pretty ashamed. But, I'm—"

Jimmy interrupted Madelyn over the noise of the ATV. "You don't have to be ashamed, Madelyn. You can make everything in your past just go bye-bye. Forever."

"I wish it was that easy, Jimmy. Consequences follow you." The visual image of Kareem flashed in Madelyn's mind.

"I know better than you think I do, Madelyn. But there's a better way to deal with consequences than staying in the same rut of what got you there to begin with."

"I'm going to get there, Jimmy. I've made up my mind. I'm going to get my teaching degree. I'm getting my life together. You'll see. I'll make Granny and all of you proud of me. Bryson needs a clean mom. I'm his only voice for greatness. His dad is too far gone."

"Nobody's ever too far gone, Madelyn. Don't buy that lie." Jimmy looked ahead and thought he saw a light, but then it went away. *Must've been a car light from the road that flashed through the trees.*

"Slow down. It's just ahead." Madelyn didn't want Jimmy to go crashing into any building. Neither of them had on helmets. Besides, the last thing they needed tonight was a hospital run for stitches.

Madelyn took the flashlight from Jimmy's back pocket and turned it on. "I know exactly where I left it. It won't take me but a minute. I'll be right back." She opened the door and shined the flashlight toward the table by the bed where she thought she had left the globe. Then, she patted around on the bedspread and lifted the pillow to check underneath. She froze. *Kareem!* She smelled his cologne on the pillow.

"This whatcha looking for, Woman?"

Madelyn whipped around quickly and shined her flashlight. There stood Kareem juggling the broken snow globe. Before Madelyn could scream, Kareem jumped at her and put a gun in her mouth. "You scream and I'll blow you to smitherines and back again." Madelyn's legs went limp. She felt faint. She knew this was not going to be good, but she feared more for Jimmy than herself.

"Who's yo friend? Oh, you can't speak. That's right. You got a gun in your mouth. Here's whatcha gonna do. I'm gonna take this gun out of ya mouth and ya gonna call him in here."

Madelyn shook her head in objection. She would go anywhere with Kareem, but she didn't want Jimmy harmed.

"Oh, yeah, ya are. And if ya don't, I'll take care of him right in front of ya. Ya gonna take me to the jewels 'cuz we got business with the big boss at midnight. I'm gonna move the gun, and if ya do anything funny, ya ain't never gonna see that boy again. Got it?"

Madelyn nodded her head. She had to think and quick. Kareem moved the gun, but before Madelyn could say anything, Jimmy yelled out to her.

"Did you find it? Hurry up, girl. It's spooky out here. You know how squeamish I get. If you need some help, just yell."

Kareem tilted the gun motioning Madelyn to yell. Madelyn whispered in a firm, feisty manner. "If you hurt him, you'll never find those jewels. I'll never tell you a thing. Is that clear?"

"Ya don't get to call this one. Ya got it?" Kareem grabbed her arm and squeezed hard, pointing the gun under her chin.

"Then you'll have to answer to your big boss, then. Let him go and I'll go with you and we can talk about the jewels." Madelyn had to buy Jimmy's life with whatever it took.

Kareem knew her well. She'd defy him to the hilt. "Get him in here. I won't hurt him." Kareem let go of his grip and pushed her back on the bed. He positioned himself to the side and behind the door.

"I can't find it, Jimmy. It's not here. Go on back and I'll meet you guys later when I find it." Madelyn was praying Jimmy would not walk through that door because she didn't trust Kareem at all.

Jimmy dismounted the four-wheeler and made his way to the door of the cabin. He opened the door and Madelyn aimed the flashlight at his chest rather than blinding him in his eyes. She was shaking her head trying to warn him to run. Her fear-stricken face confused him.

"Madelyn, what's wrong? Are you okay? You look like you've seen a gho—" Jimmy fell to the floor. Madelyn screamed and jumped up to check on Jimmy. Kareem stopped her midstream grabbing her arm and twisting it behind her. Madelyn caught glimpse of the blood on Jimmy's head from the whack by the gun.

Madelyn began to struggle, but Kareem tightened the grip. She broke loose and turned to kick Kareem, trying to temporarily debilitate him. He gave her a left hand to her face and then a fist to her right. Madelyn collapsed on the floor of the cabin. He picked her up and threw her over his shoulder. He stepped on Jimmy's hand and gave it a twist with his size 15 shoe. He turned on his flashlight and made his way to his getaway car with Madelyn as hostage. He would take her by the apartment first to see if he could convince her his way to come clean about the jewels. After that, she would be delivered to Boss. What he did at that point was his business. Kareem was done with her and the Willinghams.

827 VICTORY DRIVE, GRACE'S FRONT PORCH, OCTOBER 16, 8:56 P.M.

"I'm sorry if that was awkward with Valerie, James. I didn't want to invite her to stay if she was unaware of our history. Obviously, I'm not that familiar with—I'm not at all—I just—"

"Carmen, it's okay. I understand what you mean. She doesn't know. Yet. I haven't decided if I want to tell her. That part of my past is over. It's forgiven, thanks to you, and I'm working on the rest of it. Mama always told us, 'Sins can be forgiven, but sometimes you still have to live with their consequences.'" James kept his gaze straight ahead as he rocked in rhythm with the night.

"Well, that's kind of what I need to talk with you about, James–the consequences. And before I say anything else, let me just remind us both what Mom always said about how you handle consequences after sin. Help me out if I misquote her. 'When we allow God to fix our mistakes, *expect a lesson* and–"

"...*and a blessin'* is exactly right." James gladly finished his mama's quote. We've had a few of those in the past twenty-four hours, haven't we?"

"Yes, we have, James. Gladys was precious tonight! Did you feel as blessed as I did watching her?" Carmen could only measure Gladys's progress from the past reports from Grace.

"She's not the only one who morphed," James admitted. Those kids have their acts together much more than the adults. I mean, you're excluded in that lot. You're an amazing woman, Carmen. It's really odd that you're not blood daughter, because you are the child who took on more of Mama's personality and character than Gladys or myself. How did that happen? Don't get me wrong. I don't mean to sound critical or jealous or anything at all. Grateful. It's an anomaly I think."

"I was one of those mistakes of a mom and dad. But I was also the benefactor of the *lesson and the blessin'*. God took a really horrible thing in my life and look what He did with it. But I chose to capitalize on how He fixed my circumstances, James.

I think that's the key. We can make matters worse by repeating mistakes or even creating a few new ones to complicate life more. Or, we can really look for the lessons in our mistakes, or those mistakes that others make on our behalf, and develop depths of character. One can leave your heart angry and bitter, the other can open your heart to love. 'Life looks better on the blessings side of love,' as Mom always said."

James let that roll around in his heart for a moment. He didn't know what Carmen was leading to, but he certainly needed to hear what she was saying. "Carmen, I'm ready for some of my mistakes to turn into blessings. I've made a mess of my life. I sat watching my children tonight. They're great kids. Madelyn has a good heart, too. She needs to be loved. I failed them all. Mama is the only reason they recognized their potential. She was the blessing to them for my mistakes. I've been a fool, Carmen. I have been such a fool." James struggled to hold back the floodgates of emotions. They had been held hostage since Annie's death. He was confident Carmen's shoulder could bear the burden, but he needed privacy. His attempts at crying in the past had been restrained. All guards were down. He would have a time for real cleansing. And it would be sooner than later.

"Well, I have one for you, James."

"One what? I'm sorry?"

"A blessing. It's an amazing blessing, James. It *has* been for me. But only because I chose to accept the consequences of poor choices others made for me. The blessing changed my life. And it will change yours." Carmen looked intently at James's face. He truly wasn't connecting the dots.

"I'm ready for the lesson, Carmen. If you can give me some

tips on how to look at my mistakes differently, I'm all ears." James kept his relaxed rocking tempo.

Carmen reached over and rested her hand on top of James's. "Nick. Nick is your blessing as well as mine."

James stopped abruptly, as though his chair had been cemented to the floor. He sat in undisturbed silence. Carmen allowed him the opportunity to try and process the news rather than continuing to talk. She wasn't sure what else she could say at this point. She realized something would have to break the barrier of the hush, but her heart was at a loss for the time being. Perhaps this was exactly how the moment should play out.

Several minutes passed. James leaned forward and rested his elbows on his knees. He buried his face in his hands and held it tight. He took a deep breath and leaned back in his chair. "I don't even know what to say, Carmen. I'm at a loss for words. Mama knew. Didn't she?"

"Yes, James, she did. And she wanted to tell you." I was the one who asked her not to say anything to you. And we all know what a confidante she was. Maybe I was wrong, James, but I didn't want to further complicate your life."

"Maybe my life would have been different had I known. Did you think about that?" James was irritated at himself more than he was Carmen, but his tone didn't define its intended target.

"Or maybe not. Who's to say, James? We can't go back and change the what-ifs. Mom did get me to agree that if you or Gladys came to her and told her what had happened, she could tell you. And, she would have taken either or both of you to visit me and Nick in California. She prayed you would talk to her about that day until she died. She never gave up on either of you, James. Never."

"I wanted to, Carmen. I can't tell you how many times I wanted to. I was going to finally come clean with that part of my life the morning I found her." James stopped. He couldn't go there. If he did, his emotions would spill out in front of God and Carmen and the night.

"You were dealing with your own grief and–and–" Carmen was interrupted by James's awareness.

James rose from his chair. "And I wasn't even taking care of the kids I had." His irritation turned to anger. But, how can you be sure Nick is mine, Carmen? There were three of us, you know." James hung his head in total disgust and shame when he vocalized the thoughtless assault of three young boys against one innocent girl.

"We're eighty percent certain. Mom insisted on doing what testing was available then. As technology advanced, so did Grace. She wanted to know. If you want to do DNA testing to be absolutely certain, there won't be any objection from me. I certainly understand why you would want to. And so would Nick."

"Does Nick know?" James threw his head back and stuffed his hands deep into his pockets. He leaned against a column. He was grateful for the dimly-lit porch. Carmen didn't deserve to see his wrenched-out emotional countenance.

"He does. We didn't tell him for a very long time. When he became a man, he wanted to go on the search for his biological father. Mom and I knew it would be a lot for him to forgive unless I explained to him why I made the decision that I did. I spent a lot of time in prayer about this, James. It was a personal struggle that I wrestled with for a very long time. Please understand that

I meant no one to get hurt, especially Nick. He doesn't deserve any fall-out from this." Carmen's tone was pleading. She wanted to protect her son at all costs.

"You mean more than he's already experienced. He grew up not knowing his father." James innocently set himself up for Carmen's response.

"Neither have your other children, James. But you have taken the initiative to change that. Each one of them shared with me what you did today before the funeral. They couldn't be more excited about the possibilities with establishing a deeper relationship with you. I'm very proud of you, and I know Mom would be, too." Carmen moved closer to James and touched his arm to bring some sense of comfort to his tousled spirit.

"Seems like I didn't quite make my rounds. Do you realize, Carmen, this means that I have fathered every one of the heirs of the Willingham clan?" James huffed a patronizing laugh. "I must be a real joke to those kids. I already know I am to the rest of the world, but I need to redeem myself to the ones who matter most." James grabbed the column with both of his hands and wrapped his arms around it. "Mama was as sturdy as this column, Carmen. I will never match her greatness."

"You don't have to match it. You just have to pick up where she left off. We all do. It's going to take every one of us to carry her torch, James. The three of us children may not outrun her, but those five kids and the ones yet to come will." Carmen leaned on the column and James moved his right arm wrapping it around his sister instead of the column. The siblings stood looking out over the acreage that Grace had accumulated. Its outcome was yet to be determined. Neither spoke of the fortune or the future it involved for the family, but the thoughts coursed through each of their minds.

"To quote a remarkable lady, Carmen," and James took a deep sigh, "'Everything will be all right.'"

"Good timing. There comes Madelyn and Jimmy." Carmen was grateful her time with James had not been interrupted."

"No, it's not Madelyn. It's just Jimmy. Something's wrong. They've had an accident!" James rushed down the steps with Carmen on his heels yelling for Nick. "Jimmy, are you all right? Where's Madelyn?"

"She's gone! Dad, Kareem took her! We've got to help her!" Jimmy was breathless and shaking from his own trauma.

"Jimmy, what happened? You're gushing blood. Nick! Nick!"

Nick rushed out of the door onto the porch fully prepared to rescue his mother from James, but not expecting to see what he did. "Where's Madelyn, Jimmy? What's happened to her?"

Nora and Valerie joined the group bringing their own set of drama. Jimmy explained all that he knew, and the last thing he remembered. "It has to be Kareem. She was trying to warn me to leave. I just didn't get it. He had to be waiting on her in the cabin. I'm sorry, Dad. I didn't know. I should have gone in myself and looked for the globe."

"Don't, Son. Who knows what would've happened. You can't second-guess these things. Nora, go grab Mama's first aid kit. Valerie, go get some wet cloths." James had taken control before Nick could give orders. "Jimmy, I think you're going to need some stitches. It's a pretty nasty gash."

"Don't worry about me, Dad. We have to get Madelyn. Here's what's left of the snow globe she went after. She must have dropped it and the flashlight in the struggle." Jimmy held up the shattered globe and Carmen took it from his hand. She clasped it and held it to her chest and began silently praying for Madelyn's safety.

"We need to call 911, Nick." Carmen wanted immediate intervention.

"I'm calling Masters. He's sitting at the end of our drive. Ashley called me. Said she was pretty certain it was him in an unmarked car. She didn't stop. Said he had her tailed, and I'm sure Ralph and Gladys, too." Nick had dialed Masters's cell phone.

"Nick. Well, I suppose Ashley alerted you that I'm watching you," Masters was slow and taunting.

"No time for this, Masters. We need you. Get here. Now." Nick hung up and immediately saw the lights of Masters's vehicle. Apparently, he had moved in closer after Ashley spotted him.

Bruce Masters exited his car. He left the door open and scurried over to the group. "What's a-going on here, folks? Well, well, what have we here? Got a little injury, do we?" He glanced around the crowd. The girls had returned with wet cloths and first aid, but some of the gang appeared to be missing. "Where's Madelyn?"

Nick took the reins. "Pretty sure it's Kareem. Jimmy doesn't really know, because someone knocked him in the head. We don't know what he used."

"It's Kareem, Bruce. He's taken Madelyn. I'm sure of it." James spoke up boldly, but wasn't willing to incriminate himself.

"How can you be so sure, Jim? I mean, if the boy didn't see who hit him, ya might be jumpin' to some conclusions there, eh?

Maybe she went peacefully. Or, maybe it was her who hit Jimmy in the head?" Masters was hoping to snag Jim into a good lead for his other case he'd been working on for almost two years.

"Kareem's the likely candidate, Bruce. Let's don't waste time on chitchat. Let's get going and find my daughter." James was adamant.

Bruce took note of "daughter." *Strange you'd be trumping that card this late in the game, Jim, ol' boy.* "Let's, as in let us? You and me? Is that what you mean" Bruce found humor in James's suggestion.

"Yeah, I'm going with you. We can't waste time." James persisted.

"Nope, don't think so. I've got this covered, Mister Mayor. You stay here with your *family.* And, folks, y'all, please, just stay put. Don't complicate things more than they are so far. Besides, we're watchin' all of y'all. Just in case ya might be curious. Madelyn is probably not kidnapped or in any kind of danger. She's probably in on this whole theft. I've said that from the beginnin'." Bruce tipped the bill of his ball cap and strutted back to his car as he engaged his hand-held radio to contact dispatch. "I need an APB on Kareem Reynolds. Repeat, Kareem Reynolds. Be on the lookout for him. Allegedly has abducted Madelyn Willingham. Both are suspects. Repeat, both are suspects. Either or both could be armed and dangerous."

Masters took his cell phone and speed-dialed Ricks. "Ya seen any suspicious behavior at Ashley's place?"

"Negative." Ricks responded. He reported he had seen Ashley drive in her complex and enter her townhome. Best he could tell through the window, she was home alone.

"Well, do a knock-and-enter. Ask if she's seen Madelyn. Watch her expression. She can stone-face ya, so keep zeroed in on her eyes. Heard anythin' from the other family members?"

"The Murphys? They're home. Not a peep from those folks. Turned out the lights about five minutes after they walked in the door." Ricks had gotten the report from Jarrod Phillips earlier.

"Keep an eye out for those two, Ricks. Something's up with those jewels. This is the big moment." Masters put his phone on the seat. He was headed to Kareem's apartment. It seemed the most logical place to take her. He picked up the phone again and dialed Ricks.

"Me again. Hey, put someone on Turner's. The thief may come back to the scene of the crime. Put someone at Ashley's and you head to Grace's to watch. Keep me posted, and don't leave your post." Masters set his blue light on the dash of his unmarked car and sped down Victory Drive. His long week was coming to an end. *What a rotten way to put a good woman to rest.*

Chapter 44

ASHLEY WILLINGHAM'S TOWNHOME,
OCTOBER 16, 9:20 P.M.

Ricks sent a quick text to Jim Willingham: Gaston 12. Madln n hand. Jwls? He sent the message not knowing if Jim would get it or not. Masters didn't indicate that Jim had left the homeplace. He presumed not. If not, Jim was well aware of Madelyn's status. He said he'd be with the family. If he didn't show tonight, Boss wouldn't be happy. But at least Ricks had the text messages to prove he had done his job.

Ashley knew she was being watched, but who was ringing her doorbell? She finished brushing her teeth and ran downstairs. She looked through her viewer and saw Officer Ricks. "Who's there?" she cattily inquired.

"Ma'am, it's the police. We need to speak to you."

"We? Who's with you, Ricks?"

"Oh, well, sorry. I'm alone, Miss Ashley. Could I come in, please?"

Ashley reluctantly opened the door. She tilted her head to the right and peered at Ricks. "What do you need, Ricks? It's been a long day. I'm ready to settle in for the night."

"It's Madelyn, ma'am. She's missing." Ricks kept his gaze locked on Ashley's eyes. He knew Masters was right about her skill at not giving away emotion.

"What!" Ashley had not heard. She glanced over at her phone laying on her foyer table. She had silenced it at dinner and forgotten to turn it back on. There were several alerts of missed calls and texts. "What do you mean she's missing?"

Ricks had seen all he needed to see. Ashley was clueless. She obviously had not heard. "Do you mind if I take a quick look around, ma'am?"

"I do mind, *Officer*. Without a search warrant, get off my property." Ashley wanted to get rid of Ricks so she could find out what was going on with Madelyn. The sooner, the better.

"Wow. You're testy. I just want to take a quick look and make sure the suspects—"

"Now! Or I'll have your badge."

"Yes, ma'am. Thank you." Ricks left the premises and Ashley closed the door and locked it behind him. She grabbed her phone and ran back upstairs returning Nick's call as she did. She wanted to get out of the earshot of Ricks in case he was hanging around outside her door.

"Nick? I'm sorry. I had my phone on silence. Where's Madelyn? What's happened?" Ashley winced when Nick relayed the story. "Is Jimmy all right? Has someone taken him to the emergency room?" She couldn't believe all of this was happening on the day of the funeral. Everyone was exhausted, but a sudden surge of energy was summoned and plans were being made. "I'm on my way back. There'll be an officer following me. I just kicked him out of my place. They really think one of us has the jewels, Nick. And they think it's Madelyn. Do you?" Ashley didn't want to doubt her better judgment, but she couldn't dismiss the fact that perhaps it was a setup all along. She would do some of her own questioning of Jimmy when she got back home. "Who's got the baby? Nora knows nothing about babies. Nor does Valerie. I'll be there soon. Thanks."

*   *   *

GLADYS FAYE WILLINGHAM-MURPHY'S HOME, OCTOBER 16, 9:15 P.M.

"I don't want to alarm you, Gladys, but there's a police car outside our house. Well, a County cop. He followed us home." Ralph felt Gladys deserved to know they were under surveillance for whatever reason.

"Are you sure? Whatever for? Let's turn out the lights. I don't want them looking in at us. Get the candle and let's light one and we can go to the back of the house." Gladys didn't like the sounds of someone snooping around their home. *Are we in danger? Did I say something at the interview that gave Detective Masters a reason to suspicion me?*

Ralph was more than surprised that Gladys was leading him back to her bedroom. She had never *invited* him to her room. "What do you make of it, Gladys? Why would they be here?" Ralph knew Gladys had wanted to leave for a long time. He had seen her Tuscany brochure laying on her dresser one day. It was worn. It was obviously a long-time dream. When she would leave the house, he would go in her room and smell her perfume, open her closet, and touch her clothes. She would sometimes leave her scarfs laying on the dresser. He would pick them up and smell them so that he could feel close to her. He would fantasize about how he could love her if she would allow him into her cold, dark heart. He could save her from her despair. But she never gave him a chance. Rather than feel rejected, he loved the only thing that kept him warm—his dear friend, Jack Daniels. *But would she stoop so low as to steal her own mother's jewels just to get away? My Gladys wouldn't do that. I don't believe that. I won't believe that. I can't.*

Gladys stood looking at Ralph's blank stare as he held the lighted candle between them. He didn't respond to her answer. She wasn't quite sure what to make of that. "Did you hear what I said, Ralph? Why are you looking at me like that?"

"I'm sorry, Gladys. What did you say? I didn't hear you, I suppose."

"I was being funny saying that I don't know, unless they think one of us stole Mother's jewels."

"Huh-huh-huh." Ralph did a poor job at faking a chuckle. He shifted the candle away from his face.

"Why were you looking at me like that, Ralph? What were you thinking just now when you didn't hear me?" Gladys's boldness was unexpected. Ralph was struggling to keep his nerves together after not having had a drink all day. He was a good five hours past his bewitching drinking time. He was dealing with it better than he had anticipated, but to say he was not noticing withdrawal symptoms would be less than honest.

"I was thinking of you, Gladys. I was thinking of how sorry

I am for what I have done to complicate your life." Ralph was saying things he had thought of before, but clearly not sharing his immediate thoughts. If he shared those with Gladys, she would have thrown him out the door as fast she invited him in.

"You didn't complicate my life, Ralph. I complicated yours. I totally used you. I used you in a ploy to get back at Kyle Hardee, and it backfired on both of us. I wasted your life, and for that I am truly sorry. I need your forgiveness for that." Gladys never intended to say any of the words that just exited her mouth, and certainly not the forgiveness part. The healing that had happened to her heart since hearing those words from Carmen was welcoming and transforming. The least she could do was to transfer the healing to someone else she had hurt.

"Gladys, don't ever think you destroyed my life. I meant what I said at the altar. For me, it was for better or worse. But, I didn't mean to give you the worst end of the deal. It's me who needs your forgiveness." Ralph's eyes filled with tears. His emotions were raw. He surmised it was due to loss of his friend Jack.

Gladys felt awkward and walked over to sit in the bedside chair. She reached down, took off her shoes, and began rubbing her feet. Ralph set the candlestick on the nightstand beside the chair and sat on the floor in front of Gladys. He took her foot in his hands and began massaging. "I used to be really good at this, Gladys. Don't know if my hands are as smooth as they were when I was a young boy, but let me give it a try." He held his breath waiting for Gladys to object by removing her foot from his hand. She didn't. Instead, she leaned her head back on the chair and relaxed.

"You haven't lost your touch, Ralph. That feels great. My feet are miserable after the long day at the funeral. Could you believe how many people showed up for Mother's service? I'm still in shock. I've never shaken so many hands and hugged so many necks in my entire life. I never knew what a revered person my mother was. I feel like I really cheated myself." Gladys closed her eyes.

"Yeah, I thought my grin might freeze into place after about the first hour. It was quite an honor to be a part of such an outpouring of love and affection. She must have been quite a lady. Like her daughter. Not Carmen. I mean you." Ralph kept rubbing Gladys's feet. She didn't say anything. He kept his eyes down, not daring to look up. Her toenails were painted red, just like her mother's. He found that sweet. *Just acknowledge me, Gladys. Ignoring is like objecting. Objecting is like rejecting. My heart can't take anymore rejection. I'm doing my best here. Help me out.*

Ralph heard really heavy breathing. He looked up and saw that Gladys had fallen fast asleep. He gently let go of her foot. He turned back the covers and fluffed the pillow. He knew it was the side Gladys slept on. He was familiar with her smell. He reached under her and lifted her out of the chair. She put her arms around his neck of her own accord. Whether she was subconsciously accepting of his kindness, he couldn't tell. He laid her in the bed. He managed to loosen her skirt and jacket and slip them off without disturbing her. It was the first time he had seen her in her lingerie. A less respectable man might have taken advantage of an opportunity from his wife. He stood beside her and caressed her in his mind. He visualized kissing her lips, nibbling her ear, and whispering his grandest contemplations of love for her. He stopped at the boundaries of fantasy. Crossing the lines she had drawn years ago would mean losing her forever. He pulled the covers over her and kissed her on the forehead. He whispered softly, "I love you, Gladys Murphy. I always have. I always will." He picked up the candlestick and quietly walked out of her room.

Gladys opened her eyes and watched as the lone shadow moved down the hallway. No cabinet doors opened. No bottle clanged against a glass. Soon the light disappeared from sight, and Ralph shut his bedroom door. Gladys closed her eyes in peace. Tonight there were no thoughts of freedom or luster of life or Tuscany waiting patiently. Gladys was content. She placed her fingertips on her forehead where Ralph's kiss was fresh. *Love. Such a strange phenomenon. It manifests even out of deceit. It lives always and forever. It transforms into forgiveness. What might it do to a cold, dark heart…if allowed?* Gladys fell asleep with the thought of escape at her fingertips.

Chapter 45

Sweat was dripping from Kareem's brow and upper torso. He had struggled carrying Madelyn through the woods. The configuration of Grace Willingham's property ran wider from east to west rather than longer north to south. That was a very good thing, considering Kareem had entered on the south side of the property toward the coastline. He was a strapping man, but to carry Madelyn another ten feet, his endurance would have let him down. He was beginning to be concerned that he had turned off the girl's lights forever. She was dead weight. She never moved a muscle, even when he stuffed her into the trunk of the car. The fence had been his biggest obstacle. She groaned when he threw her over it to the other side. Actually, he had been relieved to hear the sound of life from her. Now, she was kicking and screaming in the trunk, and he was even more reassured of her wellbeing. At least he hadn't hurt her too badly. If she cooperated and told him where she had stashed the jewels, she could save herself a lot of pain in the end. He knew, however, even if she did turn over the jewels, it would not save her life. Once Hawk got what he was after, there would be no further use for the mayor's daughter.

Kareem was fortunate to have learned about the back entrance to the Willingham property. When he and Madelyn had first gotten together, she had innocently pointed it out to him. She had shared stories with him about how she and her siblings would run through the woods to the edge of the property. They would climb on the fence and wave to the cars while they sat and watched the world go by. He remembered how she rambled on and on about their dreams of visiting different countries. Her dream was of Australia. Apparently, her granny cranked up her grandchildren's imaginations. He thought how juvenile and boring he found their pastime to be. He grew up roaming the streets with his friends, shooting hoops, and playing marbles. The only dream he had was to get on a college and pro basketball team. He was really good, and everyone knew it. With a little coaching and half a chance, he could have held his own with the best. Once he was introduced to the gang, he had no need for dreams.

For now, his day consisted of getting her grandmother's jewels. At midnight, he had an appointment with Hawk. He didn't intend to lose his life because of her. He steered his car toward his other place—a townhome. Madelyn never knew he had a separate home apart from where the two of them lived. She was never as street smart as she gave herself credit. Kareem had been at this longer, much longer. He never involved his women in his business, anyway. They were only the recipients of the drugs he trafficked. He kept them happy that way. They kept him happy other ways.

His decision to bring Madelyn to his secret place was because it was too risky to go back to their own. The law would be swarming the area around Abercorn expecting her to show up there. If she had hidden the jewels anywhere near that place, he would have to figure things out from that point through the help of his peons. The hardest thing he had to do was to get her to talk, and to talk fast. If she wouldn't talk to stop her own pain, he would threaten her with the boy as a lure to get the jewels. He knew her heart for Bryson would loosen her tongue. Although, harming Bryson would never be a part of Kareem's plans. This was his only son. Kareem's best hope was that she didn't know him well enough to recognize the soft layer that weakened who he was.

Kareem kept a close check on his rear-view mirrors for any sign of law enforcement. He had never driven this car, so no one would recognize the vehicle. To his knowledge, the police knew nothing about his nice place. He used a different name. It was a decent neighborhood. No one came there but him. Hawk had set it up for Kareem. It was clear he was becoming his right-hand man. He didn't want any attention brought to himself in this neighborhood. He had to keep Madelyn quiet somehow so as not to create any drama. He had to keep quietly focused. Gaston by twelve was his destination–with or without the jewels. After that, Madelyn would be in the hands of Hawk. Her fate was out of Kareem's control at the stroke of midnight. Whatever happened was none of his concern. Overdosing was easy to pull off, unless there was facial damage. With Hawk's men involved, that was a given. By the time they were done, she would be at the bottom of the Savannah River. Whoever it was he knocked out at the cabin couldn't verify he was there. He never saw him in the darkness. After that, all he saw was stars. The law would have trouble linking Kareem to Madelyn's disappearance. All Kareem would have to worry about was Bryson. He would be the surviving parent, and that satisfied him. The way he saw it, his boy was the best thing that came from the whole Willingham ordeal and his only reward for having to put up with her obstinate, strong-willed determination.

The garage door opened and Kareem pulled his vehicle inside. Madelyn couldn't be knocked out again. The clock was ticking. Gagging her would be adequate. She would let him know when she was ready to talk. He looked through his garage shelves for rope and duct tape. Then, he grabbed a hammer, screwdriver, a razorblade knife, and a pair of pliers. Those could do some damage to a pretty face and fingers. He stepped inside his kitchen from his garage entrance. He grabbed a straight-back chair and placed it in the bathroom. He laid his tools beside the chair and took the tape and rope with him. His gun was concealed under his shirt between his pants and his bare back. When he opened the trunk, Madelyn would be staring face-on at a gun. If she opened her mouth to scream, he'd offer it as a pacifier. She'd calm down quickly enough. It was a twenty-minute drive to Gaston from his place. He had to act hastily in order to retrieve the jewels. Kareem preferred to show up for his appointment with them. He knew Hawk would be much happier if he did. Kareem was only one among many who understood the need to keep Hawk that way.

*   *   *

827 Victory Drive, Grace's Homeplace, October 16, 10:03 p.m.

"*Déjà vu.* I feel like I've been down Grandma's road a few times already. Because I have! I need sleep!" Ashley pounded the steering wheel. She had intended to remain condescendingly calm, but her frustration was mounting beyond control. As a little girl, she had talked to herself. Now that she lived alone, she found herself doing it more and more frequently. Driving seemed to bring out the most frustrations in her day. Crazy and slow drivers would often send her into a small fit of rage. She would never go so far as exercising road rage, but she was probably mistaken for a crazy person herself when other drivers caught sight of her at a red light.

Ashley was also known to possess a little of Nora's drama. Grandma Grace said what she and Nora were guilty of was "throwing little hissy fits." This was one of those moments her grandmother would have earmarked as such. Ashley took her right hand off the wheel, webbed her fingers together stiffly, and thrust her arm up to the roof of the car repeatedly. Her voice escalated and she was grateful for the darkness in case a passerby should overhear her loud screech. "Madelyn, what were you thinking? How did you ever get to this station in life? You had the same upbringing as the rest of us." She paused, then added. "Well, I guess that's not entirely true."

Ashley backed off her yelping because she realized Madelyn had the most difficult childhood of all the grandkids. Her inflection turned into pity and concern. "But you had Grandma Grace's guidance. Ugh! This is so frustrating. Kareem's gang is nothing to mess around with."

Ashley grabbed the steering wheel with both hands and

pulled her forehead to the top, then tapped her head lightly. "If indeed you are not in cahoots with Kareem on the jewel theft, you are in trouble deep, Girl." Ashley could think of little else she needed more than sleep, but the immediate order of business dictated Madelyn's safety. She didn't want to alarm the rest of the family, but she felt it her obligation to let them know the imminent danger Madelyn faced.

Ashley got out of the car and saw everyone in the family room through the lighted window. She ran up the porch steps recognizing a feeling she had never experienced at Grandma's. Trouble and anxiousness had not been part of her visits here. Not ever. Grandma's was a place to come and relax. It was the safe haven, the refuge, the sanctuary, the escape. It was where you came to find solutions to the chaos apart from here. This was the place you came because there was no chaos. Life, yes. Chaos, never. Grandma Grace hadn't even been in the ground twelve hours and already there was pandemonium–at her house! Ashley took a deep breath and opened the door.

"Jimmy, what happened to you? You have to get that taken care of. It really needs a stitch or two." A nauseated feeling came over Ashley. She dealt with the calmer side of law. She was not used to the blood, guts, and the gore. That shield was not by design. She realized it was a matter of time before her number was called to experience that kind of case.

"Ah, just a little bump on the head." Jimmy winced and grabbed his head. He got the sympathy from Nora and Carmen he was eliciting.

"We're getting a plan together to go and look for Madelyn. We could use some advice about what to do, quite frankly,

Ashley. Masters told us to stay put. I informed him I wanted to go with him and help find Madelyn, but he laughed at me." James scowled at the lack of respect Masters had shown for his position as a father and the mayor.

Nick quickly retorted a hardy objection as well, but took it a step further. "We're not staying home. We have no restraining order against us. Only a verbal command by Bruce Masters. Who does he think he is anyway? It's our sister whose life is in danger."

James and Carmen cut their eyes at Nick and their thoughts were duplicated. *Did you just say what I thought you said?* James was speechless and hoping it felt familiar enough to be overlooked. Carmen didn't want to give anyone time to camp out on the comment. "We wouldn't be breaking the law or anything, would we, Ashley?"

"You don't have a cease and desist or restraining order from a judge or the prosecutor's office. So I'd say let's go." Ashley was charged up and incited over Masters's indignation toward her father, as well as his throwing the law around with no authority on paper. "She's in real danger, guys. I hate to break it to you, but he's bad news."

"No, no, no, no. None of my girls are going. Too dangerous. In fact, I really want to go alone." The time was not appropriate for James to confess why he knew Madelyn was in harm's way. He needed to do this alone. His concern for Jimmy had distracted him from what his gut instinct told him to do. "Val, I'll be back as soon as I can. If you want someone to take you home, you can do that, or I'm sure you can bed down here somewhere." James lightly kissed Valerie on the lips, which proved a bit awkward for his kids who were within her age range. Carmen gave a curt shake to the head to dispel the rolling of their eyes.

"Sleep? Who can sleep with this going on? I'm going to wait right here on you and keep these girls company. Please, be careful, Jim. I don't like this. Let me say that from the get-go. I don't like it at all." Valerie wouldn't let go of James's hand. She was clueless about her husband's more tangible involvement in this spectacle, but it felt criminal enough with Jimmy's gashed-open head.

James broke loose from Valerie's grip and turned to walk out the door while still commanding orders. "Carmen, you should probably go with Jimmy to the ER. The rest of you girls stay put. Nick will be here with you. Lock the doors and don't let anyone in. I don't care who it is."

"Well, I'm not staying at the hospital. I want to get back in the house. Will you open it for me, please?" Jimmy was comically squeamish.

James kept walking toward the door and yelled back, "Check for facial hair before you do. He turns into a werewolf at midnight."

"Dad! Don't give my secrets away." Jimmy yelled back and laughed. "Ouch, that hurts."

"Oooh, you poor thing." Nora reached over to rub his hair. Jimmy ducked before she could touch his head, but grabbed her hand and patted his face with it.

"Mom, I'm going with James. Can you girls swap this around a bit? Nora, there's GPS in my car. It's set for the closest hospital. Just tell it where you want to go. You take Jimmy for stitches." Nick tossed his keys to Nora as he turned the door handle. "Ashley, I hear you're the expert with babies. You've got Bryson."

He gave Ashley a quick wink.

Ashley was getting ready to correct him as far as her knowing about babies herself, but caught herself. She remembered her own objection to Nora and Valerie taking care of Baby B. Overloading her mouth happened to her only occasionally, but seemed to happen more when Nora was involved than anyone else.

Nick paused before exiting the door. "Mom, I'd feel better if you'd stay here. No offense to anyone else. But, I would personally feel more secure." Nick closed the door behind him. "James, hold up! I'm coming with you."

James had stopped to answer a text and was just opening the door to the car. "Nick, I don't think that's a good idea. At all. Please, let me do this. She's my daughter." James was adamant.

"And she's my sister." Nick didn't bat an eye while looking straight into James's.

This was going to complicate things. A lot. But the family was bound to find out how deep into a dark side of life he was. There was no time to argue. "Get in, Son." *There. I said it.* It felt strangely *comfortable* for James, but it had to be done at some point. Now seemed as good a time as any.

"Thanks." Nick closed the door and James hit the gas pedal. Time was wasting. Madelyn was not in good company, and James was well aware.

*   *   *

ABERCORN TERRACE APARTMENTS, #14, SAVANNAH, GEORGIA, OCTOBER 16, 10:08 P.M.

The knocking turned to banging on the door of Kareem and Madelyn's apartment at Abercorn Terrace. Bruce Masters was tired of waiting. He turned the handle expecting it to be locked. It wasn't, and the detective quickly retrieved his gun from its holster. "Hello? Anybody home? Madelyn Willingham? Kareem Reynolds? Need to talk to you." Masters continued to talk as he checked each room, carefully aiming his gun in front of him. The place had been ransacked by someone. Apparently, they were looking to find Madelyn's hiding place. "Well, well, seems Miss Madelyn has been a bad little girl. And I was just beginnin' to believe your cute little aunt. Somebody's not going to like this. You've bought yourself a whole lot of trouble, little missy. You really don't know how much. Yet." Masters stepped out of the apartment and grabbed his cell phone. "Ricks, what's your 10-20?"

"Victory Drive. Followed Ashley Willingham to her Grandma's. She left pert-near after I did the knock-and-enter. I don't think she knew, Bruce. I'm sittin' in the driveway off to the side. There's some scuttlebutt going on in there as best I can tell. You want me to search their place? Kinda keep my eye on them for a while?" Ricks had some time to kill before the midnight appointment. He wanted to make sure he was the officer on duty at Gaston. He got no objection anytime he bid for street duty there. As much as officers like action, only the ones involved with Hawk survived. Provided he had no beef with them, of course. He saw Mayor Willingham exit the house and text someone before he got into his car. He heard a text message come in while Masters was talking to him and assumed Jim was alerting him to something.

"Watch the house, Ricks. Don't leave your 10-20. If anyone

leaves that house, you call me and we'll get 'em covered. I have officers posted around the periphery of the property. There must be another entrance somewhere. Either that or Kareem walked in from Victory and the folks just didn't know it. The ol' lady needed a watch dog in the worst kind of way. You had any reports of Kareem's whereabouts? They seem to think he has Madelyn. I think she's in cahoots with him myself, and they've probably done split up at this point to try to lose us. Or, maybe they're a hundred miles down the road. Who knows?"

"Nunh-unh, that ain't likely, Bruce." Ricks spoke with authority in his answer. It piqued the curiosity of Masters.

"Why you say it like that?"

"Like what?" Ricks wasn't sure what Masters was getting at.

"Oh, I dunno. You sounded kinda sure of yourself, that's all. I'm goin' to the station for a few minutes to check on some things. Again, do not leave your post. If this investigation is to get over with, people need to stay put, including the officers. Alert me. I'll be on it." Masters had executed a good plan, if folks like Ricks would just follow it. It had been a problem in the past. He hoped everybody would cooperate now that things were winding down.

"10-4. I'm stickin' right here. I'll keep in touch." Ricks ended the call and was pulling up the text message when he saw lights coming toward him. He had no idea who it was. He wasn't watching because Bruce had distracted him. The mighty oaks kept any sign of moonlight out. There would be no mistaking, however, that his dead give-away vehicle was a commission. The vehicle never slowed down. As it sped past, he caught the silhouettes of two people appearing to be men. There had been three in the house. He'd be willing to bet one of these was Jim Willingham.

He looked at his text message. Mayor had texted "No harm 2 grl. She has no jwls. I do. 12. Gaston."

Ricks went to his contacts and hit "call." The voice on the other end was more than harsh. His tone indicated he didn't like being disturbed with news–bad or good.

"This better be better than good."

"Got the jewels." Ricks's stunted ego was inflated to be the first to report. He needed all the points he could get with Hawk.

"In hand?"

"Well, not exactly, but—"

"Then you don't have them," and the phone went silent.

Ricks stared at his phone until the screen went black. *That didn't go as well as I planned. The man sounded irritated. When will you learn patience, Ricks? Doofus!*

Bruce Masters sped down the road to Victory Drive. The others were looking for Kareem and Madelyn. Ricks was watching Grace's place, where The Honorable Mayor would be. Something was up between the two of them. He had seen their exchange in the church. The big florals were a terrific camouflage for a spying soul to watch questionable personalities. He had suspected Ricks for some time of being in collusion with the Mayor. He had noticed an exchange between the two at the funeral home, as well. Someone on the force was a snitch. He'd had too many plans cave because somebody leaked information. Bruce hadn't been able to put his finger on it until now. If Ricks left his assigned post, he'd be right behind him. He had brought his wife's car tonight. His cover was more than secure. Even if the chase didn't lead him to Kareem and Madelyn and the jewels, he could blow the lid off of the inner ring of corruption in the city. *If I could cap off my career with cracking two major cases, that'd be awfully sweet.* Bruce kissed the tips of his thumb and his index finger and sent the taste of sweetness flying in thin air. *Only one minor detail, Bruce. Who can you trust as backup?*

Chapter 46

Ashley took her cell phone from her purse and walked into the kitchen area. She dialed her dad's number. There had not been enough time to adequately inform him of what he might be facing should he find Madelyn. It seemed like a futile effort for them to go on a search for her. She could be anywhere in the Savannah area, or three counties over for that matter. How he might know where to begin looking was a wee bit peculiar in her attorney way of thinking.

"Ashley? Is everything all right? Getting a call so soon after leaving was disconcerting to James.

"Yeah, everything's fine, Dad. I didn't mean to alarm you. Hey, I felt like you should know what you're walking into. You and Nick could be in real danger. Kareem Reynolds is a notorious—" Ashley didn't get to finish her description.

"I know. He's as wicked as they come— Well, actually, there are those even more vile than him. But, I understand what you're saying, honey. I appreciate your concern, but I don't want you to worry yourself over this. Okay? Promise?" James was tender and caring in his solicitation of an agreement.

"Daddy, I'm serious. I hear things out there. Do you have a way to protect yourself? You know the police are looking for them. I'm really wondering if maybe you shouldn't let them do their job. I mean, I'm sure they're looking all the places you're familiar with that Madelyn might be. You just need to be careful, Daddy. Really, you do."

"I have a gun. I can handle myself." James glanced at Nick to see if he reacted. Nick never flinched a muscle. He kept looking straight ahead, scanning the streets and parking lots to see any sign of police or suspicious activity.

"I'm sure you have a license, right?" Ashley inquired.

"Yes, ma'am, I do. No need to worry about the legality of my gun." James winked at Nick.

"Have you considered that she might be in on it, Daddy?" Ashley let that settle for a split second and quickly added, "I don't want to suggest anything criminal about Madelyn. I do feel we should explore the possibility, though. Have you given thought to that?"

"She didn't, Ashley. I refuse to believe that. Madelyn has lived a rough lifestyle for the past several years. I certainly am not one to judge. But, I know she loved your grandmother. She was all Madelyn had. I don't believe she would dishonor Grandma by being a part of stealing her jewels. I–I–I won't allow myself to believe it. And if I don't believe in her now, Ashley, who will? I may be her only chance of getting her out of this mess she's in. And right now, she's in a heap of it." Every fiber in James hurt to think of his daughter in the hands of Kareem or Hawk. He had to find her whatever the costs.

"You're right. She doesn't have anyone but us. Please be careful. Don't do anything foolish. 911. I'm just saying."

"Thanks, Ashley. I appreciate the call. Just be praying for the situation. That's the best thing you guys can do. Everything will be all right." James ended the call and looked over at Nick. "There's another one in the glove compartment."

"I'm sorry?" Nick wasn't clear what James meant.

"There's another gun in the glove compartment. They're registered. Do you know how to handle one?"

Nick reached behind his back and pulled out a Glock 23. ".40 caliber with magazine pouch. Light weight. Easy conceal. Comes in handy."

James reached behind his back for his concealed weapon. "Like father, like son. Nice choice." It was an awkward moment, but what time wouldn't be to broach such a sensitive subject. James gulped in an attempt to push his heart back down into his chest. Then, his spirit began praying on his behalf. He knew he would need strength and wisdom.

Nick turned his head to look out the passenger window. He had waited a long time for this moment. He thought the encounter might be in a different setting, but what that might be suddenly seemed insignificant.

"Nick, I really haven't had much time to process what your mom just told me. But I can tell you that I have had many years to regret the senseless, despicable and immoral act of the reckless young man that I was. I don't even have the words to say how deeply sorry I am for having hurt your mother. She's an amazing woman. She always has been. She didn't deserve anything that happened to her. The fact that she could forgive to the degree she has is remarkable. But, let me add to that. If all mistakes turned out as incredible as you, there would be a silver lining to every sad story. I'm one of those mistakes in life by my own design. I'm hoping to find the silver lining and remedy some things I've made a mess of. In the words of a very wise woman who has taken on more of the character of our mother than either of her own blood children, 'I need your forgiveness.' Can I count on that, Nick?"

Nick turned to look at James. "Of all your children, I have less to forgive than anyone. You've only known you were my father for less than an hour." Nick took his hand and gave a light punch to the top of James's right arm.

"It wouldn't have mattered if I'd found out sooner, Nick. My heart wasn't ready until about twenty-four hours ago. Your mom questioned herself as to whether her decision to hold off was her doing or God's. The Lord's timing is perfect. He sees to infinity and beyond. Grace always said, 'Patience comes when you relinquish your plans and learn to trust that God has time-stamped the answer to your prayer.'"

"Yeah, she always told me that 'He's a right-on-time God.' She knew Him well. James, I'll be honest with you, I might not ever feel comfortable saying the word *Dad.* I don't know. I've given that a lot of thought, but so far, it doesn't feel like a fit. I acknowledge that you are. Don't get me wrong. I not only acknowledge, I don't even begrudge it anymore. I did for a long time, not knowing who my father was, or if I had one out there that cared. It was tough. But I had it better than the rest of your kids. I had a mother. Mine didn't die and she cared for me and loved me with all her heart. She was a great dad-by-default. She couldn't do everything a father does for a kid because they desperately need that paternal influence only a father brings. But she was a great compensator. She has the best of hearts. But, again, don't be offended if I don't call you *Dad.* May not ever happen." Nick smiled and lightened the tenor of the conversation. "After all, I have called you James for the last five years. But, I believe we can work at a relationship. It'll have to be a long-distance one, though. I'll be heading back to France soon. Got a girl there who has my heart."

"Well, congratulations. I can't wait to hear about her." James surrendered the moment to silence. The two rode down Abercorn looking for signs of Madelyn. James was stalling for time. He knew where he had to be by midnight. He didn't know what poor Madelyn was suffering in the meantime. But he knew if it was the jewels Hawk was after, they wouldn't harm her initially. He had dealt with them long enough to understand how the system worked. It would have been James's preference to come alone and not involve Nick. He was here upon his own insistence. How things unfolded from this point forward was up for grabs. But Nick deserved to know the reality of what could come down when the clock struck twelve.

"Nick, I've made some pretty bad choices in my life. I've gotten tangled up with a few people that I'm not proud to be associated with. But I've been trying to disengage myself for a while. Financially, I've been in over my head."

"Gambling can do that to folks." Nick was matter of fact in his conclusion of the source of James's troubles.

"You knew? How? Does everyone?" To say James was surprised would have underrated his emotion.

"I sat and watched you gamble a life savings away a couple of nights. I had a business acquaintance who wanted me to meet him in Vegas and discuss designing a building for him. I saw you there. He and I parted ways. I followed you from the restaurant to the casino. I don't know what moved me to do that, but it was therapeutic for me in the end. I came to peace with being okay to have grown up in a single-parent home and without a dad's involvement in my life. I realized I had been spared from exposure to a world that was foreign to me. The first night wasn't the charm, but the second night settled all the left-over issues. It finally dawned on me what Grandma Grace was trying to tell me when I confided in her about my pain of not having a father. This was before I knew about you. She talked about God's protection and that sometimes He sheltered us in ways we didn't always understand. She told me, "Kids will generally produce the same fruits that fall from the trees around them." The second night it clicked. You were a drunken, boisterous, and angry mess. You lost the farm that night. Lady Luck had your number, and she picked your pocket. I got up and walked away feeling a very blessed man to have missed that part of your life. I was in a better place, thanks to two really strong women. If you're in a better place now, then you're ready to be a father and grandfather. You're the only one who can prove that, James. As Grace always told us, 'In order to get there, you have to start here.' I believe we all want the legacy of Grace Willingham to be carried on. It's not too late to pick up where she left off."

"I feel better. I think. That was hard to hear." James cleared his throat and took a deep breath. "There's something you probably need to know, Nick. We're about to face some real undesirables. Because of my misfortune in Vegas, I made a bargain with Satan. That night two men came and escorted me from the craps table. They took me to a private room where a gentleman made an arrangement with me. Apparently, he'd done his homework. Thought I might be an heir to some novel jewels. I guess when you have the kind of money he does, your hobbies become your career. He collected unique items. He looked for royal vestiges with stories attached. Albert's is quite the story.

"In hindsight, I believe it was a setup from the get-go—the invitation of an all-expense-paid vacation to Vegas because of my position as mayor. They even gave me some gambling money to get me started. I was hooked instantly. It was an escape from pain. I loved alcohol, and they fed me all I wanted. By the time I left, I was in debt up to my eyeballs. He mentioned the jewels. They held no sentiment to me. I was angry at the world, and the biggest part of my world was Mama. I sold my birthright that night." James took a deep breath and shook his head. He kept his eyes on the road, but he wasn't looking for any signs of Madelyn.

"So, how does Madelyn fit into this, then? Why is she getting the blame for something you did?" Nick was curious and a little feather-ruffled at the thought of his sister taking the fall.

"I got the debt reduced considerably. Then, Valerie helped me pay it off. She doesn't know that's what I did with the money, of course. She has no clue I ever got involved in something like this. But this man has a big part of the law enforcement at his mercy, too. It's a big mess. Before I could get the debt paid, I was his puppet. I helped people get off for drug crimes. I used my powers as the Mayor of Savannah in a deceitful way. I'm not proud of that, but he has that over my head. But I have been cleaning up my act lately. I know it was only because of Grace who stayed on her knees for me. She and my administrative assistant. But, I could do some time for this."

"So when you were no longer indebted, they had to find another way to get to the jewels. That's where Madelyn came in. She was a setup with Kareem?" Nick had a strong unsettling feeling about poor Madelyn's involvement. On the surface, it sounded as though she was a mere victim of circumstances. She had probably never factored in that her desperation would lead to this destination. He was praying for a miracle for her. He was certain his mother was doing the same.

"I'm afraid Madelyn was the lure, Nick. I never wanted that to happen. I know I disengaged myself from her, but I would never want to see her harmed. I hope you believe me." James was feeling the weight of his shame. "I don't know if she can ever forgive me."

"I understand. But like Grace used to say, 'Respect is best found resting between the pages of love.' Madelyn is starved for love. A little of it will send those walls crumbling at her feet." Nick could tell James was sinking fast. He needed encouragement to keep his peace of mind. And for the predicament they were apparently going to face, Nick wanted James's focus on the business at hand, not feeling defeated.

The two rode in silence for another stretch of their journey. A lot of information in a little bit of time had been exchanged between them. Emotions were raw given the circumstances of the day, and a lot had transpired since dawn's early light. The two were weary. Neither were aware of the other's lack of rest, outside of the fatigue on their faces.

"Where are you taking us, James?" Nick had not traveled this part of Savannah. It was one of the warnings he had gotten when he first came into town.

"Gaston."

"Gaston! Seriously? Isn't this a pretty wicked side of Savannah?" Nick's apprehension surfaced immediately.

"It's wicked because the cops that hang here are. All the others never make it out alive. You wouldn't want to bring your mother here, let's just put it that way." James tried to be casual in his description but still get his point across. Apparently, Nick had been given fair warning by someone else.

"Gees, James. You did keep some shady friends. Madelyn is involved with this? I've worked on a few bodies that came from this place. They're practically unrecognizable." Nick was feeling more than uneasy about the impending event.

"Midnight. We'll see Madelyn at midnight." James was emphatic.

"How do you know we will? Who told you that?" Nick really wanted the answers. James ignored his questions.

"I'm going to park a distance away. You stay in the car. I'll send Madelyn running this way. As soon as she gets in the car, you get out of sight. Don't worry about me. Just get back home as fast as you can go. And don't dare stop for any law enforcement. Let them chase you down to a respectable part of town if anyone comes after you. Got it?"

"I've got *something*. I'm not liking any of this, but I've got your back." Nick tilted his seat back to get more comfortable. He placed his hands behind his head and changed topics. "So, we have some time to kill. Let me tell you about my Abrielle."

Nick began talking about the love of his life. James sat and listened and his thoughts took him back to how he had loved Annie. The two girls sounded very similar, both having a kind spirit about them. Abrielle had obviously stolen Nick's heart and had given hers in exchange. The girl was in love. Anyone who would wait on a young man for five years was a woman of great purpose. She was a keeper.

James listened as Nick spoke of his life in France. In the meantime, he prayed for God's protection on his son and daughter. Neither of them deserved to be caught up in his disarray of life. The bewitching hour would soon come and pronounce a sentence on squandered years of a prodigal son. As the minutes ticked by, his mind was attentive to the precious time between him and his newly-announced son. But his heart was tying itself into a thousand knots of regret.

* * *

SECRET HOME OF KAREEM REYNOLDS, OCTOBER 16, 10:47 P.M.

"You gonna tell me where you hid the jewels?" Kareem was in Madelyn's face with the razorblade knife. She was sitting in a straight chair, her hands tied behind her back, and her mouth duct-taped. Before he tied her up, she tried to run and almost got away. When he caught her, he lost control and started beating her. Her face was red and stinging from the blows she had received. Her left eye had been blackened. Her ribs were hurting from blows to her midsection. There were bruises and gouges in her arms where he had used a pair of pliers and a screwdriver to hurt her. He took off the duct tape, again trying to get the needed information from her.

"I'm gonna ask ya one more time, woman! Where did you put the jewels?"

Madelyn responded by spitting in Kareem's face, which bought her another blow and bloodied her nose.

He took the razorblade knife and brought it in closer. He placed it against her cheekbone. "It won't hurt my feelings one bit to scar up this pretty face enough that your son will be scared to death to look at you." Kareem was losing his patience. He glanced at the phone to check the time and saw he had a stream of text messages from Ricks. The bottom one caught his eye–Mayor. He picked up the phone to read his texts.

Madelyn didn't like hearing Bryson brought into this. She feared for her life right now. She didn't know anything else to say other than what she had–she didn't have the jewels. Kareem didn't believe her, and there would be no convincing him. Madelyn began to cry. She wanted to watch her baby grow up. The thought of him being turned over to Kareem was more than she could stand. She had to get away from him. She was wriggling her arms, struggling to get out of the rope that bound her. Another tug or two and she would break free. She looked around to see if there was anything within reach that she could hit him with. She twisted her hands again. One more tug and she was free.

"Looks like ya lucked out, pretty girl. Seems like Daddy came to yo rescue. He got the jewels. But you gonna be the bait to get 'em." Kareem pulled at Madelyn's arms and released her from the chair. Her hands were still tied, but loosely. She prayed he wouldn't notice. He pulled another piece of duct tape and placed it over her mouth. "Don't want you screaming and disrupting my fine neighborhood here. Didn't know I had this nice spread, did ya?"

Madelyn looked around. She had no idea this was Kareem's place. What a lie he had lived. He rationed out money to her and she was barely able to get by, especially since the baby had come. Her thoughts went back to Victory Drive and where she was last night as opposed to tonight. The safe haven of home had been hers again for a while. Kareem was pushing her through the plush house. She snorted through her nose and bloodied up his white carpet. He kicked her in the back pushing her on the floor. She took the opportunity to rub her bloody face as a good reminder. *Here's another souvenir, jerk!*

"Back in the trunk for you. You'll be nice and cozy." Kareem slammed the trunk and Madelyn's world became dark again. She had no idea where she was going, but James Willingham was involved. Her mind went back to what he had said at the church earlier today. *And to think I actually believed you! I am so gullible. I'll fall for any line thinking someone might actually love me. You're as despicable as they come. Lord, if You're really up there, I could use some help here. Granny said you were the God of Impossibles. Well, this is pretty impossible. What is my baby going to do? I'm not worthy, but he is. You have to protect him. Please don't let Kareem happen to him. Please, Dear God.*

Chapter 47

"How many stitches did you get?" Carmen met Jimmy at the door.

"It's ugly, Aunt Carmen. It's ugly. There must be twenty stitches under this bandage. I thought he would never finish. And the shots, they were the worst!" Jimmy placed his arm over Carmen's shoulders and she helped him over to the couch.

"Oh, you poor dear. I didn't know it was that bad." Valerie came along the other side of Jimmy to assist and patted his back to comfort him.

"It's four. Four stitches. It took five minutes from the time the doctor walked in the room. We were lucky the place wasn't crowded. I mean, clearly, it didn't take us long at all." Nora was catching on to Jimmy's vie for attention.

"Four! Are you sure? Felt like a lot more to me. I mean, I still have quite a headache," and Jimmy grabbed his head as he plopped onto the couch.

"I'm sure you do, Jimmy. I'm sorry it had to happen. You

were really lucky, Jimmy," Carmen consoled.

Ashley quickly interjected. "Lucky isn't the word. Blessed. You were blessed. Kareem Reynolds is one of the most notorious criminals in Savannah. They believe he's been responsible for multiple deaths in the area, but they can never pin anything on him. He makes it look like a drug overdose or a self-inflicted death. He's in with a really sinister gang. The law enforcement agencies have joined ranks and all worked really hard to bring it down. Apparently, there's some corruption within the system. That has cost a lot of innocent lives of some very fine officers. It's really bad, guys. I hate to lay this on you, but you should probably know."

"Wow, I guess I am lucky. But hurt. Still really hurt, Aunt Carmen." Jimmy broke into a grin. Carmen patted his knee and nodded as if to confirm that his injury was acknowledged.

"You poor, poor dear." Valerie welcomed an opportunity to focus on Jimmy again. Ashley's comments took her thoughts to Jim, but they centered on more than his safety. Another deep, wrenching concern tugged at her gut. She didn't want to think of Jim in the way she was. The "corruption within the system" Ashley spoke of pierced her heart. She had suspicioned Jim being involved in some covert behavior. She could never put her finger on it. His desperate need for a large sum of money was the red flag. He passed it off as a real estate deal gone sour and having to ante up with some investors. He was secretive with his texts and walked out of the room for some of his phone calls. Any good wife would do what she had done. Accountability is important in marriage. She hired an investigator who got copies of his phone records. It appeared that no women were involved, and that was a relief to Valerie. His contacts were cops. A couple numbers were from the Vegas area. She knew he had been to Vegas a few times before she met him. Apparently some mayor convention was when he "fell in love with the city." He left her confused when she asked him to take her there. He had not visited the city he loved since they had been married. His other phone contacts were businessmen. She knew because she had personally called the numbers to see who would answer. She had justified her action because she was married to him. It was the right thing to do because it was her duty to protect her marriage. She flirted but was true to him and him alone. She expected no less. Part of her wanted to believe that Jim's pursuit of Madelyn had everything to do with his newfound faith that had swept over him. He seemed radically different. But why? Was it real? Or was it a diversion? Could she trust that he was having a come-to-Jesus moment in the parking lot of East Savannah Christian Church all night long? Really? Or, was he secretly meeting one of his contacts about the jewels? She couldn't help but revisit the thought. Agitation began to stir within her. His sweet family didn't need to witness her display of behavior when she found herself in this frame of mind.

"You look worried, Valerie. I didn't mean to burden you. Nick is with Dad. They'll be okay. I think they felt a little helpless hanging around and not feeling like they were involved in finding her. I'm sure they'll be okay. Both of them, Carmen." Ashley should have probably kept her concerns to herself. She knew if the two of them met up with Kareem, it could be dangerous. She would silently pray for their safekeeping.

"I can't get the look of Madelyn's face out of my head," Jimmy said. "It was really brief. I saw her, and then the lights went out, if you know what I mean."

"Oh, you poor, poor thing," Valerie reiterated. She patted his head and Jimmy ducked and held up his hands to keep her from touching his bandages. Instead, she patted his face and he rested it in her palm.

"It really hurts. Really." Jimmy touched his head gingerly, then sat up straight. "I'm scared for Madelyn. Someone she feared was there. I don't think she's in a safe place. I know that detective thinks she's in on this, but I'm telling you, her face was not the look of someone who was. I will never forget the horror. And I couldn't even see her that well, if you get my drift."

Carmen got up off the couch and walked to the window. "I haven't had a good feeling about Madelyn all day. I couldn't put my finger on it at all. It grieves me that something vile has happened again at Camp W'ham."

"Again? What do you mean? What else happened there?" Ashley targeted the word immediately. She had never heard of *another* incident ever. *Again* had to be qualified.

"I–I–I– Never mind. I didn't mean to— I'm just upset for Madelyn. I misspoke. I apologize." Carmen wanted to crawl in a hole. She didn't mean to say it that way. The thought had been with her since she and James saw Jimmy's condition. She didn't even realize she had spoken it out loud. She kept her face toward the window so no one could see her expression.

Ashley didn't buy it. She saw the reflection of Carmen's expression in the window. Carmen had been thoughtful with her words. It was an innocuous comment. But as innocent as it was, it was no mistake. There was definitely a story behind the *again.* Tonight was not a time to press the issue, but she would use her probative skills to uncover the mystery. She would get to the bottom of it sooner than later.

"Is there anything we can do? I mean, the baby is asleep, so someone has to stay here. But a couple of us could go looking, too." Valerie was willing to do anything. Sitting and waiting for someone to call and give an update seemed futile.

"Well, if you go anywhere, you might not get past that cop sitting in the driveway," Nora informed.

"A cop? Seriously? Maybe that's good. Maybe they're here for our protection." Valerie wanted to assume the best of intentions on the part of law enforcement.

"That's not why they're camped out. They're watching our every move." Ashley spoke with authority.

"Why are they watching us? It seems they would be watching *out* for our safety and wellbeing. Surely they don't think we had something to do with Madelyn's disappearance or the theft of the jewels, do they?" Valerie's concern was mounting.

"Well, if they do, that's ludicrous!" Jimmy's exclamation reminded him that his head really wasn't ready for intense volume.

"Guys, officers take precaution. Masters wants to bust this case. He's worked on it diligently." Ashley tried to explain the nature of the law.

"Which case? The jewels or Madelyn's apprehender? Seems like Kareem's a pretty questionable character, if you ask me." Nora's question was more valid than even Ashley imagined.

"Well, I was speaking of the jewels, but your point is well taken, Nora. Kareem was the worst thing that could have happened to Madelyn."

"I know what you're saying, Ashley, but when we look at Baby Bryson, we can't say that God didn't make something beautiful out of a huge mistake that happened in her life." Carmen spoke with the voice of experience.

"Ah, that's so sweet." Valerie was gushy sweet and still trying to distract herself from her negative thoughts of Jim. "So, we need to just sit tight and not go looking or anything? Just be held captive to fear? I mean, I feel totally helpless."

"Me, too, Valerie. I wish Madelyn and I had never gone down there in the dark." Jimmy grabbed his head being reminded of his pain. "What would Grandma say in a time like this? I've been trying to think of something. Maybe my head is too whacked out."

"Good question, Jimmy. And I'm sorry I haven't pulled a Grace treat out of the bag. Mom would have said something like this, 'The ancient anchor holds secure in times of disquieting commotion.' Or maybe something like, 'When you measure the realities of life against the strength of the Lord, all life's challenges are but victories in your history.'"

"Yeah, and I remember her saying, 'When you create the want for need, you lose the need for want.' That was beautiful to me." Valerie was proud of herself for recalling another gleaning from Grace.

"What does that have to do with this?" Jimmy looked a bit perplexed.

Valerie gave a bit of a ditsy response. "I don't know. I just remembered something she told me one time. That's all." Then, she giggled with delight and tapped Jimmy's knee.

"There's one I remember that really stuck with me. And,

Valerie, this may not be really pertinent either, but it is classic." Ashley sat down in a chair to relax. Thinking of Grandma always brought peace. She was glad that Jimmy brought the focus to Grandma. "When I struggled with decisions, Grandma always told me, 'Things which matter most must never be at the mercy of things which matter least.' That stuck with me. Now, I always weigh every choice I make by that scale."

Carmen saw headlights in the driveway. She had a surge of excitement thinking it could be someone bringing Madelyn home. Then, the car turned and all she saw was taillights. "Our guard has left his post. That can mean only one thing. Maybe they've found Madelyn."

"Or there's some emergency," Ashley suggested. Hopeful eyes drooped at her comment. "I mean, it could be that, but let's don't get our expectations up just yet. Did he have his emergency lights on?"

"Not that I could see. Just turned around and left. Okay, Valerie, there is something that we can do. And, we should have already." Carmen took Grace's kneeling pillow and brought it to the center of the room. She knelt and reached out her hands. "This is what we should have done immediately. It's what Mom would have done. Anybody want to join me?"

One by one they grabbed throw pillows and placed them on the floor to form a circle. Carmen watched as the next generation of Willinghams assembled to pray for a family member in peril. Grace had patterned a proclivity for prayer. This would have been her posture in this type of situation. "Mom always said, 'Life is only as hopeless as it seems.' When her hands were tied, she used her knees. Let's pray."

*   *   *

Officer Ricks's patrol car, October 16, 11:37 p.m.

Sergeant Ricks had texted Kareem multiple times to tell him not to harm the girl. He hadn't heard from Kareem until now. He had to text rather than call because he didn't need his conversations to be picked up by police scanners. He didn't need to be texting and driving. Now, he was pushed for time to get to the Gaston side of town. If Jim had the jewels, he would want the girl in one piece. If he didn't have them, Heaven help the man.

Ricks put on his blue lights without the sirens as he approached Victory Drive. He had to make up time. He really wanted to get to Gaston early and situate himself. Bruce Masters was grateful for the lights. He could lag behind yet keep Ricks in sight. He wanted to know where the man was headed. He had not been relieved of his duties, nor had he assigned another officer to cover his post. That in and of itself was enough to raise suspicion. For Masters, it raised more than he had already.

The speed dial for Ricks's number was engaged on Masters's cell phone. Bruce thought it might go to voicemail, but finally Ricks answered. "Anything goin' on there?"

"Nope. Perty quiet. Bruce. A car came in, but it was a couple of the kids—male and female. Cute chick. Guy was bandaged." Ricks was matter of fact.

"Well, stick around. Give me a report if anyone leaves or comes in. We're going to tail them, remember? You didn't let me know about the boy and girl." Bruce sounded irritated.

"Sorry, Bruce. I sure will. I just forgot, I guess. But, I hadn't seen or heard nothing else. It's perty calm here. Guess they're all tired." Ricks made no mention of the first car leaving. After all, he couldn't be absolutely positive if Jim Willingham was one of the passengers or not. And he certainly wouldn't want to alarm Masters if he was.

Chapter 48

Kareem's car was slowing down. Madelyn knew whatever he had in mind for her could be nothing short of disastrous. She had stopped struggling on this second trunk journey. Not because the fight wasn't in her, even though she was dreadfully hurting from her suffering at the hands of Kareem. She was calm because she had been thinking and crying. Her thoughts consisted mostly of her baby boy. Bryson was her world. And now, what would his world be like without her? For all intents and purposes, she had grown up without a mother herself. Madelyn scarcely thought of her mom, and she surely wasn't the ever-present person in her mind now. The only stability in her life had been her granny, and now she was gone.

No one else in this whole wide world cares about you, Madelyn Joy Willingham! No one. Granny's gone. Who do you have now? The family? Silly girl! You spent less than twenty-four hours with them after not having had a relationship for years. And James Willingham wanting to be the caring father all of the sudden.

Seriously? After all this time? Right! Well, where are you now, Daddy? Apparently, you're in on this! Madelyn's thought turned to sarcasm, then anger. Life could have been different for her. Life *should* have been different. The tied-up hands behind her back had always been bound in a sense. Then, she remembered what Granny Grace had told her many times: "When your hands are tied, try your knees." *I'm sorry, Granny. I'm sorry I let you down. If I had listened to you, I wouldn't be in this mess right now. My sweet baby wouldn't be facing a world without his mommy. Now, he's going to be left to be raised by a man who would kill his own mother! And worst yet, I let God down. Please, Lord, please find favor with me. I don't know how You could save me and give me another chance here on Earth, but if you see fit, please do. If you hear my voice and answer this prayer, I will, Lord, I promise I will serve You forever. I said it and I meant it.* Madelyn recalled a memory verse Granny encouraged her to learn as a child. '*... being confident in this, He who began a good work in you will carry it on until completion until the day of Christ Jesus,' Philippians 1:6. Please, let me complete what you began in me, God. I'm begging you. I'm a mother. I want to be there for my son.* Madelyn's quiet tears turned into deep sobs. She leaned her face toward the floorboard of the trunk. Breathing while sobbing so profusely was extremely difficult. The duct tape was so tight around her mouth that she couldn't rub it off with the trunk. Her face hurt from the bruises inflicted at Kareem's hands. Now, she was adding carpet burns to her injuries trying to work the tape free to help her breathe. Desperately trying to survive, she began working her hands with the rope again. Why had she forgotten she was almost free? It was as if the lid of the trunk had closed on her good sense as well. She continued struggling with the rope, but Madelyn's thoughts went back to the dire business at hand.

Lord, if You see fit not to spare my life now, please forgive me for walking away from what Granny taught me. Please have mercy on me. I don't want to die, not this way. But more importantly, I don't want to die without the promise of Heaven. Please let my son know how much I love him. Protect him. Send him a Grace Willingham to offer him hope in this life. I do love you, Lord. I really do.

Madelyn broke free from the rope holding her hands. She ripped the duct tape from her mouth, then struggled to reach her legs. She heard Kareem open the door of the car. She pulled her legs up closer trying to reach the duct tape restricting her legs. She felt like a contortionist trying to position her body in an extremely tight place. She wasn't sure Houdini could have done much better in such a limited space. She found the frayed edge of the tape and began pulling. She heard Kareem's voice. Apparently, he was talking on his cell phone to someone. She had to work fast. One last tug and— There! She got it. She prayed wherever Kareem had parked that it was dark enough. She resumed her twisted fetal position, this time with her legs toward the opening of the trunk. She turned her head toward the floorboard. The trunk popped and the lid opened slightly. If there were street lights, Madelyn couldn't tell. It appeared to be dark outside of her temporary prison. Kareem was ending his call. His plans included her—the girl.

Kareem's fingertips cupped under the lid of the trunk and Madelyn's prison door opened. As uncomfortable and stuffy as the trunk had been, she knew it was a much safer place than where she was about to be taken should she fail to get away. She was grateful for the darkness that surrounded her assailant. Kareem leaned into the trunk to grab Madelyn, but was not prepared for the greeting by his fiery hostage. Madelyn brought both feet up and kicked Kareem full in the face with her hard-sole shoes sending him hurling to the ground. She practically floated out of the trunk with such ease that she amazed herself. Kareem was in pain but trying to get up off the ground as Madelyn's feet hit the pavement. She quickly assessed the area. There was only one exit out of the alley. She started screaming and running as hard as she could. Kareem's footsteps were close behind. He was shouting obscenities at her. Then she heard a shot. She glanced back. Kareem was close, but his gun was pointed in the air and not at her. She needed as much speed, endurance, and wit about her as she could muster. She had no idea where she was. Should she take a right or a left at the end of the long alley? She would go left. It felt like the correct direction. The moon provided enough light to guard her steps, and she could see a dim street light at the end of the alley. She was almost there. But once she reached the street, what next? Would there be a place to hide?

A couple more steps, and then, I'll just make a break and pray for the best. Madelyn rounded the corner to the left and ran smack dab into the middle Ricks. He wrapped his arms around Madelyn to restrain her. Madelyn let out a blood-curdling scream."

"Hold on there, Lil' Missy. What's your big hurry?"

Madelyn realized she had run straight into the arms of a uniformed officer and started pleading her case. "Help me! Please, help me, Officer! He's trying to kill me," Madelyn shrieked as she looked back at Kareem. Ricks continued to hold her but never took his gun out of his holster. Madelyn was only confused for an instant. She immediately melted through the arms of Ricks and sank onto the ground at his feet. Kareem approached and with mighty force gave a swift kick to her back and ribs. Madelyn gasped for air and moaned. She knew some ribs were broken. Her pain was more than she could bear. She tried to stay lucid but everything went black and she collapsed to the ground.

"What are you doin'? I told you not to hurt the girl!" Ricks screamed at Kareem.

"She didn't break your nose!" Kareem yelled back. He took his sleeve and wiped the blood from his swollen and somewhat displaced nose.

"Let's get her to the back of the alley. Hawk will be here any minute."

"I ain't carryin' her no mo'. I done carried her through the woods. If you want her, you get her." Kareem was irritated. He muttered under his breath as he walked to the back of the alley, "You don't wanna mess with 'Reem. I could lose you and never blink an eye. What's another dead cop anyway!"

Ricks didn't have the strength of Kareem. He picked Madelyn up underneath her arms and began dragging her backwards into the alley. *Hawk is gonna be here any minute. If this poor girl is still out cold and can't talk, it ain't gonna be none too perty for Kareem. Or me. Then, Jim Willingham is on his way. If he has the jewels on his person, it ain't-a-gonna matter one way or the t'other. If he don't and he sees what's happened to this girl, there ain't no telling how this scene is gonna go down. I'd like to be anywhere else but here right now.* Ricks reached the back of the alley none too soon. He wasn't used to heavy work. He was huffing and puffing. And worried stiff. He had just straightened up his aching back when headlights blinded him. He held his hand up to shield his eyes from the brightness. The driver stayed in the car, leaving the car running and the high beams glaring. Three figures silhouetted the alley–Hawk, or Boss, and his two bodyguards.

*   *   *

Jim Willingham's vehicle, October 16, 11:56 p.m.

"Did you hear that?" James sat up in his seat.

"What? The scream or the gun shot? Yeah, I heard it." Nick put his hand on the door handle.

James grabbed Nick by the arm. "No, no, Son. You stay here. We have a plan. Remember?"

"I don't feel comfortable with you going alone." You need me as a backup. I've got my Glock. *Remember?"* Nick was equally as adamant.

"Nick, don't. Gotta run. Please, let me handle this. Stay here. I'll send Madelyn your way. Get her in the car and get out of here. Oh, and don't call the cops. If you get the wrong one, it could be bad. For all of us." James handed him the keys and opened the door.

"O-kay. Gotcha." Nick watched as James crossed the street and walked to the next block. He took note of how cautiously he approached what appeared to him to be an alley, not a street.

He exited the car to get into the driver's seat so that he could drive, hopefully, the three of them away at the appointed time. He closed the door quietly and looked around. Something startled him. He was sure he heard another car but didn't see any sign of lights. Nick reached behind his back and took his gun. He had never been in a situation that demanded self-defense, but if push came to shove, he would protect himself and his family. He went to take a step and heard voices. In the distance, James was still cautiously approaching, peeking his head around the corner of the building and pulling it back again. Obviously, Madelyn was where the voices were coming from, and James had zeroed in on them. Nick sighed. James knew exactly where to come for the trouble. It was a mixed emotion he was feeling—a bit of relief and a touch of grief.

GLADYS FAYE WILLINGHAM-MURPHY'S HOME,
OCTOBER 16, 11:57 P.M.

Gladys screamed so loudly she frightened herself and Ralph, who had come running into her room. "Gladys, honey, are you all right? I've never heard you so frightened from a dream." Gladys was sitting straight up in bed and sweat had formed on her brow. Ralph came over to her bedside. She moved her legs over to the other side of the bed so that Ralph could sit beside her. He put his arms around her for comfort and said, "There, there. It's okay. I've got you. You're fine." Gladys was trembling. He held her tighter.

"I am, but James isn't. Something's wrong with James. I just know it, Ralph. I just know. I had a dream. He's in trouble. He's in an alley somewhere. It was dark. I don't know where or why he's there. But he needs help." Gladys was fitful. Her hands were shaking as she drew them up to her face. "He's in trouble, Ralph. We've got to go see about him. Can we go? Now?"

"Gladys, honey, it's almost midnight. I'm sure he's sleeping soundly. It's been a very long day for everybody. It's just a dream. He's okay I'm sure." Ralph stroked Gladys's brow and temple area. He would try to reason with her, but he wasn't sure he was going to be able to talk her into calming down. He had never seen her as jittery as she was just now.

"He's not all right. I don't know why I know, but I do. I'm scared for him, Ralph. Something terrible is wrong. Will you take me to him? Please? I need to tell him—" Gladys stopped in midsentence. She wasn't prepared to say she needed to apologize to James. And she had never pleaded with Ralph, or anyone for that matter. In fact, what was occurring in her bedroom had never happened before. The two of them were exchanging concerns like a husband and wife should. Had Ralph not been so concerned for Gladys, he would have rejoiced all over himself! This was the kind of moment he had longed for.

"You know I will, Gladys. I'll take you anywhere you want to go. But if we wake James up, do you think he'll still love us in the morning?" Ralph pinched her chin and smiled.

Gladys chuckled through her fears. "I don't think he's home. I don't know why. I think he's in some kind of danger. I wouldn't even know where to go. I know it's silly. Isn't it?"

"I don't think it's silly at all. If my sister was that concerned for me, I'd feel pretty honored. You want to pray for him?" Ralph didn't know why he offered the suggestion. He had never prayed out loud before. But if this is what his wife needed from him, he was more than willing to muddle through it somehow.

Gladys's countenance lifted immediately. *Pray? Ralph said pray?* "Well, sure. That would be … nice."

Ralph took Gladys's hand in his and he bowed his head. Gladys should have bowed hers and closed her eyes, but she couldn't help but watch this man, her husband, this gentle person sitting at her bedside praying with her about a silly dream of hers. His words were choppy and broken, very childlike, but mostly sincere. What she was witnessing touched her heart like nothing she had ever imagined could. This man's tenderness was enchanting. His concern sturdy. His willingness to step into unknown territory was electrifying. She felt the mountains guarding her heart moving at the legitimacy of his appeal. Her ears ceased hearing Ralph's pleas for James's safety and protection. Instead, they clung to Ralph's focus on her and the special lady she was, her heart for others, and how sweet his wife was to be concerned enough to pray. Soon, Gladys was hearing nothing but her thoughts overriding the petition of a man she barely knew. *What have I missed by shutting this man out of my heart? Will he let me in his? I think I could love. I want to love. I need to love.*

"Amen." Ralph finished the prayer. He opened his eyes and raised his head. The look on Gladys's face alarmed him. *Did I say something wrong? What? What are you thinking, Gladys?* Ralph started to get up from the bed, but Gladys grabbed his shoulder.

"Don't move. Just stay right there." She slipped closer to Ralph and threw her arms around him and pulled him closer to her. She whispered in his ear, "Thank you. That was beautiful." She didn't move. She continued to hold. *One thousand one, one thousand two, one thousand three, one thousand four.*

Ralph fought his desire to thrust his arms around Gladys. Instead he moved them up slowly, caressing her back as he did, and then returned her embrace. Sensations began to pique within him when Gladys began nibbling on his neck. *Easy, Ralph. Take this easy. It has to be her idea. Follow her lead. Just don't stop, Gladys. Please, don't stop now.*

Gladys didn't stop. Her advances became an invitation to love. Ralph accepted the offer with a gracious spirit. Afterwards, the two fell asleep in each other's arms, leaving God to settle the troubling alarm regarding James.

*   *   *

GASTON, SOUTH OF SAVANNAH,
OCTOBER 17, 12:01 P.M.

"You have my jewels?" Hawk was succinct. He wanted to get what he came for and leave. The other business could be handled by the ones he gave instructions to.

Kareem looked at Ricks. Ricks looked at Kareem. Both scratched their heads but neither spoke.

"The jewels. Where are they?" Hawk's voice was low and harsh. The bodyguards flexed their chests and stood up taller beside him.

Kareem looked down at Madelyn and gave her leg a light kick with his foot. "She can't say right now, but I could probably bring her 'round if you give me a minute." Ricks started to speak and Kareem gave him the mean eye encouraging him to keep quiet for now.

"Whatever it takes." Hawk was impatient.

Kareem pulled a flask out of his pocket. He reached down and poured the contents in Madelyn's face. She came to her senses coughing and spitting. Kareem yanked Madelyn up by her arm, and she let out a squeal. Her ribs were so painful she didn't want to stand.

"Boss wants to know what you've done with the jewels." Kareem was stalling. If Jim Willingham had the jewels, he wasn't here to turn them in. Madelyn would have to be the offering instead of the jewels until he showed up. Boss would be more than happy to do away with her until he could track down Jim.

"You, Officer. You said the girl's dad had them. So where is he? Somebody has the jewels. And if you can't produce them, somebody's gonna pay." Hawk's words queued his guards. Each made a fist with his left hand and thrust it into the palm of his right. The threat left no ambiguity of its intended targets.

Kareem grabbed Madelyn by the arm and began to shake her. "The man wants his jewels. Now, what did you do with them?"

The lights were blinding her, but she looked straight ahead at the man making threats upon her life. "I don't have the jewels. I never had the jewels. Let me go. I want to go home to my baby. Please, sir. I don't have the jewels. You have to believe me." Madelyn was pleading through her tears.

Hawk took two steps forward, then stopped. "Well, if you don't have them, who does?"

"I do." James Willingham stepped forward from the back of the alley. He had his gun aimed at Hawk. "Let her go, Hawk. She's not who you want. I have the jewels. You can take it up with me."

"Well, Jim. Glad to have you join the party." Hawk turned around. His bodyguards took a step forward, but Hawk held them back and he shook his head.

James moved in closer to the fray. "Let her go, Kareem. Now." No one moved. "You will never get your jewels, Hawk, if you don't let my daughter go. Now."

"Oh, now she's your daughter, is she? How sweet. I didn't know you cared so much, Jim. You surprise me." Hawk's pretentious tone left James cold.

"Now. I told you I didn't want her harmed. She's hurt. I'm not happy. Let her go. Then, I'll take you to the jewels." James's stance was unwavering as he held a steady hand pointing the gun directly at Hawk.

"Let her go, Kareem." Hawk yelled back but never turned around.

Kareem gave Madelyn a push. He raised his gun, and Jim started to redirect his aim but was interrupted.

"I wouldn't do that, Kareem. You won't live to rejoice in your kill. I'm a mighty good shot." Nick's unexpected appearance was perfectly timed.

Madelyn kept running. "Daddy! You don't have to—"

James never looked at Madelyn. He kept his eyes pierced on Hawk and his guards. "Don't stop, Madelyn. Run. Nick, get her out of here. Both of you go. Now. I'm fine."

Nick handed the keys to Madelyn and pointed her to the direction of the car. Madelyn reluctantly followed his command. She was startled when she saw another uniformed officer. She hadn't had good luck with those guys tonight. Bruce Masters put his finger to his mouth to hush Madelyn. She knew he was a good guy at that point. He motioned to her to go around him and keep running. She did as directed.

"Jim, I don't want any trouble. I just want the jewels. I'm sure you could use the money I'm willing to pay for them. I hear you're not even in the ol' lady's Will anyway. Let's strike up a deal tonight. Why don't you get in my car and let's go to my hotel and we'll leave on amiable terms."

"I don't owe you any money, Hawk. We're all settled up. So, why would I give you my mama's jewels?"

"Because you promised them to me. You agreed, remember?"

"Read the contract, Hawk. It was contingent upon whether I couldn't pay you back. You have your money. I want you out of my town."

"Jim, Jim, let's not be unreasonable. It's you against all of us." Hawk pointed out.

"And me," Nick yelled out.

Hawk threw back his head and gave a hardy laugh. "Oh, yeah, and you." He motioned to his guards who immediately pulled out their guns. Ricks and Kareem pulled theirs, as well.

"Seems like the odds have it, Jim. You may not care about what we do to you, but I don't think you want this little punk friend of yours harmed, now, do you?"

"He's not a punk. He's my son. Don't ever talk about him like that again." James spit back venom. He couldn't let Hawk know how hopeless he felt in the situation, even though he had prayed for God's mercy and protection.

"Well, aren't you quite the busy man. Didn't know you had *another* son. I guess now we can take out all of them. I have some guys watching your mother's place right now. Let's see, you have a sister, two of your daughters, your *other* son, and a grandbaby there, too. Quite a nice family you've produced. If you want to keep them alive, you're going to give me what I'm after."

"You do that, and your little world will crumble, Hawk." James's heart was in his throat, but he did his best not to let Hawk know. He couldn't bear the thought of harm coming to his family.

"Well, you know how cleverly I cover up things, Jim. It helps when you have half of the justice system on your side. Things just get swept under the carpet. It makes for less headaches on the business end of things. Now, the jewels. I want them." Hawk's heartless nature was surfacing.

"I'll go with you, but you have to let Nick go, too. I won't get in that car alive unless you let him go. And if I'm dead, you will never find those jewels."

"You drive a hard bargain, Jim. Okay, go on, *young Nick.* Daddy's bought your life." Hawk chuckled at the thought.

Bruce Masters stepped into the alley. "You're not goin' anywhere, Mayor. You're walkin' away with your son." Masters looked down to the back of the alley and offered a greeting. "Ricks. You shouldn't have left your post."

Hawk looked a bit more concerned, but still tried to keep his wits and collectiveness about him. "Gee, I'm sorry, Officer. I don't believe we've met."

"Don't intend to, Hawk. I don't romp with just any ol' body." Masters was as cool as they come. He was confident in his position. James and Nick were hoping his confidence was going to pay off in a big way. After all, they were still outnumbered.

The three men held guns in place. There were four pointing back at them. Then, the chauffer stepped out of the car and made it five.

"We can do this peacefully, or we can make this a really sticky mess. It's your call, Hawk." Masters continued to talk as he and Nick moved forward to team up with James.

Ricks and Kareem began moving in closer as well. Ricks spoke up first, "Bruce, you shouldn't have come here. You're not on this side of the fence. You know what happens to those who aren't."

"I should've trusted my gut on you, Ricks. I've had my eye on you for a while now but kept giving you the benefit of the doubt. You're too good of an officer to go bad, Ricks. You can still step out of this, you know." Masters would have loved to save Ricks from the inevitable. He was going down, either way. The justice system would send him to prison, or Hawk would take his life. Ricks had been too sloppy. Hawk would never tolerate it.

"I ain't steppin' anywhere, Bruce. I really liked you, you know. I'm hatin' what's about to come down with you, man." Ricks started walking towards the three men facing them. "Let me have the honors, Boss."

"Sure. I won't stop you," Hawk abdicated.

"Don't be stupid, Ricks." Masters drew his gun and put his finger on the trigger. "We both have families. Let's not challenge this."

Jim and Nick looked at one another. "I'm sorry, Son. I told you to not to come."

"Like a fine lady, who we both loved, always said, 'Everything will be all right,'" and Nick winked at James.

"I'm warning you, Ricks. Stop where you are." Masters

pleaded with the officer, but he kept pressing forward.

Six FBI officers stepped around the corner—three from each side. Ricks opened fire and so did they. Hawk ducked behind the door of his limousine. He let the men with the guns fight it out. He yelled at his chauffer to get in the car and drive. He followed his command. He put the car in reverse and began backing out of the alley. Nick and James shot the tires of the vehicle. It didn't stop them from driving off, but it certainly slowed them down. Two officers jumped in their unit and took off after the vehicle. They apprehended the two men a half mile from the scene. They had abandoned the vehicle and were attempting to run. Hawk and the driver were apprehended, handcuffed, and taken away in a squad car.

One of the FBI officers had grabbed Masters's two-way. "10-00, 10-00. Officer down, officer down. Location, Gaston. Repeat, officer down. 10-52, 10-54, Stat flight and EMS needed A-S-A-P. Send several units."

James and Nick looked around to assess the scene. Kareem, Ricks, and both guards were on the ground. Masters was, too. Ricks knew where to shoot to get around his bullet-proof vest. The Willingham men ran over to Masters, and James knelt by his side. "Bruce, I'm sorry. I really am. I had no idea things would come to this."

"I just need to know, Jim, in case I don't make it, do you have the jewels?" Masters coughed and laid his head on the pavement.

"I don't, Bruce. I have no idea who has the jewels. I only wanted to save my daughter, and I would have taken the fall for it." James took Masters's hand. "Dear Lord, my friend here needs your protection. He's a great man. He has a family who needs him. We know that's important to You. You are the great healer and protector, God. Please, watch over Bruce, give him the strength he needs to not just survive, but to recover completely. Restore him, Lord. He's among your best. We all need him to live. If it be Your will, show favor on your servant tonight. Amen."

"Appreciate that, Jim. I really do. Glenna." Bruce took a deep breath and closed his eyes. "Bruce! Bruce! Hang in there, Buddy!" James heard the sirens of the emergency medical unit and saw the emergency helicopter landing. He put his fingers on Bruce's neck to find his pulse. It was faint but still there. One of the officers moved in and told James he would take it from here.

"Daddy! Daddy! Are you all right?" Madelyn was breathlessly running to James.

"Hey, my Maddie. Yeah, I'm fine. You're hurt. Here sit down. Just rest. The ambulance is almost here." James sat down beside Madelyn and put his arms around her and held her tight. He brushed her hair back from her eyes and rubbed his hands over her blackened and bruised face. "I am so sorry you got involved in this, Maddie. I never meant for this to involve you. I hope you believe me."

"It wasn't you, Daddy. That was my stupidity. I should have never gotten involved with Kareem. Granny tried to warn me. I should have listened to her." She looked around and saw the officers looking at Kareem. She didn't want to see anything, and she turned her focus back to James. She had taken note that he called her Maddie. She felt he had earned the right. She tried to take a deep breath and shrieked with pain. "I think I have some broken ribs. It really hurts."

"I know, Sweetheart. They're almost here. Just hang in there.

We'll get you taken care of." James remembered Hawk's comment about his family. "Nick! The others!"

"Got it covered. And so did the FBI. They've already apprehended the ones lurking around the house. Everyone is okay. Talked to Mom. They weren't even aware that anything was going on. They were all praying while it was happening. Leave it to Mom." And Nick smiled with relief.

James glanced back at Masters and saw the EMTs were working on him. "How did the FBI get involved?" James was curious.

One of the officers overheard him and gladly offered the answer. "This good man right here. He's a great detective. Masters is a very calculated man. He called us earlier this morning. We were at the funeral, by the way. He said he prayed about what to do and felt *urged* to call us. The stolen jewels have made a lot of noise. We've been waiting in the wings to move in on this case. Didn't know we were going to crack an even bigger one. No disrespect meant, Mr. Willingham, but your mother's case involves jewels. This one involved saving lives."

"No offense taken, sir. No offense taken." James turned his attention to Madelyn.

Masters was stat-flighted to Memorial University Medical. Their Level 1 trauma center was the best in the Southeast. The EMS units arrived and began taking care of Madelyn. James asked Nick to take the car back home and report to everyone there. As for him, he would ride to the hospital with Madelyn. Ricks, Kareem and one of the guards were taken to the hospital, but pronounced DOA. The other guard was in critical condition. If he survived, he had a warrant for his arrest waiting in the wings.

Nick was glad to stay behind with the Federal agents. He

asked who was in charge and was directed to the lead investigator, Shawn Davidson. "I know you're busy here, but could I have a few minutes with you? I need to share several facts that might be of interest to you."

Investigator Davidson responded quickly, "Oh, sir, you *will* have a word with me. I need to get statements from you and James Willingham. We'll catch him at the hospital. Just step aside and I'll be right with you."

Nick did as he was asked. He looked around at the desolate area. He had never witnessed anyone killed before. It was more than unnerving to think it could have been three of the Willinghams that might have joined Grandma Grace. *We were blessed today, Grandma. Thanks to the prayers of one smart detective and who knows who else, but we were blessed indeed. But what a horrific way to end a glorious day.*

Chapter 49

Carmen pulled duty with Baby Bryson and allowed the others to rest. He had slept through all the events of the night and was fully reinvigorated. He had no recall of rousing and smiling when his mommy stroked his head and hands and then laid her face against his at four a.m. this morning. He only knew he was hungry and ready for a new day to begin. For the moment he was content to sit in the front-porch rocker with his Aunt Carmen. He was thrilled watching the squirrels scamper in the trees, the chipmunk's ritualistic visit to Annie's memorial, and the birds feasting on the sunflower seeds the two early risers had scattered for them.

Carmen stroked his hair tenderly as he pointed to the animals and negotiated indiscernible nonsense with the aid of his pacifier. She saw a reflection of innocence in his eyes. In no time at all, the sweet season of childhood would be gone. The carefree world that revolves around him would soon be entangled with issues of adult reality, like the children in her home back in California.

Carmen pulled Bryson closer for a hug and said, "You, Little One, have a better chance at life now. Your mommy is beginning to understand the responsibility that comes automatically with being a parent. But mostly, an unexplainable love has captured her heart, and *it won't let her go.*" Carmen touched the tip of Bryson's nose, and he grinned showing his little teeth behind his pacifier. He kept his eyes on Carmen as if he appreciated every word she was saying. She often wondered what went on inside the minds of babies and how much they truly absorbed of conversation they hear. For certain, they welcomed genuine love and had a keen sense for when to fear.

Carmen rocked. Bryson seemed content to have her attention and the audience that his great-grandmother had enjoyed for many years. "You would have loved your Triple G, Bryson. Your Great-Grandmother Grace would sit and commune with God's creations for hours. She would read her Bible and pray for every one of us. You included," and she kissed the top of the baby's head. "She was a special one, that Triple G. You two would have been instant friends."

No one would stir until after eleven in the morning. James and Valerie had gone home, as had Nick. They would be back later in the afternoon and everyone would congregate for dinner. James would call Gladys and invite her and Ralph. She knew there would be some unfinished family business that needed to be discussed. And, of course, the story of the drama from last night's events.

Whereas Carmen knew the basic details, she was looking forward to the play-by-play account of everything that happened. She wasn't sure how much the participants would feel comfortable in revealing. Their nerves appeared to have been ambushed. She would not pressure them for more than they were willing to share. Likewise, she would warn the others–mostly Nora–to not ask questions either. As for herself, she was thankful for their safety. Madelyn had been brutalized at the hands of Kareem, but it could have been disastrous for the girl. Prayers for her protection had been answered, and that should be sufficient for everyone concerned. Carmen's heart was broken over the senseless deaths, one being Bryson's father. It would be a history the child would inquire about someday. Carmen was well versed in the querying minds of children who needed to know their biological roots, even when somewhat tainted.

When the day settled down a bit for her, she would visit Bruce Masters in the hospital. She wanted to call on his wife and children and offer comfort to them. Whether Bruce could respond to her or not, she wanted to thank him for his heroism and pray for him. He was the link to life for her son, niece, and brother. She had never had occasion to personally appreciate the sacrifices of the men and women who serve in a law enforcement capacity, although had heard the stories of the rescues of the children back home. But those kinds of ransoms on the part of the law don't stop at the ones who serve. They spill over into the families, as well. She said a silent prayer for Bruce and his family as she continued to entertain and watch over Bryson.

*   *   *

BAY STREET, OCTOBER 17, 11:25 A.M.

The news of the night's events made the front page of the *Savannah Daily News*—"Officer and Hero in Critical Condition after Solving Case of Corruption, Missing Jewels Still a Mystery." The downtown streets paraded their usual Monday busyness. But the talk of the day was Grace Willingham's jewels and how the theft helped to bring down the ring leader of crime and corruption not only within Savannah but many cities across the nation. Bruce Masters was being touted as a hero for saving the Mayor's daughter, but falling short in not solving the mystery surrounding the Willingham family's missing jewels. Concern had mounted as the morning progressed and the officer's condition remained unstable. But the City of Savannah could rest a little easier today with the Gaston area, the black eye of the city, being devoid of a few less criminals.

In a matter of minutes, Emmet Park would be buzzing with lunchtime visitors wishing to enjoy the beautiful day, taking in the fresh air, and vying for a place to retreat for an hour. The park bench overlooking Bay Street occupied by only one would soon surrender its privacy to some audacious individual in need of a spot to read. The paper was folded neatly again so that another might enjoy the depiction of the detective's bravery and the continued mystery surrounding the novel jewels of Grace Willingham.

It's no mystery to me. Albeit, the events from last night have more than complicated things. Could I be linked to that in some way? Nah. It would be a stretch for any prosecutor to bring charges against a person like myself for crimes I was not involved in at all. But, I suppose it could be a possibility. The law delights in finding ways to implicate the indirectly involved. Then again, what will the long arm of the law be able to effect in a far-away country? Tsk-tsk, too bad. No jurisdiction. The thought was settling and induced a smug smile.

Just as anticipated, a working woman interrupted isolated contemplation from the world. "Anyone sitting here?" she inquired?

A shake of the head and a welcoming gesture with the left hand invited her to join the park bench. "Nice day we're having."

"Yes, it is," she replied, shoving the newspaper aside. "I try to get some fresh air after being cooped up in a store all day talking to customers. Excuse me while I escape." She unwrapped her sandwich, took out her Kindle, and immediately engaged in chapter twenty-two of her book. The lunch-break hour would come and go. The two would sit without dialogue. She collected her belongings and got up from the bench. Common courtesy dictated a casual, "Have a great day," receiving a mutually polite nod of thanks. She tossed her trash in a nearby can and hurriedly distanced herself from the park.

The daily check of the jewels had found them intact. The rope was still securely attached to the box that held the enthralling treasure. But, one last check and chat before departing the park would be comforting. Communing with the jewels was a necessary part of inspiration for their new owner. Sitting at the base of the tree and tossing nuts to the squirrels, reassuring words were quietly shared. "Tomorrow I take you home with me. Plans are in place. When streets are quiet in the early morning hours, you, my precious gems, will be rescued from your shallow dwelling. Then, we'll take a leisurely drive from the beautiful East Coast to the West coastal area. We'll spend a few days taking in some sights of America along the way. The chances of returning are not likely. From the Los Angeles airport, a temporary home will be secured in Spain. From there, who knows? But as Grace used to say, '*Everything* will be all right.'"

*   *   *

HOME OF GLADYS FAYE WILLINGHAM-MURPHY, OCTOBER 17, 11:42 A.M.

"James, are you okay? I have been worried sick about you." James had finally returned Gladys's call. She eagerly answered when she saw the caller ID light up his name.

"I'm sorry, Gladys. I didn't want to disturb you last night. I should have called before you saw anything in the papers or heard it on the news. Honestly, I just came home and crashed. Valerie and I haven't been up long. I could use a little more sleep, but need to get some things done at the office before we gather at Mama's this afternoon. You'll be there, I assume?" James sounded exhausted but very much at peace.

"Absolutely. Ralph and I wouldn't miss it. I want to visit with those kiddos of yours anyway. They're all precious, James. I know you're pressed for time, but can you tell me what happened last night? I mean, I know what the paper said, but it's very sketchy. And, obviously, the jewels are still a mystery. What's going to happen with that now that Bruce Masters is kind of out of the case?" Gladys knew James wouldn't want to broach the details with her, especially with his schedule so tight. But for the first time in many years, she felt comfortable speaking casually to her brother. They had not been this carefree and open with one another for a long time.

"Well, Gladys, all I can say is someone was praying for us. Our coming out alive was nothing short of God's intervention at multiple levels, and I'm talking about from Bruce Masters on down. I know Carmen and the kids were praying. Valerie was pretty impressed by it all. It was a new experience for her." James couldn't see Gladys nodding with acknowledgment of being impressed by new experiences of prayer. She didn't share with James what she and Ralph had done. It was enough that God knew.

"And how is Madelyn? She apparently went through a lot." Gladys sounded genuinely concerned.

"Doing remarkably well. She's made of good stock. That Willingham blood runs deep. I'll share the details tonight. I'm sure everyone will want to hear them. But I need to tell you something, and I don't want you to hear it along with everyone else. I probably should do this face to face, but time-wise, I can't make that happen today. Do you mind?"

"Well, of course I don't mind, James. Go ahead." Gladys was apprehensive. Her immediate thought was that James was the one who had taken her mother's jewels. Her heart would be broken should he confess that, even though she had pointed fingers at him to Bruce Masters. If her finger-pointing was true, it could change everything in the course of the family. The paper had not alluded to anything of the sort, but what could James have to tell her that couldn't wait?

"Hello? Did I lose you, Gladys?" James had asked a question that was blocked by her thoughts.

"I'm sorry, James. Yes, yes, I can hear you now. Go ahead.

Please."

"I said I don't want you to in any way bear the responsibility of what I'm going to say. You do understand that I am accountable for my own actions?"

"I do, yes. I understand." Gladys conceded.

"Nick is my son." James had initially thought he would go into a more eloquent prelude. That was certainly his intentions. Why did he simply blurt it out? The words spilled forth before he even knew what he had done. He felt foolish and cold-hearted.

Gladys closed her eyes and sat silently. James didn't press her for a response. He was busy kicking himself for his abrupt announcement. "I know," was her quiet refrain.

"You know? How? Who told you? Did Mama tell you?" James was flabbergasted at Gladys's confession.

"No one told me. Somehow I've just known it. When Mother brought him for summer vacations, his mannerisms were like yours. I would sit on the porch with Mother and watch the children playing. He was unmistakably you. He looked like Carmen, and still does. But he is a thumbprint of your personality, James. I mean, of course, when you were at your best," Gladys teased.

"I–I don't know what to say. Why didn't you say something to me? Or to Mama?" Had James not been shocked by Gladys's foreknowledge, he would have readily understood why Gladys would not have felt comfortable to share her observation with anyone.

"James, I would give anything if I had said something to Mother. Or even you. But I can't bring that time back now. It's over. If I allow myself to get swallowed up with what I should have done or could have done and didn't, I can't move forward with my life. I'm tired of being a prisoner to my past, and I don't want to be a refugee in the present. I have to be pardoned for the future. I've wasted too many years, James. And so have you. Let's put this stuff behind us and make the best of the time we have left. We have a legacy to carry on." Gladys surprised herself at the message of her heart.

"Sounds like you and I have arrived at the place Mama mapped out for us all along. It just took us a long time to get there. And to think, the one we hurt through our selfish acts is the very one who helped to heal our self-inflicted wounds. Carmen is amazing. We owe her a lot." James was gentle and obliged in his thoughts.

"And she did one terrific job with your son. He's quite an impressive young man. Handles himself very well." Gladys paused for a second, and then resumed with an observation. "I guess you realize you have fathered—"

"Yeah, I know. Crazy isn't it? It's a mixed bag of emotions, Gladys. I feel very ashamed for the somewhat incestuous act. It'll be a huge scandal, you know."

"And that's where I *am* responsible." Gladys felt an attachment to James's shame.

"I told you that I'm accountable for my sins. Not you. I don't want you worried. I'm willing to take the fall. I don't know how the public will take all this. I can't worry about that. Like you said, what's done is done. There's a lot I could be taking a dive for, Gladys. I'll tell you up front that I'm sorry for the embarrassment it could cause you and the rest of the family." James's remorse was evident.

"I'm sure we can work through it, James. We'll take it one

day at a time. I'll see you this afternoon at Mother's. Give Valerie our love."

"Thanks, Sis. Love ya. Oh, and the jewels? Still a mystery. But, we're alive." James hung up the phone. He paused at the tenderness in Gladys's voice today. Something was different about her, vastly more so than last night. Whatever it was, she was apparently embracing the idea of Ralph. He put his phone in his pocket and whispered to himself, "'Send Valerie *our* love.' Mama, your legacy lives on."

The clarity of James's statement evaded Gladys. She couldn't imagine what her brother could have been involved in that could be of such concern. But, she knew Ralph would partner with her in prayer. She could hardly wait to share with him how effective his prayer for James had been. She glanced at Ralph. He was sitting in his chair reading the paper. The two of them had been like giddy school kids all morning. Her heart was full. She felt content. Marriage looked normal to her for the first time ever. It had been just as amazing to Ralph. The transition was too instant to feel anything short of a dream for now. If it was a dream, Gladys didn't ever want to wake up.

Chapter 50

MEMORIAL UNIVERSITY MEDICAL CENTER, INTENSIVE
CARE UNIT, OCTOBER 17, 2:07 P.M.

Glenna Masters sat with a cup of coffee in hand holding the warmth against her chest. A teenage girl sat next to her with her head on her mother's shoulder. The young man sat across in a chair playing a game on his iPad. Earphones reverberated the music his foot tapped beat to. Whether the escape on his face was due to his father's critical status or he was in his normal state of rejection of his surroundings couldn't be discerned by Carmen. It had been easy to recognize the family. The daughter was wearing an oversized Chatham County Sheriff's Department sweatshirt. Occasionally she would pull the neck of the shirt up to her nose and take a long whiff of her daddy's aroma. Her mother would pat her leg and cup her face with her hand in a consoling gesture.

"Mrs. Masters?" Carmen approached the family.

"Yes." Glenna looked surprised that anyone had called on the family. It had been a lonely day. Several officers had dropped by in the early morning hours, but by midmorning visitors had ceased and the lonely wait was on.

"Please, don't get up. Keep your seat. May I?" Carmen pointed to the chair beside her.

"Certainly."

"I'm Carmen Willingham, ma'am. I'm the sister of James. The family sends their love and concern, and this sunshine basket that will hopefully provide a little sustenance while you're waiting. A hospital can be a lonely place, especially at night. "

"That's very kind. James? James? Oh, Jim, Mayor Willingham, of course. I'm sorry. I'm not thinking clearly right now. You'll have to excuse me." Glenna readjusted her position hoping to clear her mind.

"I understand. I know you're exhausted, and very concerned. And you're?"

"I'm Rachelle. He's Brayden."

"It's nice to meet you," Carmen shook her hand.

"Brayden. Brayden!" Rachelle shouted. "Your manners?"

Brayden pulled the earphones from his ears. He got up from his chair and came over to greet Carmen. "Brayden. I'm the recluse. I keep to myself. A lot. Not trying to be rude. Just trying to escape."

"Oh, Brayden. You'll have this lady believing you. Stop it," Glenna gently scolded. "Our oldest daughter, Jessie, and her husband and children were on vacation. They're on their way back."

"I'm very sorry. I know it's difficult on all of you," Carmen comforted.

"It's nice to meet you, ma'am. I'm sorry, you'll have to tell me again who you are. I was blasting Cold Play in my ears." Brayden's good instructions kicked in.

"I'm Carmen Willingham. I'm the sister of Mayor Willingham, the one your father saved last night. Nick is my son, and Madelyn my niece. He saved their lives as well. What an incredible act of valor on his part. I don't know how we can ever thank you. Gratitude doesn't seem to suffice for the sacrifice you all are feeling right now. He's a very brave man."

"He's less than three months from retirement. We thought we were home free. He's been blessed through the years. And so have we." Glenna's eyes filled with tears through her glorious smile. "He's a good man. I'm not sure if you guys ever got to see that side of him. He can be a prickly pear when it comes to his cases. He takes his job very seriously."

"A little too seriously sometimes," Brayden added. "We hadn't seen him for days while he was working on some jewel theft case."

"Brayden. Mind your manners, Son." Glenna knew it was innocent because Brayden hadn't connected the dots, but she could have crawled in a hole. "Please excuse—"

"Don't apologize. I know it's been all-consuming for Detective Masters. I know I speak for all of the Willingham family when we say we would have rather none of this to have happened."

"And forgive me, please, ma'am. I'm sorry for the loss of your mother. Right? You said the Mayor was your brother, did you?" Glenna was still trying to shake the cobwebs from her head.

"Yes, Grace Willingham was my mother. James, or Jim, and Gladys Murphy are my siblings. Grace is the one whose jewels were stolen, Brayden. And I can assure you, she would have given them to someone to keep them from stealing them, especially if she knew this would happen to your father." Carmen touched the shoulder of Brayden and looked him in the eyes. She knew he had innocently stepped into the puddle, but she wanted him to understand the spirit of her mother.

"Oh, I didn't know it was your mom. Sorry about that." Brayden hung his head.

"Don't be ashamed. Pick up your countenance," Carmen said to the young man as she placed her fingertips underneath his chin and lifted his face. "It was very honest on your part. I only stress that because your father's spirit mirrors that of my mother. She would give her life for a noble cause. That's the kind of person your dad is, too. From everything I understand about the great majority of our law enforcement, they sacrifice an awful lot. But it doesn't begin or end with the officer. People have no idea of the personal costs to their families. Your father has a long record of public service, a character of impeccable integrity and tremendous courage, and one that is dedicated to the profession. I can only imagine how demanding his job must be, not to mention dangerous. He wore his uniform and his badge with pride, not because he did his job well, but because he wanted to make his family proud of his accomplishments. I only met him briefly, but even then, he spoke fondly of his family. And when he did, he lit up like a beacon and his tough veneer softened. It was obvious where his real world revolved."

"Thanks, Ma'am. I probably needed to hear that more than anyone. I guess we sometimes forget that they really do love us more than the force." Brayden looked contemplative. He knew he had been more than a challenge for his mom and dad in the past couple years. He blamed his dad for not being around. Truth was, when his dad was there, he wasn't interested in being with him. He used his absence as an excuse. It was a cop-out in the lamest sense of the term.

Carmen visited with the family for the better part of an hour. Glenna brought her up to speed on the prognosis. It was worse than Carmen expected. To add to the stress, the nurse had placed restrictions on the time they could spend with their loved one. Ten-minute increments, one at a time, with a break in between. The rules were adding to their frenzy. Carmen encouraged Glenna to insist on staying and ask for the doctor to demand no visitors other than by the immediate family. As long as there's no rowdiness in the room, it should be perfectly acceptable. Glenna seemed genuinely grateful for the encouragement to find her backbone. Her gentle, kind spirit typically didn't buck the system. Her backbone stiffened, and she was charged for any opposition.

Carmen rose to her feet and gathered her belongings. "If there is anything I can do for you all, please call me. Here's my card. It's a California number, but I'll be in town for a couple more weeks. Please allow our family to help you in some way. We realize we're not responsible for the acts of criminals, but we are terribly indebted to your husband and father for his heroism."

"Thank you, Carmen. I appreciate it. I know Bruce would be touched." Glenna was kind and sincere. She had gotten up from the couch to say goodbye to their guest.

"Do you mind if I pray with you before I leave?" Carmen had determined she would not leave without a prayer. "And, if you don't object, I'd love for us to gather around Detective Masters and do that together."

"That would be great. We need all the prayers we can get." Glenna picked up the phone to call the nurses's station. "Yes, this is Glenna Masters. I know only one is allowed in at a time, but do you think we could possibly bring the kids in with me and a guest. We just want to have a quick prayer with Bruce, and we'll be gone after that." And kind voice gave an affirmative response, and Glenna replied, "Oh, thank you."

The double doors opened and Glenna pointed the way to the ICU room that housed the brave detective. She stopped to speak to the nurse at the desk. Carmen walked into Bruce's room. Monitors and IV solutions were in place. Oxygen was being administered. He was still in an unstable situation. His attending nurse had been taking his vitals. She whispered to Glenna, "Only two minutes with this many. You're welcome to come in yourself as long as you want."

"I want my children in here, too," Glenna was insistent. "I have a call in to the doctor to get clearance for them to be here with me at all times. No more increments of time. He's my husband and their father."

"If the doctor says it's okay, we'll make the exception. There were too many in here through the night. Your husband is a very sick man, Mrs. Masters. He doesn't need any sort of confusion."

"I understand, ma'am. We're not having a party in here. He is their father and my husband. We *are* going to be with him." Glenna was kind but rallying support for the rights of the patient's immediate family. She winked at Carmen and then joined them in the room.

The nurse walked back to her station. Bruce's family members gathered around his bed in silence. Carmen stood at the end of his bed looking at the picture of utmost sacrifice. This was a man who was willing to lay down his life for the safety of not only people he scarcely knew, but for a community to be free of dangerous recidivists. But this man was shot by one of his own who had turned criminal.

"Hey, Honey. You have more company. Carmen Willingham is here. She wanted to personally thank you for saving her family last night and tell you what a hero she thinks you are. Of course, we knew that all along. We love you, Sweetheart." Glenna was soft and tender with her husband.

"I love you, Dad. You're my hero, too," Brayden echoed his mother's choice of sentiment.

"Daddy, I need you. Please get well. I want you to come home." Rachelle began sobbing softly. Glenna patted her and shook her head trying to get her to maintain control.

"Detective Masters, I bring thank-you's from all of the Willinghams. Your bravery is unsurpassed. We didn't deserve your sacrifice, but it is acknowledged and greatly appreciated. I just wanted to have a word of prayer with you." Carmen held out her hands. Brayden and Rachelle joined hands with her. Rachelle took her mother's, and she joined it with Bruce's. Brayden held Bruce's other hand.

"Dear Lord, We praise You for all good and perfect things. We know Your creation began with excellence, and man corrupted it when we invited sin into our lives. Yet You still loved us. You didn't separate us from Your love, only from Your Garden. You cast us into the world of sin that we chose over You. And throughout history, we have compounded sin upon sin. Because of what we compromised, evil runs amuck in the world today, and even those of us who strive to do Your will fall prey to the schemes of evil men. Bruce Masters is one of Your very finest, Heavenly Father. He gave everything because he cares. And now, we stand beside him today because we care. If it be your will, Lord, restore him to complete health. Heal his body as only You can. Guide the doctors, Lord, so that they know what to do to bring about healing. Bless his family as they stand beside him. May they reflect on the love and devotion each has shared in unique ways with this man—their husband and father. Let not time erase the memory of the sacrifices he has made in every walk of life, but especially this sacrifice in his prominent career as an officer to uphold justice. He gave in large part because of the love he has for his family. It was his desire to create a safer environment for them to live. Bless him, bless them. May Your will be done, Lord. And in so doing, please give us a spirit of understanding for how You orchestrate our lives. In Your precious Son's name we pray. Amen."

Carmen left Bruce Masters's loved ones gathered around his side. He had regained consciousness only for about an hour after his surgery. Glenna and the children had to share that time with his fellow officers and the lead investigator of the FBI. They only had a few moments with Bruce alone before he took a turn for the worse. Internal bleeding had complicated his recovery, and he was taken back to the operating room again. The doctors were pleased he lived through the second procedure, but could not give Glenna any expectation for survival. Carmen was heavy-hearted as she watched a family holding onto only a thread of hope.

*   *   *

827 VICTORY DRIVE, GRANDMA GRACE'S BACK PATIO,
OCTOBER 17, 4:30 P.M.

"I know it's here somewhere." Jimmy was plundering through Grace's recipe drawer to find the special barbecue sauce formula. His head was feeling better today. He thought he would try his luck with ribs for the family gathering. The Willinghams had enjoyed tasty ribs on many family occasions. Mr. Morris's special barbecue sauce was the best. Grandma's friends from the neighboring town of Rincon had shared the recipe with her years ago. The peanut butter-and-vinegar-based recipe was to die for. It had been five years since Jimmy had cooked or eaten any of the delicious ribs. "I know I can do this if I can find the recipe. It's got to be here. Bingo! Got it. Oh, yikes. I have to squeeze lemons, too? And cook the ribs for three hours? And baste them every ten minutes? No wonder they're good. This is a lot of work, guys. Are you sure you want—"

"We want the ribs, Jimmy!" Everyone shouted in unison. Jimmy had whetted everyone's appetites for the ribs, now he had to live up to his mouth. The dish was a favorite of everyone's. It would be a grand way to celebrate family and get Madelyn's mind off of the trauma she had gone through last night. She had already been begging Jimmy not to make her laugh. It hurt too much. Her condition was still tenuous. Everyone insisted she take it easy, and she offered no resistance.

Bryson had been the sweetest to Madelyn. He would rub her face and arms and say, "Boo-boo, boo-boo," and then, lean over and kiss her injuries tenderly. Madelyn had seen his look of concern before when Kareem had roughed her up. Through her sadness for what happened, she found delight in the fact that her son would never have to witness that kind of abuse again.

The imagery of last night's events would intermittently flash in and out of Madelyn's head. She knew it would be quite a while before the nightmare would cease invading her thoughts. But she was grateful to be breathing, as painful as it was. Her prayer had been answered, and she had a promise to fulfill. How she would serve was yet to be determined. One day at a time. As her Granny Grace used to tell her, "Put your best foot forward while standing tall on the other one." Her internal dialogue had been trying to redirect her from the negative conversations she had been having with herself. She would remind herself of Grace's advice to keep her on the positive track: "Be careful how you talk to yourself. People will come to know you for who you believe you are." Today she had a new promise of tomorrow. She would get a plan, a backup plan, and even an alternative one should the backup plan take a foul turn. It was one of Granny Grace's secrets to contentment. She never had a plan to fail. It simply made way for another one.

"So, what's the point of our get-together tonight?" Nora inquired.

"The point? Does there have to be a point?" Ashley fired back.

"Calm down. I just asked. I mean, are we going to be talking about dividing up GG's belongings, or laying claim to some things we wanted? I mean, wouldn't this be a good time to do it if it's not the intent of the gathering?" Nora continued to make her point.

"We have to have a death certificate before we can probate a will, Nora. There are provisions the law controls. That's one of them," Ashley pointed out.

"Well, I figured there would be some sort of restriction. But, I mean, Jimmy and I can't stay here forever. Neither can you, Aunt Carmen. Right?"

Carmen didn't hear Nora. Her thoughts were with the Masters family. "I'm sorry. Ask me again, Nora."

"When are you headed back to California? I know Jimmy and I can't stay here forever. We'll need to be moving on soon."

"Hey, speak for yourself, Nora Jean. I might just stick around forever and let the natives come to me. They'd enjoy hanging out here on this acreage, don't you think? It'd be a nice change of pace for them." Jimmy's comment was tongue in cheek, but he had entertained staying in the States for a few years. The last year had been rough on him in Zimbabwe. He hadn't shared with anyone how tough the mission field was right now. He'd been attacked by a group that wanted to do away with him, not once but several times. In fact, they had targeted him at least once a month, if he was lucky, for the past six months. Sometimes he was visited twice in a month's time. He was exhausted and needed a respite from the mission field for a while. He didn't want to give it up, but felt a change might be good for his soul.

"Oh, stop it, Jimmy. No one can tell when you're serious or kidding anymore. We know you love Africa. You'll decide you're going to be there forever, and eventually, you won't come home as often, and then, we'll never see you again." Nora's dramatic description of Jimmy was somewhat true. She just had no idea how close he had come to not seeing them again ever.

"Well, I might need to find me a woman before I leave again. I want children. I need a mini me. I'm just considering it, that's all." Jimmy was divulging more of himself than he had planned, but it seemed a natural setting for him to be real.

"Married? You? I don't ever want to get married. It'll mess up everything. I like my freedom." Nora was almost convincing.

"Being unmarried is not all that it's cut out to be, Nora." Carmen spoke with the voice of experience. "I make myself content because I'm not going to live my life miserable. I'm going to make sure that I stay busy for the Lord. But I would like to have a companion. Especially now that Nick is gone. And he's been gone for a while. I got really busy with the children's home about the time he left for college. Before I knew it, I found myself married to me and my children's home. I'm passionate about it, but quite honestly, when I go to *my* home at night, I would love to have someone to share the day's events with. I had a difficult time trusting men. Mom Grace always told me, 'Trust is on loan.' She said, 'It only belongs to you until someone decides to take it back.' She was right. Once it's gone, it's hard to give it back to the one you took it from. I am responsible for the trust I convey to others. It's the only trust I can control. So, now that I've come to learn that lesson late in life, I'm ready to embrace love myself. I think life demands to be loved and to love. I believe I have that capacity within me. I'm ready to give it a try."

"Wow, Carmen. I've never thought about it that way." Nora was captivated by the idea of trust being the individual's responsibility. "My idea has always been to transfer the responsibility entirely to the one wanting to be trusted. Did I just say the same thing you did in a different way and from a different perspective? Anyway, it's something to think about, so thank you."

"I love how you said that, Carmen. I'm ready, too. I've put off love long enough. I've had several suitors interested. I haven't been ready. I hate it that Grandma didn't live to see any of her grandchildren married. I find that sad. She would have loved that." Ashley felt melancholy for the first time today. Grandma had always encouraged her to love, but was patient with her. She knew Ashley would grow into the idea someday.

Nora wanted to get back on topic. "So, Grandma's Will. When can we get that probated? Do you know, Miss Attorney?"

"It all hinges on the death certificate. When it arrives, the Judge will probate it, then the reading of the Will can be held. *As* soon as we get that, it can be done anytime," Ashley informed.

"Well, wait no more. I have Grandma's Death Certificate in hand." Nick had walked around the house and was listening to the conversation.

"Nick, I didn't hear you come up at all. How are you, Son?" In light of what he had been through the night before, Carmen was delighted to see him refreshed.

"I'm fine," Nick assured. "A little sad. Just left the hospital. Bruce Masters is really bad. I don't think he's going to make it."

Eyes turned to Madelyn. She had been greatly disturbed over the news of Masters. As miserable as he had made her life the past few days, he had spared hers last night. He was incredibly brave, and she would be indebted to him forever.

Ashley changed the subject. "How did you get the Death Certificate so quickly?"

"Well, think about it. Grandma's funeral dragged out a couple of days longer. Also, I let them know we had out-of-country family members, and they put a rush on it for me. It worked. I'm putting it in your capable hands, Miss Attorney. I'm glad to pass it on." Nick took a deep breath. He fixed himself a glass of sweet iced tea and sat in a patio chair.

"Will everyone be here? Did anyone call Aunt Gladys?" Ashley asked.

"Done. Gladys and Ralph will be here. Da—James and Valerie will be here. It'll be a full house. But, that's totally our call, Ashley. If you're prepared to do that, you let us know. Or, if there has to be a more formal procedure, we can do that. We are at your mercy, My Lady." Nick was hoping that everyone had overlooked his Freudian slip. He wasn't ready to call James "Dad," if he ever would. Why it slipped out of his mouth, Heaven only knew.

"Okay. We can do that tomorrow if everyone is ready for that. I'll just need to get to my office and get some matters taken care of. Personally, I would prefer Grandma's attorney, Richard Thomas, do the honors. He would need to do that, being her attorney, although I did help her draw it up. I'll have to see if Mr. Thomas is free tomorrow. If not, I can, but there are a few things that need to get in order first."

"So, you already know what's in GG's Will? How fair is that?" Nora snipped. Ashley was an attorney, but Nora felt there was a real conflict of interest surrounding her involvement. No one questioned Grace's motives. Out loud, at least.

"Yeah, I'm thinking we'll wait for Richard Thomas." Ashley had expected objection from Nora.

"I'm in charge of the main course. You guys just sit. Relax. Don't mind me. I'm laboring and sweating over these ribs. It's no big deal. I have stitches in my head. It's throbbing from squeezing all the lemons. But don't mind me at all." Jimmy was busy talking as he was coming down the stairs and tripped over his feet. He went spiraling out of control with the sauce in hand. Everyone jumped up and squealed. "Just kidding," Jimmy said. "Had it all under control all along." He grinned and walked over to the grill to apply the sauce to the slow-cooking ribs. It was going to be a feast. All the Willinghams would be in place for the second night in a row. The family circle had a missing link. Physically Grace was gone. But in the hearts of all who loved her, her presence was as real as her memory.

Chapter 51

James and Valerie Willingham stood at the double doors of the intensive care unit at Memorial University Medical Center. The doors opened, and they approached the desk. Nurses and interns filled the station attending to details of their assigned patients. Nurse Sandra Burkhart was busy with her own tasks but stopped and greeted them with a smile. "Mayor, Mrs. Willingham, so nice of you to come. Mr. Masters's wife, children, and grandchildren are in with him now. It's not looking good. They've called their minister to come. I think they could use some support. Although they might not acknowledge it now, they'll remember it later. But, I wouldn't hang around too long. It is a very private time for a family."

"I understand. We'll just be a few minutes." James took Valerie's hand and with indebted hearts, they walked into the room where Bruce Masters lay dying. James looked at Glenna Masters as she leaned in close to her husband. His son stood at his left side. His daughter Rachelle was sitting in a chair with her head laying on Masters's left hand. His oldest daughter, Kathleen, had arrived and gathered close beside her sister. It was a heartbreaking scene of a family losing their patriarch. James fought back the tears. His legs felt encumbered at the weight of his heart. His bottom lip quivered and his voice cracked as he tried to speak to the failing hero's wife. "Glenna, I–I'm sorry. I don't–I'm at a loss for words."

The brokenness of a woman in love losing her soul mate looked at James and Valerie. They would have understood if she had asked them to leave, or spewed venom from her mouth at the audacity of their appearance. That would have been the expected salutation from the wife whose husband's life was ebbing away. Especially given that his last week was devoted to bringing about justice for the family that stood before his death bed. Instead the kindness that was projected epitomized the beauty within her. "Your presence speaks volumes. Thank you both for coming." She turned her focus back to her husband. "Bruce, look who's come to see you. You're a loved man. The Mayor and his beautiful wife are here to cheer you up." She continued looking at her husband but addressed James and Valerie. "He hasn't been too talkative the last few hours. He did decide to wake up and respond to us a little bit. Got to hug and love on everyone. It was special. Then, he got tired and decided to go back to sleep." Bruce exhibited all the signs of death. Breathing had become more irregular and was slowing. His airway was congested and he had begun the death rattle. Mottling had appeared on his cold hands and feet. His nail beds and lips were turning blue.

"You're welcome to say something to him, Mayor. They say hearing is the last sense to go. We've been talking his ears off.

I believe he's enjoying it. He's such a stinker, you know. He's going to beat us all to Heaven. Except your mom. She got there just a little earlier than my Bruce will. God's getting two really fine people in one week. I hope Heaven can handle it. Of course, as if He didn't already know, He's getting a good taste of how stubborn my man is." She managed a soft giggle and kissed Bruce lightly on the lips.

James marveled at the lady's strength. She was preparing her children for the loss in a true mother's nurturing way. He knew firsthand that the loss of a spouse is one of the most soul-wrenching experiences a person faces. The other is the loss of a child. James had stood at the threshold of the latter—once at the birth of Jimmy, and again last night with two adult children who, ashamedly, he barely knew. Even so, James was willing to lay down his own life for their safety. Annie had given hers in exchange for Jimmy's. But this man gave his life for the cause of all families in a community, leaving behind the one he cherished most.

James moved in closer and stood beside Glenna. Valerie stepped in behind Glenna and placed her hands on the weary wife's shoulders. "Bruce, buddy, you cracked the biggest case in the history of Savannah. You helped clean up a corrupt system in this community. We're all indebted to you. This case will be the crème de la crème of your illustrative career. You have a spotless record. It goes without saying that I owe you my life and the lives of my two kids. I've never seen anything more heroic than what you did last night, Bruce. I could never repay you. But I promise you this: your family will be taken care of till you get back on your feet. I'm going to make sure of that. I'll check in on them regularly for you. You can count on me."

Bruce managed an ever-so-slight nod. Glenna put her hand to her mouth to keep her garbled cry from being heard. She wanted to be strong until the end. The children's tears were flowing more freely.

Valerie had remained quiet. The opportunity to observe people cross from this side of life to another had presented itself with her several times, but of much older men. She, however, felt a fervent indebtedness to this man. This would apparently be her only opportunity to express any sort of appreciation to him directly, so she seized it. In her high-pitched Southern drawl, she tenderly spoke her heart. "Officer Masters, I need to say that what you did was the most selfless act I've ever known. But for you, the picture could be me grieving today." James closed his eyes and held his breath. He so hoped that Glenna would understand Valerie's intentions. She continued, "I am not worthy to have been spared the grief. I don't hold a candle to your sweet Glenna, but she has inspired me to love the man you saved like she loves you. Thank you. I …" Valerie struggled to finish her sentence. She was crying with the others. "I will never forget you."

"We're going to leave you guys alone for now. If you need us, here's my card. I'm a phone call away." James handed Glenna the card. She continued to hold Bruce's hand up to her mouth as she took the card and nodded at James. He patted her shoulders. Valerie reached down and hugged her tightly. The two walked around to the Bruce's children and hugged the girls and shook Brayden's hand. There was little response from them. They, too, remained focused on their hero dad.

As James passed the nurses's station, Nurse Burkhart stopped him. "It won't be long, if you wanted to stick around outside for a few minutes."

James thanked her. He and Valerie had the waiting area to themselves for another thirty-two minutes. Their concern for Bruce and his family was upper most in their minds. In the meantime, James shared more particulars of the events surrounding the night. He had shared the highlights on the drive home from Grace's, including the news about Nick. Valerie asked explicit questions, challenging James's appreciation for detail.

"Can I say something?" Val asked.

"Of course. You can say anything to me." James assured her.

"Thank you. Thank you for telling me about Nick and Hawk and everything. That took a lot of courage, too. I'm proud of you. I'll be totally honest with you, though, Jim. It's a lot for a girl to digest. I feel a bit deceived—actually, I feel a lot deceived. I should be absolutely furious with you. But for some baffling reason, I'm not. It scares me senseless that I'm not. I can't explain that. But, whatever is coming over us, do you think we could find a way to keep it up? What do you say?"

Valerie could not have said anything that could have thrilled James more.

He was searching for a comeback to match her sensitivity when the doors to the ICU area opened and Nurse Burkhart exited. "It's over. He's gone. If you want to give the family a few minutes alone, I think they would really appreciate some comforting arms shortly. No other family members or ministers have arrived yet."

"Thank you. I appreciate your courtesy." James and Valerie sat back down. James laid his head on the back of the chair. He knew he wasn't directly responsible for this death, but he bore a burden for the man's demise nonetheless.

"You want to pray?" Valerie's sweet voice broke James's moment of despair.

"Yes. Yes, Val, I think we should." The couple joined hands and both prayed for the family who was left to grieve the loss of a father and husband. Their prayer was brief, but restorative. It brought a sense of peace that is difficult to find when life's questions leave doubting moments. They waited an appropriate time and reentered the ICU area. The Masters family had exited the room where Bruce Masters's lifeless body lay. The curtains were drawn and the staff was preparing the body to be taken away. James and Valerie approached them with open arms. Bruce's wife and children welcomed the comfort the newfound friends provided. Tonight would be an especially lonely time at the Masters homeplace. James could attest that every day for the rest of their lives would be introduced with a void. As life progressed, the void would not leave them as breathless as the day before. But arriving at those more yielding times would be a long, arduous journey.

*   *   *

827 VICTORY DRIVE, GRANDMA GRACE'S PATIO, OCTOBER 17, 6:17 P.M.

Nick slid the dial on his cell phone to accept the call from MUM. He hesitated, not wishing to hear who had deceased. "Nick Willingham. Yes, ma'am. I'll get someone there right away. Thank you for your call." Nick returned his phone to his pocket and sat staring into space with his hands folded at his mouth.

"Everything all right, Nick?" Carmen noticed his withdrawal.

"Bruce Masters just passed away. Turner's is handling his funeral." Nick couldn't help himself. He turned his face away from the crowd as his tears were flowing freely. He pulled his handkerchief from his pocket to accommodate the streams of grief.

Carmen held her finger up to the others who had made an advance toward Nick in order to console him. "Give him a moment. We all should take one. Madelyn, how are you?"

Madelyn sat staring off into space herself. She visualized the very spirit of Bruce Masters being welcomed into Heaven's gates. Tears flooded down her cheeks. She didn't want to cry uncontrollably. It hurt too badly for her to breathe deeply. She had much more pent-up emotion that needed purging, but she preferred her privacy. Now was not the time or place. She didn't want people's pity. She only wanted to talk to God and Granny Grace.

"Madelyn?" Ashley coddled. "You need me to help you upstairs? We understand if you need to be alone."

Madelyn accepted Ashley's sisterly understanding as a soothing balm. "Thank you. I'm okay for right now. I'll let you help me later. In fact, I'd love it if you would help me later."

Ashley made a thoughtful suggestion. "If it's okay with everyone, why don't we hold off on discussing Grandma's business until tomorrow? Can we just enjoy one another tonight and not think about anything else? I think everyone's nerves could use a break."

"Wonderful idea, Ashley. I'm all for it." Carmen inaudibly applauded Ashley's maturity.

"I think it's the least we could do," Nora added.

"Tell you what, guys." Jimmy laid down his baster and dish-cloth. "Why don't the four of us circle around and have prayer on behalf of Bruce's family. Nick and Madelyn, you guys stay right where you are but know that you're in on this, too. I'll do the honors."

From the Heavens looking down on the Willingham acre-age, the celebratory smoke from the grill drew attention to a steeped heritage. It was a legacy of faith. It was a belief system that had seen years of trials and tribulations, scores of losses and sufferings, and multiple victories and blessings that remained unshakable upon the firm foundation of prayer. Grace Carissa Willingham would be proud to know her family had caught the vision of what she demonstrated in her daily life. From the Heavens looking down, she and Bruce Masters were sharing an understanding about the truth about the jewels that had solidified many family legacies.

Chapter 52

There was a somberness attached to the evening. The reprise of last night's trauma with the death of Bruce Masters left everyone gloomy. The ribs were the highlight of the meal and a great conversation diversion. The taste conjured up memories of gatherings on Grandma Grace's patio. She had taught each of her boys the art of grilling the delectable meats that could be dowsed with the distinctive South Carolina-style sauce, and passed on the Morris family recipe to her girls. Jimmy had outdone himself and served up an appetite-pleasing rendition of the family favorite.

After getting primed, the conversation remained light. The concentration centered on catching up with one another's lives. Jimmy shared tales of Africa. The persecution of Christians was alarming to his family. He wondered if their obliviousness was because they were not mission-minded or due to their absence from church altogether. Ashley and Carmen apologized for their neglect of his passion and promised to become more involved. The others attentively pondered the details, but whether they buried in their heart or was a passing revelation was yet to be determined.

Nora enthusiastically expressed her zeal for Spain. The picture she painted on the canvas of her years in that country was intended to leave everyone absorbed and awestruck with the life she had assembled for herself. She was beautiful, successful, ambitious, and removed. Behind the charade of sonata was a chord of disharmony within her soul. Something was missing. Underneath Nora's veneer of achievement was a layer of emptiness. Her life and love evolved around herself. She was a self-made icon who could only be accessed at her invitation.

Ashley was more modest in updating the family regarding her law practice. Nick boasted of her claim to fame within the Savannah community which brought her merited respect and some enviable competition among her peers. Ashley reminded everyone that she was blessed. She assured them she could have done nothing without the help of the Lord. Her focus on Him kept her fixed on her goals. Anything she had accomplished was to His glory.

Madelyn's account of her life began with an apology to the family. It was painfully emotional for her to tell and others to hear. There was a veil of uncertainty as to what would possess Madelyn to reveal the traumatic episode at school. She had never told anyone. She had been convinced that no one cared and wasn't willing to compromise the relationship of the only person who did—Granny Grace. She explained how the wreckage cluttered up her life and disrupted her goals. Madelyn declared to her family that Bryson would have a mother he could be proud of. She asked for their prayers and support as she would become a teacher. She knew it was going to be difficult as a single mom, but many women before her had reached the goal. Additionally, she and Bryson would go to Sydney. She had promised that to Granny Grace on the day of her funeral. Madelyn pointed to Bryson playing in his activity center. She confessed that she had almost aborted him and believed it was her family roots that kept her from crossing that boundary. She couldn't imagine life without him.

It was Nick's turn to talk about himself. He was not quite prepared to reveal some aspects of his life, especially his future plans. He realized the family knew very little about his life in France or his love for Abrielle. They had limited knowledge regarding his accomplishments as an architect. They were simply willing to accept the fact that he was a mortician. He would not breathe a word about his purpose for being in Savannah. There would be a time to disclose his objective. He was fairly confident no one in the group would fully appreciate the intent. However, in order to be a participant in the family spirit, he began by asking for their confidence and prayers regarding a potential buyer for Turner's so that he could move back to France. He spoke with ease of his love for Abrielle, but judging from the looks on their faces, the relationship was difficult for others to understand.

Gladys and Ralph had been showing affection for one another, and it was noticeably refreshing. Each made an apology for wasted years. Forgiveness was in place. Ralph pulled a worn-out brochure from his pocket and announced their upcoming plans. The two would ask Pastor Webster to renew their vows the following Friday at East Savannah. Everyone was invited to attend. After that, their plans were to stay in Tuscany for six months at a charming one-hundred-year-old stone cottage in Riolo, a quaint picturesque village near Tuscany. Hugs and loves and congratulations were the next order of business. The picture of life exuding from Gladys warmed the hearts of everyone, especially James and Carmen.

Carmen spoke of her passion for her children's home for which she was founder and president, its fragile beginning, and the dreams she had for its future. Her promise was to make up for lost time of not visiting her family in Savannah as her short time here had been a reminder of how important they were to her.

It was a perfect segue for James to introduce the history behind Carmen's life in California. This was a place he never wanted to be in life—confessing to a conspicuously offensive act as a young boy. Darkness had long settled on Grace's backyard. The lanterns and sconce garden torches illuminated the patio, but reduced visibility was enough to disguise the startled, disappointed, and possibly disgusted expressions from his children's faces. Carmen added a good measure of leveling agent to the shameful incident. Her gracious spirit was a welcomed interjection for James. Valerie sat with a tender hand on the back of James's neck to show her support of the man she loved, and planting an occasional kiss on his cheek. Gladys was grateful she had communicated the saga to Ralph earlier in the day. He sensed her uneasiness for the part she played, even though James did not reveal her role in the drama. He was proud when she spoke up and assumed responsibility. It was a huge step for her to confront her demons. He breathed a sigh of relief when she finished. He knew the past that haunted her had been put to rest once and for all.

"So, Nick is your son? That's what you're trying to tell us?" Nora had been wanting to be the first to define the mystery behind the estrangement in the family. She wouldn't dare interrupt until more of the details had been exposed. But before James could make the announcement himself, she stole his thunder. "It all makes perfect sense now. I knew it. I just knew there was something really twisted here."

"Nora! Your choice of words leaves me cold." Ashley had never wanted to pop Nora in the mouth more than she wanted to now. As shocking as the news was to Ashley, she was sensitive to the fact that the three siblings had healed from years of an obvious unfavorable separation. Yet Nora was quick to remind them of how perverse it was. *Sometimes thoughts are best kept to oneself.*

"Ashley, you have to admit it is somewhat—" Nora was going to defend her position, but James interrupted in an attempt to be the diplomat.

"You're right, Nora. It is. I'm very ashamed of what I did, but we have to remember that—"

"But we have to remember—" Jimmy stood up and walked over to his father. He stepped behind him and placed his hands on his dad's shoulders. He dug in his fingers in a massaging fashion. "We have to remember God's grace made provisions for even the worst of sins. God doesn't look at one man's sin any differently than he looks at mine, or yours. In His eyes, sin is sin. Consequences of sin is where the difference of the degrees of sin come in. These three siblings have been suffering consequences of what happened for years. None of us know the private hell each of them has gone through. And the way I see it, their consequences are not over entirely. People will talk. They'll be unkind.

They always are. But we are family. We are Grace Willingham's family. Grandma knew about this for a lot of years and didn't say a word. Yet, she didn't stop loving unconditionally. That's grace with a little "g," and our Grace, with a capital "G," demonstrated it." Jimmy held up a finger and took a deep breath. "No one talk yet. I'm not done."

He walked over to Nick. He had been especially tolerant as the family secret was being laid bare. Jimmy placed his hands on Nick's shoulders and massaged a couple of times. "On Grandma's Wall of Remembrance is an inscription. It's written in Grace's handwriting and signed and dated by Nick. It's Romans 8:18: 'And we know that in all things God works for the good of those who love him, who have been called according to His purpose.' Nick may have been a mistake by the world's standards, but to God, Nick has a mighty purpose." Jimmy paused. "No one talk yet. I'm not done."

Jimmy walked back to his chair, but he didn't sit. He stood behind the chair and addressed them all, scanning his small familial audience and connecting with the eyes of each one intermittently. "I've taken some time to study Grandma's Wall of Remembrance. You should, too. Each verse assigned to us as her children and grandchildren had specific significance in our lives. Ashley, Jeremiah 32:17: 'Ah, Sovereign Lord, You have made the Heavens and the earth by Your great power and outstretched arm. Nothing is too hard for You.' It was your encouragement to keep pressing on always drawing from His strength. Madelyn, Philippians 1:6: 'Being confident of this, that He who began a good work in you will carry it on to completion until the day of Christ Jesus.' Grandma knew you would search for your identity and question your worth. Nora, John 5:30: 'I can do nothing on my own. As I hear, I judge, and my judgment is just, because I seek not my own will but the will of Him who sent me.' She knew you would be more self-absorbed. I'm sorry, but you are. One of mine was Proverbs 19:11: 'Good sense makes one slow to anger, and it is his glory to overlook an offense.' I spent years being angry at my dad. She knew it was my weakness. Dad, Aunt Gladys, Aunt Carmen, you guys had your weaknesses. She had us all pegged! She knew us intimately. She knew what our weaknesses were. Grandma understood that because of those weaknesses, we would face our greatest struggles in life. She not only prayed for us to overcome our flaws and to find strength to endure the struggles, she equipped us to do that ourselves. She knew that one day we would be on our own, that she wouldn't always be here, and that while she was, we wouldn't always listen to her godly advice. She created a legacy for each of us because she knew days like yesterday and today would come. If she were here, Grace Carissa Willingham would be quoting 1 Timothy 6:20-21: 'Guard what has been entrusted to your care. Turn away from godless chatter and the opposing ideas of what is falsely called knowledge, which some have professed and in so doing have departed from the faith.'

"Nick, perhaps you knew or maybe you didn't realize at all that one of the verses bearing your authentication of hiding it in your heart had been earmarked for you by Grandma. But it was. She assigned that one to you first. You are the personification of how God fixes man's mistakes. You knew the story. To what extent, I don't know. I'm assuming you already knew everything that we've heard tonight for the very first time. And even though you have lived with this shocking secret all these years, you stood by this family. You put your life on the line for Madelyn and for Dad. You were equipped, like each one of us, by the anchor of this family. I loved it thinking you were my cousin. I'm digging it even more knowing you are my brother." Jimmy took a deep breath. "No one talk. I'm not done."

Jimmy took his knife and clanged it against his glass. Then, he picked up the glass and held it high in the air. "I'd like to propose a toast. Raise your iced tea glasses." Everyone followed Jimmy's command. "A toast to Grace Carissa Willingham, a woman who faced fears with victory going before her, whose priceless wisdom brought us inestimable value, who questioned the norm and defied the odds, who didn't place any more expectations on you than what the Lord demanded, who gave without seeking return, who was humble, confident and optimistic, who never intended to be remarkable,… she just was. To Grace, who knew God's grace was sufficient for her sins and mine."

Not another word was necessary. Everyone tipped their glasses toward the Heavens in honor of their matriarch. The remainder of the October night held warmth and love. Old memories were revisited as new reminiscences were created. A designated time was set for the following day to meet at Ashley's office to reveal the contents of Grace Carissa Willingham's Last Will and Testament. A great foundation had been laid for civility. Ashley, knowing the assignments of the estate of Grace, was somewhat disconcerted in her spirit. Everything that is except for the jewels, which, for the time being, at least, was a moot issue. As she drove away from her grandmother's homeplace, she looked in her rearview mirror and saw her family saying their warm, loving goodbyes. She couldn't help but think, *But will you love me tomorrow?*

Chapter 53

The rope was still secured to the box. A good tug at it broke loose the soil that covered the rope, but the container would demand more effort. Three days didn't seem long enough for the ground to become hardened. But given the sunny days that followed the rain on the morning of the treasure being buried, it was understandable some hard digging might be required.

Lights from a car passing caused alarm. Giving the appearance of a homeless person resting against a tree for the night was a great disguise to ward off any curious onlookers. Once the lights faded into the distance, the digging resumed. The hand-held garden shovel clanged against metal. *There you are. I told you I'd come for you. Just a couple of more times around with this shovel, and you'll be safe.*

Another set of car lights triggered positioning against the tree. The car had slowed down. Slightly opening one eye to see that it was continuing to its destination brought relief. The digging recommenced. Finally, the box holding the jewels was uncovered.

The edge of the small garden hand tool was used to provide lever-age to lift it out of its shallow grave. The box was then placed in a piece of carry-on luggage along with the hand tool. The bag was closed, zipped, and picked up by its handle. Once reaching the sidewalk, the luggage was set down, the retractable handle released, and the jewels were in the custody and control of the third individual to assume possession of them.

The hollow spot at the foot of the massive oak appeared for-saken. The hideaway for the gift of royal favor bestowed upon the widow of a hero was now a disheveled remnant of an unsolved mystery. The wind began to blow in from the distant coastline and off the Savannah River. Autumn leaves swirled around, finding refuge in the shallow pit. The rope tied to the root of the sturdy ancient oak began blowing against the twinkling backdrop of sky and river. From pirates to pilfers, the thieves continued to provide another tale to add to the legacy of its chronicles. If trees could talk, would they tell the secrets they've been entrusted to?

*   *   *

ASHLEY WILLINGHAM'S LAW OFFICES, OGLETHORPE SQUARE, SAVANNAH, OCTOBER 18, 1:03 P.M.

The law offices of Ashley Willingham were located in an impressive building in the historical district of Savannah, Georgia. She purchased a perfectly appointed building and had it renovated by the prestigious architectural firm of Lott & Barber. Nick had taken a keen interest in the firm and praised their architectural and restoration skills. His judgment validated Ashley's research and their pristine reputation. The resulting aesthetics had captured the essence of her dream. Lott & Barber had apprehended simple elegance with modern embellishing to the building's historical core. The uniqueness of her retro building was the guest quarters and entertainment room attached. Her desire was to create an atmosphere for her clients to be able to situate themselves comfortably during a short or lengthy trial. The community room could be used for gatherings of casual or stylish celebration. The facility was open to their families, as well, for memorable visits to Savannah's twenty city squares and to enjoy the stately mansions, the towering oaks drizzling with silvery moss, and the timeless sparkle found in the crown of Georgia's coastal area.

After her multi-million-dollar verdict, Ashley sought creative ways to invest her funds. Grandma Grace had provided great counsel to the triumphant counselor. Grace was a woman who lived frugally but invested abundantly. Her grandmother also understood the importance of positioning oneself in a location to be a servant to the masses. Her attendance at East Savannah Christian Church was the acid test by which she evaluated rewards of investment. She could have attended a much more conveniently located church, and one that was suitably established. Instead, she sought out East Savannah to invest, and a thirty-member congregation grew to an imposing beacon within the community in large part due to what she believed a small contribution of her efforts. One of Grace's favorite mealtime teachable moments was to remind her family about time, talent, and thriftiness: "Successful investing is not that you alone profit, but that others will yield from your outlay as well." The concept had worked out well for Attorney Ashley Willingham.

Apart from Nick, no family member had visited her new offices. Her dad had promised to drop by, but he didn't even make her ribbon-cutting ceremony. She couldn't help herself—she was excited that the ones most intimate to her would get to appreciate her accomplishments. As she considered the idea, her confining thought was she hoped "appreciate" would be the settling sentiment.

The Willingham clan began assembling at the law office. Gladys and Ralph were the first to arrive—an hour early. Carmen, Jimmy, Madelyn and Bryson came shortly thereafter. James and Valerie were timely. As each arrived, greetings from a gracious Southern-speaking middle-aged receptionist/paralegal cozied them in for their appointment. She elongated her words with a dainty canary-like voice. "I'm Donna Kay. Ashley will be *riiiight* with y'all. She's just getting some loose ends *tiiied* up. Can I get y'all something to *draaank?*" Her Southern twang gave the appearance of an uneducated woman, but she was far from it. Donna Kay was a striking woman with long, shapely legs and strong cheek-bones. She had her master's in business and was nearly finished with her law degree. Her plans were to join Ashley's firm once she passed the Bar exam. She exchanged pleasantries with the family, and offered condolences for the loss of their loved one. She continued her conversation, interrupting only long enough to welcome each family unit as they arrived. "I don't usually sit *heeere,*" she explained. "I'm usually tucked away in the *baaack.* I've been pulling double-duty for Tanisha. She's our *reeegular* receptionist. She's currently on *FMLAAA*—that's the family medical leave of absence. She's having her third baby! I can*not* imagine. Can y'all? Two did me in. I told my husband no more. I had to *quiiit.* I couldn't keep up with those little *raaascals.* They're big rascals now." She giggled and greeted the last to arrive of the Willinghams. Nick had been meeting with Bruce Masters's widow regarding arrangements for his upcoming funeral. He apologized for running late. Donna Kay hit the intercom and announced to Ashley that everyone had arrived.

"Tell them I'll be right out, Donna Kay. Thank you." Ashley signed the last letter and placed the file in her outbox. She took a key from her purse and unlocked her bottom desk drawer. She thumbed through the folders until she found the one labeled "Grace Willingham" and pulled it from the drawer. She laid the folder on the desk in front of her, closed her eyes, and had a silent prayer for the meeting about to occur. To the best of her ability, everything was in order. There had been a lot of scurrying on the part of herself and Donna Kay to get all the i's dotted and the t's crossed for the appointed hour. Everyone had received an official notification by courier midmorning that per agreement of the family members the reading of the Will would take place at the law firm of Ashley Willingham. That was not necessary, but Ashley wanted to make certain she covered every base, so she asked the family attorney, Richard Thomas, to execute that. The Order had been prepared earlier in the morning for the probating of the Will. Before the Judge would sign it, his law clerk did inquire as to the "big hurry." Anticipating the question, Ashley had informed Counselor Thomas of the out-of-country relatives who needed to get back to their affairs. She had attached the expedited Death Certificate to the Order. Affidavits had been prepared for the witnesses to Grace's Will to sign attesting to the fact that they knowingly and willingly witnessed the execution of the Will on the attested-to date, and that Grace Willingham appeared to be of competent mind and sound memory. It was a blessing they were alive and still located in the Savannah area. It was a bigger blessing they were loyal employees of the family attorney. Richard Thomas was able to get those executed and file-stamped by the Court's clerk, as well. Ashley had made Thomas's job in presenting Grace's Will to the family a breeze. Everything was in impeccable order. The Judge determined everything to be proper and considered the Will officially probated. Now, the Executor or Executrix could be appointed.

Thomas planned to be present, but Ashley asked that he show up thirty minutes later than the others. That way, she would have time to give them a quick tour and then get them settled in the conference room. She was aware that she was the appointed Executrix. She had helped Grace draw up the Will. Of course, Attorney Richard Thomas would be the one opening the copy of the Will and reading its contents.

Ashley felt Grandma Grace had been extremely fair in her distribution. That is, except for the mystery surrounding who would inherit the jewels. Since those were nonexistent at the present time, that should not be a huge issue. Should the gems be recovered and the thief brought to justice, the issue would have to be revisited. That part of her estate was an unknown variable for the time. She was holding out the hope that Grandma was going to bequeath the jewels to her care, custody, and control. After all, she had promised that Ashley would inherit them, and Grace always kept her word. If that was not revealed in some fashion today through a codicil that Thomas held, Ashley was at a loss as to the disposition of the precious gems.

Ashley was concerned about how the family would take her being appointed as Executrix, especially in light of the fact she helped her draw up the Will. She realized it could cause hard feelings in the family, and that it could be challenged. She met all the qualifications–she was of age, a resident of the State of Georgia, wasn't a convicted felon, and was mentally competent. So was everyone else. But, surely they would understand why Grace had selected her. She was the one with the law degree in the family. It made sense that she should be the overseer of her estate. As far as being Grace's favorite, which everyone would suspect, that remained to be seen upon assignment of the jewels. As for her responsibilities, she would perform her job as Executrix in a very professional manner. If that included the jewels, sobeit. For now, there was little need to be anxious about something so uncertain.

*   *   *

ASHLEY WILLINGHAM'S LAW OFFICES, OGLETHORPE SQUARE, SAVANNAH, OCTOBER 18, 2:30 P.M.

The family was gathered in the conference room and waiting on Grace's attorney. The tour had been received graciously by all. The family seemed genuinely happy for Ashley's success and her superior taste. James glowed like a beacon. He lagged behind and took Ashley by the hand. "I want you to know how proud I am of you. This place is amazing. I don't even know what to say about me missing your opening day ceremony. It was inexcusable. I hope you can forgive me for that."

"Dad, that's water over the proverbial dam. It's over. You're here now. Everything's fine. We're all going to do better. It's a new day for us." Ashley tried to convey her best spirit of forgiveness. She wanted desperately to release her father of any encumbrances he had so he might get a fresh start. She was uneasy of what he might be facing regarding any repercussions of his involvement with Hawk. He didn't need to worry about the family's past any longer. As for her, she was trying to get used to the news of Nick being her brother and the circumstances surrounding that. If she spoke forgiveness and moving on out loud, she felt it would help her get to a softer landing place sooner. "We'd better get to the conference room. The attorney will be here any minute."

*   *   *

ASHLEY WILLINGHAM'S LAW OFFICES, OGLETHORPE SQUARE, SAVANNAH, OCTOBER 18, 2:47 P.M.

"Sorry I'm late, folks." Richard Thomas walked into the conference room and set his attaché case on the table in front of him. He was a handsome man, in his early sixties. The archetype of a true Southern gentleman. He was slow and methodic in his speech. He believed in not rushing matters of importance. The proper introductions were made as he took documents out and laid them on the table. He set his case on the floor and got comfortable in his chair. He pulled out his glasses and laid them beside Grace Willingham's Will.

"I know I told you at the funeral home how sorry I was for your loss. Grace is going to be missed, not just by you, but by everyone. She was a remarkable lady. All who knew her loved her. She was that one-of-a-kind personality that only comes around once in a century. And each one of you has a part of her within you. You couldn't know Grace and not get some of that goodness rubbed off on you. It just didn't happen." Mr. Thomas chuckled, and Grace's family members agreed.

"The Last Will and Testament of a person is likely one of the most important documents he or she will ever execute. It is, likewise, the greatest gift a loved one can give to the grieving family. It's an essential element in estate planning. It's used for all sorts of reasons from appointing a probate executor or executrix to divvying property, assets, and personal belongings. Sometimes burial preferences are listed in them. Grace had a separate codicil drawn up for that. I appreciate how Nick handled the execution of her wishes. Nick, you did the best you could with the circumstances surrounding her services.

"The most important aspect, as I see it, for having a will is so that the family doesn't have to make decisions or bicker and fight over what's left. Grace wouldn't want that for any of you. Her family was too important to her. The designated person appointed by the deceased to be the probate executor, or executrix, whichever it is, will be responsible for handling the estate that is set up after the reading of the Will. That person is going to have a lot of responsibilities associated with it. It can be a full-time job in and of itself. You have to take inventory of the assets, get property appraisals, pay outstanding debts, file a final tax return, and, of course, distribute the assets to any named beneficiaries. Now, because this is such an encumbering position, it would behoove you to understand that the estate executor, or executrix, will be compensated for his or her duties. The family can agree upon an hourly rate, a flat fee, or a nominal percentage of the estate's value. I'm sure if Grace didn't designate how that is to be handled–I can't imagine her not defining it down to a frog's hair–then the family can surely come to some amiable agreement as to a fair and equitable calculation for those purposes.

"I would highly recommend to you as a family that you embrace and support the designated individual to handle Grace's estate. Whoever that person is, I trust that person will work hard to locate all probate assets. I'm confident, as well, he or she will get with a reputable estate planner and establish trusts in keeping with Grace's desires as set forth in her Will. The objective is to avoid as much inheritance tax as possible and to minimize estate expenses so that beneficiaries get the largest distribution possible. You wouldn't want all of Grace's wise stewardship to go to dear ol' Uncle Sam or to get caught up in some needless family dispute. So I hope you carefully consider those things as we go through Grace's wishes in this Last Will and Testament.

"Let me remind you all that Grace loved every one of you equally. It would be an apostasy to her legacy if any of you should take issue with what she had bequeathed to you individually or others corporately. She was of sound body and mind on the day she drew up this Last Will and Testament," and Thomas held up the document, "or any codicil that might be discovered hereafter. Why can I say that with such assurance? Because Grace Willingham was of sound mind on the day she died. You know it, I know it, and her world around her knew it. She was one sharp cookie."

Attorney Thomas picked up the copy of the probated Will and put on his reading glasses. He cleared his throat and took a drink of water. "Now, without further ado, I am going to read Grace's Will. I don't think I have ever been accused of going too fast for anyone's hearing, but if you think I need to slow down or repeat anything, you let me know and I will gladly accommodate you."

The family sat as though they were frozen in place. Bryson was looking around trying to understand in childlike manner why everyone was so quiet. Madelyn patted him on the head to reassure him everything was fine. He sat in attention with the rest of the family, as though he knew this was another significant event in his family history.

Richard Thomas began the ritualistic procedure. "This is Article One: 'I, Grace Carissa Willingham, being of sound mind and disposing memory, and residing at 827 Victory Drive, Savannah, Georgia, declare that this is my Last Will and Testament.'

"Article Two: 'I revoke all other wills or codicils executed prior this one.' Those are pretty insignificant and straightforward. Don't think you have any problem with those." Richard Thomas cleared his throat and continued.

"Article Three: 'I have three living children: Gladys Faye Willingham-Murphy, James Albert Willingham II, and Carmen Lola Willingham. Further, I am survived by five grandchildren: Nicholas Albert Willingham, Ashley Renee Willingham, James Albert Willingham III, Nora Jean Willingham, and Madelyn Joy Willingham, who will, likewise, be beneficiaries of the assets of my estate.'" Attorney Thomas interrupted the reading. "Now, I can read through all this legalese, or gobbledygook, if you want me to. They are perfunctory formalities. They're things like, 'All references in this Will to child or children or issue include all of the above child or—'"

Nora was the first to speak up, but others were eager to. "No, no, no. Please, spare us all the legal mumbo-jumbo. Is that okay with everybody?"

"Works for me," Jimmy agreed. It was a unanimous consent.

James spoke up. "Gladys, Carmen, do either of you have any problem with Richard just cutting through the chase and spelling out the bottom line that I think everyone wants to get to, anyway?" James was under the impression that he had no cause to be here. He had been sliced out of Grace's Will. He was here in support of the family. He really was not concerned about the prospects of any inheritance. He had prepared Valerie for the possibility as well. Although she seemed somewhat disappointed, she was in support of whatever he wanted to do. James felt any omission by Grace was well deserved on his part. He was beginning to realize the wealth his mama had left behind had nothing to do with monetary value.

"It's fine with me," Carmen interjected.

"I suppose that would be okay. I can't see any harm in that. Do you, Ralph?" Ralph shook his head in support of Gladys's decision. "Ashley, honey, you're the lawyer. Do you think it's necessary?" Gladys didn't want the family to be shortchanged in any way, but felt everyone would trust Ashley's opinion.

"I know that if there's anything Mr. Thomas feels like we need to know, he'll make us aware of that. I'm confident in his judgment."

"Absolutely, I will, Ashley. And thank you for your confidence. Folks, I was your mother's attorney for a lot of years. I feel as loyal to you as her family as I did to Grace personally.

May I?" Richard sought permission from Ashley.

"Yes, please, go ahead. I think we're fine," Ashley nodded.

"And, I'll be happy to get everyone a copy of this, if we could impose on Ashley's good graces here. You can take it home and look at it and inspect every word. But I'm going to cover the ground that needs covering. It's pretty short and sweet, as you can see. One of Grace's most abundant attributes was her succinctness. You didn't have to worry about where she was coming from. She said it point blank and in as few of words as possible." Thomas received hardy "amens" and laughter at the depiction of Grace.

"So, what y'all really want to know about is who gets what, to put it bluntly. Let's see, I'll get right down to it here." The attorney mumbled through some words, and finally arrived at the language he was looking for. "Here we go." He cleared his throat again and took another sip of water. "Article Four: 'I give, devise and bequeath my real property, which comprise eighty acres, to be equitably divided by the eight heirs outlined herein above, with the—'"

There were gasps of joy as well as concern that emanated from the group. If thoughts had been visible, the majority of the dismay stemmed from dividing up the homeplace and disrupting its stability. The concern would erupt over who would be getting the house, the Sugar Shack, and Camp W'ham. Wrapping minds around the equitable division of that was going to be iffy at best. Nora and Gladys were the outspoken ones.

"I don't see how that's going to work. Who's going to get the ten acres with the house on it? That seems a bit unfair." Nora slapped her hands in her lap and began straightening her skirt.

She was noticeably already agitated.

"I believe that's what Mr. Thomas was speaking of at the beginning–that the family will work out these details with the Executor," Gladys added.

"Or Executrix," Mr. Thomas interjected.

"Or Executrix." Gladys nodded. She assumed it would be her, as the oldest daughter of Grace Willingham.

"I'm just the messenger. That will be for you all to hash out. If I may continue," Richard looked at the crowd with a questionable expression. Everyone agreed he should.

"'…with the understanding that the acreage will not be disturbed, divided, or sold to any person or entity outside of the James Albert, the First, and Grace Willingham lineage. Should any beneficiary decide he or she is not interested in keeping the property intact or desire to participate in the upkeep and maintenance of said property, their percentage of their property will be abdicated to the remaining heirs. This will continue until the last heir deems it necessary to liquidate. Any proceeds derived will go to a legitimate facility that rescues child abuse victims, including but not limited to the California Children's Home.'" Mr. Thomas lifted his head and waited for any objection or comments. He thought Nora was going to make a comment. Instead, she pulled on her skirt. The group was silent, so Mr. Thomas pressed on.

"I'll continue. 'I devise and bequeath one-tenth of the value of my liquid assets of my Estate, i.e., my cash, checking or savings accounts contents, to be given to East Savannah Christian Church to be used in the furthering of God's Kingdom and mission work as the church leadership sees fit, with the only stipulation being that the church will seek the consultation of a reputable Christian financial advisor.'" Attorney Thomas didn't look at the expressions but paused for any comments. Had he looked up, he would have seen Nora mouth to Madelyn, "A tenth?" She brushed a hair from the shoulders on her blouse and then smoothed out her skirt. Hearing no objections, he continued.

"Continuing with Article Four: 'I devise and bequeath to each of my children and grandchildren, to be divided equally among the eight heirs, the proceeds from any stocks, mutual funds, savings accounts, certificates of deposit, investments, insurance policies, or any other investment I may have overlooked to be equitably divided among the heirs, with the stipulation—"

Rumblings gurgled from the family. Ashley watched the others. She was pleased to see exuberance and satisfaction in the comments and on the faces. James bit his lip to keep from breaking into a huge grin and simply nodded his head as to thank his mama for undeserved favor.

Richard banged his hand on the desk. "If I may. '... with the stipulations that, one, the monies will be set up in a trust by a trusted estate planner to be mutually selected by the person designated as Executor, or Executrix, of my estate in conjunction with the alternate designated Executor, or Executrix, of my estate. And, two, it will not be distributed in any sort of increments unless and until an entity is formed that will honor the Creator in some fashion, i.e., a ministry, a children's home, a magazine, a building, a teaching facility, etc. If no legitimate entity is formed, the gift will be passed from generation to generation of the heir until such entity is established.'" Richard Thomas looked up from the document as if to invite any objection or comments. There were no audible ones. Nora slapped her hands in her lap and straightened her skirt.

Mr. Thomas resumed. "Continuing with Article Four: 'I hereby bequeath that one of my accounts be liquidated and the following be bestowed upon my children and grandchildren as follows: Gladys Faye Willingham-Murphy, James Albert Willingham II, and Carmen Lola Willingham the monetary gift of $1 million each, and to Nicholas Albert Willingham, Ashley Renee Willingham, James Albert Willingham III, Nora Jean Willingham and Madelyn Joy Willingham the monetary gift of $100,000 each with the—"

Jimmy clapped his hands, Madelyn began crying, Ashley and Nick were silent, and Nora slapped her hands in her lap and straightened her skirt. The three children of Grace Willingham sat quietly content.

Mr. Thomas peered over his glasses, "If I may. '… with the stipulation that …'" and he paused and peered over his glasses again. He had to chuckle when he saw the change in expressions. "'… with the stipulation that should the recipients deem it prudent, they may incorporate it into his or her individual trust, and further stipulated that each would seek the guidance of a professional and reputable financial advisor regardless of the individual's decision.' Any comments? Questions? Emotional outbursts?" Mr. Thomas's more charming side was surfacing. Ashley smiled. She had seen this side of him before and found it terribly endearing.

"I'll move on. Grace made a list of individual items from the home that, apparently, she accumulated on trips. Those are to be divided among the family members, and she has designated to whom they are bequeathed. The Executor, or Executrix, will go through all of those with the family. They seem to be fairly non-incidental–small items, a guitar, a figurine, a vase, little things. I believe you will find within that document that Grace's wishes were that the home remain undisturbed so that the family could enjoy it as a getaway and reunion place. Any questions?" No one responded.

"I'll continue. 'The account designated estate planning will be set aside and used exclusively for any expenses, to include a respectable salary for the Executor, or Executrix, performing the duties necessary to oversee my estate.' That's my Grace. I thought she might cover that one, as she well should. It's a really big responsibility." Mr. Thomas waited for any protest. Hearing none, he continued.

"Article Five: 'I designate my granddaughter, Ashley Renee Willingham, as Executrix of my Estate. If for any reason she is unable to perform her duties, I designate Nicholas Albert Willingham as alternate Executor of my Estate.' I'm quite sure you all trust the abilities of your successful family members, Ashley and Nick. Grace obviously did, and really, that's what matters." Thomas was matter of fact in his comment. No one dared object, not even Gladys, whether it settled well or not. The matriarch of the family had spoken.

"Then Article Six goes on with, 'In addition to any powers or elective rights conferred,' blah, blah, blah. A lot of legal jargon follows that, and I'll be happy to read it. Or not." Mr. Thomas looked at Ashley for a response.

"Thank you, Mr. Thomas, I think that's sufficient. Does anyone need anything repeated? I'll have Donna Kay get copies for everyone." Again, there was no objection from anyone. Attorney Thomas began gathering his belongings and pushed his chair back to leave. He thanked everyone for their attention and indulgence. He then laid a stack of business cards on the table and encouraged anyone with belated questions or concerns to contact him, and he would be glad to help them if he could. He shook Ashley's hand, made his rounds to the others, and then started walking out of the conference room.

Nora looked around waiting for someone–anyone to speak up about the jewels. No one dared or cared–she wasn't sure which it was. But she did care and would dare. She stood up abruptly and raised her voice over the others' chatter. "What about the jewels? There was no mention of the jewels at all, Mr. Thomas. I mean, that's a pretty significant piece of our grandmother's heritage. I know they're missing, but surely they're going to be recovered." Nora looked back at her family members hoping for some help. "Am I the only one who is concerned about the jewels at all? Why is no one mentioning them? Help me out here. Is there something I'm not privy to?"

Gladys spoke up first. "You're right, Nora. I wondered, too, but I guess I wasn't clear if we should say anything since Mother didn't mention a word about it in her Will. It's almost as if she knew the jewels would be stolen. I mean, I know that sounds preposterous, but it is odd. Isn't it?" Gladys looked around the room to include everyone in her question.

Mr. Thomas turned to address the group. "Well, I was wondering if anyone was going to address that minor issue." He chuckled lightly and shook his head from side to side. "Seems like Grace made provisions in a separate codicil for the jewels. She asked that I turn that over to Nick. So, Nick, it's all yours,

Son. You folks have a blessed day." Mr. Thomas walked out of the conference room and all eyes were on Nicholas Albert Willingham, the firstborn grandson of Grace Carissa Willingham, custodian of the missing novel jewels which originally belonged to Queen Elizabeth II.

Chapter 54

Nick Willingham stood looking at the bewildered faces of his family, but his mom's was the one he targeted. There was bound to be family fallout when the final tally was delivered. He was prepared for that, at least from Gladys and Nora. Whereas he didn't want to damage any relationship, it was the one between him and his mother that was most important to him. Nick encouraged everyone to take a rest break and replenish their beverages. The group dispersed and he took a moment to compose himself.

It had been almost a decade that he had treasured Grace Willingham's wishes in his heart. She had entrusted him with this critical decision of hers. He had been true to his promise that he would reveal it to no one, not even his mother, until the appropriate time. His mind flashed back to Paris and the dinner at *Le Meurice*. It had been a glorious time with Grandma Grace. They had spent many wonderful times together in Paris, but *Le Meurice* was her favorite place to dine. It was where he met Abrielle. Grace had introduced him to her. Grace shared her faith with a stranger in the elevator and, from that chance meeting, a romance was spawned. *Le Meurice* encounters were the introduction to critical beginnings for Nick—livelihood, love, and legend.

*   *   *

PARIS, FRANCE, SEVEN YEARS PRIOR,
LE MEURICE HOTEL RESTAURANT, 7:30 P.M.

"Beautiful young maiden, Nick, inside and out." Grandma Grace was an excellent judge of character.

"Quite charming, Grandma."

"A young man would do well to pursue her. She's eager to learn more about Jesus. I'll expect you to follow up on that. We're going to meet again tomorrow before I leave. I'll do what I can, but if she's left unattended, the seed I planted may waste away. Here's the phone number she gave me. I'll pass it on. I put it in my cell phone contacts already." Grace laid the folded piece of paper on the table and patted Nick's hand.

"I'll see what I can do, Grandma. I'll at least invite her to church. How's that?"

"It's the best place to begin." Grace winked at her grandson. "Let's order dinner and enjoy it, and then there's a small matter I need to discuss with you."

"Sure, Grandma. You know I'm always here for you." The two ordered dinner, enjoyed catching up on life since her last visit, and then, the business at hand ensued.

"Nick, it's time."

"Time? Time for?" Nick was confused.

"Our agreement. It's time to begin making preparations for that." Grandma took a sip of her espresso and dabbed at her mouth with her napkin.

Nick felt a surge of concern. "Grandma, is everything all right? Are you trying to tell me something other than—"

"No, no, I'm healthy as a horse. But, I want to give you plenty of warning. Two years. Can you clean up your loose ends in two years? I can't tell you how long you'll have to be in Savannah, but if I'm not dead in five years, we'll talk then. How does that sound?"

"This is hard stuff, Grandma. I don't like talking about this with you, but I understand we have to. I have a huge project that will be completed this time next year. I have very capable men in my office now. I'm in a position that I can monitor my work offsite. I've done the due diligence for mortuary school already. I'll check on reciprocity. Shouldn't be too much difference in embalming bodies from one country to the next."

"Morbid thought." Grandma grinned.

"Hey, you're the one who started this whole idea." Nick pointed his finger at Grace and then laid his hand tenderly upon her aged fingers. She was a beautiful woman, even in her senior years. Graceful, elegant, but simple. There had never been any pretense with Grace's charm. It was the purest, and the spring of her youth kept flowing from deep within her soul. Her faith, her goodness, her love for people held her beauty in place. Nick had never seen a pretty dead person, but he was convinced her loveliness would not fade with her last-drawn breath.

"Something else I need to address with you. They're ready

for your safekeeping."

"I'm sorry? What's ready?" The connection was slow for Nick. He was hanging out at the thought of taking off his architect hat and putting on his mortician one.

"The jewels. I'm passing them on to you."

ASHLEY WILLINGHAM'S LAW OFFICES, OGLETHORPE SQUARE, SAVANNAH, OCTOBER 18, 3:48 P.M.

"Nick, is everything all right?" Carmen's hand was gentle on Nick's back. He had turned facing the credenza in deep thought.

"Oh, Mom, thanks. Yeah, it has to be. Pray for me, Mom. I don't want to lose the trust I have with my family, but mostly you. I wanted to tell you all this myself, but I promised Grandma Grace." Nick's handsome face reflected his inner turmoil.

"Hey, you don't owe anyone a justification for what you did. All of us know that Grace had her own agenda. Her business was between her and the Lord. Everything she did was prayed over. Whatever it is you have to tell us, say it. Whether it goes well with the soul of everyone here is beside the point. If it's Grace Willingham's wishes, we live with it." Carmen was tender and supportive. She had Grace's understanding for life, love, and the Lord.

"Thanks, Mom. I needed that."

"Hey, remember what Grace used to always say: 'Everything will be all right.'" Carmen hugged her son. The other family members were reassembling. Carmen found her place at the table. Nick did a quick-study of faces to assess the demeanor of Grace's family tree.

He hadn't calculated that Ashely would be struggling with what was about to happen. *What has Grandma done? Why didn't she say anything to me about this? Did she feel like she couldn't trust me? I don't quite know how to digest this, Lord. Please take this hurt, this sense of betrayal out of my heart. Is she going to give Nick her jewels? She promised them to me. Her eyes began to water. Stop this, Ashley. You'll look selfish.*

Madelyn flowed easy. If she was disappointed or apprehensive at the next unveiling of the family saga, no one could tell. Her focus was on Bryson. "You've been such a good boy today. Yes, you have. Mommy's so proud of you." Bryson clapped his hands, applauding his praise. Madelyn pondered her future. *I don't care what happens with the jewels, Baby B. You and I are going to make something of ourselves. Granny gave us a beginning. And a dream. Today I start from here to get there. I have her memory. She promised me the jewels, but knowing her, she probably promised them to everyone else, too. Whatever happens, she figured it out. And so will we, Baby B. So will we.* Madelyn brushed her hands through Bryson's hair and kissed him on the crown of his head. "Pay attention. Look at Uncle Nick." Bryson turned around and devoted his attention to his uncle and his pacifier.

Jimmy was indifferent but pleased. Whatever his thoughts were, Nick was certain they were noble. *Leave it to you, Grandma, to leave a tenth to God. You go, Girl! But, you did your tithe, then you did your offering. Ministry, children's home, magazine. You're a piece of work. All will be to God's glory or it just won't be at all. I love you. You knew how to live, but you really showed us all how to die.* Jimmy brushed away tears from his eyes. However, Nick took note of the smiles behind them. The tears were not bittersweet. They were obviously syrupy sweet.

Gladys was the surprisingly mellow personality. No objections or groaning showed their ugliness at all. Everyone was a bit amazed at her turnabout disposition. No questions were asked. No one dared pry into the personal affairs of Gladys. But the display of affection coupled with the announcement of a trip to Tuscany, it was more than apparent that Gladys had discovered the missing link to life—love. *I can't blame you, Mother, for not appointing me Executrix. I wouldn't have either. But you freed me up. How did you know I would need that right now? I wouldn't want to be encumbered with having all the details of your estate. I'm on my way to Tuscany with a man that loves me for who I am. And always has. I didn't know anyone would accept me like that but you. And God. But I wouldn't even let Him, because I didn't like who I was. Love has set me free. But then, you always told me it would.* Gladys took a deep breath and looked at Ralph. She leaned over and kissed him on the cheek. He reached under the table and grabbed her leg and gave it a squeeze. Her hand slid into his and they kept them locked in unity.

As best as Nick could get a read on James, he was happy he wasn't overlooked. He was right. James was content. *Had I not been so self-absorbed, Mama, I would have remembered that you never operated the way the world does. You didn't slice people out of your life. Yet you still loved us when we walked away from you. Who cares what you decided to do with your jewels. You left me so rich with your wisdom that I don't need diamonds or rubies to recognize your wealth. I didn't deserve you, but I sure am glad God saw fit for me to be a part of your legacy.* James took his chair and slid it closer to Valerie. He leaned into her ear and whispered, "I love you, Val. You're all the jewels I need." The approving glance from Valerie warmed his heart. She moved in to snuggle closer to her husband.

Nora sat staring ahead. She was the one Nick was most concerned about. He hadn't had much occasion to be around Nora, and even limited as a child. She seemed to be more caught up in the world and herself and, unfortunately, material possessions. Her thoughts? Nick didn't want to go there, but they could be a bit distasteful. *I'm not discounting my chance at being the recipient of those jewels, GG. You always told me that I would inherit them. You never gave me a reason to doubt your word. Nick is probably the messenger you appointed to soften the blow to the family. And even if I don't get them, which I know I will, you were gracious with your gifts. But, magazine ministry? You were talking about me, weren't you? I'm not so sure about that. I guess I'll have to wait and see how much is involved in that. That's selfish, I know. These people think I'm self-absorbed. Jimmy flat-out told me that last night. Kind of hurt my feelings, but it kind of made me stop and analyze myself. You always warned me about that yourself, GG. I don't want to be. I really don't.* Nora felt emotion kicking in. She wasn't about to let her family see one of her weak moments. She slapped her hands in her lap, straightened her skirt, and gave her attention to Nick.

"Everybody settled?" Nods gave Nick the approving signal to proceed. He took a sip of water, a deep breath, and ushered in his comments.

"Grace Willingham was the most unique individual any of

us will be privileged to ever know. And she was our mother and grandmother. Ralph, Valerie, she thought of herself as your mother, too, not just an in-law. That's our Grace. Everything she did was not just well thought out, but it was bathed in prayer. She took matters before the Lord and left them at His throne. Sometimes it was years before her petitions met resolve. But she was patient. Thoughtful. Trusting. Dependent.

"Dependent. Now, that's an adjective we don't equate with Grace Willingham when we think of her. Most of us, especially her grandchildren, saw Grace as a rock. Self-sufficient. Financially stable. Someone who never experienced adversity, or loneliness, or regret. Mom, Dad, and especially you, Aunt Gladys, you all know better than us kids, that Grace had more than her fair share of trials and tribulations. She hurt, cried, and was familiar with loneliness. Her heart wasn't made of stone. It bled from pain. It mourned with loss. It rejoiced with others' victories. What I loved most about Grace Willingham, and I'm sure you all will agree, is that Grace was constant. She didn't waver in her faith–not in her belief in each of us, and especially her faith in God.

"Grace appeared to be a rock because she stood on the Rock. I'm sure you probably heard her say, as did I, "Truth often stings the ears and can even cause the heart to bleed, but in the end, it is Truth which saves the soul." Grace not only believed that, she lived that. We have never witnessed anything else but truth come from the person each of us hold so dear to our hearts. And we miss her with every breath we take." Nick's voice broke and his eyes smarted. He dried his long, wet eyelashes, and regained his composure.

"In keeping with her promise to each of you, that being that you would inherit the jewels, Grace took it before the Lord for His wisdom. She got a plan, presented it to me, and I was part of the execution of that plan. I think it's important that you all understand why I, Nicholas Albert Willingham, became the engineer of her train ride. I was the one who landed on Paris as the country to visit. Had it been any of you, you could have been standing here today. I wasn't her favorite. She didn't play those kinds of games."

Ashley lowered her head slightly. She felt a tinge of shame sweep over her earlier doubting thoughts. She lifted it immediately, as though Grace herself had her finger underneath her chin and was raising her countenance for her.

Nick continued his explanation to the family of why he was chosen as Grace's messenger. "I fell in love with Paris and the architectural school there. That's where I chose to live. I'm sure you all recall Sergeant Benton, Albert's comrade who was with him in London when he died. Like myself, Mr. Benton fell in love with a beautiful French maiden. He settled there. He worked at *Bulgari's*, a prestigious jewelry store there. God networks in mysterious ways. He alone knew the story and how it would play out. He knew Albert would die and The Queen would feel so indebted she would give Grace expensive jewels. He knew Benton would live in Paris and become a jeweler. He knew I would live there and could monitor the progress of her plan. And He knew Grace would put all the puzzle pieces together because she always trusted Him to show up and show off how He had orchestrated His ordained days for our lives. She didn't have to figure things out. She simply had to trust Him to show her His plan for her life. That was our Grace.

"Long story shortened. Grace took the jewels to Mr. Benton with the plan. They took pictures and made an exact replica of the jewels made from cubic zirconia. The jewels that were stolen were fake. The joke is on the thief."

Everyone gasped initially, then broke out into a raucous roar. It took a few minutes for everyone to settle down. Nick was doubled over with laughter. Jimmy danced a jig around the table. Ashley's tears were flowing freely leaving black tracks on her beautiful cheeks. Madelyn got up from her chair, stood Bryson on the table, grabbed his arms and helped him dance on the tabletop. She grabbed his hands and they clapped and shouted with glee. Gladys high-fived James and Carmen. Nora was giddy with delight as all she could do was make a fist and yank her arm down to her side repeatedly, and say, "Yes! Yes! Yes!" Donna Kay stuck her head in the door and asked, "Is everything okaaaay with y'all?" Ashley, who was laughing hilariously, gave her a thumbs up, and Donna Kay closed the door behind her.

The group settled down. A few chuckles surfaced. Jimmy continued to tap his feet on the floor with amusement. Nick grabbed the stapler from the credenza and tapped it on the table to get everyone's attention.

"There's more. There's more," Nick said, hoping to quieten his crowd.

"Well, I hope so. We still don't know where the real jewels are," Nora was quick to remind everyone. It brought order.

Nick bent down, took his attaché case and set it gently on the conference table. He opened the cover so that it faced his audience. No one could see the treasure that lay inside the case. He took out an envelope. "This is an envelope that has a number one on the front. Observe." Nick held the envelope out and allowed everyone the opportunity to see the big "#1" on its face. "And, in true Grace style, it is sealed with red wax and a "W" insignia on the back." Nick pointed to the wax seal.

"Grandma always made things look so beautiful." Madelyn observed.

"She really did, Maddie," Carmen agreed.

"Grandma could make anything look good. I mean, she could take a pile of p—"

"Stop it! Don't go there, Jimmy!" Ashley pleaded. "We know where you're headed with that."

"What? You guys have such little faith in me. All I was going to say was pickles, put a bow on it, and everyone would love it." Jimmy winked at Ashley and broke out in his signature mischievous grin.

"Okay, okay, get back to it. The letter. Please," Nora begged.

"It has never been opened by me. You will witness what's inside at the same time I do. Is it okay if I do the honors, or would someone else like me to pass them the envelope and—"

"Just open the envelope!" Jimmy yelled from the back of the room. "You're killing me with suspense." He laughed and everyone joined in the plea to open the contents of the envelope. Nick reached in his attaché case again and took out a letter opener. "I try to always be prepared," he jested. It was refreshing to see the lighter side of Nick. He slid the letter opener in the slot of the sealed envelope and began to slice a clean cut. He reached in and took out the contents.

"It appears to be a letter in Grace's handwriting. Would you like for me to read it or would you rather I—"

Voices screeched in unison, "Read it! Read it!"

"Okay, okay. Testy." Nick smiled. He unfolded the letter and began to read the last penned sentiments of the woman who had loved each of them uniquely and the same:

"Successful investing is not that you alone profit, but that others will yield from your outlay as well. As always, I invested the decisions for my life, and yours, in prayer. Each of you will recall that I promised you would become heirs to my jewels. I remained true to my word. You have.

I was blessed beyond measure in life. Not that the blessings came at no cost, mind you. My heart longed for Albert until my last breath. Now, the two of us celebrate life again in a better place than we started out. His death brought a treasure from the world's perspective. But the world's riches fade. The real gem in our lives was what the two of us created—a legacy. Each of you will create one. But be reminded, you will carry on ours. The legacy upon which you stand now is built upon the Rock. Its foundation is firm, unshakable, and full of hope and promise for the greatest riches one could ever desire to acquire.

I did my best to fulfill the intentional commitment Albert and I made together to The Lord. Each of you have inherited our most valuable jewels. Albert could have done a much better job, but life happened and I had to trust God with a different plan. I doled out God's riches at Christ's expense every opportunity I had. I laid the foundation in each of your lives. For that, I have no regret. Now, it's up to each of you to trust Him with the jewels you hold in your heart. Little pieces of grace – not me, but Christ's grace – that you will pull from when you're on a mountain top or at the bottom of a deep, dark pit. These are the jewels I bestow to you equally, without favoritism, and with a measure of love that only the heart of a true parent and grandparent can appreciate. You hold the jewels of where real life and family values connect. Take them. Wear them well. You have a crown awaiting you that is priceless. I love you.

In battle for His cause,
Grace.

The Kleenex box was like a popcorn kettle shooting out tissues for the runny noses. No one moved after the noses were clean and the tears were dry. Instead, they allowed the words of Grace to filter into their hearts. Their souls digested the richness of their worth. They basked in the quintessence of the selfless love of Grace Willingham.

James was a little unnerved by it all. Valerie noticed his hands trembling. She wrapped her other hand tightly around the one she held. She assumed it was the emotional loss that was affecting him. James's thoughts were those of remorse and regret heaped on top of sorrow. *I should have been the patriarch of the family standing before Grace's heirs. I should have been the man Mama prepared me to be. Instead, my son–a picture of redemption–is doing the honors for my mother. God, I solemnly vow before You and my family that no mistake of mine will ever bring harm to another soul. If Nick is a portrait of how You make beauty from ugliness, I am sold out one hundred percent to that kind of redeeming grace.*

Gladys sat somewhat numb. She watched Nick Willingham as he conducted himself with dignity and professionalism. A very handsome man with a vision for his future. She couldn't help but think: *You are a product of my conniving jealousy. You are how God fixed my mistake. I want to be a part of that kind of restoration. If He can do that for you and Carmen, I'll let Him take over my life, too. I have wasted my last day. I have a lot to make up for in the short time I have left here.* Gladys squeezed Ralph's leg and smiled. Contentment was taking hold of her life. That alone was more valuable than anything she could have hoped to receive.

"The other letter, please. That was number one. That means there are more." Nora felt she must keep everyone on track. "What else does GG have to say?"

"Letter number two. Again, same red wax with insignia, unopened until now." Nick opened the second envelope and pulled out another letter. He began to read:

In further keeping of my word, you will each receive the jewels I wore as a gift from Queen Elizabeth II. Mr.

Benton was a trusted friend of Albert's. He and Monica became mine, as well. You have heard Albert's story, and by now Nick has shared with you how Mr. Benton is further steeped within our family legacy.

The original jewels have been disassembled. Yes, they no longer exist in their original state. (It's really okay, Nora. Elizabeth and I shared a cup of tea. I have her blessing.) The jewels are in safekeeping. I trust Bulgari's. I trust my Attorney, Richard Thomas, even more. He has scripted a binding contract with Bulgari's which will secure the jewels until the last one is expended through your children and their children. They should last for many generations to come.

Each of you will receive at least one each of the priceless jewels—a diamond and a ruby. A ring has been designed for each of you. God made us unique. In light of that, Mr. Benton has crafted a suitable piece to match the personality description I provided him.

With these jewels, you not only have a history of royalty enmeshed within them, you have a legend of great sacrifice. No riches come without tremendous cost to someone.

Take them. Wear them well. Wear them with pride. Tell your children the story. But build your legacy around the jewels I spoke of first, inspiring their hearts to live up to the standards by which these were passed on to you. The Apostle James said, "What is your life? You are a mist that appears for a little while and then vanishes." I say: Make your legacy worthy enough to endure. Soon, you, too, will fade away.

In battle for His cause,
Grace

The mood went from humble to more self-effacing. Grace Willingham's charge to her family continued to be indicative of the life she lived. Grace had lived the abundant life, but she lived it frugally. She stored up, but she gave more away than she could amass for herself. She had learned the art of living—you can't out-give God.

Nick reached in his attaché case and pulled out eight envelopes. He laughed and exclaimed, "I feel a lot like Santa Claus right now."

"I think you'd be more like the elf delivering from Santa," Nora corrected.

"Touché," Nick acknowledged. "First envelope is for Gladys. Grace has them numbered in order of delivery, by the way." Nick would deliver the envelope to Gladys and each recipient until all envelopes were gone. The rings were exquisitely fashionable and uniquely personal. With each piece of jewelry there was a personal handwritten note from Grace. Benton had used the gold from the original jewel settings to create the rings for Grace's three children. He was well versed with the craze for platinum with the younger adults and designed their rings accordingly, unless otherwise instructed by Grace.

Gladys's ring was set with a ruby and a diamond. Her note

was simple: "Peace and contentment will be yours." Within Gladys's envelope was a piece for Ralph. He was especially moved to have received a simple band with a diamond. A note accompanied the ring thanking him for his provision of Gladys and encouraging him to reclaim his worth, his manhood, and his faith. He was a mere mush-puddle when he read Grace's heartfelt inspiration.

James's envelope also held two tokens. His ring was a suitable masculine setting with a bit of flash and encased two diamonds. Grace had etched the words, "God loves you and can fix everything for you." No one was more surprised than Valerie to receive a ruby ring with a simple heart encircling the stone. Astonished that the ring fit perfectly, she found herself breathless at the display of accepting love. The card attached was in Grace's penmanship with the simple word, "Dance." Valerie closed her tear-filled eyes and took herself back to Fanfleezie's. She could envision Grace's face as she told her, "A heart never hears the song it doesn't dance to."

Carmen's ring was a tri-band display of a diamond and two rubies. Her words from Grace: "A good man needs your heart. Make it a covenant relationship—you, him, and God."

Nick's was next. He opened his package. He felt especially blessed to see a single diamond setting in his simple platinum band. A loose ruby nestled in a box against the black velvet. The note read: "Add a diamond. Don't let her get away. She has a heart for God. She's a keeper."

Ashley's ring was perfectly elegant. A single platinum band but not meeting in the middle. Instead, it was separated by the edges of a diamond and a ruby stone. Encircling the band were beautiful small diamonds to add a movement of sophistication. Her encouragement from Grace: "Keep the faith and a reserve for true love. It never fails."

Jimmy danced another jig when he opened his envelope. Like Nick, he had a loose ruby stone and a simple band bearing a diamond. His note from Grace read: "You know the standards. Find her. God has prepared her heart for you."

"Nora, this is what you've been waiting on," Nick announced. Nora couldn't wait for Nick to come to her. She raced to meet him and grabbed her envelope. Benton had designed a single-band ring that divided but circled back around and wrapped a beautiful ruby snugly. Like Ashley's, the band was completed with smaller diamonds to complete the elegance of the setting. In a small box was a lone diamond. Nora was apprehensive to open Grace's message. Nora could hear GG correcting her as a younger child and especially in her teens that "Heart-voids can only be filled with a *you*. Too much of *me* digs its own holes." Although Nora loved the unusual design, she was confident its intent was to reprove her about her self-absorption. She slowly opened the small elegant card bearing Grace's initial on the front. The note quickened Nora's spirit. It simply said, "He loves you most. Find a man that loves Him, and he will, too." Nora smiled and hugged the note to her chest.

Madelyn had patiently waited. Being the youngest in the crowd, aside from Bryson, of course, had taught her a lot of patience. She was anxious to see what Granny had done, if she remembered her passion.

And, Miss Madelyn. Last but certainly not least." Nick handed her the package and gave her a kiss on her blackened cheek. She could have called it a day at that. To have Nick's approving tenderness was significant. His stoic demeanor had given her the impression that he didn't agree with her taste for body art. She was beginning to learn how wrong she had been to assume a lot about her family. She thanked Nick and put the package in front of Bryson so that his tiny eager fingers could help open. Madelyn pulled out the box with the ring. She couldn't contain herself. "Yes!" she yelled. "Oh, sorry." Madelyn didn't realize how flashy her excitement had been. She saw the gold and that pleased her sufficiently. She had always talked about the beautiful gold in the necklace of Granny's. She had always been a gold girl. You wouldn't know it from her multiple earrings and piercing jewelry. She couldn't afford gold. She had to settle for the cheap stuff. Granny really surprised her with the ruby set in the ring, and one diamond pierced earring, perfect for a single piercing. There was another package in her envelope. The package was earmarked for "Baby B." Bryson's note said, "Set your feet on God's path. We have so much to talk about!" Baby Bryson clapped for glee as if he knew Grace was planning on seeing him someday in Heaven. There was an additional note designating a diamond for the first great-grandchild of Albert and Grace Willingham. It could be claimed at his twenty-first birthday. Madelyn's note was sweet. It would go in her box of memoirs. "Your life lessons will be great teaching tools for you soon. You will return. You belong to Him. My heart will be with you in Sydney."

Nick calmed down the wagging tongues and the flashing of ring fingers. "There is one more envelope here. It just says for me to read this verse of Scripture to you before you are dismissed.

It's 1 Timothy 6:17-19, and it says, 'Command those who are rich in this present world not to be arrogant nor to put their hope in wealth, which is so uncertain, but to put their hope in God, who richly provides us with everything for our enjoyment. Command them to do good, to be rich in good deeds, and to be generous and willing to share. In this way they will lay up treasure for themselves as a firm foundation for the coming age, so that they may take hold of the life that is truly life.'"

To no one's objection, Nick continued to lead the forum. "Grace left no stone unturned. Leave it to her to find a way to outsmart a crook. I'm not sure she had the premonition that this might occur, but knowing Grace Willingham, I'd bet she did." Multiple agreeable voices chimed in to affirm Nick's speculation. He continued. "Likewise, leave it to Grace to find a way to stick to the promise she made to all of us to inherit the jewels. Brilliant!" Again, he got hearty affirmation.

"But if we miss the concept that Grace was getting at because we wear our perfectly-sized and aptly-suited pieces of her novel jewels, we will have missed the essence of Grace's life. Grandma's jewels are priceless. Her gems hold more value than a thousand pieces of Queen Elizabeth's could ever consider matching. The worth of the jewels she left behind for each one of us is incalculable. And they're all right here, injected within my heart and yours. Her pearls of wisdom are Grandma's jewels. Her ruby red love is Grandma's jewels. She was a diamond in the rough, but when God got through with her, nothing compared to the brilliance of Grandma's jewels.

"I don't know about you, but when I look at this rendition, this remnant of the jewels she wore, I won't think of its monetary value. I won't even think of the novelty of its original owner. But, I will consider the sacrifice behind the love that created a legacy that you and I can be proud of. I will contemplate the burden that is now upon my shoulders and yours to continue what Grace Willingham began and so appositely pulled off. Because like it or not, tag, we're it. I will look at this ring and the one I will place on Abrielle's hand and take to heart all of Grandma's jewels and the legacy behind them."

Chapter 55

"I'm sorry, ma'am, the jewels are worthless. Both stones are nothing more than cubic zirconia." The gemologist at *Bulgari's* had spent hours examining all 136 jewels of the necklace, not to mention each and every stone in the bracelet and the earrings as well. He had charged a hefty price for his time. After his initial examination, he immediately told the couple the jewels were worthless–the rubies and the diamonds, mere zirconia. They insisted he examine each individually, so he named his price to examine every gem. They accepted.

"I don't believe you. You are mistaken. We know that these stones come from royalty." The woman was adamant that he look at them again. The gemologist gave no indication he was willing to do so.

"Don't, Melissa. It doesn't matter. They're not real. This is the third store we've been to. It's no use. They're fake."

"Now what, Benny? We've traveled all over the place for six months just letting the dust settle. We've spent my life's savings

and yours. We're broke. I don't know if we can even get home."
To say Melissa Fitzgerald was fretful with the dilemma she and her
live-in found themselves would have been a grave understatement.
But her frustration didn't hold a candle to Benny Fulkerson's.

When Melissa came to him with her scheme to snag Grace
Willingham's jewels, Benny's initial thought was to run. But after
Grace had humiliated him with the end of the barrel of her gun,
he wanted to make her pay. Melissa had taken a huge risk on
presenting the proposition to Benny. She and Benny had secretly
fooled around for years, but she knew his heart belonged to Grace.
Grace never loved anyone but Albert. It was pathetic, but sweet
as far as Melissa was concerned. She would have given her right
arm for a love like that. Benny became her pursuit.

Melissa stayed connected with Grace. The lady was constantly
trying to save her soul. She finally walked the aisle to appease
Grace. She cleaned Grace's house and kept her children for her.
Melissa never took a thing from Grace's home. Had she done
so, Grace would have been the first to know. The woman knew
when anything was out of place in her ordered-up home. Melissa
wasn't mean to Grace's kids. She just wasn't nice. Melissa never
liked children. When they ratted her out for being cantankerous
and Grace confronted her, Melissa confessed she was having a bad
day and reined it in. Grace Willingham gave everyone the benefit
of the doubt, so Melissa Fitzgerald never gave her any more cause
for concern. But she wanted Grace's jewels. She had never laid her
eyes on them, and never could find where Grace hid them away.

Benny Fulkerson was the most logical person to help pull
off the grand theft Melissa Fitzgerald contrived. He was familiar
with the funeral home. He wasn't happy that Nick had bought

out Turner's. He had plans of taking it over himself, and Nick ruined that opportunity for him. He knew how to access the attic and turn off the camera. He had unlocked the basement earlier in the day. It was a cinch because he had never turned in the basement key. Even with all the renovations, they didn't replace the basement door.

Benny had hoped that Nick had simply laid the jewels on the body. It is the customary way to do things because it's much easier to turn them over to the family at the end. Nick didn't. He fastened them, probably because of their "extreme value." He struggled a bit, but Melissa had kept the family busy chatting about the antics of Grace. He walked out of the viewing room, and in no time Gladys was screaming. The cops left their posts, and Benny entered the basement. He should've kept walking then and dropped the Melissa snag, but he was too afraid she would squeal before he could get out of the country. But all in all, the whole thing was all too easy.

Benny began to laugh. *How stupid, Benny. Burying the jewels, watching over them in Emmet Park, and then retrieving them in the middle of the night. A pile of cubic zirconia! You always were smarter than the average, Grace Willingham. Why do you think I loved you so much? I just wanted a part of you. I should've settled for your cup of tea and talk of Jesus. Instead, I went after your jewels.*

"Benny? I'm talking to you? What now?" Melissa was trying to catch up with his fast pace as he walked down the street and distanced himself from *Bulgari's.*

Benny yelled back at Melissa, "I'd say we'd best learn to speak Spanish and get a job." Benny threw his head back and laughed out loud again.

"Benny. Why are you laughing? This isn't funny! What now?" Benny shoved his hands in his pockets and continued to walk faster than Melissa's legs could keep up. Behind him he could hear Melissa's voice fading. Eventually, he heard her no longer. She had gotten lost in the crowd, and so did he.

* * *

Chatham County Sheriff's Department, Chief Griffin's Office, 2:57 p.m.

"Well, I appreciate your cooperation, sir. I have the descriptions. Two other jewelry stores have called me today, as well, but they didn't have a good camera shot. If you'll send my office the video surveillance, we would greatly appreciate it. Our office learned of the replicated jewels shortly after Ms. Willingham's death. We hadn't let it become public knowledge here, though, because we still wanted our thief—or thieves. The jurisdiction isn't ours in Spain, but they'll be back in town. And when they are, we'll have a few jewels here waiting on them ourselves. Thank you, sir. You have a great day."

Chief Griffin hung up the phone. He sat back in his chair, threw his feet up on the desk, and placed his hands behind his head. "Well, Bruce, I don't think either one of us would have suspected the likes of these two. You didn't lose a big case after all, buddy. But, I'm kinda guessin' that Grace Carissa Willingham has shared that little gem with you already."

The End

the Legacy Pendant

Grandma's Jewels and the Legacy Behind Them stirred within me a desire to have a pendant crafted to pass down to my children and grandchildren. I asked master jeweler, Jim Jackson, owner and founder of *Aesthetics in Jewelry* in Louisville, Kentucky, to design the heirloom piece I don on my "About the Author" photograph.

The heart is fashioned using my maternal grandmother's wedding band. My initial perception proved true—it was a very inexpensive piece of jewelry. It was dull and not too impressive. I was right about its worth, but then again, can one place a value on sentimental items? *Aesthetics in Jewelry* not only breathed life back into the band, they shaped it into the abstract heart you see here. Then, birthstones were placed to fill and complete the heart. My birthstone centers the piece, with my mother's directly below mine, then my grandmother's at the tip of the heart. My two daughters' stones are placed to the left and right above mine, with stones designating their children surrounding them. Diamonds from my family jewelry are placed as filler stones throughout. Should my daughters add to their immediate family, a birthstone

the Legacy Pendant

can replace one of the diamonds. Or two, or three! The heart is open to welcome generational expansions of love to our family unit.

The heirloom piece will be passed down in some creative manner at the appropriate time. In the meantime, I am enjoying wearing my one-of-a-kind Legacy Pendant. My philosophy, and what I have taught my children and grandchildren to understand, is that a heart loves best when it is open to receive. Consequently, I have named my Legacy Pendant *"Receptive Heart™."*

Let the master jewelers at *Aesthetics in Jewelry* design and preserve timepieces of your family history. A generational legacy, the master jewelers at *Aesthetics in Jewelry* has more than 100 years of prestigious skills and experience. To secure your "Grandma's Jewels," contact *Aesthetics in Jewelry* to craft it for you at www.aestheticsinjewelry.com, 800-729-7498. Your family legacy deserves recognition and commemorations.